Explorations
in Film Theory

EXPLORATIONS IN FILM THEORY

Selected Essays from *Ciné-Tracts*

EDITED BY

RON BURNETT

INDIANA UNIVERSITY PRESS

Bloomington and Indianapolis

The essays in this volume originally appeared in *Ciné-Tracts* between 1976 and 1983.

© 1991 by Indiana University Press

The paper used in this publication meets the minimum requirements of American National Standard for Information Sciences—Permanence of Paper for Printed Library Materials, ANSI Z39.48-1984.

Manufactured in the United States of America

 ™

Library of Congress Cataloging-in-Publication Data
Explorations in film theory : selected essays from Ciné-tracts / edited by Ron Burnett.
        p. cm.
ISBN 0-253-31282-5 (alk. paper).—ISBN 0-253-20612-X (pbk. : alk. paper)
1. Motion pictures—Philosophy.   I. Burnett, Ron.
II. Ciné-tracts.
PN1995.E98 1991
791.43'01—dc20   89-46337
                                                                        CIP

1 2 3 4 5 94 93 92 91 90

CONTENTS

FOREWORD

Kaja Silverman

Between 1976 and 1983 seventeen issues of *Ciné-Tracts* were published under the general editorship of Ron Burnett. What is not generally known, although it is fundamental to any understanding of the journal's seven year history, is that the conditions under which these issues came into existence were almost unimaginably difficult. Because *Ciné-Tracts* had no real funding, virtually every aspect of production had to be performed by hand, either at the Burnett residence in Montreal, or in the print shop at Vanier College. *Explorations in Film Theory,* which provides a kind of *Ciné-Tracts* reader, represents a deluxe edition by comparison.

Although Canadian artistic and academic ventures normally have better access to national funding than do their United States counterparts, *Ciné-Tracts* received such assistance only for Number 17, which was guest-edited by Bruce Elder. Significantly, that issue presents itself as entirely "Canadian"; all of its essays are written by Canadians and most of the films addressed by these essays have been made by Canadian filmmakers. The issues edited by Ron Burnett, on the other hand, address a wider readership, as was evidenced by the journal's far-flung subscriptions. (*Ciné-Tracts* had [and continues to have] a substantial readership not only in North America and Britain, but in countries as geographically and culturally remote from Canada as Italy and Australia.) Moreover, Numbers 1–16 of *Ciné-Tracts* are contextualized within the framework of important Anglo-American debates, within which they also frequently and significantly intervene. This is not to say that these issues do not regularly concern themselves with Canadian work, or raise questions around nationhood. As the present collection makes clear, *Ciné-Tracts* contains some essays of seminal importance to the ongoing investigation into the representational bases of national identity, essays which often look directly at the Canadian film "scene." However, I am suggesting—and I speak here as someone who has lived and worked in Canada, and for whom that experience has been vital in many respects—that Burnett wisely decided not to localize *Ciné-Tracts* either within Canada or within the province of Quebec, and for that he paid a heavy price. The Canada Council refused to fund Numbers 1–16 of *Ciné-Tracts*, even though it was subsequently to provide generous support for Al Razutis's short-lived and narrowly partisan *Obsis*.

The irony of *Ciné-Tracts*'s funding situation is that it did for Canada what *Screen* was doing at the same time for Britain: it not only revitalized film studies, but framed alternative film practice in new ways. It also helped put Canada on the map, giving that country the visibility for which it is always looking. Despite the poverty of its means, *Ciné-Tracts* was ahead of almost all of its American counterparts; it

was *Ciné-Tracts* after all, rather than *Wide Angle* or *Film Quarterly,* which published many pivotal essays from the Milwaukee film conferences, and *Ciné-Tracts*
was one of the first film journals anywhere to go so far in challenging the principle
of disciplinariness as to include general theoretical essays like Teresa de Lauretis's
"Semiotics, Theory and Practice: A Critical History of Italian Semiotics," or
Stephen Heath's "The Turn of the Subject." Like *Screen* and *Camera Obscura,*
Ciné-Tracts has contributed significantly to the definition of what many of us now
think of "film theory"—a potent synthesis of feminist, semiotic, Marxist, and
psychoanalytic theory, centrally concerned with questions of subjectivity and
spectatorship.

It has been with great interest, but also with considerable surprise, that I have
reread the essays included in this volume. I had been expecting those essays to
transport me back to the late seventies and early eighties, to have a kind of "period"
flavor. However, what I discovered was that the issues they articulate are still those
that concern us today. In many instances, our theoretical investigation has not
proceeded past the highwater mark left by the articles assembled here, and in others
it might even be said to have regressed. I think in this respect most particularly of
the dossier on identification, which includes among other major essays, Stephen
Heath's brilliant critique of Althusser's theory of ideology, with its call for a greater
psychoanalytic specificity in conceptualizing the subject ("The Turn of the Subject"); Thomas Elsaesser's ground-breaking "Primary Identification and the Historical Subject: Fassbinder and Germany," which still remains the most theoretically
sophisticated account of historical and national identification, as well as one of the
best readings of Fassbinder ever to have been written; and Mary Ann Doane's
provocative schematizations both of identification and female spectatorship ("Misrecognition and Identity"). However, *Explorations in Film Theory* also encourages
us to think about the place of sexual difference within primitive cinema, and
spectatorial closure within the musical comedy. It interrogates the formal, sexual,
national, and historical status of the documentary film, and investigates the perceptual parameters of camera movement. The essays contained in this volume
remind us as well that film history cannot be thought apart from its industrial
determinants, and that the discourses through which we construct that history can
never deliver it up in its "totality." Finally, *Explorations in Film Theory* never lets
us forget that the cinema and its various theories are irreducibly political. In 1990,
this is a crucial reminder.

ACKNOWLEDGMENTS

Over the years many different people were associated with *Ciné-Tracts*; they helped the journal by nurturing its intellectual growth and establishing the network of contacts so crucial to the development of the magazine. More than that, they stood by the journal during some of its most difficult periods and in no uncertain terms contributed to its success. They include Martha Burnett, Hart Cohen, Chandra Prakash, Phil Vitone, David Crowley, Jacqui Levitin, Bill Nichols, Donald Theall, Martin Walsh, Chantal Browne, Paul Fournier, Hans Speich, John Berger, Nicole Chèné, George Mitchell, Kevin Roch, Thomas Waugh, David Allen, Saul Landau, Bruce Elder, Rick Thompson, Ron Abramson, Alison Beale, Bram Herlich, Sophie Bissonnette, Zuzana M. Pick, Teresa de Lauretis, Patricia Mellencamp, Stephen Heath, Noel King, Judith Mayne, Peter Ohlin, and last but by no means least, Peter Harcourt, whose unswerving support for *Ciné-Tracts* transcended his and the Canadian film community's own apprehensions about its editorial direction. My heartfelt thanks.

Finally, I want to thank my two daughters, Maija and Katie, for enduring the nonstop work and commitment which comes with editing a journal, and Martha, whose loving support during the most difficult of times never wavered.

INTRODUCTION:
PLENTY TO SEE EVERYWHERE

Ciné-Tracts began in 1976 with a burst of creative and collective activity. The idea of starting a Canadian based film journal was largely the work of four people, and in some respects *Ciné-Tracts* could not have been created without the bonds of friendship, the emotional, philosophical and ideological ties which are the foundation upon which projects like *Ciné-Tracts* are built. More than just a magazine, *Ciné-Tracts* was a *project* because we originally saw the journal as a tool for political debate, a context where a community of scholars, filmmakers, and students could engage in a form of praxis somewhat alien to Canadian cultural life. This idea, this ideal of a place where the artificial divisions between intellectual and practical work could be redrawn was only realized in a marginal way, not because of a lack of desire but because the fundamental changes which we envisioned could not be created within the context of a journal.

In the beginning *Ciné-Tracts* provoked more incredulity than faith among the members of the film community in Canada. After its first two issues it was ostracized by filmmakers, rejected by most of the people teaching in colleges and universities, and looked upon with disdain by other publishers. At the same time the journal exploded in the rest of the world. Subscriptions, enquiries, and manuscripts came pouring in from the United States, England, Italy, Germany, Australia, India, etc. This rather strict division in support lasted for the life of the magazine, and though we tried to 'locate' ourselves more fully within the community we most wanted to address, it quickly became clear that the politics of Canadian culture operated in a very different way from what we had expected.

In an ironic parallel to the way in which the cinema operates, we were most fully present as an absence in Canada. As much as we attempted to resist it we were slotted (by funding agencies, for example, and by other media who rarely if ever examined what we published either critically or in a supportive manner—in fact, when the journal stopped publishing it was a British magazine, *Framework,* which wrote an emotional article about our demise) into that tiny and peripheral spot most fully expressed by the word "theoretical." As "theorists" we were supposedly divorced from practice; in fact we were accused of perpetuating the very divisions which the magazine had been created to dispel. This question, which still today haunts the teaching and creation of the cinema and television (in Canada and elsewhere), is perhaps the most artificial and politically suspect of debates, and yet it remains tenaciously enshrined in the very curricula which should be disputing its premises.

Many schools, all production houses, certainly most universities remain locked into a division between practical and theoretical and historical approaches to the media of film and television. Ironically, media professionals regard universities with distrust, rarely engage in debate, rarely believe that debate per se need be a serious part of their work. When they do get involved it is in the promotion and financing of schools where the "craft" of filmmaking, for example, is taught from within the "bowels" of the technology as if in some mysterious way the technology has transcended both its own history and the discourses which have enabled its practitioners to understand and use it. Universities and colleges share the same problems. There are untold numbers of "practical" courses now available to students. Their identity is dependent on their perceived difference from "theoretical" or "historical" courses. What is demeaned by these divisions is the discourse available to students with which to examine their own interests in the media, but what is undermined at a deeper level is the very notion of practice itself. It is as if the act of using a camera can be divorced from the user, since this kind of pedagogy relies on the mystification, if not the elision of discursive practices which underlie the complex relationship between subjectivity and creativity.

Once *Ciné-Tracts* was identified as a "theoretical" journal it was quickly accused of using a language which no one could understand and thus divorcing itself from the community. Symbolically it came to represent that division between theory and practice which the community itself was installing. I was astonished by the vitriol which was often directed our way, mostly by members of the Canadian film community. I was often taken aback by the lack of institutional and subscriber support in Canada. I still believe that it was of great value to struggle with these problems, but what I didn't realize was that the journal was fragmenting from the inside because of them. As the pressure increased, many of the core members of the editorial staff began to look for a different intellectual and discursive model for the magazine. Ironically, when our subscriptions zoomed over the one thousand mark they questioned the direction of the journal more and more. As the journal became increasingly well known throughout the world, as between ten and fifteen manuscripts began arriving every month, as suggestions for issues poured in from everywhere *but* Canada, the group running the magazine disintegrated.

I mention this here because *Ciné-Tracts* was conceived as a collective and political activity; once the former disappeared, the latter weakened as well. If we are to understand the extraordinary success of *Ciné-Tracts* we must also understand how the pressures on the journal and on its editors finally succeeded. Those pressures were enframed by a profound anti-intellectualism, by the divisions mentioned above, and by preconceptions as to what role a journal should play in the community from which it springs. The following collection of essays brings together all of the strengths and reveals few of the weaknesses of *Ciné-Tracts*. History is present in the selection, represented by the obvious desire to both explore and articulate the conjuncture of politics and theory, the growing awareness of gender as a central issue, the profound influence of feminist thinking. History is absent because the process through which the journal decided on the publication of these articles cannot be rendered in anything but a skeletal form.

The following remarks are somewhat pesonal, which I feel is important, crucial. Hopefully *Explorations in Film Theory* adequately represents the legacy of *Ciné-Tracts* and also the legacy of one of the most important periods in the very recent history of the discipline of film studies.

Plenty to See Everywhere

What did you see, wanderer?

I saw a pleasant landscape; there was a grey hill against a clear sky, and the grass waved in the wind. A house leaned against the hill like a woman leaning against a man.

What did you see, wanderer?

I saw a ridge good to position guns behind.

What did you see, wanderer?

I saw a house so tumbledown that it had to be propped up by a hill, which meant that it lay in shadow all day. I passed it at various hours, and there was never smoke rising from the chimney as if food were being cooked. And I saw people who were living there.

What did you see, wanderer?

I saw a parched field on rocky ground. Each blade of grass stood singly. Stones lay on the turf. A hill cast too much shadow.

What did you see, wanderer?

I saw a rock raising its shoulder from the grassy soil like a giant that refuses to be beaten. And the grass standing up stiff and straight, proudly, on parched ground. And an indifferent sky.

What did you see, wanderer?

I saw a fold in the ground. Thousands of years ago there must have been great upheavals of the earth's surface here. The granite lay exposed.

What did you see, wanderer?

No bench to sit on. I was tired. (Bertolt Brecht)[1]

I have lived in the same area of Montreal for over twenty years. My desks have always been in front of large bay windows facing onto one of the few parks in the east end of the city. Over time the habit of staring out of those windows, sometimes for minutes on end, became an everyday part of my work routine.

Strangely, as the years have passed, the experience of observing the park has not led to any certitude about what is actually going on. I don't mean that I haven't taken notice of the many events in the park ranging from all manner of sports activities to people picnicking, to children playing, etc. I mean that often, it is looking through the windows themselves more than the events outside which has fascinated me, leading to a rather strange sensation, full, yet empty, a sense that my knowledge was, is, and always will be very fragmentary.

The events which I have observed don't lead in a "natural" manner toward a synthesis, toward a preferred narrative, though I could always invoke some kind of broad cliché about the "passing parade." In other words, to tell the story of my relationship to the park more is needed. The events themselves raise questions about my own status as an observer. A history of that process will inevitably be a meta-discourse and it will in effect rewrite the past. The join between language and observation will thus be under stress, but it is precisely this tension which the act of looking, the activity of being a viewer, a spectator, brings into the foreground. Interestingly enough, the "more" that is needed is discourse, which necessarily acts as an arbiter between my viewing and my efforts to reconstruct the history of what I have seen.

Continuously, repetitively, the act of looking through the windows raises questions about "what" I am seeing, and there is an endless interplay between memory and vision. For example, did I see a tall man with long hair flying a kite? Were there one or two large dogs chasing each other at high speed past sunbathers and frightened squirrels? The effect is not dissimilar to the experience of viewing a film where the activity of viewing is perpetually enframed by the knowledge that something has already (before any realization about the act of viewing comes to consciousness) *been* viewed. It is this difficulty, the present slipping away into the past and the past into pastness, an endless regression through which images, for example (and our thoughts about them), exist within memory almost as quickly as they have existed in fact, which Bertolt Brecht's poem "Plenty to See Everywhere" explores and which is at the root of one of the major concerns of this book. Questions of subjectivity, sexual difference, identification, and viewing, questions which go to the heart of how the cinema both produces meaning and is understood are a central theme of the essays which follow.

Bertolt Brecht's poem was written during one of the darkest periods of his life and one of the darkest moments of the twentieth century (1938–1941). To me the poem is about the precariousness of seeing and the inseparability of the act of viewing from thought. While this may seem obvious, it is precisely the hidden ambiguities of the *obvious* which Brecht's poem explores. A fold in the ground cannot be *seen* for what it is without also investigating its history. History cannot be explored without overcoming the temptation to equate the act of viewing with knowledge. For every landscape or object or person the wanderer sees, there is inevitably a story, and the story develops into a metaphor about the "scene" as well as a statement about the viewer, about the wanderer; what is inevitably questioned is the manner in which the metaphor replaces the event and comes to represent the act of viewing, the moment of experience.

Following on from this argument, I could create a story about the events in front of my window. I could hypothesize a whole series of things about the people I have seen and with time fit those elements together into a narrative. Limited only by my imagination, this narrative would come to "stand" for my knowledge of the park. Its meaning would be derived in part from my experience, but only in part; yet, depending on the manner in which I chose to communicate the narrative, it could develop into a replacement for the experience. The dilemma would always be: was there some finite moment when the narrative was not there? Or does the act of looking inevitably generate narrativity—the ongoing creation of a story? Does the window stand for a perpetual activity of replacement where what is seen is being continuously altered by a plethora of processes that are never "out there" or simply in my head?

Substitution (ranging from the construction of narratives to the act of writing to the creation of a painting) is an inevitable and perhaps desired outcome of the activity of viewing, but what are the boundaries between the "replacement" and what I have observed? Does the narrative necessarily depend on the experience of observation?

In Brecht's poem a ridge, part of a "pleasant landscape" is transformed into an emplacement for guns. Initially, a house in this pleasant landscape is shown to be a shack propped up by the ridge. That the house never has smoke rising from it suggests that the people who live in it can't afford food or fuel. As the poem develops the landscape changes into a parched field. Increasingly the poem focuses on the deterioration of the environment until it is only the rocks standing above the soil which resist the dry emptiness, which resist the obvious fact that these are killing fields. They hold the dust of the soldiers who have died.

The field is covered by an "indifferent sky" and it hides the history which has determined its look. For it is not natural forces which have created the landscape, but human beings. Yet that history is not part of the "visuals," suggesting that it is metaphor which will allow us to grasp and perhaps understand what has happened. It is the capacity of language to break down the visual, to "break into" the screen of images which will determine how much of the history can be reconstructed. But it is also the capacity of language to subvert the very terms of its own enunciation which brings the poem closer and closer to a rewriting of history.

The windows have now become a screen. It is the very arbitrariness of the events in the park which has allowed me to define their usefulness for this introduction. If, to some degree, arbitrariness is at the heart of the process of substitution, then the windows have shown that substitution, per se, need not be an unproductive outcome of viewing. Given that this book is appearing during a time of intense discussion about postmodernist theories, I would like to initially situate some of its emphases by examining what is "different" about this collection, what distinguishes it from and perhaps puts it in opposition to many of the concerns of postmodern theorists and cultural analysts.

Substitution (which should not in this instance be equated with representation but without which the latter would not be able to communicate meaning) suggests how language and seeing, for example, are inseparable, how narrativity and knowledge are indivisible, how what Jean Baudrillard describes as "simulacra" are merely the continuing torrent of sign-systems which arise with every act of interaction with the world. In a more hysterical yet derivative vein, Arthur Kroker, by now a "classical" postmodernist, virtually equates the process of substitution with death, the death of culture, the viewer, and the possibility of social change. But if it were that simple, if for example the bay windows were my only contact with the park, or, by extension, if the media were my only contact with reality, or if images were my only vehicle for understanding the world around me, then processes of substitution would indeed represent the danger which Kroker, Baudrillard, and Jean-François Lyotard have suggested.[2]

Clearly, as Brecht's poem so beautifully points out, the ability to narrativize what one sees (among many possible strategies) transforms the seen into one of a number of fragments in a continuous chain of signifiers. The danger is not that these signifiers initially stand for the real and then in an endlessly regressive sense lose contact with the reality upon which they depend. Their link to reality (the word 'real' on its own is a 'sign' of this) as Umberto Eco has often pointed out is through the activity of semiosis.[3] Sign systems don't produce meaning outside of the social and cultural context from which they have developed. The "appearance" of autonomy is just that, and, though signifying systems often seem to take on a life of their own, that "illusion" persistently breaks down through historical activity. Substitution, representation, and signification are inherent to the activity of communication and are never, singly or as a whole, imported into reality, nor do they come to determine or overpower the real. The division, for example, between reality and representation is more a matter of degree with neither the former nor the latter in a privileged position, since they are inseparable to begin with.

In the world of Jean Baudrillard the viewer of a film becomes the screen as an *effect* of the screen itself. The driver of a car becomes an effect of the car. Objects signify in order to manipulate and overpower subjects. Signification creates a world beyond the control of those who, so to speak, bathe in its waters.

> Harrisburg, Watergate, and *Network* form the trilogy of *The China Syndrome*—an inextricable trilogy in which we cannot tell which is the effect or the symptom of the others: is the ideological argument (the Watergate effect) only the symptom of the nuclear (the Harrisburg effect) or the information model (the *Network* effect)?—is the real (Harrisburg) only the symptom of the imaginary *(Network, The China Syndrome)* or vice versa? Marvellous indistinguishability, ideal constellation of simulation.[4]

The world of simulation precedes the real, and thus history, in a paradoxical and undialectical twist, has already *been* written. It is as if the future has overpowered the present, rendering all human activity, praxis, into an overwhelming and oppressive pattern of predictability.

> What else does the media dream of if not raising up events by its very presence? Everyone deplores it, but everyone is secretly fascinated by this eventuality. Such is the logic of simulacra: no longer divine predestination, but the precession of models, which is no less inexorable. And it is for this reason that events no longer have any meaning: not because they are insignificant in themselves, but because they have been preceded by models with which their own process can only coincide.[5]

As Robert Hughes has so eloquently put it, "The machinery of 'communication' communicates little except itself. Baudrillard is something of a McLuhanite; not only is the medium the message, but the sheer amount of traffic has usurped meaning."[6]

It is the usurption of meaning, the emptying out of the vessel in favor of the vessel itself, which leads toward the mystification of media control, media effect. Outside of human praxis, unaffected by histories which have, so to speak, already been written, the universe of the simulacra becomes a place without subjectivity, unchangeable, unattainable, truly the universe of the Gods, a restatement and reinstatement of an all-powerful patriarchy.

"What did you see, wanderer?" It seems that in the case of images, very little. For it is an altogether extraordinary paradox that as more and more images have spread their way through our culture, as more and different types of stories have been told through images, the antipathy to the world of images has actually grown. This is particularly the case with postmodernists who would somehow like to proclaim the death of meaning in much the same manner as surrealists in the 1920s proclaimed the death of language. Surrealism, however, was a strategy to language, a way of rebelling against the use to which language was being put in an increasingly bankrupt culture, while postmodernism, most fully represented by Jean Baudrillard, sees the death of meaning as an inherent and inevitable part of cultural processes in late twentieth-century society.

In contrast, in regard to the spectator, I would argue that viewing is a creative act, never just consumption, rarely passive. This is because there is no absolute moment without signs, without language, without, in other words, a whole host of mediations between seeing, experience, and knowledge. The mediators can take many forms, can act in many different ways, but they remain, as do signs, part of a multi-tiered process. For analytical purposes it may be necessary to isolate the sign, to decontextualize its role and placement in the construction of meaning, but at no point does the sign transcend context or create a world independent of the material reality within which it plays so definitive a part. This would be like saying that language did not develop through, and as a result of, human history or that the images which surround us have somehow come from outside the social and cultural processes which made them possible in the first place.

The collection of essays in this book originated in *Ciné-Tracts Film Magazine* and it seems appropriate to quote some of the central aims of the journal from its first editorial, "[*Ciné-Tracts* will try and link] . . . together the issues of self-reflexivity, subjective positioning and hegemonic social structures, [and] propose the outline of a possible theory of culture which embraces both the critique of ideology and the problematic of praxis."[7]

This was a rather broad if not pretentious goal, but one which nevertheless guided the magazine for many years. It grew out of a desire among the first group of editors associated with the journal to publish a "political" magazine and to bind (if not to "suture") theory with practice, not only as a way of critiquing dominant ideologies, but also as a prelude to altering the way in which film institutions functioned in our society. In our second issue Teresa de Lauretis and David Allen continued this line of thought:

> Within the general problematic of positioning the subject in relation to a hegemonic social structure operative in the institution of cinema in general and in the cinematic apparatus in particular, the papers presented here examine the perceptual and conceptual codes established by that apparatus, including self-reflexivity, excess, and the relation of image and sound-tracks. Explicit or implicit in these discussions is the critical awareness of the irreducible, insuppressible dimension of the socio-historical context in the film text, i.e., the social foundation of the most "personal" or "original" work. These problems are addressed in both general and specific terms, and examined in the perspectives of cinema as institution, of the codes established by a particular genre, or of the textual strategy of a single film.[8]

In large measure as the essays in *Explorations in Film Theory* detail, the journal remained faithful to the direction suggested by the above editorials. The division of this book into four parts along thematic lines was arranged not only for clarity, but also to properly represent the main ideas which the magazine pursued. By the time we reached our tenth issue we had published authors like John Berger, Saul Landau, Peter Harcourt, Barbara Leaming, Jean-Louis Comolli, Sandy Flitterman, Anthony Wilden, Bill Nichols, Michael Silverman, Laurence Benequist, Douglas Gomery, and Kristin Thompson, among many others. None of the above writers is in this collection, not because they didn't deserve a place, but because from an editorial point of view the selection was designed to highlight those debates which most fully suffused the journal during its seven-year existence.

Explorations in Film Theory opens with an essay by Patricia Mellencamp on the way in which the classical Hollywood cinema codifies meaning in order to design a particular position for the viewer of narrative films. Her far-reaching discussion examines the many different techniques through which the "look" of the spectator coincides with the process of identification. She examines the work of Stephen Heath, Christian Metz, and Jacques Lacan, all with the aim of explaining how narratives, in this case musicals, create a context for viewing and in a reciprocal manner how spectatorship is contained within the very look of one character to another. Many of the questions which she raises are at the center of modern debates in film theory, but in particular she suggests further research in sound-image relationships as a necessary base for understanding viewer position. This essay both supports and prefigures later research in feminist film theory.

Mary Ann Doane discusses identification through a historical overview of the way in which film theory has appropriated notions of identification from psychoanalysis. She discusses sexual difference and spectatorship in the cinema, the way in which the classical Hollywood cinema is, in a sense, a mirror for the male viewer, a privileged port of entry for the male which restricts and prevents women from gaining the mastery over the image which men have. Her conclusion, that identification is not an ideologically neutral term, foregrounds the difficulty which psychoanalysis itself, as well as film theory, has had in coming to grips with the relationship between sexual difference and processes of representation.

In a long and complex essay Stephen Heath traces the historical development of the term 'subject" as it has been used by film theory. He explores the origins of the concept of 'subjectivity' and the universalization of the bourgeois individual into a unified representative of all 'subjects'. Historically, the homogeneous manner in which subjectivity has been discussed is described as a symptom of idealist presumptions about ideology in which ideology simply defined subject-position as if neither, over time, had in a dialectical manner influenced the other. He emphasizes the heterogeneity of the psychoanalytic model as discussed by Lacan, and crucially the subject (divided by relations between the symbolic and the imaginary) is seen as undergoing continuous change. This is most fully exemplified by the way in which the imaginary is never a reflection of ideology, never reducible to ideology. The subject is a historical construction. Language and processes of signification all contribute to the constitution of subjectivity. They do so through historical and social activities which are not immediately apparent or visible, but this does not mean that they are absent. There is an effort in Heath's essay to avoid cause and effect arguments, to enrich the notion of subject-position in order to avoid the pitfalls of earlier arguments by, among others, Louis Althusser. His aim is to describe subjectivity as a site of struggle; it should be noted how profoundly this contrasts with postmodernism.[9] His argument attempts to avoid the closures of an overly determinist position, and he thus brings to the term 'subject' exactly the kind of historical overview which is most often avoided in its actual use, particularly in film theory.

Linda Williams explores the way in which the cinematic apparatus has used and represented the human body and the manner in which the apparatus has intensified and supported the voyeuristic placement of the female body onto the screen. She does this by examining the early cinema of Eadweard Muybridge and Georges Méliès to see if their employment of female and male bodies reveals codifications similar to the ones used in the classical Hollywood cinema. She conclusively shows how Muybridge's female bodies, ostensibly there for purposes of experimentation, are continuously placed in typically feminine contexts and postures. Muybridge's "scientific" and supposedly neutral exploration of the body turns out to be very biased and contains within it representational strategies similar to, if not a duplicate of, more modern approaches to "femininity" in the cinema. Méliès uses the female body in order to show his mastery over the representation to, as Williams puts it, "disavow" the potential threat of castration posed by women's bodies and to more fully eroticize and fictionalize that which in reality would threaten male power. Williams concludes her essay by stating that even at its earliest stage of development the cinema became just another means of asserting power over the female body, another representational device designed to fetishize an unthreatening form of sexual difference.

It should be clear by now that it is the feminist voice in film theory which reverberates throughout *Explorations in Film Theory,* an echo whose creative and political voice has transformed the very way in which "theory" as such is written. Yet this fits with the history of *Ciné-Tracts* itself, where debates among the editors and between editors and writers centered on such issues as gender, psychoanalysis, voyeurism, and the screen. Clare Pajaczkowska's article on pornography was the focus of many discussions leading to an extended analysis of the antipornography film *Not a Love Story* in a later issue.[10] It is not without consequence that it was the editors who wrote about this film and that we came to similar conclusions about its dangerous "moralisms." In large measure we were indebted to Pajaczkowska's distillation of the entire problematic of pornography as representation. For, as becomes clear in her essay, sexuality is never outside of signification, never beyond representation. While obviously not supporting the sadistic use of women in pornographic films, she raises questions about how porno films communicate meaning, how and why male spectators are aroused by them, and where exactly female viewers fit in, if at all. Her model of spectatorship is a highly active one. She refuses to equate the image with the viewer; that is, she refuses to create an equivalence between what is on the screen and what the viewer sees. In fact it is the dilemma of "what" is seen, a dilemma which cannot be explored without reference to theories of the unconscious which the article scrutinizes. At the same time Pajaczkowska suggests that many of the paradigmatic accounts of subjectivity in psychoanalytic theory are ahistorical, an idea which links up with Heath's earlier assertions and which then leads her to examine the work of Eugénie Lemoine-Luccioni. Pajaczkowska describes Lemoine-Luccioni's skepticism about the primacy of the castration anxiety in women and the need to rethink the role of the Oedipal complex in general in relation to both men and women. For Pajaczkowska the work of Montrelay, Kristeva, Irigaray and Lemoine-Luccioni represents a departure in psychoanalytic theory, a shift in which pornographic representations, for example, can be rethought, "Not simply to refuse these representations in a mental anorexia but to use them to ask ourselves: What are our sexualities, our desires? And 'What do we want'?"

Thomas Elsaesser rounds out Part One by linking his discussion of identification with the films of Fassbinder and showing how Christian Metz's use of primary and secondary identification as a way of explaining what happens to a viewer in the cinema may be fraught with error. This is simply because the distinction itself may not be applicable to the act of viewing but also because primary identification in the Freudian sense describes a process which "ties the spectator to a regressive state, in an endless circuit of substitution and fetishization." Fassbinder's cinema is particularly appropriate given the continual and overwhelming concern on the part of the characters in his films with seeing and being seen. This brings Fassbinder closer to Bertolt Brecht, to a desire to play with the very experience of identification, to persistently question viewer position, to experiment with bringing the viewer closer and closer to a film and then to create the conditions for their estrangement. For Elsaesser, Fassbinder's efforts to stretch and toy with narrative form allow Fassbinder to foreground the voyeurism of viewing while still retaining the potential pleasure of being a spectator. Fassbinder's self-reflexivity is related by Elsaesser to the context of modern-day Germany, where to raise questions about voyeurism is to do more than just experiment with cultural artifacts: it is to question the repressed history of Germany's relationship to fascism.

Part Two of *Explorations in Film Theory* consists of a series of debates on the documentary cinema. Jeanne Allen and I ask questions about the legitimacy of the distinction between documentary and fictional film, all with a view to reopening a debate which has haunted film theory throughout its history. For, as Raymond Williams points out, the heart of the discussion may not be whether a cultural representation is real or not but whether there is an adequate historical base for examining the relationship between a film and its context. The iconic authority of the image is effective only in those circumstances properly suited to the spectacle of the cinema. This performative power will affect the message and means that the documentary cinema cannot be thought of purely in terms of its content nor simply as a function of its presumed intention. The fetish of the visible and the equation of the visible with the real lead to a cinema which presumes that it has found the formula for the relationship between the production of meaning and human understanding.

Two of the essays in this section deal specifically with Quebec cinema. There are many reasons for this, but the most important is that one of the key purveyors of the documentary form in the world is found in Montreal, The National Film Board. It is with a critical eye toward the traditions which the NFB has put in place and supported that much of Part Two either directly or indirectly addresses itself.

There was no room in *Explorations in Film Theory* to include a long interview with the documentary filmmaker Johan Van der Keuken, whose cinema is as much a theoretical exploration of the genre as it is an effort to self-reflexively transform the way the documentary cinema is made and performed. I have included a short quote from that interview because it so effectively highlights the questions which are raised in Part Two.

I fictionalize in order to arrive at truth. In *Springtime*[11] you have people speaking and there is the pretension of truth—because that is the commitment of the filmmaker—to go and see these people, listen to them talk etc. . . . I cannot guarantee that what they are saying is true but I can establish relationships between the people speaking. In this way I try to create a comprehensive framework for the different speeches, and where the framework is foregrounded the use of the means is made clear. In relation to my film *The Palestinians,* there is, at the beginning of the film a photo of an old Jew in the Ghetto. I had each frame printed five times. It is on the screen for two minutes with a small text and phase-like music. I think that this in itself goes against the ethos of the documentary tradition. Here the image is totally flat, it cannot deliver more information than it did at first glance. So you are presented with an image which empties itself out so to speak, and the text that is spoken by me has the characteristic of being a text spoken by a person. I think that in this way you establish a very different relationship to the documentary. It is quite clear that the photo is not there for two minutes to prove anything. It only gives a material basis, an image and a text to the spectator. It also leaves things open, it leaves things unsaid which the spectator can fill in and which establish a framework in which the more truly recorded elements find their place. Also, what I have tried to do in *The Palestinians* with the commentary was never to present commentary as such, over a determined action but to make a separate place for the commentary so that it would speak over the more aesthetic, passive elements in the film—not dynamic elements. In that way the commentary itself would never interfere with the action itself. I think these are some tools which may enable an audience to see that here there is no pretense to a claim to history or authenticity.[12]

The documentary cinema's claim to authenticity and truth is based in large measure on its filmmakers' rather limited understanding of the viewing process and on their efforts to reduce the complexity of subject position to a function of intentionality. Thus, of the many thousands of films made at the NFB during its fifty-year history, very few incorporated the kind of self-critical and experimental approach which a film like *Man with a Movie Camera* took. Part two traces out the various dimensions of what I have called a crisis of meaning because, although there are more and more documentary images in circulation, the concern for the relationship between form and medium (for example, that between iconicity and the means of communication) is more often than not marginalized by the films themselves.

Of all the essays in *Explorations in Film Theory,* Judith Mayne's is the most fully reworked from the original, and though she does not categorize *Man with a Movie*

Camera as a documentary film it is clear that its effort to describe "a day in the life of a Soviet city" both implicates and sets it apart from the documentaries of the 1920s. Dziga-Vertov's experiments with the genre, which Mayne characterizes as an investigation of the relationship between perception and representation, are also, as she suggests, an exploration of gender and social formation in a society in transition. Mayne generates a powerful argument to explain the film's use of male and female workers. She describes how Dziga-Vertov's images explore the ideological and formal foundations of the cinema while also highlighting the connections which link the activity of working with representations of it. She concludes that *Man with a Movie Camera,* though profoundly self-reflexive, cannot evade the male point of view which governs its filmmaking. This is an argument which needs to be applied to the documentary cinema in general where discussions of realism tend to overwhelm a more historical overview of gender position as it influences both the production and comprehension of films.

One of the first definitions which I encountered when reading about the cinema in the early 1960s was "moving pictures in time." I was in the first instance attracted to the simplicity of that explanation since it linked duration with the pictorial process. But what does the definition actually mean? Movement presumably refers to change or to development, though that still explains very little about the suggestion that there is movement *in* time. I was puzzled by the way in which the cinema both uses and is used by time. Ironically the discontinuities between production, performance, and viewing do not distort time; instead they give a film the appearance of harmony, a "sense of the present." Films, particularly narrative ones, manage time very effectively despite their inherent fragmentariness. It is this management of time which is at the heart of narrativity. Different mediums have different ways of producing narrative forms, but in Margaret Morse's essay in Part Three of *Explorations in Film Theory* she examines the conjuncture of narrativity in the novel and film. She finds similar unities of space and time and suggests that the transparency of narrative film, that is its capacity to tell a story without explicit reference to the production mechanisms which have made that telling possible, are not dissimilar to the novel. In particular, identification and seeing are inherent to the process of reading, and novels are, after all, mechanically produced visual media. Morse extends this dialectic of fragment and whole to a variety of different experiences in the late nineteenth and early twentieth centuries, from telegraph to train to telephone to the generalized use of electricity, to the relationship between the automobile and perception in space and time, and then of course to the photograph and cinema. All of these technologies have different ways of overcoming the manner in which they break the visual and auditory into fragments and each has creatively accommodated the need for some sense of unity. But it has been left to the novel and to the cinema to incorporate all of these diverse experiences into their formal structure, to in fact structure their form around the unification of difference. And in so doing both the cinema and the novel have tried to create a reality-effect as a way of integrating and harmonizing their narratives. Morse ends her piece by questioning whether this strategy will work anymore given the present proliferation of stories and images, the interface between fiction and reality, the influences of television. She claims in fact that the imperative to faithfully record the experience of everyday life through the cinema and the novel has become impossible.

The context for this change is explored in greater detail by John Fekete, who scrutinizes Walter Benjamin's pivotal position in modern cultural studies. Benjamin's concern with the patterns of discontinuity manifested in culture and society parallels his efforts to revolutionize and overturn what he saw as bourgeois traditions of realism and narrativity. Benjamin's aphoristic prose presages the work of McLuhan, though Fekete is careful to distance Benjamin from McLuhan by pointing out how Benjamin's concerns were derived from a creative mix of Marxism, The Frankfurt School, and Bertolt Brecht. The aphorism was an intellectual counter-strategy toward ideological totalizations, a reflection of the need to find a new language for talking about the many different and radically innovative cultural forms of the twentieth century. It is in the relationship between the new technologies and their language of expression that Fekete finds the most fertile example of Benjamin's contribution to cultural theory. Benjamin recognized the potential of the cinema, for example, to revolutionize an audience's understanding of the world, and while he can be accused of over-optimism he at least tried to situate and contextualize the potential effects of the new mass media at a time when critics like Theodor Adorno were disparaging their very existence. Even more importantly, and in line with the concerns of Bertolt Brecht, which are examined in great detail by Ben Brewster in chapter 15, Benjamin was very attentive to the position of the audience and concerned with their capacity to creatively and critically respond to the experience of the new media. For him it was a matter of democracy, of the democratic right to challenge the unidirectionality of the then rapidly developing new technologies. Fekete critiques Benjamin's precarious assumption that there is a certain rationality and potential to mass audiences. He also questions Benjamin's desire to produce a new future, an apocalyptic *"novum"* which will wipe out the past and put a new and more democratic society in place. The revolutionary impulse is what differentiates Benjamin from other cultural critics, though this in and of itself doesn't guarantee that Benjamin will escape the theoretical pitfalls of a kind of mysticism about the effects of mass media communication which can lead to an overinvestment in their potential for radical change.

Part Three contains the second essay by Stephen Heath in this book. The essay was written after the death of Martin Walsh, one of the founding editors of *Ciné-Tracts*. It was originally presented in the context of the first Martin Walsh Memorial Lecture, an annual talk given during meetings of the Film Studies Association of Canada. Heath's analysis of the image looks at the contradictions of equating the visible with meaning, of reducing signification to a function of what can be 'read' on the screen. This is because Heath's emphasis is on the role of the imaginary, on both its creative and disruptive potential. He asks: How can images be resisted? How can the regime of identification be overcome? How can the implication of the spectator in a circuit of desire and narrative completion be foregrounded? As alternatives he mentions some of the films of Straub-Huillet and Godard. For Heath the resistance to meaning is a potential act, one which works against the seeming inevitability of the cinema's narrative machine, against its use of the female body, against its repeated support for the imperatives of the male gaze. The image in the narrative cinema depends for its very coherence on a relay of looks, with woman at the center, in a kind of specular exploitation often hidden under the guise of entertainment. Heath's radical redefinition of the image is in large part rooted in his desire to historicize not only the place of the image in the production of meaning, but the very notion that images are at the heart of how meaning operates in films. He thus poses the possibility of a different kind of analysis of the cinema and joins that, as does a filmmaker like Godard, with the assertion that a political cinema must reevaluate the context for the statements which it makes and the epistemological basis for its use of images.

The echo of Bertolt Brecht's ideas can be heard throughout *Explorations in Film Theory*. Ben Brewster attempts to distill the particular and often contradictory relationship which Brecht had with the cinema. One of the most important ideas which Brewster brings out is Brecht's concern with pedagogy. Brecht was quite aware of the many contradictory effects which his plays had. He puzzled over the gap between performance and comprehension. He wanted to produce a revolutionary art which would entertain and instruct at the same time, but which would not reduce the complexities of class conflict, for example, to a simplistic struggle between good and evil. In the twenties and thirties he came up with a model for a "learning theater" and wrote pieces which he labeled "learning plays." These were intended to radically alter the performance of a play. In fact they were to be performed by the audience so that the content of the plays would be something which the audience would both feel and be able to reflect upon. Brecht knew that this kind of approach could not be applied to the cinema, and in some respects he despaired of the cinema as a medium precisely because of its inflexibility in regard to performance. Brewster tries to show, with reference to some specific examples, how the cinema often subverts its own premises from within and how entertainment films, for example, can end up creating a new knowledge base for their audience within the parameters and restrictions of the cinematic presentation. The distribution and exhibition of films need not end up supporting the closures of performance, and it is Brewster's conclusion that part of the solution will ironically be found in Brecht's ideas and proposals for culture in general.

Teresa de Lauretis, who was a member of *Ciné-Tracts'* editorial board from its second issue on, was a key figure in the history of the journal. Her contribution extended far beyond the essays which she wrote. Her suggestions for articles and her sensitivity to the complexities of putting out a magazine were a continuing source of inspiration to the editors in Montreal. I consider her article in this collection to be of central importance if we are to understand the evolution and history of the theoretical concerns which have so heavily influenced an entire generation of film theorists and writers. It is significant that she begins her essay with a distillation of the centrality of semiotics for cultural theory. Much maligned, not very well understood, semiotic theory can, I believe, be appropriated as a politicalizing influence for the analysis of cultural objects like film. It is true however that some of its formalist and empirical tendencies have been taken up by film theory (e.g., close or frame by frame analysis of a film). But, as de Lauretis points out, a history of the semiotic enterprise reveals as many conflicts between formalists and materialists, for example, as might be found in any other discipline. Thus a good deal of her article is devoted to uncovering the history of one such set of conflicts as they arose in Italy from the fifties and sixties on. De Lauretis explores the appropriation by Italian theorists of early structuralist thought and their transformation of structuralism into the semiotic enterprise. She sees that transformation as a positive thing, as a political act of some import in line with a desire to examine and more fully understand the workings and effects of popular culture on Italian society. In Italy the alliance between semiotic inquiry and the study of ideology was a crucial component in the exploration of how sign systems construct and communicate meaning. Communication and signification, often studied in isolation from each other, are shown by de Lauretis, via Umberto Eco, to be interdependent since communication can never occur outside of a specific historical context and since signs gain their meaning as a consequence of social and political processes. May 1968 keeps reappearing throughout de Lauretis's essay as a fundamental, almost apocalyptic event. Italian semioticians experienced it as a crucial shift in the way in which the political and cultural fabric of their society could be understood. May 1968 pointed out the necessity for new models, for a new approach to signification, for a more radical understanding of how bourgeois ideologies both failed and succeeded in a moment of crisis. "The emphasis is no longer on the sign systems as mechanisms that generate messages (i.e., on the sign systems seen as the "machinery plants" of semiosic processes); instead semiotic research focuses on the work performed through them, which constitutes and/or transforms the codes, the subjects using the codes (i.e., perform the work), and, however slowly, the systems themselves." Crucially, raising the problematic of how "subjects" use the codes means that questions of sexual difference must be included in debates about semiotic theory. De Lauretis ends her essay by calling for precisely that kind of intellectual endeavor, later to be realized in her book, *Alice Doesn't.*

Part Four has six chapters, and they all, to varying degrees, dwell on problems of film form and film history. Will Straw, for example, questions the methodological track record of film history itself. He lays bare the often innocent use of archival materials and asks whether the archive is itself no more than an imaginary construction designed to support historical research. Archives don't house the past in a simple empirical sense but are themselves subject to the context during which they were created. For film history this is particularly important because archival material classifies information on the cinema as if the archive were a source of truth, and in some cases this can overwhelm the way in which the films of a certain period are understood and interpreted. One of the problems in the writing of film history is the ephemeral nature of the object itself. Straw discusses the way in which the archive can fill in the gaps and how this can have a detrimental effect on historical research.

George Mitchell has, so to speak, plumbed the depths of the archive, and his article on the consolidation of the film industry in the United States during the early part of the twentieth century is full of the detail which was often missing in earlier histories of the cinema. As Straw points out, it has been in the area of economic history that the greatest advances have been made in film historiography. Mitchell describes how the demand for films between 1910 and 1920 was so extreme that in response the film industry was essentially made up of small firms guided by the spirit of entrepreneurial capitalism. A large number of films were made and many were political and took an overtly pro-working class stance. The consolidation of the industry was as much an economic concern as it was an ideological one. It affected the internal organization of the production process and it led to a dilution of the power of the director in favor of a more industrial model with the real power in the hands of bankers and producers. It is Mitchell's thesis that this had profound effects on the content of the films which were made, and it is certainly a thesis which Peter Watkins upholds in his piece on the media.

The move toward almost complete monopoly ownership in the media has been a central part of the 1980s. Though there have been many efforts to establish alternative film and television production and distribution mechanisms, only a few have succeeded and only in the face of tremendous odds. The range of political activities in relation to the media has increased, but actual access has only marginally improved. This is what makes the film *Song of the Shirt* so interesting and the efforts of the Film and History Project in Great Britain so important. The film was made collectively. It was designed not to be shown in one sitting in a cinema. Its style is fragmentary and full of self-reflexive commentary. It is both narrative and anti-narrative at the same time. It challenges the viewer and then interrogates the validity of its own motives. It reconstructs historical events and then foregrounds the difficulties and potential pitfalls of a cinema which attempts to reconstruct the past. The result is a pastiche with the past as yet one other discourse among many, with history stripped of any possible relationship to some kind of transcendent truth. Yet another and more radical kind of history comes out of this film, a history which takes the suppressed voice of women and restores what has been elided. Even more important is the way in which a new history is written, one which is unafraid of its own ideological premises, which in fact takes great pleasure in revealing its political priorities. Alison Beale ends her article by showing how the encounter between psychoanalysis and feminism influenced the film and how its search for a new way of talking to its audience could only have been possible through that encounter.

While many of the essays in *Explorations in Film Theory* mention television, Phil Vitone's article takes up the debate about the role of television in our culture through a comparison of the pedagogical strategies which conventional T.V. and educational T.V. use to address their audiences. There is a tendency in the latter to presume an almost direct relationship between information and understanding. This fundamental reduction of the complexity of viewing which has also been challenged by film theory is shown by Vitone to be at the heart of the formal strategies which educational broadcasters use in the production of their programs. The link then between the formal and the ideological characteristics of film and television emerges as a major theme of *Explorations in Film Theory*. The need to understand the production of meaning as a discursive and practical activity governed in large part by institutional and political imperatives is a part of many of the articles in this book. Most importantly, what emerges out of so many of the essays is the importance of foregrounding and theorizing the role of sexual difference as an integral part of any history of the cultural forms of mass media, especially in relation to the cinema. And without a clear step in that direction, studies of the spectator, of subject position, and of films themselves will inevitably reproduce precisely the idealism and the politically regressive stances of so much that has stood for film analysis in the past.

NOTES

1. Bertolt Brecht, *Poems: 1913–1956*, ed. John Willett and Ralph Manheim (New York: Methuen, 1976), pp. 358–359. Reprinted from *Bertolt Brecht: Poems, 1913–1956* with the permission of the publisher, Routledge, Chapman and Hall, New York.

2. See Arthur Kroker and David Cook, *The Postmodern Scene: Excremental Culture and Hyper-Aesthetics* (Montreal: New World Perspectives, 1986); Jean Baudrillard, *The Evil Demon of Images* (Sydney: Power Institute Publications, 1984); Jean-François Lyotard, *The Postmodern Condition: A Report on Knowledge* (Minneapolis: University of Minnesota Press, 1984).

3. Aside from Umberto Eco's many books I would refer the reader to a recent interview, Umberto Eco, *Magazine littéraire* 262 (February 1989), pp. 18–33.

4. Baudrillard, *The Evil Demon of Images*, p. 19.

5. Ibid., p. 21.

6. Robert Hughes, "The Patron Saint of Neo-Pop," *New York Review of Books*, vol. 36, no. 9 (June, 1989), p. 29.

7. *Ciné-Tracts*, vol. 1, no. 1 (Spring, 1977), p. 5.

8. David Allen and Teresa de Lauretis, "Introduction," *Ciné-Tracts*, vol. 1, no. 2 (Summer 1977), p. 3.

9. For an important critique of poststructuralist notions of subjectivity, see Gillian Rose, *Dialectic of Nihilism: Post-Structuralism and the Law* (London and New York: Blackwell Publishers, 1984).

10. See *Ciné-Tracts*, vol. 4, no. 4 (Winter, 1982).

11. Part of a trilogy by Van der Keuken on the impact of modern technology on everyday life.

12. "A Dossier on Johan Van der Keuken," *Ciné-Tracts*, vol. 1, no. 4 (Spring-Summer, 1978), pp. 12–29.

I

The Turn of the Subject
Psychoanalysis/Feminism/
Identification

I

SPECTACLE AND SPECTATOR
LOOKING THROUGH THE
AMERICAN MUSICAL COMEDY

Patricia Mellencamp

> And we; spectators, always
> everywhere,
> looking at everything and never 'from'
>
> Rainer Maria Rilke

This paper assumes that the musical comedy is a subcategory of classical Hollywood cinema, having significant codifications of conventions which warrant labeling it a genre. These codifications create a movement between narrative and spectacle, shifting the position of the spectator from the "once upon a time" of the fictive narrative to the "here and now" of the performed spectacle. The spectacles, enclosed units which mirror the larger structure of the film, often reveal both the repressed cinematic apparatus and the suppressed "family romance" thematic, thereby repositioning the spectator within the text. Thus, three problems will be addressed: the musical comedy as classical narrative; the codes operative in the spectacle which precipitate the shifting position of the spectator; and the functioning of that shift. The notion of the fiction film as a process operating with and on the spectator will underlie both sections of the paper. The critical model assumed here is derived from the constructs of classical narrative evolved by Christian Metz and Stephen Heath.[1] Genre is defined in accordance with Tzvetan Todorov's approach as codifications of procedures and responses which represent codes shared by the writer and the reader.[2] These three theorists emphasize the relationship between text and reader, film and spectator, as an active process of shared conventions.

Classical Narrative

Classical narrative, dated by Metz as 1933–1955, creates and preserves film's illusion of "reality, of verisimilitude as 'truth'," the truth of vision. Formal spatial

3

and temporal elements are subordinated to the consuming process of the narrative, centered on the human figure, actor, or character as the dominant focus in a linear cause-effect chain. In his essay, "Narrative Space," Heath describes this process: "The fiction film disrespects space in order to construct a unity that will bind spectator and film in its fiction" (p. 101). The spectator is thereby located in a position of intelligibility, temporally and spatially stabilized by the form's adherence to the 180 and 30 degree rules, eyeline matches, and other "invisible" continuity editing practices. Moving inexorably to resolution through an intricate balancing of symmetry, by constant repetitions and rhymings on the sound and image tracks, classical narrative meticulously follows the rules of its conventional game. Pleasure is provided by the play of these shared conventions: relays of anticipations and delays which alternately create expectations and provide gratification for the spectator. This process is concluded by the narrative's resolution; the spectator, voyeur of a hermetic world, is led to stasis, "The End."

This operation, the "work" of the narrative which "sutures," "finds," and "contains" the spectator in the fiction, is dependent upon the suppression of the spectator's awareness of the film mechanism and of the cinematic machine as an institution of social regulation.[3] Thus, the narrative overlays and contains the revelation of the mechanism's operations and consequently the spectator's awareness of self. Film theorists Jean-Louis Comolli and Jean-Louis Baudry have illustrated this ideological process. Comolli argues that the dominance of the ideology of the visual in Western representational art contributes to this concealment.

The camera, "a reduced model" of the machine, is the only visible component. The invisible elements of cinema, among them "the processes of grading and sound mixing," are located in the "hidden and unreasoned areas of cinema." In Comolli's detailed historical essay, he concludes: "It is to the mutual reinforcement of an ideological demand ('to see life as it is') and the economic demand to make it a source of profit that cinema owes its being."[4] Baudry, adopting similar premises, expands the model of the cinematic apparatus and asserts: "Both specular tranquility and the assurance of one's own identity collapse simultaneously with the revealing of the mechanism, that is, of the inscription of the film work."[5] Christian Metz advances this argument in "The Imaginary Signifier." "The cinematic signifier does not work on its own account but is employed entirely to remove the traces of its own steps."[6] Heath elucidates the process that results in the suppression of the filmic mechanism for the spectator: "Classical cinema does not efface the signs of production, it contains them, according to narrativisation. It is that process that is the action of the film for the spectator."[7]

This suppression of the mechanism through a set of "invisible" techniques—more precisely, "visible for the narrated" (Heath, p. 90)—enables the narrative to dominate classical cinema. The fiction emerges and the overriding theme of this narrative is "family romance." The End restores patriarchal structures, the restitution of a briefly disturbed system of Law and Order. The resolution spirals back to the beginning.

Musical Comedy as Classical Narrative

The narrative of musical comedy coincides with classical narrative. In fact, musicals depict a literal version of "family romance," a thematic often embedded within another "story" in other genres. Musicals virtually reenact the ritual of re-creation/pro-creation of the privileged heterosexual couple, the nucleus of patriarchal society. As in classical narrative, the work of musicals is the containment of potentially disruptive sexuality, a threat to the sanctity of marriage and the family. A youthful couple loves at first sight, meets and overcomes obstacles, and unites in the end. The rise-to-public-success story often parallels the romance. A surrogate family surrounds the central couple and serves several functions: ensuring that the couple couples; providing comic elements; and reversing, parodying, or rhyming the relationship of the privileged couple. Actual parents, authority figures, and children are usually absent, impotent, or relegated to off-screen space. Unlike other genres, the Oedipal drama is often resolved before the film begins. (In *Gigi* Gaston's father is dismissed in the dialogue; Gigi's mother is silenced by closing the door on her off-screen singing. Annette Kellerman's father in *Million Dollar Mermaid* loses his job, sickens, ages, and finally dies.) Love and fame, or sex and money as interchangeable commodities, are ultimately bestowed upon the privileged couple as a reward for "true talent" and for proper, socially accepted behavior. The End is the beginning of a new family. Love and marriage do go together like a horse and carriage.

The dominance of the "family romance" theme as exemplified by the privileged, altar-bound couple is ensured by many codes, among them center framing through camera placement, reframing by camera movement and editing, elevated height of "stars," and the presence of an on-screen audience remaking centrality. Marginality is a place from which the characters within the film look. Centrality is the space in which one is looked at. These are among the "invisible" codes that "bind the spectator in place, the suturing central position that is the sense of the images" (Heath, p. 99).

A brief analysis of the function of these codes in two musicals, *Singin' in the Rain* (1952) and *The Bandwagon* (1953), illustrates how they generate the narrative. *Singin' in the Rain* creates the privileged couple by eliminating the male buddy, Cosmo Brown, from the initial triangle of the opening shot and hence, from the film's conclusion. After the MGM logo, the film begins with a full shot of Don Lockwood, Kathy Selden, and Cosmo Brown in yellow raincoats and hats against a blue backdrop singing the title song. Titles then re-mark the triangle: first, Gene Kelly; second, Donald O'Connor; third, Debbie Reynolds. After this initial equivalent framing and titling, Cosmo is repeatedly shoved to a marginal position, but not because he fails as does Lina Lamont when occupying the central place. In fact, as musical director and as performer, he initiates much of the film's action. It is immediately one-half of the central couple. Upon his arrival at the Hollywood film premiere, Brown is pushed to frame left, a viewing place of marginality. Lockwood's centrality is marked by center framing, intercut closeups during the "flashback" montage, and by his role as narrator, which grants him the supreme authority of the voice. However, this system of framing alters when the two friends are alone together, talking or performing. In these instances, e.g. in "Moses" and "Good Morning," they share center frame. Lockwood even serves as audience for Brown's solo performance, "Make 'Em Laugh." The most overt examples of Brown's marginality occur during the encounters with R. F., the producer, and Lockwood. While Brown is making artistic decisions, he is center framed by camera placement, re-marked by the marginal placement in the mise-en-scène of R. F. and Lockwood. After suggesting a solution, Brown is immediately pushed to a marginal position. Secondary players can occupy this privileged center space only for brief moments. The key to the complexity of Cosmo and to the conventions of framing is his and the spectator's awareness and apparent acceptance of his marginality.

The interchangeability of Kathy and Cosmo and his implied asexuality is an exchange that further reinforces his marginality and foreshadows his inevitable elimination. In "Make 'Em Laugh" Cosmo dances with a dummy, an action repeated in "Good Morning" which in many ways is the rhyme of "Make 'Em Laugh." In the raincoat segment, Kathy dances a hula, Don mimics the steps of a Spanish toreador, and Cosmo dances with his raincoat as a dummy while wearing Kathy's hat. After this spectacle, Cosmo stands in front of Kathy, miming her voice. This action is rhymed at the end of the film when Cosmo replaces Kathy behind Lina Lamont and sings. After Lamont's humiliation, Lockwood rushes out, reclaims center stage, and calls Kathy up to the stage while Cosmo descends to his marginal position of conductor of the orchestra and the union of the couple. He is totally eliminated in the final images of the film as the privileged, heterosexual couple kiss in front of a huge billboard promoting their film and their love. The "suturing central position" of both the couple in the frame and the spectator to the film is "the sense of the images," the family romance thematic.

The Bandwagon, in contrast, partially displaces the spectator's accustomed position by a system of symmetry and asymmetry that alternates centrality and marginality. Displacement occurs because in this film it is the "star" instead of a secondary character who undergoes the ordeal of marginality before achieving the resolution of total centrality. The first instance of "star" marginality is Tony Hunter/Fred Astaire's encounter with Ava Gardner at Grand Central Station. Hunter is framed left, watching with a quizzical look. This asymmetry is immediately rhymed by symmetry: the marginal moment is followed by a centered "By Myself." Hunter walks and sings the song, the tracking camera following him while unaware porters move in the opposite direction. The spectator is thus granted a privileged position which demonstrates the centrality and "talent" of the star. This song is repeated during the film's resolution. Hunter hums the tune in his dressing room while his valet adorns his slim body in the proper Astaire attire, tails and a top hat. Hunter carries the melody backstage, meets the acclaim of the play's cast, and receives the promise of marriage in the kiss of the woman. The restoration of the "star" and the re-creation of the couple occur at the same moment. The spectator is led to stasis, in this instance the resolution of the framing dilemma which in many ways replicates the privileged couple/family romance thematic. The end reverses the beginning.

This alternation of marginality and centrality is maintained throughout the film, particularly in Hunter's scenes with Jeff Cordova, the "genius" producer/director/actor. In their initial encounters, Hunter is marginal and Cordova central. For example, during Cordova's play, Hunter is in the wings, watching. He is placed frame left in the long shot, excluded from the frame as the camera dollies into a medium shot of Cordova and the Martons, and repeatedly ignored in the dialogue. When the four move backstage to discuss their new "show," Hunter is seated in a white chair frame left, again watching. Cordova walks and talks while the camera follows him, often exluding the marginal Hunter from the frame. Hunter eventually asserts his individuality by standing; the two men then meet mid-frame. But after this brief frame equality, Hunter again sits, in a marginal place, while Cordova remains standing, retaining control of center frame. Round one to Cordova. This segment is rhymed in the latter half of the film during the beer party sequence with the chorus and the Martons. Cordova is seated frame right, while Hunter stands in control of center frame. They meet mid-frame, resolving the final shift of authority. The frame has passed from Cordova to Hunter, the rightful heir to centrality, a heritage granted him by his role in the privileged couple.

The spectator's sense of displacement or discomfort during Hunter's moments of marginality is created by prior knowledge of Astaire as "star," but most importantly by a series of privileged glimpses in the film. Among these are the already mentioned "By Myself," Hunter's center framing between his friends, Lily and Lester Marton, and the "Shine on Your Shoes" spectacle. The Martons have left Hunter after the walk down a decaying Broadway. Thus, no continuing characters in the film witness this spectacle which again presents the "truth" of the Astaire/Hunter talent. The anonymous audience in the penny arcade mirrors the anonymous, average viewer in the movie theatre, in league with each other and with the omnipotent camera as purveyor of the truth of vision. The spectator knows. It's only a matter of time before the world of the film will confirm it. This moment of recognition is the film's conclusion, the resolution of the framing ordeal and the restitution of fame and the family. The framing system of "Shine on Your Shoes" is identical to that of the resolution: Hunter is center framed, reframed by camera movement and editing, dominant in height on the shoeshine platform, a centrality re-marked by the presence of an on-screen, appreciative audience. The frame is righted; the star is knighted. However, the operation of these codes that precipitate the shift in the position of the spectator is designed to be "invisible." As Baudry suggests, the inscription of the film work is concealed. Up to this point, musicals obey classical narrative rules.

The Spectacle

Narrativization, which "contains," "binds," "sutures" the spectator into the fiction, is usually a covert operation with concealed codes. The spectacles in musical comedy overtly function as enclosed units within the larger narrative, rupturing the perceptual transference of the spectator to the filmic illusion of "reality" by an interaction of codes that momentarily displace or halt the forward movement of the diegesis. Spectacles are the literal, visible enactment of "that moment of closure that shifts the spectator as the subject in its terms" (Heath, p. 99). It was argued earlier that musical comedy is a literal version of "family romance," a thematic usually embedded within another story in other genres. In an analogous fashion, the alternation between narrative and spectacle is a literal, dramatic version of the spectator's shifting position vis-à-vis the text.[8]

Spectacles are closed units within the larger narrative, set off by a system of brackets. First and most importantly, spectacles are bracketed by complete musical scores. Music is a foregrounded code which symmetrically reoccurs as "functional" scoring in the narrative segments and under titles, thereby either anticipating or recalling the spectacle. Singing and dancing are the usual performance modes but not a necessary component of the genre. Because music is the dominant code, the performer can sing, dance, skate, or tumble to its rhythms. Hence the term, "musical comedy." When the music concludes so does the spectacle.

The opening and closing musical notes are re-marked by another system of mirrored bracketing shots. Identical shots of theater stages, curtains rising, orchestras and conductors and/or on-screen audiences open and close the spectacles. This theatrical iconography refers both to the origins of the genre and to the spectator in the movie theater, usually a proscenium stage with an inserted, reflective screen. For example, the "Girl Hunt Ballet" spectacle in *The Bandwagon* opens with a long shot from the stage down on the conductor, the orchestra (two flutists) and a "theater" audience behind the orchestra pit. The spectacle closes with the same shot. Modified bracketing shots, cuts to high angle long shots, track-ins past balconies, railings, etc., operate in a similar mirrored manner, opening and closing the spectacle.

Within these clearly bracketed spectacles, the performer denotes "to-be-looked-at-ness." Four interacting codes operate to sustain this central position, the "point of the film's spatial relations" (Heath, p. 99) for the spectator:

(1) Center framing of the performer by camera placement.

(2) Reframing of the performer by camera movement and editing. In the spectacles these movements are choreographed to the rhythm of the music which parallels the movement of the performer.

(3) Elevated height of the performer. Performers are often placed on "real" stages, as in the "Girl Hunt Ballet," or functional equivalents of stages—the shoeshine stand in "Shine on Your Shoes," the desk and chairs in "Moses," the stairs and tiered levels of Lockwood's house in "Good Morning."

(4) Presence of an audience. This audience can be a "real" theater audience ("Girl Hunt Ballet"), a chorus ("Broadway Melody"), a single viewer (Lockwood in "Make 'Em Laugh," the vocal coach in "Moses"), the spectator of the film (by direct looks and gestures addressed to the camera as in the conclusion of "Good Morning"), or a combination of the above. Whatever the source of the look, the

camera, the characters within the film, or the spectators, all looks are funneled to the performer as "star."

The erotic messages of the spectacles, however subdued by Hollywood convention and regulation, are celebrations of the body and the voice, intensified by the interaction/duplication of visual and aural codes. Mise-en-scène, camera movement, editing, and sound rhythmically re-mark each other with a high degree of redundancy. These bracketed and rhythmically marked spectacles, set in and apart from the overall movement of the narrative, accord the musical a particular status in the category of fiction film. Musicals make explicit and even exhibit in their textual organization certain operations that other genres of classical narrative suppress.

The Spectator in the Spectacle

In "The Fiction Film and Its Spectator" Metz draws on analogy between film and dream that lends insight into the function of the spectacle within the narrative:

> The spectator of a novelistic romanesque film no longer quite knows that he is at the movies. It also happens, conversely, that the dreamer up to a certain point knows that he is dreaming—for instance, in the intermediary states between sleep and waking . . . and more generally at all those times when thoughts like "I am in the middle of a dream" or "This is only a dream" spring to mind, thoughts which, by a single and double movement, come to be integrated in the dream of which they form a part, and in the process open a gap in the hermetic sealing-off that ordinarily defines dreaming. (p. 77)

Through the redundance and repetition of codes, through the revelation of usually "invisible" codes such as music, thereby alerting the spectator to the fact of filmic illusion which is mirrored in the illusion of the spectacle within the narrative, spectacles in musicals may be said to "open a gap in the hermetic sealing-off that ordinarily defines" classical narrative film. The spectator is awakened to the "here and now" of performance and to the awareness that the events of the "once upon a time" of the fictive narrative are not "real." (Gene Kelly and Donald O'Connor are really dancing, but Lockwood and Brown are only acting.) Moreover, as Metz states: "Certain nightmares wake one up (more or less), just as do certain excessively pleasurable dreams" (Metz, p. 78). Spectacles can be considered as excessively pleasurable moments in musicals, awakening the spectator to the fact of filmic illusion. Ironically, then, the moments of greatest fantasy and potentially greatest identification would coincide in musicals with the moments of maximum spectator alertness. But this seeming contradiction must be examined further.

Just as musicals literally enact both the "family romance" thematic and the process of shifting the spectator's position, so do they dramatize the look. The privileged couple falls in love "at first sight," a drama which overtly signals the significance in the spectacles of the classical recipe of looks, the mechanism which creates identifications which locate the spectator in the text. First, all looks are funneled to the performer. Second, the sealed code of looks is often broken, the performer acknowledging the presence of the camera as spectator, present at the "immediate" moment of performance. And third, there is an absence of point of view shots or shot-reverse shots from the performer's position. The look turns into a stare, the drama of vision becomes the spectacle of vision. The performer denotes "to-be-looked-at," not "to look"; the passive exhibitionist arouses the active voyeur in the spectator. *The Bandwagon* demonstrates the tension that occurs when the characters' and the camera's look work in opposition to the spectator's look and consequent identification and the resolution that results when all looks work in unison.

The look not only positions the spectator in place enabling a permutation of possible identifications; it is also a source of sexual pleasure, the pleasure of scopophilia in relation to the "star" which "takes other people as objects subjecting them to a controlling and curious gaze."[9] Sexuality is coded by the performer's movements, the love lyrics, and an often lush mise-en-scène which intensify the pleasurable fantasy of the body and the voice.

According to Metz and other film theorists, the look as a source of identification is predicted on the Lacanian mirror phase. The spectator of the film, like the child in front of the mirror, is in a submotor state, perceiving a reflection of self, yet a more complete, capable self: "there is no break in continuity between the child's game with the mirror . . . and certain localized figures of the cinematic codes."[10] In film, this immobile spectator in front of the screen can identify with actor, character, camera, projector, screen, and finally, with self as the source of the look. According to Metz, "the spectator is the searchlight . . . duplicating the projector, which itself duplicates the camera, and he is also the sensitive surface duplicating the screen which itself duplicates the film strip."[11]

In Metz's phrase, "the spectator identifies with himself . . . as a pure act of perception" (p. 51). This accords with Mulvey's description of the functioning of the mirror phase for the child: "This is the moment when an older fascination with looking . . . collides with the initial inklings of self-awareness."[12] Two factors emerge from the analogy: the spectator's immobility and silence in a darkened theater; and the identification (recognition/misrecognition) with a superior body and/or voice. During the spectacles, the discrepancy between the spectator's immobility and silence and the performer's and/or camera's heightened mobility plus the foregrounded music/voice can result in awareness of that very immobility and silence—the place of the spectator as spectator in a movie theater. At the same time, intensified identification with a superior self capable of fantastic athletic feats can occur, drawing the spectator further into the spectacle's fantasy. Tension results; the movement of the diegesis is ruptured by both possibilities, and the spectator is no longer completely sutured into the fiction. This gap is analogous to the gap of the dream, "the intermediary states between sleep and waking." Furthermore, the drama of that first vision of self in the mirror is reenacted as literally as the couple falling in love at first sight. However, the difference consists in the spectator's awareness, an awareness that was not present in the first encounter with the mirror, and that wakes the spectator up by momentarily fracturing the "illusion of reality" of the larger narrative. Spectacles are momentarily subversive fantasy breaks in the wished-for "illusion of reality" of the narrative superstructure. These breaks displace the temporal advance of the narrative, providing immediate, regular doses of gratification rather than delaying the pressures until The End. (Spectacles satiate the spectator with several "Ends" as well as feeding the pleasure of repetition.) Through this play, the psychical energies of the spectator are granted freer movement and the signifiers are less suppressed.

However, the spectacles are ultimately contained by the process of narrativization. Just as the policeman must stop and censor Lockwood's sexual explosion in the cold shower spectacle, "Singin' in the Rain," so does the narrative regulate, order, and contain the spectacles for the film's (and the spectator's) climax preserving the sealed impression of reality. As Metz states, "all diegetic films, quite apart from their content and degree of realism, play on this impression."[13] The circulation of the codes of "star," framing, and music/voice throughout both the narrative and spectacle segments maintains continuity, indicating that the spectacles mirror rather than rupture, at once anticipating and delaying the resolution of the narrative. It might be said by analogy that the secondary processes of the narrative and the "invisible" filmic apparatus control the primary processes of the erotic spectacle—the pleasure of looking at the performer as sexual object of unbounded exhibitionism, and the excessive style of the spectacle. In this sense, the spectacle functions as a strip tease: spectacles are a tease, but finally part of a strip of classical narrative film.

The preceding analysis attempts to describe the musical comedy as a theoretical genre, a "specific version of process," or "excess" of classical narrative, "a series of relations with the spectator it imagines, plays, and sets as subject in its movement" (Heath, p. 97). The central hypothesis advanced, that musical comedy displays certain of the processes of classical narrative usually more rigidly contained in other genres, suggests several crucial problems or areas for further study:

(1) The interaction between sound and image. Figure and voice interaction is an instance of complex exchange between codes. Other genres, war or horror films for example, which are dependent on foregrounded music, might function in the same manner as musicals, without the comedy.

(2) The relation of spectacle to narrative. The potentially disruptive alternation of spectacle and narrative exists as a possibility for radical cinema. This relates to the first question, voice-image interaction; both are largely uncharted, unexplored problems.

(3) Applicability of the theoretical model for musical comedy proposed here. The form is open to variation, as illustrated by several recent films. Is the variation only a matter of historical evolution, the process of the genre becoming progressively less literal but functioning in the same way? Classical musicals, manufactured by the same industry that produces other narrative films, play the same game, varying the rules during the spectacles. Within a capitalist society, there seems to be only one commercially viable, visible game in town. Conventions might vary but the process stays. That's entertainment.

Postscript

Looking back, fourteen years after I researched musicals, I note what is missing from this account, including detailed analyses of at least fifteen additional musicals I used as data—from the various versions of *Showboat* through all the Astaire-Rogers films and Esther Williams's swimming extravaganzas. Crucially absent is any account of sexual difference— particularly critical given that the male body is often on display in musicals as the object of the gaze, but portrayed differently, an athletic or comic or inventive body, a body of mastery, of action, of control, of skill and not an available body, a sexual body. Male narcissism is self-contained as prowess, as genius and talent rather than vanity; it is there for itself as demonstration or reassurance rather than needing approval or mirroring by an other. (If another is necessary, as in *Cover-Girl,* then Kelly will dance with himself, his own reflection.) In *Singin',* Kelly's obsessive domination of the image in constant close-ups and his control of the voice, beginning with the voice-over of "Dignity, Always Dignity," is the result of the star system and his determinant and not very generous role in the real conditions of production as codirector/choreographer. His continual centrality which wipes other characters off the screen again and again becomes an obsession, a real vanity, when the system is noticed. This then becomes the joke while Lamont's speechlessness and humiliation become quietly embarrassing, truly not at all funny. This spectatorial switch took time, which is history.

Along with critiquing the acceptance and approval of advanced male narcissism as normal, talented, humble, and logical rather than obsessive, domineering, and stingy, I would begin my 1990 analysis of *Singin' in the Rain* by looking at the relationship between Lina Lamont and Kathy Selden, which is, among many other issues, a question of language and an issue of the real versus the imaginary. Lamont is comic, is stupid, in the film because she believes her publicity, the image, with Selden representing the real, the down-to-earth. Like the rest of the film's contradictory logic, this is doubly inverted; it is Selden who buys into romance in the end after declaring herself outside it; Lamont suffers the consequences of romance for women who overstep its boundaries by stepping outside illusion.

Sexual difference in this film works its power by dividing women against each other, resulting in the public humiliation of Lamont, held outside language, being spoken for by Don Lockwood during the first third of the film (with even modern audiences not aware of her silence, her acquiescence, her place as mere adornment), her bad and nasal speech there as both a joke, eliciting laughter from film audiences, and a narrative dilemma, how to get rid of her. The status of women and language is displaced onto the historical issue of cinema's transition to sound film. This good riddance represents the place of women in film histories, a problem which historians have ignored (and solved) by going to empirical data. The price of Selden's fame and happiness (marriage, not work) is Lamont's humiliation and defeat. Rather than her bad voice, Lamont's real crime, however, might be wanting power, control over her own life, ironically linked to Mary Pickford (and her role in

United Artists) in the scene in R. F.'s office where she reads a real and famous Pickford review as hers and declares her independence by citing her contract; now possessive of a voice, she invokes, correctly, the law. This connection between Lamont and Pickford should give pause to the comedy of her dismissal and our response.

Like the ideological operations of a text which conceals while coyly pretending to reveal its workings (including dubbing in a singer at moments for Debbie Reynolds), woman against woman is an old tactic of envy applied to women—one that is culturally difficult to discern given its common practice. Imagine another film in which Selden and Lamont unite, a scenario in which neither woman is lacking in either looks or sounds. This is a very different story, one which has yet to be shown on a big screen.

Another unexamined cultural system, along with the dyad of envy working for the triad of jealousy of two women/one man, is chronological difference, the older man and the younger woman, with women measured by a more rigorous calculus of difference than men, the Gene Kelly-Debbie Reynolds problem perpetuated in many other musicals. How this system of disavowed difference—entwined with concepts of sexual attractiveness and beauty which forever hold women to youthful standards of appearance and perpetuate manufactured desire for daddy—contours the body and molds the narrative action according to a Freudian scenario in which the little girl is passed from father to another man would be for me, older and maybe wiser, a central focus today. I know the 1990 revision would be a rewrite with little resemblance to the original, just as the films no longer grant the same satiation. In many ways, musicals engage with scholars' fantasies of romance, taken into deconstruction or history, yet remaining intact by surrounding the object with scholarship, making it more legitimate. To perceive something is not to change it. I believe that the operations of romance have been internalized in even many feminists; more radically than uncovering the apparatus, which revelation we believed, in the 1970s, would result in change, romance needs to be wrenched from our experiences, from our unconscious. It is not, after all, only a movie.

NOTES

1. Stephen Heath's essay, "Narrative Space," *Screen* 17 (Autumn 1976), 68–112, is frequently cited. However, other concepts were gained from two intensive seminars conducted by Heath at the University of Wisconsin-Milwaukee, Spring 1976 and Spring 1977, under the auspices of the *Center for Twentieth Century Studies*. The specific texts of Christian Metz used here are "The Imaginary Signifier," *Screen* 16 (Summer 1975), 14–76, and "The Fiction Film and Its Spectator: A Metapsychological Study," *New Literary History* 8 (Autumn 1976), 75–103.

2. Tzvetan Todorov, *The Fantastic: A Structural Approach to a Literary Genre* (Ithaca, New York: Cornell University Press, 1975).

3. For clarification of the notion of "suture," see Heath, pp. 98 and 99.

4. Jean-Louis Comolli, "Technique and Ideology: Camera, Perspective, Depth of Field," *Film Reader* 2 (January 1977), 132 and 138.

5. J. L. Baudry, "Ideological Effects of the Basic Cinematographic Apparatus," *Film Quarterly,* vol. 28, no. 2 (Winter 1974/75), p. 41.

6. Metz, "The Imaginary Signifier," p. 44.

7. Heath, p. 97.

8. The concept of "shift" is used to indicate that meaning does not arise from an object relation but from the position of the spectator in relation to the film text. "What moves in film, finally is the spectator, immobile in front of the screen. Film is the regulation of that movement, the individual as subject held in a shifting and placing of desire, energy, contradiction. . . . This is the investment of film in narrativisation" (Heath, p. 99).

9. Laura Mulvey, "Visual Pleasure and Narrative Cinema," *Screen* 16 (Autumn 1975), p. 8.

10. Metz, "The Imaginary Signifier," p. 58.

11. Ibid., p. 53.

12. Mulvey, p. 9.

13. Metz, "The Fiction Film," p. 79.

II

MISRECOGNITION AND IDENTITY

Mary Ann Doane

In the theorization of the cinema, the term "identification" has consistently been used to indicate a blockage of any active work of deciphering on the part of the spectator. Identification as a mechanism is conceptualized as reducing the gap between film and spectator, masking the absence upon which the cinematic representation is founded. Image and sound, reconfirming each other's depth, proffer to the viewer a lived space inhabited by bodies similar to his or her own. Nevertheless, although the film's task may appear to be that of drawing the spectator in, of obliterating a distance, it must not be too successful—as indicated by the anxiety elicited by incidents which seem to act as witnesses to the completion of identification. James Naremore describes one of these: "In November 1960, a nineteen-year-old boy from Milwaukee stabbed a girl to death. He entered a plea of not guilty by reason of insanity; just before the stabbing, his lawyers explained, he had seen *Psycho*."[1] Regardless of the validity of the lawyers' theory of determination, the incident's description evokes the horror of a representation which fails to "keep its distance," a representation which appears to break down and merge with the real. The boy, in claiming in some sense to become Norman Bates, operates a perversion of the mechanism of identification—the film is made too present. Cinematic identification can only operate "properly" on condition that a limit is acknowledged and a distance maintained. Rather than effecting a complete collapse of spectator onto character (or film), identification presupposes the security of the modality "as if."

Nevertheless, the vague reference to a certain closeness or adherence of spectator to film appears to be the only characteristic which the various usages of the term "identification" hold in common. The concept disperses itself across a number of different registers and has been used to indicate a variety of relationships from emotional bonding to epistemological mastery. At least three different instances of identification in the cinema can be readily isolated: (1) identification with the representation of a person—the spectator is given double access to this represented person, through the concepts of character and star; (2) the identification of particular objects, persons, or actions as particular objects, persons, or actions. Identification here is a form of classification or categorization and involves the replay of what is already known; and (3) the type of identification which Metz refers to as "primary"—"primary," because it is the "condition of possibility of the perceived."[2] Here, the spectator identifies with "himself" as "look"—as pure capacity for seeing. It is the very institution of the cinema which, by positioning its spectator as punctual source of a unified image, posits simultaneously the coherency of subject and scene. The spectator becomes *the* unified ground of knowledge, of the knowable. Hence, for Metz, this is the fundamental form of identification in the cinema—the form which makes all other types of identification possible and throws the cinema ineluctably onto the side of the imaginary. While the three types of identification just outlined may appear to be drawn from entirely different and alien problematics, they are inextricably linked.

It is the first form of identification—that involving character and star—which is, perhaps, not only the most familiar but the least clearly defined. Dependent as it is on the notion of the integral person filmed, this "secondary" (in Metz's classification) mode of identification presupposes a disavowal of the two-dimensionality of the image and an investment in the reality-status of the diegesis. For the connection established between spectator and character is vaguely one of empathy, sympathy, or even, if the identification is truly successful, substitutability—not "I am like the character" but "I am the same as the character in this respect at least." More accurately, perhaps, it is a position with respect to narrative actions and depicted experiences which becomes exchangeable, and it is this very exchangeability which tends to break down the boundary between spectator and scene.

The mechanism of identification with a character in the cinema pivots on the representation of the body. Narrative is a *mise-en-scène* of bodies and while images without bodies are perfectly acceptable within its limits, it is the character's body which acts as the perceptual lure for and the anchor of identification. In psychoanalytical theory, the ego is the site of identity, conceivable only in terms of the form or limit offered by the bodily envelope. The tendency toward unification which is characteristic of the ego is strongly linked to an image—that of the body. This is the case not only in the Lacanian description of the mirror phase but in Freud's somewhat enigmatic formula in *The Ego and the Id:* "The ego is first and foremost a bodily ego; it is not merely a surface entity, but is itself the projection of a surface."[3] In this sense, it is not only the protagonist of a film who initiates the mechanisms of identification, but any represented body on the screen—offering, sheerly by means of its recognizable form, a reconfirmation of the spectator's own position and identity.

Overlaying and inseparable from identification with the character is identification of and with the star—where the codification relating body and identity is particularly strong. Grounded in the pleasure of tautology, this kind of identification relies on the pure recognition of the star as star. In the words of Stephen Heath, "the star is exactly the conversion of the body, of the person, into the luminous sense of its film image."[4] The star, as "a piece of pure cinema,"[5] reasserts the power of that cinema, its hold on the imaginary of the spectator. The presence of the star insures that I do not identify with the character as "real person" but as superperson, as "bigger than life," as part of a spectacle performed for me. What is involved here is less an identification with a person than an identification with a moment of cinema. The entrance of Rita Hayworth in Charles Vidor's *Gilda* is exemplary in this respect. A shot in which Ballen/George MacReady asks his new wife, "Are you decent?" is immediately followed by an empty frame whose function is simply the establishment and holding of a space. Gilda/Rita Hayworth, tossing her hair back with an almost violent gesture, rises into the frame and answers, "Me?" (later adding, after a reverse shot of Johnny/Glenn Ford and as she pulls her dress strap over her shoulder, "Sure, I'm decent"). The affective value of that moment, strengthened by both lighting and the movement into the frame, is tied to the spectacle of the recognizable face—the very ability of the cinema to manufacture the pleasure of recognition. The film itself prepares the gap which Rita Hayworth fills. And the fact that there always appears to be more of the spectacle, and hence more of the cinema, in the representation of the woman is not without ideological implications. Gilda moves into immobility; the woman is given all at once in the totalization of the fetish.

Identification of and with the star bleeds over into the second type of identification outlined above—identification of objects or recognition of the represented. This type of identification is taken for granted, given the potential for iconicity which the narrative film necessarily exploits. In fact, it is this type of identification which can most accurately be said to situate the cinema in the realm of the imaginary—perpetuating as it does the idea of a one-to-one correspondence between sign and referent. Metz, in *Le Perçu et le nommé,* goes so far as to suggest that even in the case of the abstract or avant-garde film, there is a kind of drive to recognize on the part of the spectator, to translate visual forms and sounds into the familiar. To recognize is to trace back to something already known, and the cinema perpetually exploits what Freud isolated as the compulsion to repeat. The condition of recognizability is not the accretion of metonymic detail which would add up to a realism but, as Metz points out, the reference to the "pertinent traits"[6] which are coded as defining the object, so that in caricature, for instance, a particular stroke of ink is capable of evoking the recognition of a famous nose. The narrative cinema relies heavily on the economy offered by such a system as well as the potential fascination contained in its dialectic of concealing and revealing. For Bazin, this was the fascination of the sequence shot in *Citizen Kane* in which Susan Kane attempts to commit suicide. The camera is located behind a night table on which appear a large glass (taking up almost a quarter of the image, as Bazin notes) with a spoon and an open medicine bottle. Susan's bed is in shadow but her labored breathing is audible. The door of the bedroom is visible far in the background and a knocking sound is heard. Bazin points out the fact that spectatorial recognition is here more strongly related to auditory space than to visual space.

> Without having seen anything but a glass and heard two noises, on two different sound planes, we have immediately grasped the situation: Susan has locked herself in her room to try to kill herself; Kane is trying to get in. The scene's dramatic structure is basically founded on the distinction between the two sound planes: close-up,

Susan's breathing, and from behind the door, her husband's knocking. A tension is established between these two poles which are kept at a distance from each other by the deep focus.[7]

For Bazin in this analysis, to 'recognize' is to make the image readable as a scene. Implicit in his description of the scene is the notion that its "art" is constituted by a reduction in the number and kinds of signifiers necessary for recognition. And this particular scene is exemplary in the extent to which it is the sound which constitutes its readability, its recognizability, rather than the image.

Nevertheless, despite the extent of the contribution of sound to the cinema as we know it, the third type of identification outlined above is founded on a visual analogy—that of the mirror. Metz claims that it is "primary." Metz attempts to demonstrate how the positioning of the spectator in the cinema is analogous with the positioning by the mirror in the Lacanian schema. The mirror phase of the imaginary order reveals that there is a fundamental lack of reality in the image which constitutes the child's first identification. That image is only a reflection (and a *virtual* one) and although it reassures the subject that he is indeed unified, that reassurance is a misleading one and has no knowledge value. Similarly, the cinema presents us with more to perceive (when compared with the other arts), but it is characterized by a founding absence—what is there to be seen is not really there.

> The unique position of the cinema lies in this dual character of its signifier: unaccustomed perceptual wealth, but unusually profoundly stamped with unreality, from its very beginning. More than the other arts, or in a more unique way, the cinema involves us in the imaginary: it drums up all perception, but to switch it immediately over onto its own absence, which is nonetheless the only signifier present.[8]

Since the mirror phase can be understood as the primary identification of the subject, it would seem that it could valuably be used as a model for the understanding of cinematic identification. And this is precisely what Metz does. However, there is an essential difference between the mirror phase and the situation of the cinema. Anything may be "reflected" on the screen except the spectator's own body. Since the spectator cannot identify with his own image, Metz poses the question, "With what does the spectator identify?"

Metz briefly considers the possibility of identification with a character, but rejects it because character identification can only take place in the case of the narrative-representational film. Since Metz is interested in the "psychoanalytic constitution of the signifier of the cinema as such," these identifications, when they occur, must be secondary. But in the viewing of any kind of film, the spectator understands that he can simply close his eyes in order for the film to disappear—that he is, in a sense, the condition of the possibility of the film. The projector behind him and the camera before it are also recognized as conditions of the possibility of the film and the "looks" of all three coincide (they all face in the same direction). Metz concludes that the primary cinematic identification is the spectator's identification with his own look and, consequently, an identification with the camera. This is, most importantly, an identification *of* the viewing subject as a "pure act of perception."[9] Metz's description of primary cinematic identification here rejoins contemporary film theory's obsession with assigning the spectator a position—a project which brings to bear on its object such Freudian concepts as scopophilia/exhibitionism, fetishism, and the meta-psychology of dreaming. The spectatorial position described by film theorists is not a geographical but an epistemological position, one which dictates a particular relationship between subject and object. Coherency of vision ensures a controlling knowledge which, in its turn, is a guarantee of the untroubled centrality and unity of the subject.

All of these concepts utilized by the discourse of positionality in film theory rest upon the assumption that the spectator's investment in the film is based upon the activity of *misrecognition*. The spectator mistakenly identifies discourse as history, representation as perception, fiction as reality.[10] And the film is described as promoting this misrecognition, exploiting its pleasureable effects. For the pleasure of misrecognition ultimately lies in its confirmation of the subject's mastery over the signifier, its guarantee of a unified and coherent ego capable of controlling the effects of the unconscious. This is, essentially, a guarantee of the subject's identity. Thus, there is a sense in which the concepts of scopophilia/exhibitionism, fetishism, and the dreamer/spectator are subsumed beneath that of primary cinematic identification. Primary cinematic identification entails not only the spectator's identification *with* the camera but his identification *of* himself as the condition of the possibility of what is perceived on the screen. The film viewer, according to Metz, is positioned by the entire cinematic apparatus as the site of an organization— the viewer lends coherence to the image and is simultaneously posited as a coherent entity.

I have argued elsewhere[11] that there are difficulties with Metz's use of the mirror analogy—most acutely in his obsession with locating a primal scene for the cinema, an original grounding event which would accurately define or delineate spectatorship. A corollary of this difficulty concerns the conceptualization of identification as instantaneous—a conceptualization which presupposes an undialectical notion of temporality in the film viewing process. Metz upholds the priority of a before/after distinction—the look of the spectator is the originary moment within his system. Finally, identification cannot be located solely in the axis of the look. Yet, Metz's emphasis upon primary identification isolates the image as the determinant cinematic unit and bestows upon perception the quality of immediacy. It is this immediacy imputed to the process of identification which needs to be questioned along with the strict separation effected between primary and secondary identification.

Nevertheless, it seems to me that the strength of Metz's analogy between the cinema and the mirror phase makes it resistant in some way to these objections— gives it a truth whose form might be compared with that accorded by Freud to the neurotic obsession. For the model of the screen as a mirror holds a certain fascination—not only "outside" the cinema, in its theorization, but within it as well. We have only to think of *Madame De. . ., Lady from Shanghai, All That Heaven Allows*. The use of a mirror within a scene strikes us as almost automatically constituting an "insight" about the cinema itself. For it aligns the cinema with specular identification which, while it may not be mechanically and formally linked to the structure of a founding "look," is nevertheless a strong constituent of the classical cinema. The idea of the mirror and its force in the imaginary of film theory—despite the fact that it privileges the visual signifier over the auditory, the moment over temporality—can be linked to the notion of visual captivation by an image, facilitated in the cinema by the darkness of the surrounding auditorium and the immobility of the spectator. The very brilliance of the screen *draws* the eye.

Identification, from this perspective, is inseparable from narcissism or the drama of the ego which the mirror implies. In its primary form identification is quite simply, as Lacan points out, the process of *assuming an image*.

> We have only to understand the mirror stage as an identification, in the full sense that analysis gives to the term: namely the transformation that takes place in the subject when he assumes an image—whose predestination to this phase-effect is sufficiently indicated by the use, in analytic theory, of the ancient term imago.[12]

The transformation effected in the mirror phase is that from a fragmented body-image to an image of totality, unity, coherency. Hence, it is not so much tied to the empirical event of seeing oneself reflected in a mirror as to the ability to conceptualize the body as a limited form. As Laplanche points out, the earliest identification is "an identification with a form conceived of as a limit, or a sack: a sack of skin."[13] Freud's description of narcissism rests on a reference to the treatment of one's own body as a sexual object. Furthermore, incorporation and introjection are seen by Freud as prototypes of identification when "the mental process is experienced and symbolised as a bodily one (ingesting, devouring, keeping something inside oneself, etc.)."[14] An image of the body anchors the ego which in its turn is the point of articulation of identification. Any "body" can be used as a mirror—but in psychoanalytical theory it is most frequently, and significantly, the body of the mother. In identification, the other—whether person or image—is used as a relay, a kind of substitute to conceal the fact that the subject can never fully coincide with itself.

The function of primary identification is, therefore, to establish an outline, a boundary between inside and outside—to trace the form of a unity capable of operating as a desiring subject (Laplanche speaks of the ego as "indeed an object, but a kind of relay object, capable of passing itself off, in a more or less deceptive and usurpatory manner, as a desiring and wishing subject"[15]). Primary identification, then, involves the very constitution of the ego and hence acts as the precondition for the attachment between subject and object which we think of as secondary identification. The history of the subject's secondary identifications is the history of its positioning in an intersubjective economy which, in Freud, is dominated by the Oedipal Complex. Identification with the father, the support of the super-ego, becomes the model for all secondary identifications. (Thus, in the classic schema, the woman's super-ego is necessarily weaker than the man's.)

Metz follows the lines of this argument in distinguishing between primary and secondary cinematic identification and therefore assumes a strict division between

primary identification which is founding and secondary identifications with characters. Laura Mulvey, on the other hand, in her article on "Visual Pleasure," leaves
room for the possibility of articulating a common space within which both primary
and secondary identification operate. In fact, in her argument primary identification
is from the beginning inflected by, overlaid by secondary identification. Instead of
specifying the misrecognition of the mirror phase as the misrecognition of an image
as a reality, an absence as a presence, Mulvey links it to the posited superiority of
the ego ideal.

> The mirror phase occurs at a time when the child's physical ambitions outstrip his
> motor capacity, with the result that his recognition of himself is joyous in that he
> imagines his mirror image to be more complete, more perfect than he experiences his
> own body. Recognition is thus overlaid with misrecognition: the image recognized is
> conceived as the reflected body of the self, but its misrecognition as superior projects
> this body outside itself as an ideal ego, the alienated subject, which, reintrojected as
> an ego ideal, gives rise to the future generation of identification with others.[16]

In this description, the first secondary identification can be traced to the "primary" identification of the mirror phase, and the opposition between primary and
secondary is collapsed. Furthermore, in all of the discussions which abolish the
necessity of the (empirically verifiable) mirror and substitute for it the existence of a
recognizable human form (e.g. the mother), primary and secondary identification
appear to merge. For secondary identification is dependent upon positing the
existence of an object "outside" the subject—an object with a recognizable, more
perfect and complete form—an object which can be incorporated, introjected,
mimicked.

Yet, the thrust of Mulvey's argument is that, in patriarchal society, this kind of
misrecognition and this kind of identity are, quite simply, not available to the
woman. Her discussion deals only with the male spectator (as articulated in the use
of the pronoun "he") and, by implication, situates female spectatorship as the locus
of an impossibility. Mulvey's division of the classical text into two components,
spectacle and narrative, and her correlation of these tendencies with the psychical
mechanisms of scopophilia and identification with an ego ideal, support her analysis
of the cinematic representation of woman as a form of reassurance of male mastery.
Built into the mode of seeing legalized by the classical text is the exclusion of the
feminine. It is necessary to relate the problematic of identification outlined above to
that of sexual difference and its inscription in the cinema in the terms of its address.

Secondary identification, in its classical description, is clearly compatible with,
and fully implicated in the mechanisms of patriarchal society. In Freudian terms it is
articulated with the father, the super-ego, and the Oedipal Complex, and in Mulvey's discussion it represents a bond established between the spectator and the male
protagonist, a bond authorizing a shared power over the image of the woman.
Primary identification, on the other hand, is more difficult—situated as it is in most
discourses on the nether side of sexual difference, before language, the symbolic
order, the Law of the Father. Does it really define a moment which is neuter, which
pre-dates the establishment of sexual difference? Can anyone look into the mirror?

The answer to this question necessarily has serious repercussions for the entire discussion of spectatorship and sexual difference in the cinema.

The work of Luce Irigaray suggests that the woman does not have the same access to the mirror-definition as the man. For Irigaray, the woman is relegated to the side of negativity. Because she is situated as lack, non-male, non-one; because her sexuality has only been conceptualized within masculine parameters (the clitoris understood as the "little penis"), she has no separate unity which could ground an identity. In other words, she has no autonomous symbolic representation.[17] But most importantly, and related to this failure with respect to identification, she cannot share the relationship of the man to the mirror. The male alone has access to the privileged specular process of the mirror's identification. And it is the confirmation of the self offered by the plane-mirror which, according to Irigaray, is "most adequate for the mastery of the image, of representation, and of self-representation."[18] The term "identification" can only provisionally describe the woman's object relations—for the case of the woman "cannot concern either identity or non-identity."[19]

Why then, in the films cited previously—*Lady from Shanghai, Madame De . . . , All That Heaven Allows*—is it the woman who is linked with the mirror? The fact that narcissism and the mirror are violently yoked to the figure of the woman (in the cinema, in psychoanalysis, and in the codifications of common sense) can only be a decoy—concealing the fact that she *is* the mirror for the male and hence has no access to the identity it proffers.

Such an analysis, however, which forces an adherence of the cinema to the apparatus of the mirror, would seem to be totalizing—permitting no possibility for the development of an alternative filmmaking practice. This is precisely why it is necessary to emphasize that the mirror-effect is not present as a precondition for the understanding of the image, as Metz implies in his description of primary cinematic identification, but as the after-effect of a particular mode of discourse which has been historically dominant but will not always be so. In terms of the aesthetic practices with which we are faced however, as Silvia Bovenschen points out, traditional patterns of representation have allowed the woman two options, equally restrictive:

> identification on the part of women could take place only via a complicated process of transference. The woman could either betray her sex and identify with the masculine point of view, or, in a state of accepted passivity, she could be masochistic/narcissistic and identify with the object of the masculine representation.[20]

In the realm of artistic practice, identification on the part of the female reader or spectator cannot be, as it is for the male, a mechanism by means of which mastery is assured. On the contrary, if identification is even "provisionally" linked with the woman (as Irigaray does), it can only be seen as reinforcing her submission.

From this perspective, is it accidental that Freud's description of identification with respect to the woman frequently hinges on the specific example of pain, suffering, aggression turned round against the self, in short, masochism? In *The Interpretation of Dreams,* it is the hysterical symptom which acts as the point of articulation for identification. Apropos of the discussion of a dream in which a woman identifies her friend with herself and then proceeds to dream of an un-fulfilled wish, Freud claims:

> Identification is a highly important factor in the mechanism of hysterical symptoms. It enables patients to express in their symptoms not only their own experiences but those of a large number of other people; it enables them, as it were, to suffer on behalf of a whole crowd of people and to act all the parts in a play single-handed.[21]

In his subsequent reference to the contagion of a hysterical spasm by all the members of a hospital ward, it becomes even clearer that, for Freud, the sign written on the body of the female hysteric is a pivot for the exchange of masochistic identifications.

While this is a relatively early account of identification, aligned with the first topography of psychoanalysis and preceding the description of the ego as a veritable sedimentation or history of object choices, later attempts to rethink identification in the context of the second topography and the intersubjective economy of the Oedipal Complex retain this link between the woman and masochism. The chapter entitled "Identification" in *Group Psychology and the Analysis of the Ego* begins with a delineation of the little boy's identification with his father as an ideal—a "typically masculine" process—and its relation to the Oedipal Complex. The little girl's case is put differently, however. As Freud notes, the mechanism of identifica-tion seems peculiarly resistant to a metapsychological definition, and it is as though Freud's text can only traverse and retraverse a number of scenarios. The first involves the identification of a little girl with her mother—articulated by the fact that the little girl assumes the neurotic symptom exhibited by the mother, a painful cough. The symptom, according to Freud, expresses the little girl's guilty desire to usurp her mother's place with respect to the father. And the imaginary dialogue Freud attributes to the symptom underlines its masochistic effects: "You wanted to be your mother, and now you *are*—anyhow so far as your sufferings are con-cerned."[22] Freud's second scenario dramatizing the relation between the little girl and identification is a simple rewriting of the scene described earlier in *The Interpretation of Dreams*—the scenario merely undergoes a change in location—from a hospital ward to a boarding school for girls. While in the case of the boy, the super-ego is the relay of identification, in the girl's situation, it is the symptom which becomes the "mark of a point of coincidence between two egos which has to be kept repressed."[23]

While these instances in no way exhaust Freud's conceptualization of identifica-tion, they do indicate a difficulty in the theorization of feminine identification which is rearticulated in film theory. Contemporary film theory delineates certain struc-tures of seeing—scopophilia or voyeurism, fetishism, primary identification—which align themselves with the psychoanalysis of the male. The woman is nowhere a spectator in the proper sense of the term. In this regard, it would be interesting to note the contours, the different registers which define the specificity of those discourses which purportedly assume the woman as addressee. In what way, for instance, does the "woman's film" of the 1940s and 50s claim to be the possession of the woman and to locate her as the focal point of its address? Films like *Mildred Pierce, Reckless Moment, Possessed, Stella Dallas, Suspicion,* and *Rebecca,* dealing with derangement, the excesses of the maternal, paranoia, and suffering, would seem to substantiate the claim that identification for the female spectator can only be simultaneous with a masochistic position. This type of text defines the woman's pleasure as indistinguishable from her pain. Nevertheless, this description can only circumscribe the specificity of feminine spectatorship *within* patriarchy. There are also the inevitable contradictions of a discourse which appeals to voyeurism, fetishism, and "primary" identification while simultaneously claiming the woman as addressee. It is the mapping of these contradictions which is essential.

To speak of identification and the cinema, therefore, is not to pinpoint a mechanism which is ideologically neutral, which resides outside of sexual definitions. It is rather to trace another way in which the woman is inscribed as absent, lacking, a gap, both on the level of cinematic representation and on the level of its theorization. As long as it is a question of mastery of the image, of representation and self-representation, identification must be considered in relation to its place in the problematic of sexual difference.

NOTES

1. James Naremore, *Filmguide to Psycho* (Bloomington: Indiana University Press, 1973), p. 72.

2. Christian Metz, "The Imaginary Signifier," *Screen* 16, No. 2 (Summer 1975), p. 51.

3. Sigmund Freud, *The Ego and the Id,* trans. Joan Riviere (New York: W. W. Norton, 1960), p. 16.

4. Stephen Heath, "Film and System: Terms of Analysis," Part II, *Screen* 16, No. 2 (Summer 1975), p. 105.

5. Ibid., p. 104.

6. Christian Metz, *Essais Semiotiques* (Paris: Editions Klincksieck, 1977), pp. 141–43.

7. Bazin, *Orson Welles: A Critical View,* trans. Jonathan Rosenbaum (New York: Harper & Row, 1979), p. 78.

8. Metz, "The Imaginary Signifier," p. 48.

9. Ibid., p. 51.

10. See, along with "The Imaginary Signifier," Jean-Louis Baudry, "The Apparatus," trans. Jean Andrews and Bertrand Augst, *Camera Obscura,* No. 1 (Fall 1976), pp. 104–26 and Metz, "History/Discourse: Note on Two Voyeurisms," trans. Susan Bennett, *Edinburgh '76 Magazine,* No. 1, pp. 21–25.

11. Mary A. Doane, "The Film's Time and the Spectator's 'Space'," paper presented at *Fifth International Film Theory Conference,* Center for 20th Century Studies, Univ. of Wis.-Milwaukee, March 26–30, 1979, forthcoming in *Cinema and Language* (MacMillan).

12. Lacan, *Ecrits: A Selection,* trans. Alan Sheridan (New York: W. W. Norton, 1977), p. 2.

13. Jean Laplanche, *Life and Death in Psychoanalysis,* trans. Jeffrey Mehlman (Baltimore and London: Johns Hopkins University Press, 1976), p. 81.

14. J. Laplanche and J.-B. Pontalis, *The Language of Psycho-Analysis,* trans. Donald Nicholson-Smith (New York: W. W. Norton, 1973), p. 207.

15. Laplanche, p. 66.

Misrecognition and Identity   25

16. Laura Mulvey, "Visual Pleasure and Narrative Cinema," *Screen* 16, No. 3 (Autumn 1975), pp. 9–10.

17. See *Ce sexe qui n'en est pas un* (Paris: Les Editions de Minuit, 1977), pp. 23–32. I am very aware of the danger of essentialism in Irigaray's work—of her tendency to refer to femininity as an essential entity defined by inherent characteristics. Nevertheless, her work also, unlike many feminist theories which do not risk essentialism, avoids the simple rearticulation of patriarchal definitions of woman (even if they are rearticulated only in order to act as the object of a critique of a process which can be seen as a never ending cycle of recuperation). The question—too complex to be dealt with in the context of this article—is whether an attempt to provide the woman with an autonomous symbolic representation is synonymous with essentialism.

18. Irigaray, *Speculum de l'autre femme* (Paris: Les Editions de Minuit, 1974), p. 93.

19. Ibid. This conceptualization of the woman's relation/nonrelation to identity and hence the process of identification necessarily problematizes certain feminists' demands for "stronger female characters" or role models.

20. Silvia Bovenschen, "Is there a Feminine Aesthetic?," *New German Critique,* No. 10 (Winter 1977), p. 127.

21. Sigmund Freud, *The Interpretation of Dreams,* trans. and ed. James Strachey (New York: Avon Books, 1965), p. 183.

22. Freud, *Group Psychology and the Analysis of the Ego,* trans. James Strachey (New York: Bantam Books, 1960), p. 48.

23. Ibid., p. 49.

III

THE TURN OF THE SUBJECT

Stephen Heath

The notion of the subject has been important in much recent work on cinema and film, work that draws on and places itself within current debates in cultural and political theory—questions of the nature and role of ideological struggle, of the development of alternative practices of representation, and so on. It may be helpful, therefore, to try to provide something of a summary account of the implications of that notion today; and this all the more so in that there is a certain sliding in the terms of much discussion, a certain difficulty (sliding and difficulty are then part of the necessity of the discussion, of the problems it engages). What follows is thus a series of clarifications (in intention at least), so many notations of the turn of the subject, the various issues at stake. These notations are given in a more or less straightforwardly didactic mode of exposition which reflects the original circumstances of their elaboration.[1]

Evidently, the summary account is at the same time the argument of a critical position, coming from and going back across and perhaps moving beyond the writings which I and others near me have published over the last five or six years. In this connection, it should be stressed that the notations, set out as numbered 'theses', have an assertive form of the kind 'x is or is not equivalent to y' that is shorthand for the idea of such a critical position and its argument, for, to express it in full, in relation to current theoretical work and understanding, we need to clarify the discussion in the following way, this way being proposed in the interests of the attempt to produce an understanding of the concept of the subject useful in— possible as a point of practical extension in—historical materialism.

(1) The subject is not equivalent to the individual.

The main source for the common assertion of the equivalence of subject and individual is Althusser's essay "Ideology and Ideological State Apparatuses."[2] Though apparently working with a distinction between subject and individual, Althusser there effectively, constantly, makes subject and individual correspond in his description of ideology and its functioning: the subject as the unitary identity of the individual. In fact, the distinction initially retained—referred to as "convenient" by Althusser—is so precisely for the benefit of the final correspondence. Ideology interpellates concrete individuals as subjects, constitutes subjects on individuals who are the given supports of this process; at the same time, individuals always

26

already are subjects, the individual in the individual/subject distinction is 'abstract', a convenience in the description of the mechanism of ideology. The terms of the constitution of the subject in ideology—and ideology *is* this constitution of the subject—are those of the specular and the imaginary (the structure of all ideology . . . is specular, the individual as subject is called to an image of her or himself in that of an 'Absolute Subject' according to a structure of recognition/misrecognition, ideology as the operation of this subject-imaginary); the subject is thus the individual always held in the identity—the identification—of interpellation: subject and individual correspond as that imaginary relation, the individual nowhere but in—only 'abstract' to—the recognition of ideology, entirely subject in its terms. Against which, work exists that has been crucially concerned to develop a grasp of the subject, and of the individual as subject, in displacement of versions of the unity of subject with individual, of the individual-subject (whether that unity be referred to God or reason or . . . ideology): work on language signification and the relations of individuals in their constitution in meaning as human beings, as 'individuals'. Althusser acknowledges Lacanian psychoanalysis, a major factor in this work, but retains only the mirror-phase and the specularity of the imaginary—the imaginary of the individual-subject in ideology, the subject as the category of that ideological imaginary. When Lacan stresses, however, that "the subject is not the individual,"[3] his conception is not that of the subject as a term of the imaginary, supported by an abstract individual; the subject is here the insistence of a complex articulation of instances and, first and foremost, a symbolic production, never a unity, a simple imaginary, a simple effect of ideology. Althusser's individual/subject distinction-for-correspondence cannot be made to agree with the whole weight of Lacan's emphasis on the primacy of the signifier in the constitution of the subject such that there is no individual as a given to be converted into a subject in ideology ("all ideology has as its defining function the 'constitution' of concrete individuals as subjects"); rather, on the contrary, subjectivity is a fact of the 'concrete individual' (to keep Althusser's phrase) in its reality as being in language, which subjectivity in its constitutive division and process cannot be contained or subsumed in any unity (the imaginary is the fiction of such unity). This problematic of the subject is radically different from Althusser's, with, potentially, quite other political effects. The gap between Althusser and Lacan over the notion of the subject and the confusion of the equation of the former with the latter can be quickly illustrated. Lacan's Other, the locus of the symbolic cause and division of the subject, of the decentering of the individual to itself in subjectivity, finds as its response in Althusser's argument the 'Other Subject', the centering of the unity of the individual as subject. Consider the following:

> Through the effect of speech, the subject realises itself more and more in the Other but is already now only pursuing there a half of itself. It will find its desire only ever more divided, pulverised, in the circumscribable metonymy of speech. The effect of language is always mixed up with this, which is the basis of analytic experience: that the subject is subject only from being subjection to the field of the Other, the subject proceeds from its synchronic subjection in the field of the Other. (Lacan)[4]

> The individual is interpellated as (free) subject in order that it freely submit to the commandments of the Subject, in order that it (freely) accept it subjection. (Althusser)[5]

> If one adds, first, that this subject with a capital "S"—absolute and universal subject—is precisely what Lacan designates as the Other with a capital O and, second, that, still according to Lacan, "the unconscious is the discourse of the Other," one can see how unconscious, repression and ideological subjection, while not the same, are materially linked in what may be called the process of the signifier. (Michel Pêcheux)[6]

The Althusser passage bears a certain resemblance to the Lacan from which it is then quite distinct. Despite Pêcheux, who is commenting on this same Althusser passage, the Subject posed as a necessary term in the description of the realization of individuals as subjects in ideology (the Other Subject is a pole in the specular relation in which the subject is produced in recognition; the subject is mirrored in the Subject) is precisely *not* the Other of Lacanian theory (which, far from being a pole in a relation of recognition, far from being a Subject, is the site of lack and desire and the whole circulation of the division of the subject: the material fact of the lack that is the place and the experience of the subject in language; with the unconscious as the 'discourse of the Other', the structuring of desire from this constitutive division of the subject in the field of the Other, in the process of the signifier). Any consequent account of subjectivity and ideology will have as one of its first steps to refuse the individual-subject-imaginary-Subject reduction and confusion. Pêcheux's wanly symptomatic "while not the same," the return of the difficulty of such a reduction, is a little indication of this.

Three sets of remarks at this point as a kind of appendix to this initial proposition, the subject is not equivalent to the individual; remarks which take up one or two issues arising from its discussion and that will be important again later:

First, the unitary identity of the individual as subject with the definition of the latter as purely and simply an ideological construction is the basis for the total sexual indifference of Althusser's account. The individual is a given, "abstract" in the theory, "concrete" in the world, and the individual-subject is a universal function without history or body, constituted by interpellation in ideology, an imaginary relation, exhausted in that. Althusser's stated overall purpose in the "Ideology and Ideological State Apparatuses" essay is to "go beyond" the "descriptive" and "metaphorical" base/superstructure model by developing a theory of the state and the means of its reproduction of the relations of production and of the labor force in those relations; hence the description of "state apparatuses," "repressive" (the apparatus formed by government, army, police, etc.) and "ideological" (the apparatuses of school, religion, family, etc.), the emphasis on the reality of ideology, embodied in apparatuses, having real effects, and so on. At the same time, however, the account of ideology and subject can only serve to confirm the most static, and politically quietist version, of the base/superstructure model. In ideology the subject is in an imaginary relation; individuals are subjects through and only through ideology, the imaginary, in total subjection to the Subject, in total subjection to a more or less infallible State power (the "immense majority" of individuals come out as good subjects, "go all by themselves" in the imaginary freedom provided for them, happy in their illusion; the majority of school teachers, for example, all but the "rare" few, have not the slightest "suspicion" of what they are really being made to do . . .). Outside of ideology (were this possible), the individual is as nothing, is just a given, a cog in the economic real. The real/ imaginary couple, with the subject in the latter mode, tightens back the base/ superstructure model into a totality that leaves no place for contradiction, action, transformation, no way of conceiving the actual fact of different struggles and actions today. Thus, exactly, Althusser's silence on questions of male/female difference and their political implications for a materialist account of subject and ideology. Thus, again, the impossibility, truly unthinkable, of a concept such as patriarchy with its critical questions to the simple terms of a fixed base/ superstructure, economic-real/ideology-imaginary description, with the force of its development in a movement within which subjectivity and sexual difference were and are important, and terms of real and effective action and transformation.

It is true that patriarchy is not too well thought of these days, that it is regarded by some as theoretically quite hopeless, if not empty, as dangerously infected with transhistorical diseases. But then it is a peculiar criticism that, overtaken by a kind of 'theoretical purism' on the basis of merely formal objections, is blind to the fact of a theoretical concept that is political; for it is political action that here commands in a directly theoretically reflected fashion, and what is at stake is *precisely* to produce *contradictions*, to transform, to advance critically, on the basis of a specific struggle and its specific and irreducible questions, historical materialism and its political theory, Marxism. To take Juliet Mitchell's well-known "we should ask the feminist questions, but try to come up with some Marxist answers,"[7] the Marxist answers are not the covering up of the questions with the reiteration of an assured position (Marxism is not a dogma or a theoretical purity) but the development of a politically materialist assumption and articulation of those new transforming questions. Patriarchy is one such question today. And the concept of the subject, it might be added, is perhaps once again, related moreover to ways of considering patriarchy, sexual difference, and so on; these notes, indeed, are finally about the possibility of that concept as such another question.

Second, anticipating here in the light of previous discussion points to be taken up under the heading of the next proposition, it must be stressed that the constitution of the subject is not equivalent to that of the ego (the identifications of the subject). Althusser, holding the subject as a simple category of ideology and imaginary, considers specularity, interpellation, place, identity as constitutive of the subject, with the individual supporting this subjectivity. Hence his reduction of psychoanalysis to a reference-source for an idea of the imaginary, leaving aside the actual concern of psychoanalysis with the history of the individual as 'individual' and the relations of subjectivity produced in and as that history. All distinction between subject and representation as 'subject' is elided: Althusser's subject is its representation, no more no less, is entirely defined in that representation. Representation in this sense, however, is the term of an identification which does not comprise the constitution of the individual as subject, but a specification of the ego, a representing of the subject. A model for this distinction—and thus for the constitutive non-homogeneity, non-unity—of the individual as subject, is the interminably sliding division in the practice of language of the subject of the enunciation and the subject of the enounced; the latter the representation of the subject in discourse that the insistence of the former as the mark of the signifying process of its production, ruins, sets in movement again, and in the very moment of the fixity posed, that representation.

Third, if we say that the subject is not equivalent to the individual, what is at stake in 'the individual'? Do we need—and if so in what sense—to retain an idea of the individual? Althusser needs the individual as support for ideological identification as subject, a kind of raw material on which ideology can work, but the appearance of 'the concrete individual' has a general inevitability beyond the particular form of his argument. It is as though in thinking of men and women as animal and human beings, 'natural' and 'cultural', and so on, a term was required to name and refer to the singular, delimitable body and existence, the fact of beings. The problems are then many and almost overwhelmingly complex: from the recognition that the reality of the seemingly obvious term 'individual' is a fully historical and ideologically full version of human nature with a definite political value (hence Marx's critique of social arguments from the individual, the stress that what individuals are is dependent on the material conditions of their production) to awareness of the difficulty of the very notion of an individual being (evolved physical organs, genetic inheritance, environmental relations of growth and development, etc.). More substantially, too, there can be no question anyway of 'dividing off' an animal from a human reality: there is no unity of either and no separation out into two 'sides'. What one confronts is "a precise constituted materiality"[8] and there is no single opposition of the type individual/subject adequate to that constitution which then demands every time a multiple analysis of instances, articulations, determinations that intersect, cut different ways, open into contradictions one with another. To say that the subject is not equivalent to the individual is one moment of a stress on such a multiplicity, of a necessary attempt to pull away from the reductionism of Althusser's essay so as to refind something of the difficulty of his given—'abstract', 'concrete'—individual. Lacanian theory is of crucial and critical help here, but is only that, is not the end of a materialist conception of subjectivity. What it offers is another account of individual and subject (the subject as implication in the process of the signifier) that is important in its posing of questions of the determinations of subjectivity in relations of language and meaning and of the construction of sexuality and difference there, while simultaneously limiting those questions in, exactly, the idea of 'the subject' it then proposes ('the law of the Other' as a purely absolute symbolic function, an eternal history of the subject in an essential phallic order);[9] with the individual left on the one side as pre-subject organism;[10] on the other as an entity also existing in a society, about which social existence there is little or nothing to say.[11]

It is as though it is necessary always to maintain the use of an individual/subject distinction in the interests of the development of a materialist description (demonstrating the specific productions of the terms of subjectivity, refusing the idealism of the subject-individual unity) and at the same time necessary always to displace and transform that distinction in its different versions in order to arrive at a properly historical materialism which takes human beings in the very fact of its complex relations of existence, the real of its precise constituted materiality.

(2) The "I" is not equivalent to the ego.

'I' is an instance of the subject in language: that is, at once of its division in the symbolic ('I' marks 'me' in the activity of language, in the process of the signifier, which 'I' can never fix, never stop as mine; 'I' itself is an element in that interminable movement, is a constant moment of exchange and circulation and nonidentity: 'I' always joins 'me' to language anew, in difference) and then of its strategies of identification, a point of the insertion of identity (precisely 'I' serves to mark 'me', my[self] possession). The ego is the function of the subject as identity, the reality of its identifications, the subject as object: "the ego is an object—an object which fulfills a certain function that we call the imaginary function."[12] The subject and the 'I' as moment of the division of the subject in language are excentric to the ego as function of the imaginary, "absolutely impossible to distinguish from the imaginary captations which constitute it from top to toe, in its genesis as in its status."[13] This excentricity indeed is the very site of psychoanalytic intervention. Freud's *Wo Es war, soll Ich werden* translated in English as " Where Id was, there shall ego be" and in French as *Le Moi doit déloger le ça,* "The Ego must dislodge the id," is rendered by Lacan as "There where it was, must I come:" psychoanalysis is to be involved not in strengthening the ego (Lacan's conception of the ego is not that of an agency assuring adaptation to reality, which was one practically influential—notably American—extraction from Freud) but in making come the 'I', the subject in the reality of its division and desire, in the assumption of its history.

The nonequivalence of 'I' and ego can be focused again from the distinction briefly mentioned earlier between the subject of the enunciation and the subject of the enounced in the practice of language. I—individual, speaking being—pose myself as 'I', the subject of a proposition, a statement, some meaning, and find myself as 'I' in the division of 'I' in language, the latter's production of the possibility of the place 'I', its excess to that product, the stated, fixed 'I'. 'I' is split, never complete, a simple identity: 'I' am subject of statement and of language. Freud indeed, already, pointed to instances of language of the kind "when I think what a healthy child I was" as examples to help understand the slipping of identity in dreams, the dispersion of the ego in the 'I' of the dream, an 'I' that is process against any unity of the subject, a point of its constant division.

There exists in the practice of language a class of utterances that can be cited in turn as providing something of a linguistic scenario of the imaginary-confusion of 'I' and ego, the closing of the split between the subject of the enunciation and the subject of the enounced: namely *performatives* (the term introduced by the Oxford philosopher J. L. Austin).[14] When I say "I promise," I pose myself as the subject of an action that is really mine in language: I accomplish the action (to say "I promise" is to promise) and, exactly, that accomplishment is the achievement of a stable, unified 'I', full of the action that is mine—only I can promise—and the holding of language entirely to that of action of mine—the utterance is the action. Subject of enunciation and subject of enounced come together: 'I' has the identity of my action that this utterance is. Thus the supreme performative, though never to the best of my knowledge discussed in the classic literature, is "I object" (in a debate, for instance). To say "I object" is to object; I may or may not go on to give reasons for my objection but, no matter, I have objected. Precisely. I have indeed *objected,* brought myself together as an identity, erect, *an 'I' object.* But then, this objectification or 'objection'—is cast in the imaginary, a fiction of the ego ("the ego is an object"); 'I' is always the mark of a subject in language, its cause there, and the split, the division, never closes; the act is also an act *of language,* the imaginary is a production *in relation to* the symbolic which always returns the process of the signifier and the implication of the subject in that process. Performatives are an example of an imaginary of the 'I', but this is to say that that 'I' is an object constructed, underrun by the process it offers to stop. It should be noted, moreover, that performative utterances are significantly supported by controlled social rituals and institutions (what Austin would disingenuously refer to as "the appropriate circumstances"), often with the possibility of reference to quite specific contractual relations between legal "subjects" (promising and "breach of promise," for example). Ego and imaginary are not and cannot be produced and sustained in the sole realm of language.

Here, we can come back a little to Althusser's essay and a problem it raises. Althusser effectively conflates subject and ego: the subject is the identifications given in ideology, realized through the agency of the ideological state apparatuses and functioning through the mechanism of interpellation ("ideology interpellates individuals as subjects"). In illustration of interpellation, Althusser proposes one or two linguistic examples: "Hey you!" shouted in the street and followed by the automatic turn in recognition that it is me thus addressed; a knock on the door, "Who's there?"/"It's me" (strictly speaking, this latter example is presented before the main discussion of interpellation begins; it is introduced nevertheless as an example of that "ideological recognition" which is exactly the effect of interpellation). Interpellation, however, cannot constitute individuals as subjects in this way; indeed, the mechanism of interpellation presupposes subjects,[15] human beings in determinate and constitutive subject relations in the symbolic, in language (not just raw material—'abstract', 'concrete'—'individuals'). The linguistic examples are then striking illustrations not so much of interpellation as of the confusion engendered in these terms by Althusser's account of what is at stake in interpellation. Interpellation on the basis of those examples, that is, is not the constitution of the subject (no interpellation constitutes the subject) but an extreme confirmation of the ego or a fantasy of 'the subject'. "Hey, you!," the voice "in the back," and I turn, become the object of that address, place myself out there, held in the sudden 'presence' of myself (Freud insisted on the link between what is heard and the production of fantasies); "Who's there?"/"It's me," me, ego, an object again, as though I were an evident identity in language, as though language were mine, another scenario of the imaginary. And, moreover, as though to underline the subject/ego confusion and the reality of the examples proposed, the reply, "It's me" is generally considered to be more or less "silly": people do not answer "me," they are not so stupid, are not simply the illusion of themselves in the mirror of "the Subject," and if they do, it is, except in what are often joked about as moments of "forgetfulness" or "confusion" (in which, yes, one touches a real of the imaginary), in specific circumstances (involving intimacy, friendship, expectation, and so on) that engage them with another as subjects in a complex play of relations within which certain imaginary effects are sustained and enacted as positions of me but which are not reducible to those effects, which effects in turn are not constitutive of subjectivity.

Interpellation is in no way the key either to subjectivity or to ideology, neither of which is to be taken as a simple instance of the imaginary: the ideological always involves relations of symbolic and imaginary and works with individuals as subjects in these terms; it does not, that is, constitute 'subjects', convert individuals into unities of illusion that run along all by themselves, but is an activity engaging the process of subjectivity in determinations of meaning—a certain performance of the subject, certain representations—which nevertheless cannot exhaust that process, its material complexity, its contradictions.

Two brief sets of remarks, further to points arising from the above discussion:

First, the distinction of subject and ego in the definition of psychoanalytic practice, Lacan's "must I come," is effectively and importantly a radical position, the refusal of a role of social repair—work. This radical position, however, which has a well-rehearsed fluency (the merest reminder of American practice or the International Psychoanalytic Association will do the trick) is, finally, itself no less questionable. It has to be asked, that is, whether Lacanian analysis and theory, refusing the reinforcement of the ego, have not then in their turn contributed to a formidable reinforcement of 'the subject', to the maintenance of a conception of subjectivity fixed in an idea of 'the subject' beginning and end of theory and practice, last instance. "The assumption by the subject of its history"—but what are the terms of this subject and this history? the dangers that in the end psychoanalysis is the containment of subjectivity and history in the fabrication of a 'history' of 'the subject', its constant assumption of that?

Second, if today, in the mesh of symbolic and imaginary that is any instance of 'I', 'I' pulls toward the confusion of an equivalence with the ego, toward the particular imaginary of the full subject, unity to itself in consciousness, that pull is not some linguistic universal but a directly historical construction. In this connection, it can be noted at once, for example, that the standardization of the term 'subject' in the analysis of language and the classification of what we now call the 'personal pronouns' as such coincide. "Subject' is a term of logic and philosophy that appears in grammars of English in the seventeenth century and is decisively accepted in the latter half of the eighteenth; the personal pronoun classification ('I', 'thou', 'he', 'she') is again present in some seventeenth century grammars and then practically standard in its current form from about 1740. The stabilization of the analysis of language in this way accompanies the move for a reform of language— the development of a regular English prose, insistence on English "refined to a certain standard," given a permanent and rational form, as the medium of educated converse—in the terms and the interests of the bourgeoisie with its economic wealth, rising political power and increasing investment in science as technological advance. The Royal Society, founded in 1662, includes necessarily a committee "for improving the English tongue." Taken up in its conception as instrument of communication (Locke: "the chief end of language . . . to communicate thoughts"), language is to be settled (regularized, refined . . . Swift talks of 'fixing') for the free exchange of ideas and knowledge, which exchange is supported by, is between, uniform and equal subjects, the subject of the universalizing bourgeois ideology (transformation of the class values of its social-economic exploitation into universal values and attributes of the natural being of 'man' now given rational expression in an achieved social organization); the subject instituted equally in political economy and legal theory (economy and law supposedly based on the rights of individual subjects freely to possess property, enter into contracts, buy and sell, and so on). Philosophy then has the task of accommodating this universal subject, clarifying the terms of its agency of knowledge (the subject as "the knower wherever there is knowledge"), founding the 'I am' of self-possession in immediate consciousness ("the groundless ground of all other certainty"). In this respect, the Romanticism of the eighteenth and nineteenth centuries can be recognized as an important but limited contradiction within the setting in place of this version of subjectivity: forcing the universal subject toward questions of the history of the individual, of the *individual history,* it returns a heterogeneous, nongiven subjectivity, with pro- gressive and radical political effects; reproducing the subject in the relation of the individual ('individual' as uniqueness, particularly), it constitutes a new unity, the subject-person-personality, which easily supports the universal subject of bourgeois order, which the latter demands indeed as the complement to its generality—the complement expressed in the received oppositions that are now so "natural" to our thinking 'objective'/'subjective', 'public'/'private', and so on.

(3) No individual is one subject.

The individual, precise constituted materiality, is not *one* but heterogeneous, a process, the term of a multiple and complex construction that is historical, un- finished, not given. To say this is to cut back across the proposition that "the subject is not equivalent to the individual" in order to stress the difficulty of any notion of the subject. And it is to touch, moreover, on the difficulty of the very notion 'subject', the function of which (as immediately preceding remarks will have suggested) has in the past been massively to found a site of unity. 'The subject' has been, that is, a basic component of idealist systems and the problem today is to exploit the material kernel of current theory and debate, to work toward an account of subjectivity that does not rest on any instance of 'the subject'.

In current theory and debate, it is psychoanalysis that offers the decisive empha- sis on this heterogeneity of subject construction. The subject is the term not of a unity but of a division, the effects of which return against every fiction of the one-subject possessed of itself in consciousness (effects which psychoanalysis recognizes in the concept of the unconscious: "the unconscious is a concept forged on the trace of what operates to constitute a subject").[16] The history of individual subjectivity is never over, never concluded (were this so, there would be no scope for psychoanalytic practice) but is interminably actual, ceaselessly going on in the

present. I do not become a subject, 'I' am the term of a structuring production in process which defines 'my' instance of subject. Thus, the subject is neither the beginning nor the end of language: language produces the possibility of subjectivity in which 'I' come again and again in a movement and slipping and difference of identity; I am never finished with language which is always where 'I' 'am' and elsewhere at once to 'me'. Critically, Lacanian theory thus proposes the impossibility of 'the subject' (every schema drawn, every reference to this or that topological figure, every knot tied and untied is an immense effort to represent that impossibility—the process, the division, the articulation of instances); finally, 'the subject' is there nonetheless as the unity that psychoanalysis gives itself as its closed area of operation and conception, its truth.

(4) The subject is produced in language.

Once again, this is an emphasis crucially developed by Lacan (perhaps the major emphasis of his theory, certainly so far as a materialist account of subjectivity is concerned). Language is the 'cause' of the subject: "Its cause is the signifier, without which there would be no subject in the real. This subject is what the signifier represents, and it could only represent something for another signifier: to which the subject who listens is then reduced"—in short, the subject is an "effect of language."[17]

Lacan himself qualifies this emphasis as materialist: "Only my theory of language as structure of the unconscious can be said to be implied by Marxism . . ."[18] What is indeed materialist is the attention, against any given of the subject or any notion of the subject simply realized on the individual as the imaginary of ideology, to the effective construction of subject in language. The subject is not before or beyond, but part of the process of signification, is in the slide of signifiers and their representation ("this subject is what the signifier represents"). Caused in language, the subject is thus not the cause of itself but, precisely, a term of division and nonidentity, with the unconscious the fact of that constitution-division.

Yet what exactly is 'language' in these formulations concerning language as cause of the subject? Language has no such abstract existence. Lacan, in fact, has a further term, the symbolic, which functions in response to this problem of abstraction (and which saves the psychoanalytic subject, the unity psychoanalysis ensures as its field of explanation and operation): language is the reality of the symbolic but the latter is, as it were, the term of the psychoanalytic description of the subject, of the order of the constitution of the subject in language, which order is the realization of the universal of the subject (the phallus as "the privileged signifier," the final and eternal meaning of symbolic exchange). Nor does language have any existence in unity. The 'unity' of language is a powerful political and ideological operation, the most striking example of which is the institution of "French" in the conjunction of the development of a centralized State following the Revolution (again, the necessity is to render uniform "the language of a great nation" in the interest of free communication, in the interest, that is, of the maintenance of the national hegemony of a particular class). There is, in fact, something of this same unity in Lacan's language-symbolic and it is not without significance in this respect that, in extreme moments, its universality seems to be a nationalism of the French language—

French-speakers have the symbolic (a good working unconscious, etc.), the English are precarious, very dubious, and the Japanese are beyond the pale (Miller: "You have already excluded the Japanese from analysis?" Lacan: "I have already excluded the Japanese, of course . . ."[19] Of course.).

The process of the subject in language is exactly that: a process, not a structure of the subject. If language is the site of the symbolic constitution of the subject in the movement of the signifier, then that constitution is always historical, multiple, heterogeneous, always specific and specifying subject effects. There is no existence of language other than in this radical complexity.

Something of what is at stake can be demonstrated with an example. Take, for instance, the sentence: *He who died on the cross to save us all never existed.*[20]

Analysis concerned with an effectively materialist account of subjectivity would have to consider at least the following:

(i) I cannot understand the sentence, "what is being said," unless I know English: the sentence is involved and involves me in the fact of the English language. But my relation to English is not a unified and uniform 'knowledge': I do not know "the English language," there is no "fact of the English language" in this sense; it is not some simply given coherence, a unity.[21] My relation is a definite history of and in language: through family and school and work to the various distributors of language available to me—to *me,* not equally and similarly available to everyone, every one person, class, sex, race, and so on—in my society (libraries, press, radio, television, cinema, advertising, etc.); a relation that has indeed a crystallization in a specific institution of English, which institution is what I know and live, including in its support and production of class division and conflict.

(ii) Repeating language, the sentence is inevitably implicated in particular discursive formations: language has no existence other than in acts of language that engage determinate forms of meaning, pose what I want to say, and the very terms of the "I want to say," in and from those forms (no one has ever spoken 'language' or 'a language'). This emphasis must be clearly guarded against idealist misinterpretation: it maintains not that language determines, is the instance of determination, but that language exists and only exists as an area of determinations, as always condition-and-effect of social practice (a dialectical conception close to that of Marx and Engels in their stress on the simultaneity of linguistic and social activity, on language as "practical consciousness"). The influential error of structuralism and post-structuralism, as of Lacanian psychoanalysis, is an ultimate *belief* in 'language', which becomes exactly the instance of determination, either as the system underlying all individual uses (but meaning was always more or less problematic in this account, left for the social taken as these individual uses and grasped as a contract for communication) or as the symbolic (with the constant meaning of the phallus, the phallus 'destined' for this role).

To recognize the existence of language as an area of determination is to recognize a complex historical reality in every linguistic act, and that complexity is multiple, diverse in its times and levels of operation. Thus, quite simply, the example-sentence is bound up in the ready-made—the preconstruction—of "He who died on the cross to save us all," the history of that. Thus, more difficulty, it is bound up with its movement with and from that preconstruction in a way that is contradictory, open in its process to different effects. The sentence moves me—speaker or listener, writer or reader—to a position, the assertion of the nonexistence of "He who died . . ."; even if I wish to deny the assertion, I must take up its—that—position. At the same time, the act of the assertion itself is involved in a recognition of "He who died . . .," an acknowledgment of an effective existence; and this is correct, since "He who died . . ." does have a discursive existence here which gathers up a whole history of Western religion, its forms today, a certain context of current argument, and so on. "He who died . . .," that is, may or may not be judged to have existed but that judgment either way is the recognition of the existence of "He who died . . ." as a discursive reality, which discursive reality is a historical mesh of past and present social practice and practices in which I am here placed and in relation to which "I am" in the sentence (and that historical mesh is not then 'extra-discursive'; its reality includes the effectivity of discursive formations, language as condition-and-effect of social practice).

(iii) The "I" that I am in the sentence is difficult again. The coming together and apart of the subject of the enunciation and the subject of the enounced is condensed in the "us" of "He who died on the cross to save us all." "Us" is an element of the enounced, of the topic with which the statement of the sentence is concerned, the universal savior; simultaneously, "us" involves me in the utterance of the sentence, the fact of its enunciation, points the address of the sentence from me, speaker, to you, or from someone to me, listener. The "us" is a knot of join and division; there is no simple position for a "me": my relation is an implication in the production of the enunciation as well as in the product of the enounced. This relation, further-more, is always for me, through and through, a historical and social relation that engages the terms of my subjectivity in the actual conjuncture of this utterance in the manner that is not the simply determined closure of a position. I am in play in any position I have in the sentence: for example, as between its anti-Christian position and its statement of that position in an assertion of nonexistence which leaves aside the question of the historical existence and significance of Jesus of Nazareth by its adoption of the "He who died . . ." formula which, in turn, traps me in the address of an "us" that, even as in the movement of the sentence I perhaps elude its religious embrace, catches me in the position of an ideology of a common humanity, the "us" of "my fellow men," that is strong in the specific institution of English I know . . . And this is to ignore the fact of the enunciation of the sentence here, that it is given as an example in a particular mode of argumentation with particular conventions of exposition, particular strategies of subjectivity, that it is derived from a particular kind of Althusserian account of ideology and subject-construction in which the reference to the Christian religion is powerful and powerfully symptomatic (of the eternalization of ideology in a necessary and invariable subject-form, "the formal structure of all ideology being always the same"), that it is quoted in an argument working in most respects against that account and in a particular journal of "film, communications, culture and politics. . . ."

(iv) 'The subject' is then this play: not one, but the subjectivity engaged in this movement, the multiple and contradictory possibilities of meaning. I am subject in the realization of language in meaning, the turn of that process; which realization is my existence, precise constituted materiality, in the historical mesh of effects and determinations, including their instance in language.

(5) A signifying practice involves relations of subjectivity.

This proposition has a number of difficulties, points where it is important, as it were, at once, for a start, to avoid misunderstanding. The delimitation of "a signifying practice" is one such difficulty inasmuch as it tends toward confirmation of a series of given and assumed unities of practice—literature, cinema, and so on. To treat cinema, for example, as signifying practice must not be its assumption as 'cinema', as some simply specific practice, unified in that specificity. Cinema in practice is beyond the definition of 'cinema' at any given moment (the definition supported and maintained by its social institution), existing in films that are always the fact of a precise social relation (which relation includes the effects of the particular social institution of cinema).

To stress that the given and assumed unity of a signifying practice does not exhaust—and in this sense, at least, is false to—the reality of its practice, which brings into play each time a definite historical and social engagement of meaning and subjectivity, is to stress a certain coextensiveness of signifying practice with sociality, with social being. Social relations are always, simultaneously with their other determinations, a practice of signification; the social is a permanent implication in meaning (attempts to identify and situate areas of experience outside this implication merely serve to endorse its strength, the very problematic of meaning; as again, in opposite and complementary fashion, does the institution of recognized and powerfully controlled areas in which the production of meanings is allowed and regularized in its potential; as, for example, literature with its accompanying and defining criticism, variously instituted in school and journal, newspaper and university).

Semiology—the semiology programmed in Barthes's *Elements of Semiology*—took something of its stand here: social and signification are in equivalence; everything signifies, from kinship to furniture; semiology, the science of signs, studying the systems of the different practices (kinship, furniture, etc.), is the necessary sociology, a socio-logics: "the universal semanticisation of uses is fundamental: it reflects the fact that the real is always intelligible and should lead finally to the merging of sociology and socio-logics."[22] The problem then was exactly the notion of intelligibility. The conception of language that semiology adopted as model from Saussure was that of a system of communication between purely given subjects (Saussure's '*sujet parlant*'); thus Lévi-Strauss defines the aim as "the interpretation of society as a whole in function of a theory of communication."[23] In this perspective, ideology is simply hidden communication, an exchange of signs concealed by a process of naturalization (analyzed in terms of connotation), and the critical role of semiology, stressed above all by Barthes, is the demonstration of intelligibility, the bringing to light of signs and their systems. All of which is to leave aside the difficulties of the very idea of communication. To declare its function to be communication is to catch up language in a teleology that essentializes it in the terms of a particular ideological conception, supporting precisely a social and political representation of free subjects in relations of free and equal exchange, with a basis in mutual understanding, a common and unproblematic intelligibility of the real.

The difficulties of communication were felt within semiology as the question of the status of language, again above all in the work of Barthes. Where Saussure had seen language as a model for semiology, one important system among other systems, Barthes saw semiology as everywhere brought up against the presence of language, language as inextricable foundation of the meanings of other systems. The consequences of this then go beyond those of a mere reversal of emphasis. If signifying practices are penetrated by and founded in language (and, with regard to cinema, no one makes or sees a film before or outside language, but always in relation to and with language), there are strictly speaking no signifying practices in the sense of semiology's distinct systems of signification. What one is dealing with as a "signifying practice" or an "institution" (remembering that meaning is not instituted from some one place) is in every instance a complex of relations, a heterogeneity (by which a signifying practice is crossed but which it may well be the point of its institution to attempt to contain). The locus of this heterogeneity, its pressure almost, is the subject, the subject not one but the realization of the process engaged, the subjectivity in play.

It should be added, recalling earlier discussion, that if language is everywhere, it is not as simple system but, exactly, as practice. One encounters not 'language' or 'a language' but practices of language; language exists only as signifying practice—"discursive formations" are signifying practices of language—and itself offers no unity to which subject and signification can be returned.

The starting proposition, "a signifying practice involves relations of subjectivity," might be rewritten, and the argument advanced, as follows: signifying practices are subject productions. What is then at stake is the need to maintain the dialectical ambiguity of "subject productions" (ambiguity may not be, as Benjamin suggested, the visible image of dialectics, but it can help at certain points of theoretical and conceptual difficulty to keep two necessary emphases in movement together): productions of the subject, productions by the subject; or better, avoiding 'the subject', subject production as a give-and-take of relations between, say, spectator and film, between precise constituted materiality and particular work of signification ('the subject', the subjectivity in question, being these relations in meanings).

The impasse of the failure to maintain this give-and-take of relations is striking and politically serious in its consequences: either the subject determined or produced, the one subject given, in passive subjection, of the subject freely creating and according meanings, pulling this way or that at active will; in the first case, no hope, it all works perfectly, in the second, lots of hope but not much to be done, since it goes the way you want already (all determinations are elsewhere, in the economic 'real').

In both cases, variants of subject-individual correspondence are operative. The second recovers and reconstitutes 'the subject' onto the individual who then confronts signifying practice from the distance of this unity, as 'given subject'. The first knows no existence of the individual other than as the unity of 'the subject' produced in ideology. Thus Althusser is led, as the very assumption of the terms of his argument in the "Ideology and Ideological State Apparatuses" essay, to the notion that individuals-as-subjects *'marchent tout seuls'*, go all by themselves, like so many automata, "in the immense majority of cases," with the exception of a few difficult subjects, a few *'mauvais sujets'*, duly brought back into line by the repressive powers of the State; hence indeed the necessity of "a scientific discourse (without subject) on ideology." Individual-subjects are by definition—that of ideology as characterized by Althusser—subjected, locked in illusion; the "immense majority"—the popular masses—have had it, pinned "in the back" like so many immobilized butterflies, with only theory, subjectless scientific discourse, and the political directives of the Party able to save them, put them right (they will have at long last the vision of the "process without Subject(s) or End(s) of history . . .").

Thinking quickly of cinema and film in this context of subject production, it is not a question of 'a' or 'the' subject 'in' or 'outside' a film; it is not a question of conceiving film on the model of interpellation, which, at the same time, is not to say that a film will not adopt and construct strong forms of interpellation; it is a question of insisting on the experience of a film, its signifying practice, as so many relations of subjectivity, relations which are not the simple 'property' of the film nor that of the individual-spectator but which are those of a subject production in which film and individual have their specific historical and social reality as such.

(6) The ideological is a political function of representation.

If we are to understand what is at stake in the conception of the ideological and of the possibility and necessity of ideological struggle, we need to pose not an eternally defining instance of 'the subject' but the question, each time, of the representation of meanings (which representation of meanings may well include, at specific times, and this is indeed part of our present history, definitions of 'the subject', a stable identity of exchange).

Recent critical work on ideology has been concerned to reject the concept of representation and hence what is characterized as "the classic Marxist problem of ideology."[24] Representation, it is argued, is inevitably implicated in an idea of correspondence, the link between representation and represented where the latter is the determination of the former which does or does not correspond (the representation represents or misrepresents the represented). To hold to the concept of representation is thus to hold at some stage to a reality given outside of its production in representation and so available to be known truly or falsely by consciousness ("the classic Marxist problem of ideology"). The moment any determining action by the means of representation in constituting what is represented is allowed (for instance, the stress in many of the preceding remarks here on the constitutive engagement of subjectivity in language, in relations of meaning, against any notion of a simple grasp of consciousness to the world, against any phenomenology of 'the real'), then the forms of correspondence/noncorrespondence are shattered and with them the very concept of representation—"the products of signifying practices do not 'represent' anything outside them."

Such a critique, however, is inadequate in its account of representation, failing—and this despite the suggestion that these are its grounds—to bring into that account the terms of subject production in signifying practice. Representation is not a correspondence (except for philosophical argument) but, in practice, a certain return of the subject: divided-constituted in language, the individual in subjectivity crosses and is in place in meanings, is a movement of relations of meaning, with representation first and foremost this process. The question of representation, that is, is not initially that of the represented (which is indeed a specific action of representation and hence not a term from which the question should be posed) but that of the subjective effect produced, the point of the action of representation, of its represented. Misrepresentation, and struggle against ideologies on that basis, need not be simply abandoned (quite the contrary). With regard to sexual difference, for example, misrepresentation is defined in the analysis of existing relations of subjectivity in meaning and of their effects from a political perspective of the demonstration of oppression; misrepresentation then being not the position of an essence but the opposition of a different practice, based on the need to transform existing relations (not to recover some precedent). Or again, cinema can and should be examined in its institution of relations and effects, its reply to the subject production of meanings, its representing of available terms—of grounds—of subjectivity.

These formulations are themselves inadequate if not filled out with a number of clarifications of their emphasis.

A signifier represents a subject for another signifier; a sign represents something for someone (these definitions are made by Lacan).[25] Signification, the relations of meanings, is the process together of these two 'sides' and it is this complex production that is at stake in representation, that is that certain return of the subject mentioned above. Representation, in other words, names the process of the engagement of subjectivity in meaning, the poles of which are the signifier and the subject but which is always a complex, specifically historical and social production that can know those poles only as theoretical abstraction and/or ideological construction (thus the problem of psychoanalysis with its assumption and confirmation of 'signifier' and 'subject'). The ideological is not in or equivalent to representation—which, precisely, is this complex process of subjectivity—but is the constant political institution of the productive terms of representation in a generalized system of positions of exchange. The stresses of "constant political institution" can be underlined: institution-language, meaning, signifying practice, representation outrun in their production any closure of an ideological position which is thus not a kind of automatic result but an intervention, an appropriation, in meanings which is the reality of the given (financed, legislated, etc.) "ideological apparatuses" (it being understood that these apparatuses cannot simply subject, engaging as they do a process of subjectivity which is not simply 'their' construction, and that the intervention and appropriation in meaning is not a conspiracy or the translation of a will but the effect of the actual and multiple determinations of social practice in a particular social formation); constant—there is no end to the process of the engagement of subjectivity in meaning, never a one position, the subject achieved once and for all, and subjectivity is indeed the liberty of that process which must thus be ceaselessly caught up, entertained (hence the ideological importance of representing machines—cinema, television and so on—and the more or less difficult problems of control they pose in our societies); political—the ideological is not representation but its political function, the modes of institution do not arise spontaneously from representation but from the political reality of the social practice (which is not to say that the ideological is the 'expression' of a subject-class but is to say that it may and will in specific social formations contain determinate effects of the realization of class struggle).

Adapting Lenin, it seems right to say, as these notes run out, that the reality with which they deal is always richer in content, more varied, more multiform, more lively and ingenious than is imagined by even the best theories.[26] It seems right not because the point is then to lay down the arms of the development of analysis and theory (Lenin's own example is sufficient indication of that) but because the need is constantly to push and rework analysis and theory into the richness and variety of experience, in order to understand and use and extend its transforming possibilities. These notes have been an attempt at something of a pushing and reworking of the notion of 'the subject', its critique in the interests of a materialist account of subjectivity. Of course, this attempt does not go very far; but the distance within which it stays, its difficulties and contradictions are part of the current theoretical and political stakes of subjectivity as a significant, indeed fundamental site of struggle.

As coda, a brief return to cinema, present here and there in preceding remarks. It is apparent now that the major error of the production of the question of cinema and representation in conjunction with an appeal to the explanatory powers of psychoanalysis has been the location of a complete subject of cinema, via the description of the latter exclusively as single apparatus, instance, or whatever. Primary identification, voyeurism, and so on have entered as static and absolute determinants, without history; in every case, there is primary identification, the all-perceiving subject, the phallic look. . . . The point is not to deny these descriptions but to insist on their historicization (and thus, in fact, on the historicization of the concept of 'subject' in the context of the terms of the engagement of subjectivity as stressed in these notes). We have to learn to understand and analyze the redistribution in specific conjunctures of the operation of the cinema, the redeployment of limits—for example, the recasting of the 'all-perceiving subject' from the reality of a film practice in its material complexity, its possibility of contradictions. Redeployment and definition of limits, since to grasp the former is to understand also that cinema is not a set of essences more or less actualized in its history (and generally more, always there), but a practice, signifying practice, only in the historical and social relations and institution of which are such 'essences' produced, and cinema held to them, to a 'the subject'.

NOTES

1. The material for this article was prepared as a contribution to a seminar taught with Teresa de Lauretis and Annette Kuhn for the *Center for Twentieth Century Studies* of the University of Wisconsin-Milwaukee.

2. Louis Althusser, "Idéologie et appareils idéologiques d'Etat," *La Pensée* no. 151 (June 1970); reprinted in *Positions* (Paris: Editions Sociales, 1976); translation in *Lenin and Philosophy and Other Essays* (London: New Left Books, 1971).

3. Jacques Lacan, *Le Séminaire livre II* (Paris: Seuil, 1978), pp. 11, 17.

4. Jacques Lacan, *Le Séminaire livre XI* (Paris: Seuil, 1973), p. 172; translation *The Four Fundamental Concepts of Psychoanalysis* (London: Hogarth, 1977), p. 188 (note that, as often elsewhere, the translation is badly in error in its rendering of this passage).

5. L. Althusser, *Positions,* p. 121; *Lenin and Philosophy and Other Essays,* p. 169.

6. Michel Pêcheux, *Les Vérités de La Police* (Paris: Maspero, 1975), p. 123.

7. Juliet Mitchell, *Women's Estate* (Harmondsworth: Penguin, 1971), p. 99.

8. Raymond Williams, "Problems of Materialism," *New Left Review,* no. 109 (May–June 1978), p. 7. William's *Keywords* (London: Fontana, 1976) contains useful details as to the histories of the words 'individual' and 'subject' (pp. 133–36, 259–64).

9. The phallus has "the privilege of being universally the index of the lack" produced from the subject's relation to the signifier; Serge Leclaire, *Psychoanalyser* (Paris: Seuil, 1968), p. 181. Sociologically (so to speak), and "with no paternalism towards women," it then only remains to acknowledge that "all community is phallic," by definition, irredeemably; Jacques-Alain Miller, "Pseudo-Barthes," in *Prétexte: Roland Barthes* (Paris: Union Générale d'Editions, 1978), p. 208.

10. "Once caught in the net of language, the relation of the organism to its environment is transfigured into that of the subject which speaks to what is called its being . . ." Moustapha Safouan, *Etudes sur l'Oedipe* (Paris: Seuil, 1974), p. 117. The entry into language submits the needs of the organism to the formulation of demands which in the fact of their formulation, their fixing of the process of the signifier, leave over the effect of that process in the subject, the desire instituted from the lack in the field of the Other.

11. As witness the fiasco of Lacan's encounter with the Vinçennes students in 1969: no way of understanding Marx until the discourse of the hysteric and the advent of psychoanalysis, society is dominated by the practice of language, revolutionary aspiration ends in the discourse of the master, psychoanalysis at least is progressive in that it will tell you what you are really rebelling against; "L'impromptu de Vinçennes," *Magazine littéraire,* no. 121 (February 1977), pp. 21–24. The issue is not that Lacan was not locally acute at several points in the encounter but that there is no possible movement beyond the assumed positions of the theory in its psychoanalytic closure, the site alone of knowledge and explanation. Or witness again the almost total absence of any historical reference or consideration of the historical in Lacan's massive work; history is simply interior to the elaboration of the theory of the subject (Miller, in his article previously cited, gives a striking illustration of this when he suddenly declares something to be "perfectly visible in history," see the *Nicomachean Ethics*—history is a reference to Aristotle, a bibliography for psychoanalysis).

12. J. Lacan, *Le Séminaire livre II,* p. 60.

13. J. Lacan, *Écrits* (Paris: Seuil, 1966), p. 374.

14. J. L. Austin, *How to Do Things with Words* (Oxford: O.U.P., 1962; second revised edition, 1975).

15. The difficulties of this have been demonstrated at length by Paul Q. Hirst, "Althusser and the Theory of Ideology," in *Economy and Society,* vol. 5, no. 4 (1976); reprinted in P. Hirst, *On Law and Ideology* (London: Macmillan, 1979).

16. Lacan, *Écrits,* p. 830.

17. Ibid., p. 835.

18. J. Lacan, "Sur l'objet de la psychanalyse," in *Cahiers pour l'analyse,* no. 3 (May-June 1966), p. 10.

19. Discussion in *Ornicar?* no. 4 (1977), p. 17.

20. This sentence is not taken "at random" (later remarks will pick up this point); it is an English version of a sentence considered by M. Pêcheux in the course of his attempt to suggest the basis for a theory of discourse within the perspective of Althusser's "Ideology and Ideological State Apparatuses" essay (Pêcheux, op. cit., pp. 88–89). I adopt elements from Pêcheux's discussion after my own fashion in an analysis that is intended to grasp a real complexity beyond the subject-imaginary-ideology limitation. (For a general situating of Pêcheux's work, see "Notes on Suture," *Screen,* vol. 18, no. 4 (Winter 1977/78), pp. 69–74).

21. The purpose and conception of the most influential linguistic theory of recent times have been defined in terms that apparently go quite contrary to such an emphasis: Chomskyan linguistics is devoted, that is, precisely to the description of competence as "the speaker-hearer's knowledge of his language." Without being able here to enter into substantive discussion, one or two points can be noted. The linguistics developed by Chomsky is indeed a problem of knowledge; it seeks to characterize the system of linguistic knowledge that has been attained and is internally represented by a person knowing some language (a further question is that of accounting for the growth and attainment of that knowledge). The procedure of this linguistics is thus the characterization of "potential systems of knowledge," while its end is an innate linguistic theory, "universal grammar," "what we may suppose to be biologically given, a genetically determined property of the species," this innate schema defining "the 'essence' of human language" (Noam Chomsky, *Language and Mind* (New York: Harcourt, Brace & World, 1968), p. 76. Between universal grammar and performance, "the actual use of language in concrete situations," competence is projected as the knowledge internalized by the speaker of a language, a realization of the "essence" as a particular language. Chomsky himself, however, is scathing on such notions as "a Language": "So what is a language? There is a standard joke that a language is a dialect with an army and a navy. These are not linguistic concepts." (N. Chomsky, *Language and Responsibility* [Harvester: Hassocks, 1979], p. 190). No serious study can have "language" and "a language," as object inasmuch as these notions have no principled reality; serious study can only be based on "the idealization to systems in idealized homogeneous communities" (ibid., p. 191). The critique of "language" and "a language," that is, serves to support the idealization of competence: on the one hand, individuals and a variability of the system or systems "in the heads" of these individual speakers in a "language community" (itself to be analyzed as a "question of power" alone); on the other, a competence that poses and presupposes a general subject-form. "Real speakers" are "individuals" who can go in all sorts of ways but they are joined at the same time in an ideal knowledge (a grammar) which is available in the linguistic intuitions of individuals and which is the only serious linguistic reality of "language." This subjectivity of the individual in language is derived from a universal subject-form—the knowledge of universal grammar—that is its very condition.

22. Roland Barthes, "Eléments de sémiologie," in *Communications,* no. 4 (1964) and translation, *Elements of Semiology* (London: Cape, 1967); cf. Roland Barthes, "A propos de deux ouvrages recénts de Cl. Lévi-Strauss: Sociologie et socio-logique," in *Informations sur les Sciences Sociales,* vol. 1, no. 4 (1962), pp. 114–22.

23. Cl. Lévi-Strauss, *Anthropologie structurale* (Paris: Plon, 1968), p. 95.

24. See especially Hirst, section E, " 'Representation' "; *On Law and Ideology,* pp. 68–73.

25. See e.g. *Le Séminaire livre XI,* p. 188; *The Four Fundamental Concepts of Psychoanalysis,* p. 207.

26. Cf. "History as a whole, and the history of revolutions in particular, is always richer in content, more varied, more multiform, more lively and ingenious than is imagined by even the best parties, the most conscious vanguards of the most advanced classes." V.I. Lenin, " 'Left-Wing' Communism, An Infantile Disorder," *Selected Works,* vol. 3 (Lawrence and Wishart: London, 1967), p. 401.

IV

FILM BODY

AN IMPLANTATION OF PERVERSIONS

Linda Williams

In the first volume of *The History of Sexuality,* Michel Foucault writes that ever since the seventeenth century there has been in the West an increasing intensification of the body both as object of knowledge and element in the relations of power.[1] This intensification has emerged in a proliferation of discourses of sexuality which have produced a whole range of sexual behavior now categorized as perverse. For Foucault this "implantation of perversions" is the result of the encroachment of power on bodies and their pleasures.

> The implantation of perversions is an instrument—effect: it is through the isolation, intensification, and consolidation of peripheral sexualities that the relations of power to sex and pleasure branched out and multiplied, measured the body, and penetrated modes of conduct. And accompanying this encroachment of powers, scattered sexualities rigidified, became stuck to an age, a place, a type of practice. A proliferation of sexualities through the extension of power; an optimization of the power to which each of these local sexualities gave a surface of intervention: this concatenation, particularly since the nineteenth century, has been ensured and relayed by the countless economic interests which, with the help of medicine, psychiatry, prostitution, and pornography, have tapped into both this analytical multiplication of pleasure and this optimization of the power that controls it. Pleasure and power do not cancel or turn back against one another; they seek out, overlap, and reinforce one another. They are linked together by complex mechanisms and devices of excitation and incitement.[2]

Foucault's argument offers a significant challenge to the commonly held notion that sex exists autonomously in nature, independent of any discourse on it and as a natural challenge to a power which either pretends it does not exist or prohibits it. He argues instead that sex is a fictitious causal principle that allows us to evade the true relation of power to sexuality. Thus, we do not escape social determination when we have recourse to the supposedly natural pleasures of the body since the particular forms these pleasures take are themselves produced by the needs of power.

Psychoanalysis has been a major force in the deployment of a sexuality that has intensified the body as a site of knowledge and power, making this body the major arena for the discovery of the nonexistent "truth" of sex. But nowhere has the deployment of sexuality, and its attendant implantation of perversions, been more evident than in the visible intensification of the body that came about with the invention of cinema. This invention itself grew out of a scientific discourse on the body in the work of Muybridge and Marey whose "chronophotography" attempted to document the previously unobserved facts of its movements. And yet, this very machinery of observation and measurement turns out to be, even at this early stage, less an impartial instrument than a crucial mechanism in the power established over that body, constituting it as an object or subject of desire, offering up an image of the body as mechanism that is in many ways a reflection of the mechanical nature of the medium itself.

The Film Body and the Body of the Spectator

In his essay on "The Apparatus" Jean Louis Baudry argues that the cinematic apparatus—considered not just as the film itself but the technical specificity of the entire cinematic process and its ideological effects—brings about a state of regression and narcissism in the spectator. Baudry suggests that this regression imitates an original condition of unity with the body of the mother. In this original state of plenitude, before the separation of the subject's body from everything else in the world, the images produced by dreams and hallucinations are taken as real perceptions. Baudry suggests that the cinematic apparatus imitates aspects of this original condition of unity by placing the film spectator before "representations experienced as perceptions" similar to those of dreams and hallucinations. Thus the cinema recreates a form of lost satisfaction from a time when desire could be immediately satisfied through the transfer of the memory of a perception to the form of hallucination.[3]

In other words, according to Baudry, the very formation of the cinematic apparatus responds to a desire to figure a unity and coherence in the spectator that has long since been lost in the spectator-subject's entrance into the symbolic of difference. But if the "invention" of the cinema corresponds to a desire to figure a lost unity in the body of the spectator-subject, what is the effect of this invention on the primary object of this spectator-subject's vision: the human body figured in the film?

To a certain extent we know what the status of this body becomes as a relay to the body of the spectator within the already formulated institution of classical narrative films and their system of "suture."[4] To a certain extent also we already know how these films constitute the male body within the film as surrogate for the look of the male spectator and the female body as site of the spectacle.[5] But we know much less about the position of these male and female bodies in the "pre-historic" and "primitive" stages of the evolution of the cinema, before codes of narrative, editing and mise-en-scène were fully established. I hope to show that this "film body," like the apparatus itself, operates to restore a lost unity in the spectator-subject, but that

this unity is a more specific and perverse response to the threat of disunity posed by
the visible "presence" of the body on the screen—that in fact, there exists, at the
very moment of the emergence of a "simulation machine"[6] capable of figuring the
human body in a dream-like "representation mistaken for a perception," a dramatic
restaging within this representation of the male child's traumatic discovery of, and
subsequent mastery over, sexual difference.

Both Eadweard Muybridge and Georges Méliès, two child-men whose work, in
different ways and at different times, was formative of the institution and apparatus
of cinema, privilege the body as pure object of truth in their work. For Muybridge
this truth is scientific—a matter of isolating the essential. He strips the body of
clothes to better reveal its musculature and movement. He isolates it against a bare
background or grid to measure it, and he tailors his frame to accommodate the
body's full extension in size. For Méliès, on the other hand, the truth of the body is
both magical and mysterious. He complicates and clutters his bodies with a vast
array of costumes, mechanized scenery, and gadgets of all sorts, and he situates all
of this within a rudimentary diegesis. But for both men the naked body of the
woman, whether boldly and repeatedly figured by Muybridge as in the plate from
The Human Figure in Motion[7] (fig. 1), or briefly and coyly glimpsed as in this still
from one of Méliès rare "stag" films entitled *After the Ball*[8] (fig. 2), poses a problem
of sexual difference which it then becomes the work of the incipient forms of
narrative and mise-en-scène to overcome.

Eadweard Muybridge

As early as 1880 Muybridge had illustrated his lectures on animal locomotion with
the aid of his own "zoopraxiscope"—a circular glass plate that could mount up to

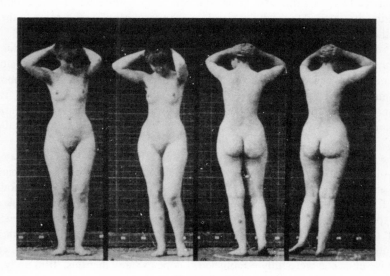

Figure 1

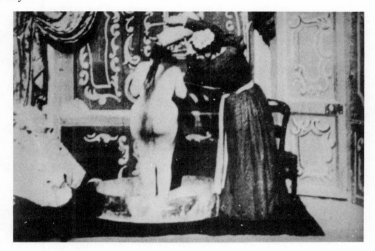

Figure 2

200 transparencies which, when revolved, could project a short sequence of movement. These projections of movement sequences, like the printed plates of *Animal Locomotion*—his vast study of both human and animal movement published in 1887—repeated very short portions of motions from side, front and rear points of view. Both the published photo-sequences and the projected movements of these sequences mounted in the "zoopraxiscope" portray an image of the body as a repeatable mechanism. This body mechanism is controlled in the published work by a whole battery of machines (Muybridge employed 48 cameras in a normal set up) capable of arresting movement for further scrutiny; and it is controlled in the zoopraxiscope by a mechanism capable of reconstructing this movement as illusion. Thus with Muybridge we encounter the very moment at which the representation of the discontinuous fragments of the still photograph begins to be reconstituted as a perception (Baudry's "representation mistaken for a perception") of continuous motion.

What is striking, however, is that with this mastery of the illusion of motion, with this near restoration of the whole body in its full perceptual force, come, in Muybridge's studies of the human body, gratuitous fantasization and iconization of the bodies of women that have no parallel in the representation of the male. And this is so in spite of the enormously simplified decor and relative absence of clothing of all his subjects.

In *The Human Figure in Motion* Muybridge divides his subjects into three categories: men, women, and children. In each category, sequences of movements are arranged to reveal a progression from simple to more complex motions. The male figures progress, for example, through various forms of walking (fig. 3), running, and jumping to more complex tasks such as throwing and catching, kicking, boxing, and wrestling, and finally to the performance of "Various Trades" such as carpentry (fig. 4) and hog carrying.

Figure 3

Women's bodies are put through a similar progression of activities designed to reveal movement in more typically "feminine" contexts. For example, we see many sequences of women walking but only one that shows a woman running. In place of the "Throwing and Catching" activities for men, we have women more sedately "Picking Up and Putting Down" to which a very brief section on throwing has been added. On the other hand, there are many variations on the comparatively passive postures of standing, sitting and kneeling.

Some of the movements and gestures in the women's section—walking, running, jumping—parallel those of the men. Yet even here there is a tendency to add a superfluous detail to the women's movements—details which tend to mark her as more embedded within a socially prescribed system of objects and gestures than her male counterparts. For example, the sequence of a woman walking (fig. 5) adds the inexplicable, and rather coy, detail of having her walk with her hand to her

Figure 4

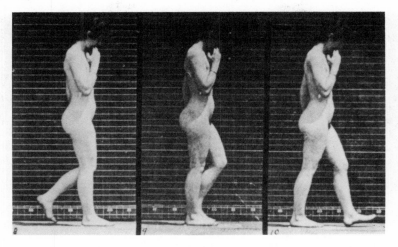

Figure 5

mouth, thus lending an air of mystery, an extra mark of difference which far exceeds the obvious anatomical difference between the male and female. Or, in the single instance in which a woman runs (fig. 6), her run is again differentiated from the male's by the gesture of grasping her left breast with her right hand. Although one could presume that this is to keep her breast from bouncing, the narcissism of the gesture is unmistakable, especially since it has no parallel among the similarly bouncing male genitals.

A frequent feature of the various male activities is some kind of simple prop that

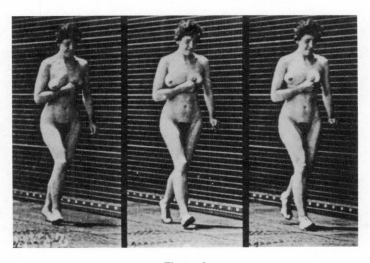

Figure 6

Figure 7

is either carried or manipulated to facilitate different muscular and kinetic activities: dumbbells, boulders, baseballs; the equipment of various combat sports such as swords for fencing; and the tools of the "Various Trades" such as spades, saws, and hammers. (Many male activities show men lifting, throwing, balancing, and carrying a simple round boulder which functions in a variety of situations to demonstrate the movements which manipulate it.) But when the women's gestures include props, these props are always very specific objects, never a simple weight that can be reused in many different situations. Lifting or carrying activities for women never use an abstract, nonspecific object but instead, two types of baskets for her head, a jug of water, a bucket of water and a basin of water—all of which engage her in specific activities of washing, watering, or giving to drink.

Although these props serve the ostensible purpose of eliciting certain kinds of motor activities, and although we do encounter some equally specific props for men as well, the props associated with women's bodies are never just devices to elicit

Figure 8

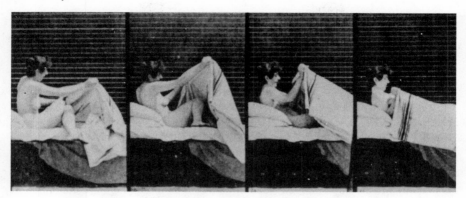

Figure 9

movement; they are always something more, investing her body with an iconographic or even diegetic surplus of meaning. For example, when a women lies down on a blanket placed on the ground in an activity that is identical to the series entitled "Man Lying Down" (fig. 7), she does not only lie down. She is provided with a narrative reason for lying down and the extra prop that goes with it: she lies down in order to read a newspaper (fig. 8). In other variations of lying down that have no male equivalent, the woman lies down in a hammock and, finally, in a bed complete with sheets and pillows (fig. 9). The latter offers the bizarre sight of covering up the woman's nudity. It is complemented, in the final plate of the women's section, by the reverse spectacle of uncovering her nudity as the woman gets out of this same bed (fig. 10).

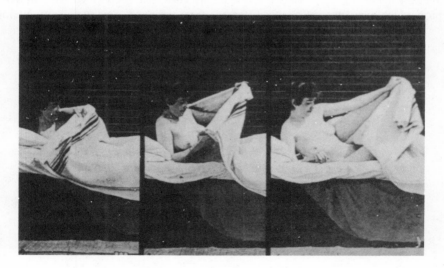

Figure 10

Figure 11

It does not seem entirely accidental that Muybridge chooses to conclude his section on women with this particular prop which in addition to its obvious sexual use, entirely covers and then uncovers the very body which the motion study seeks to reveal.[9] A similar game of peek-a-boo is played with a variety of materials or garments which partially cover—and in that covering seem to reveal all the more—the woman's body. We see this in the sequence entitled "Woman Walking Downstairs, Throwing Scarf Over Shoulders," (fig. 12), which covers only to uncover again (fig. 13). Thus the women are consistently provided with an extra prop which overdetermines their difference from the male. This overdetermination

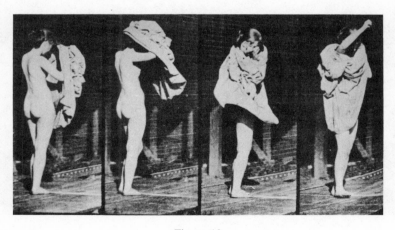

Figure 12

Figure 13

of difference also extends to such propless activities as walking and running or, strikingly, in a sequence in which the gratuitous gesture of difference, blowing a kiss, entirely defines her as a flirtatious object of desire (fig. 14).

An even greater surplus of erotic meaning runs through the group of photos which show two women in the same frame. These sequences are paralleled in the male section by such two-person activities as boxing, fencing, and wrestling, which show the men performing a limited repertoire of combat sports. It would be absurd to expect women of the period to engage in similar sports. But it is interesting that

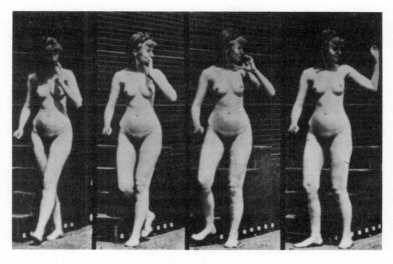

Figure 14

Figure 15

even though Muybridge makes no attempt to imitate with women the motor activities of these male combat sports, he nevertheless does attempt to create activities that women can perform together. Since he must literally invent these activities, it is not surprising that we find in them extreme instances of what can already be termed a cinematic mise-en-scène.

In one almost comically incongruous "scene," an ambulant naked woman serves a cup of coffee to another seated woman who drinks it and hands it back. In another (fig. 15) a woman stands on a chair and pours a bucket of water over another woman seated in a large basin. This second woman reacts, as if surprised by the coldness of the water, by jumping out of the basin and running away. In both examples

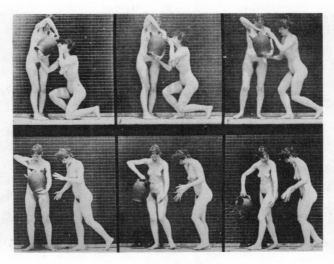

Figure 16

Muybridge has directed his female figures in what are very nearly dramatic scenes of domestic interaction taking place in a minimally defined dining room and bathroom. These scenes have a much greater degree of diegetic illusion than the less spatially situated, more purely motor activities of the men.

But even the more erotically charged are the scenes in which two women perform an atypical series of movements, as when two women dance together, or the sequence entitled "Woman Turning and Holding Water Jug for Kneeling Companion" (fig. 16). This sequence depicts the unlikely situation of a woman pouring water into the mouth of another from a large and unwieldy jug, with the added detail that she appears to spill a little water. Here, the unconventionality of the activity invests the scene with an enigmatic eroticism: why are these women playing with this large jug (no less!), and what is the nature of their relationship? The two women are defined as "companions"; none of the two-person male activities offers a similar description of the nature of the relationship between them. Another enigmatic scene, entitled "Woman Sitting Down in Chair Held by Companion, Smoking Cigarette" (fig. 17)—the very length of these titles indicates their increased narrativity—shows a standing woman leaning against the back of the chair of her "seated companion" gazing down on her almost longingly.

The cigarette in this last sequence offers a powerful connotation of both loose morals and, for the period, masculinity, both of which lend lesbian overtones to the scene which are completely unequalled in the comparable male activities of boxing or wrestling. For even though these male activities involve body contact, their purposeful and conventional nature does not allow the same erotic investment. The cigarette is yet another of the many gratuitous details which perversely fetishize the woman's body. But it does so with some insistence, as in an equally unmotivated, extravagantly lascivious "pose" of a single woman (fig. 18), or in a twosome in which both women smoke while walking arm in arm (fig. 19).[10]

Of course, one could try to explain all these props and poses by the fact that most of the women Muybridge used for his photos were professional artist's models, while the male "performers" were everyday people whose movements were linked

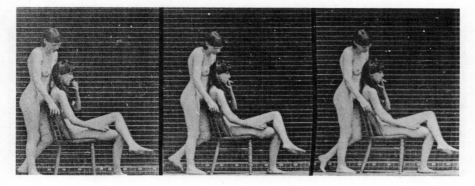

Figure 17

Figure 18

to their activities in real life, e.g., the University of Pennsylvania's "Professor of Physical Culture," and "Instructors at the Fencing and Sparring Club," etc. But all this really explains is the significant fact that even in the prehistory of cinema, at a time when the cinema was much more a document of reality than a narrative art, women were already fictionalized, already playing assumed roles, already not there as themselves.[11]

Robert Taft, who wrote the introduction to the current edition of *The Human Figure in Motion,* tries to explain the need for professional female models by the fact that many of the women were required to appear nude.[12] But even allowing for the fact that it was more risqué for a Victorian woman to pose nude than for a Victorian male and thus the need for professional models, we cannot use this same reasoning to account for the fact that the women are both categorically and numerically more nude than the men. Of the fourteen classes of human and animal subjects photographed by Muybridge during his stay at the University of Pennsylvania, the first three are of men in three stages of undress listed as 1) "draped," 2) "pelvis cloth"—a kind of jock strap, and 3) "nude." Thus the women's intermediate level of undress, transparent drapery and seminude, does not perform the same function of covering the genitals as the male "pelvis cloth." In fact, it does

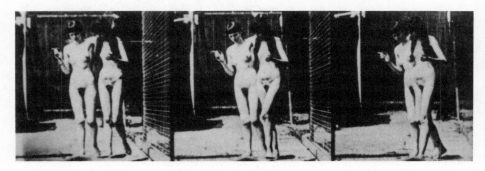

Figure 19

quite the reverse, draping the female body with a transparent veil (fig. 20) or partial garment which, like the bed covers, scarf, or dress, only call attention to her nudity all the more. These transparent and partial clothes offer a variation on what Roland Barthes has described as the erotic function of all revealing clothes: the "staging of an appearance as disappearance."[13]

The contradictory nature of the gesture which discloses the "truth" of the woman's body at the same time that it attempts to hide it is common to almost all the surplus props and gestures throughout these photo-sequences, revealing the unmistakable structure of the fetish. In its classic Freudian definition, the fetish is any object which acts as a substitute for the penis, allowing the male to continue to believe in the myth of the female phallus so as not to have to confront the threat of castration which underlies the fact of sexual difference.[14] These erotically charged substitutes often cover or connect with the part of the female body thought to have undergone castration to preserve the illusion—the perverse male fantasy—of a female phallus. Freud calls these substitutes a "disavowel" but he also notes that it is in the very nature of this disavowal[15] to perpetuate beliefs that have been abandoned, thus paradoxically reasserting the very same fears it is intended to allay.

If Muybridge's photos of naked women insist on their nakedness at the same time that they also attempt to disavow it, if, in a sense, he always gives us more to see—more of her body, more of her gestures and more objects which decorate or situate her in a prototypical narrative—this could be because of the male fear that this "more" is really less, that women pose the terrifying threat of "lack." The obsessive gaze at the naked female body attempts to re-assure itself in the very sight (and site) of this "lack" by the fetish-substitutes which endow her with a surplus of male-generated erotic meaning. By denying the woman any existence apart from the marks of difference, Muybridge exerts a form of mastery over that difference. But the very nature of the fetish disavowal also assures that the woman is defined entirely in terms that will perpetuate the nagging fear of the lack she represents. Her body can never be anything more than the two poles of this contradiction.

In this Freudian reading, the woman's body is reduced to the pure expression of desires produced in the male unconscious. But as Foucault notes, since it is law that constructs both desire and the lack upon which it is based, "where there is desire, the power relation is already present."[16] In other words, we find in the work of

Figure 20

Muybridge, long before the evolution of the cores of either the primitive or the classical illusionist cinemas, at the very inception of the basic apparatus itself, a patriarchal power which places the woman's body within a perversely fetishized structure. The cinematic apparatus thus becomes, even at this early stage, an instrument in the "implantation of perversion" whose first effect is to deny the very existence of women.

We have seen that the "presence" of the woman's body on the screen generates a fetish response on the part of the male image-producer to restore the unity which this body appears to lack. This fetishization operates on the level of the cinematic signified. But as Christian Metz has shown, another form of fetishization exists on the level of the cinematic signifier. This, too, is structured upon a similar process of disavowal. However, this disavowal is of the illusory nature of the signifier itself. In other words, part of our pleasure in cinema derives from the contradiction between our belief in the perceptual truth of the image and our simultaneous knowledge that it is only imaginary—the discrepancy between the perceived illusion of presence created by the image and the actual absence of the object replaced by the image. As Metz writes:

> The cinema fetishist is the person who is enchanted by what the machine is capable of, at the theatre of shadows as such. For the establishment of his full potency for cinematic enjoyment (jouissance) he must think at every moment (and above all simultaneously) of the force of presence the film has and of the absence on which this force is constructed . . . his pleasure lodges in the gap between the two.[17]

The fetishist's pleasure in the holding of two contradictory beliefs is doubly inscribed in the early invention of the cinematic apparatus: (1) on the level of its signified when it first comes to represent women's bodies, forever arresting the look at this body with a look at the fetish which disavows the very perception of which the machine is capable, and (2) on the level of the signifier. Here it is significant that the fetish pleasure is strongest at the moment the "theatre of shadows" first emerges, when audiences—like the audiences who first viewed the projection of moving bodies by Muybridge's "zoopraxiscope"—are still capable of amazement at the magical abilities of the machine itself. Muybridge's apparatus, present and visible in the space of projection, hand operated by its own inventor, thus revealed more acutely than the later invention of the projector the magical power to create an illusion of motion from a succession of stills. Even though this illusion would be perfected in Lumière and Edison's later invention of celluloid film and the resulting ability to film and project much longer sequences of motion, at no time would the fetish pleasure of the signifier alone be so pronounced, until, that is, Georges Méliès—that other original fetishist of the early cinema—found new ways to amaze his audiences at the capabilities of the machine.

Georges Méliès

For Muybridge the pleasure in the cinematic signifier lodged in the ability of the projection machine to produce an illusion of movement. He himself stood outside this machine as its operator. Méliès, however, redoubles and refines this pleasure in the cinematic signifier by placing his body within the machine, casting himself in the role of the magician-scientist-jester-Mephisto who manipulates its magic. Thus he makes a spectacle of his own perverse pleasure in the tricks of which his personal "theatre of shadows" is capable. In film after film Méliès obsessively repeats the same game, playing, like the fetishist, upon the contradictory knowledge of presence and absence, making the game of presence and absence the very source of his own and the spectator's pleasure, while privileging his pleasure over that of the spectator insofar as he alone, as filmmaker behind the scene and as magician on the scene, penetrates more deeply the contradictory nature of presence and absence. As typified by a frame from the 1902 film, *The Devil and the Statue* (fig. 21), his mugging delight in the game of illusion is clearly visible in each role he assumes.

But if Méliès refines and increases the fetishistic pleasure in the cinematic signifier, he also refines and increases a similar pleasure in the primary cinematic signified of the human body. As with Muybridge, the primary impetus behind Méliès's manipulation of the body is, once again, the need to master the threat of difference posed by the naked female form. And if for Muybridge this fetishization of the woman's body begins to produce a level of diegetic illusion and mise-en-scène that far exceeds the levels called for in his motion studies, then a similar fetishization, running rampant in Méliès, produces even more elaborate forms of diegesis and mise-en-scène.

Long before Méliès had discovered the illusory powers of cinema, he was already engaged in an obsessive pursuit of mastery over the human body. From 1885 to 1888, before purchasing the theater of the magician Robert Houdin, Méliès constructed a number of robots in imitation of Robert Houdin's own work.[18] These mechanical simulations of the human body allowed their inventor-operator complete control over their appearance and movements.

Figure 21

(There is a fascinating similarity here, not only between the mechanical simulation of the human body constructed in the robot and the later simulation of that body afforded by the cinema, but also between the manner of Méliès's mastery of both. According to Méliès's own account, he had seen robots on the stage of the Robert Houdin theater and had proceeded to imitate them without any prior understanding of their mechanism.[19] Thus he reinvented an invention whose trick was the simulation of the human body. This simulation of a simulation was then repeated ten years later in 1895 when, after failing to purchase the new invention of the cinematographe from August Lumière after an evening showing at the Grand Cafe, Méliès proceeded to reinvent it as well. Thus Méliès seems to have been fated to repeat the invention-construction of machines capable of ever more perfect and life-like simulations of the human body, and to repeat this construction through a process that was itself a simulation of an already existing mechanism.)

From the first trick of assembling a simulation of the whole body out of mechanical parts to the further trick of making the imaginary bodies projected on a screen appear and disappear, Méliès perfects his mastery over the threatening presence of the actual body, investing his pleasure in an infinitely repeatable trucage. This trucage offers two related forms of mastery over the threat of castration posed by the illusory presence of the woman's body made possible by the cinema: on the one hand, the drama of dismemberment[20] and reintegration performed on all bodies, and on the other hand the celebration of the fetish function of the apparatus itself, particularly in its ability to reproduce an image of the woman's body.

A 1903 film entitled *Extraordinary Illusions (Illusions funambulesques)*[21] is a typical example of mastery over dismemberment and of particular interest because it combines cinematic trucage with Méliès's original obsession with the mechanized limbs of a robot. The film shows Méliès as conjurer removing from a shallow box, obviously incapable of holding what emerges from it, a pair of legs, dummy's torso, and finally a head. He assembles these pieces into the body of a mechanical woman who becomes animated enough to turn her head to give the conjurer a kiss. He then tosses this mannequin into the air. Upon landing on the other side of the screen, she is transformed into a flesh-and-blood woman. The rest of the film shows the conjurer trying with some difficulty to maintain this apparition—the woman has a disturbing tendency to change into a chef with a saucepan—but not without a further variation on the theme of dismemberment and reintegration in which the woman is tied up in a large cloth which explodes into fragments of paper whose pieces again reform the woman. Finally, when the woman turns into a chef once again, the conjurer rips the chef to pieces and gradually vanishes himself.

Many of Méliès's early films (1898–1903) have similar rudimentary narratives based on variations of this drama of the dismemberment and reintegration of both male and female bodies. As early as 1898 *The Famous Box Trick (Illusions fantasmagoriques)* shows Méliès, again as conjurer, making another magic box appear from which emerges a little boy. The body of the boy is first conjured up, cut in two by the magician's wand, then restored to its original wholeness by the creation of two boys who begin to fight among themselves. Only after the drama of morcellation and restoration does final transformation, causing the boys to vanish, bring an end to the conflict.

Frequently this drama of morcellation takes place on the body of the magician-conjurer himself. In *The Melomaniac (Le Mélomane,* 1903) Méliès plays a magical music teacher who gives a music lesson using a string of five telegraph wires as his staff. To obtain notes he tears off his own head and throws it up on the staff. Since his head always grows back he is able to musically notate a performance of "God Save the King" sung by the infinitely replenishable supply of heads (fig. 22).

The Melomaniac is in many ways a refinement of the earlier *The Four Troublesome Heads (L'Homme de têtes,* 1898) in which the magician alternately removes and regrows his own head until the group of removed heads begin to annoy him with their singing. He then makes two of them disappear and tosses the third into the air to land on top of and merge with his current head. In both these films the magician stages the morcellation of his own body with the aid of a cinematic trick; he then restores his unity with another trick to become a kind of virtuoso performer of the drama of dismemberment and integration.[22]

In those films in which morcellation of the body is not followed by reintegration, we often find that the body undergoing morcellation can be regarded as a threat to another character who functions as a more sympathetic prototype of a hero. In these films two male protagonists engage in a crude oedipal drama ending in the dismemberment of one of them and the triumph of the other. Occasionally a woman figures as prize or cause of the conflict. In *The Man with the Rubber Head (L'Homme à la tête de caoutchouc,* 1902) a conflict between a chemist and his

Figure 22

assistant ends when the assistant inflates the head of the chemist to the point of explosion (fig. 23). In true oedipal fashion it is frequently the younger of the two men who succeeds in dismembering the older one, as also in *The Cook's Revenge* (*la vengence de gate-sauce,* 1900). In this film a kitchen boy steals a kiss from a chamber-maid, is caught by his boss, but then decapitates this boss in the ensuing chase. The film ends with the kitchen boy using the headless body of the boss as a broom to continue his work.

In all the above films we encounter a specific use of cinematic magic first to assert then to disavow an original "lack." Even when women's bodies do not appear at all (as in *The Troublesome Heads* and *The Famous Box Trick),* the threat of castration posed by their bodies seems to underlie the pattern of each scenario.

In a recent *Film Quarterly* article entitled "The Lady Vanishes: Women, Magic and the Movies," Lucy Fischer argues that the primary function of women's bodies in Méliès's films—and in many other "trick" films of the period—is to disappear.[23] Fischer takes Méliès 1906 film, *The Vanishing Lady,* as a paradigm for the magical treatment of women throughout the period. In this first use of a cinematic "substitution trick," a magician, played as always by Méliès, covers the body of a seated woman with a piece of cloth. When he removes the cloth not only has the lady disappeared but in her place is a skeleton.

Fischer is quite right to stress the significance of a magic which exerts power over women's bodies, decorporealizing it and reducing it to the status of a decorative object. But it is simply not accurate to privilege the disappearance of women in Méliès's films, any more than it would be accurate to privilege her magical appearance. In fact, there are probably an equal number of magical appearances and disappearances of men in these films, or of any object for that matter, since the staging of appearance and disappearance is the primary way Méliès exercises the illusory power of his simulation machine.

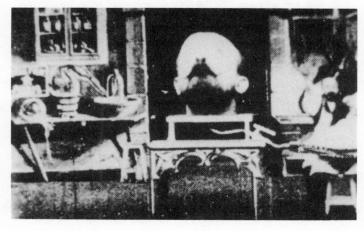

Figure 23

Fischer's ultimate point is not only that Méliès's magic makes women disappear, but that often in the process this magic acts out a drama of male envy of the female procreative power, "giving birth" to all manner of animals and objects. This latter idea is tempting in its opposition to the patriarchal notion of a female "lack,"[24] and the somewhat shaky Freudian construct of "penis envy" which sometimes accompanies it. Fischer actually reverses the process to suggest that a kind of "womb envy" is at work. But again I fear that there is not enough evidence from the films. More important than the vanishing act, more important than the imitation of procreative powers, is the construction of a scenario which gives the magician-filmmaker power over all the bodies in his domain, allowing him not simply to conjure away the woman but symbolically to reenact, and thus master through obsessive repetition, the problem of difference, the threat of disunity and dismemberment posed by the woman's body. Like the child's symbolic restaging of the problem of his mother's absence in the game of fort!/da!, making her disappear so that she may again, this time as a result of his own manipulation, reappear,[25] Méliès's scenarios of fetishistic disavowal announce his own role as magician-author-metteur-en-scène with a great flourish.

Significantly, these flourishes radically exclude his own body from the voyeuristic regime that Méliès, more than any other early master of film, inaugurates. In all the early films over which Méliès presides as magician (or as some thinly disguised variant thereof), the magician usually enters the scene, bows directly to the audience, begins an act containing many hand flourishes which call attention to the magic performed, and finally bows again before exiting. No one else in the film is allowed this knowledge of the existence of the film audience. Although it is possible to attribute these flourishes to the conventions of stage magic reigning at the time, it seems significant that even after the magician disappears from his films, Méliès retains characters, like Mephistopheles in *The Damnation of Faust* or the witch in *The Kingdom of the Fairies,* who carry on the function of the magician. If Méliès persists in this acknowledgement of the distance separating audience and scene, even going against all the emerging codes of cinematic illusion to do so, and if, at the same time he animates this scene with a multitude of characters who do not seem to be aware that they are on a scene, he does so in order to share with the audience his perverse pleasure in a visible mise-en-scène. Like the proverbial dirty-old-man who delights in showing his obscene pictures to others, part of his pleasure is in watching us watch. But for Méliès this pleasure is further enhanced by the inclusion in his own pictures of the fetish-machine that tames the threat of the female body.

It is striking, for example, just how many of Méliès's films, especially his later ones, revolve around the functioning of an elaborate machine operated and manufactured by the fictional surrogate of the original magician. These machines, whether the clocks of the 1889 *Cinderella* or the rocket ship of *A Trip to the Moon* (1902) are often associated with or adorned by the multiplying bodies of beautiful women in scant attire. The proliferation of the machines themselves—the many fantastic vehicles, futuristic laboratories, even the mechanized monsters such as the

Figure 24

giant in *The Conquest of the Pole* (1912)—are obvious ways in which Méliès celebrates and makes visible the primary invisible machinery of the cinema itself. A great many of the machines featured in these films are, in fact, optical devices: telescopes in *A Trip to the Moon* and *The Merry Frolics of Satan* (1906) (fig. 24), a fantastic camera in *Long Distance Wireless Photography* (1908), a magic lantern that turns out to be a motion picture projector in *The Magic Lantern* (1903). These devices allow their operator and the film spectator a privileged view of women's bodies, variously producing, reproducing, or voyeuristically spying upon them.

In *Long Distance Wireless Photography* Méliès plays the Marconi-like inventor of a magical camera capable of projecting life-size moving images of whatever is placed before it. This fantasy on the potential of the recently invented telegraph is an uncanny anticipation of the not yet invented marvel of television. Méliès the inventor-operator shows off the capabilities of his machine to an elderly couple in his laboratory. He first reproduces a life-size image of three identically-dressed women taken from a small photograph (fig. 25), then "televises" the movements of a live model.

In both cases Méliès celebrates the power of the apparatus to frame, tame, and reduce the flesh and blood woman to the status of a two-dimensional image. In the first case it may even be significant that the live model is dispensed with entirely as Méliès creates a life-size enlargement of what is already only a two-dimensional image of women's bodies. In the second case, a live model is present but a comic discrepancy between the seductive movements of the "televised" image and the less seductive behavior of the original model suggests a preference for the image over the less obliging reality of the original model.

Figure 25

Thus Méliès celebrates within the primary image machine of his own cinema a secondary image machine that is capable, like the first, of reproducing an image of women's bodies to the voyeuristic measure of male desire. The apparatus which makes possible "long distance wireless photography" packages the real-life bodies of women into safely proffered cheese-cake tableaux. Individual female bodies become the simple stereotypes of femaleness which uniformly differs from the male.[26] As Figure 25 amply reveals, Méliès's own pleasure is that of the purveyor of images who delights in watching others watch. The "Others" who watch in this case are the elderly couple, the in-the-laboratory audience of the film's scientific demonstration. Like the doubling of the cinematic apparatus itself, this within-the-film audience duplicates the voyeuristic structure of the relationship of primary audience to filmed image.

In *A Spiritualistic Photographer* (1903), Méliès reverses the above process to bring the two-dimensional photograph of a woman back to life. He performs a similar trick with the figure of the Queen on a life-size playing card in the 1905 film *The Living Playing Cards*. In all these films the device of the frame within the frame alerts us to the fact that everything we see, particularly the body of the woman, has been animated and produced by a voyeuristic, optical machine which safely situates the female object of desire both at a distance from and on a different plane from the male voyeur. Thus the image machine itself, through contiguous association with the woman's body and through its ability to reproduce that body as an image which disavows its inherent threat of lack, becomes the fetish-object par excellence of all Méliès's films.

Perhaps the most complex illustration of the inscription of women's bodies within the voyeuristic and fetishistic regime of cinema occurs in Méliès's 1903 film *The Magic Lantern*. In a children's playroom two clowns, a Pulcinella and Pierrot, build a giant magic lantern to which they attach a lens. When they place a light (burning torch) in it, it projects a series of circularly framed moving images upon the wall of the playroom. The progression of these images is significant: a static landscape is followed by close-ups of a man and a woman in eighteenth century wigs flirting with one another against the background of the same landscape; finally we see the clowns themselves projected in close-up upon the wall. With this progression Méliès demonstrates the power of his toy which, like the machine in *Long Distance Wireless Photography* is once again a metaphor for the cinematic apparatus. Thus we discover the ability of this apparatus to (1) document external reality (the landscape), (2) represent a fictional world (the characters in 18th century dress), and (3) confuse the categories of real and imaginary in a gesture of reflexivity (the projection of the clowns from the "real" world into the fictional space on the wall).

After this brief anticipation of the entire history of film art, the two clowns become curious about the internal workings of the machine producing this magic (or perhaps they are like the naive spectator who suspects that the machine itself houses the people and objects it produces). They dismantle the box to discover that it contains a whole bevy of beauties attired in long dresses and hats who do a little dance in front of the dismantled machine. This process of dismantling is repeated several times to yield a pair of women in clown suits who do another dance, exit, and then perform two more choruses of dances, this time dressed in scanty tutus.

The two clowns interrupt the dancers to battle with one another center stage. Soldiers with drawn sabers arrive to restore order. They march around the two clowns and force them to climb into the magic lantern. When the soldiers reopen the box, the clowns have been transformed into a single giant jack-in-the-box Pulcinella capable of extending itself to a height twice that of a normal human. As this jack-in-the-box moves up and down, the soldiers continue to brandish their sabers around the alternating elongations and retractions of the jack-in-the-box.

Once again Méliès plays with the contrast between a two-dimensional, framed image and three-dimensional reality. And once again this contrast suggests a metaphor for the machine's ability to produce women's bodies. But while Lucy Fischer emphasizes the envious male's appropriation of female procreative powers in the construction of this machine that gives "birth" to women, I would stress instead that this spewing forth of identical female bodies only calls attention even more to the status of these bodies as totally mastered, infinitely reproducible images whose potential threat of castration has been disavowed by the fetish object of the machine with which they are associated. In other words, not only can this image machine be construed as a metaphor for the womb, but also and more powerfully, it can be construed as a metaphor for the penis—in particular since, as we have seen, the fetish object is always a stand-in for the fantasy of the maternal penis.[27] In *The Magic Lantern* this fantasy penis emerges first in the proliferating bodies of the women produced by the machine and second in the phallic protrusion of the jack-in-the-box. In fact, the shift from soldiers brandishing their sabers at this jack-in-the-box to the final dance of the women around it would seem to offer yet another variation of the drama of threatened dismemberment and integration. There is probably no greater illustration of the centrality of this fetish object in all of Méliès's work than this dance of worship around the undulating phallus at the center of this giant magic lantern.

Conclusion: The Perverse Implantation

In the prehistoric cinema of Muybridge and in the primitive cinema of Méliès, the unprecedented illusion of presence of the film body acutely posed the problem of sexual difference to the male image maker. Of course painting and photography had long since set precedents for the eroticization and objectification of women's bodies.[28] In many ways Muybridge simply follows these precedents. What is particularly striking in Muybridge, however, is the extent to which a supposedly scientific study of the human body elicits the surplus aesthetic qualities of incipient diegesis and mise-en-scène in the treatment of his women subjects alone. It is as if the unprecedented perceptual reality of the female body made possible by the emerging cinematic apparatus necessitated a counterbalancing fictionalization even more powerful than what could already be found in the arts of painting and still photography.

Thus what began as a scientific impulse to measure and record the "truth" of the human body quickly became a powerful fantasization of the body of the woman aimed at mastering the threat posed by her body. This surplus of male generated erotic meaning denies the woman any meaning apart from her marks of difference from the male. As we have seen, Méliès complicates and refines this mastery over the threat of castration through the drama of dismemberment and reintegration performed on all bodies and through the celebration of the fetish function of the cinematic apparatus.

So if, as Baudry suggests, the cinematic apparatus in general affords the simulation of a lost unity with the body of the mother, then we find that some of the earliest representations of the female body within this apparatus aim at a more specific restoration of unity in the fetishistic disavowal of castration. But if the woman's body generates a surplus aestheticism designed to disavow difference, this surplus also severely limits the meaning of this body to the two contradictory poles of the assertion and denial of sexual difference. Like the fetish which it in some ways becomes, the woman's body arrests the male's gaze just short of the site of difference. Caught between these two poles of the fetish structure of disavowal, the woman's body is perversely trapped within the contradictory assertion and denial of the fear of castration. Thus the cinema became, even before its full "invention", one more discourse of sexuality, one more form of the "implantation of perversions" extending power over the body.[29]

NOTES

1. Michel Foucault, *The History of Sexuality,* translated by Robert Hurley (New York: Pantheon Books, 1978), p. 107. Original French title: *La Volonté de savoir* (Paris: Gallimard, 1976).

2. Foucault, p. 48.

3. *Camera Obscura* 1 (Fall 1976), pp. 97–126. Translated into English by Jean Andrews and Bertrand Augst.

4. As applied to film the term suture implies the process by which the spectator as subject fills in the discontinuities and absences of a cinematic discourse which proceeds by cuts, framings and the fundamental absence of the signifier itself. The term derives from Jacques Alain Miller's discussion of Lacan's "logic and the signifier." In Miller's extension of Lacanian theory, suture describes the way the "I" created by language is both a division and a joining. Divisions of the "I" are overcome by the imaginary projections of a unitary ego to produce the fiction of the subject. In a similar way, the spectator-subject of the cinema overcomes the disunity of the cinematic discourse. See Miller, "Suture: Elements of the Logic of the Signifier," and Jean-Pierre Oudart, "Cinema and Suture," both in *Screen* 18 (Winter/Spring 1977–78), pp. 24–47.

5. See Laura Mulvey, "Visual Pleasure and the Narrative Cinema," *Screen* 16 (Autumn 1975), pp. 6–18.

6. See Jean-Louis Baudry, "The Apparatus," *Camera Obscura* no. 1 (1976), p. 122.

7. Eadweard Muybridge, *The Human Figure in Motion* (New York: Dover, 1955). This is the latter of the two abridgements Muybridge made of his vast and very expensive original 1887 work, *Animal Locomotion. Animal Locomotion* is an eleven folio volume of some 20,000 photos of animals and humans in movement. Muybridge later abridged this work into two smaller volumes: *Animals in Motion,* published in 1899, and *The Human Figure in Motion,* published in 1901. All the photosequences reproduced here are from this latter work.

8. *After the Ball* (1897) stars Méliès's mistress and future wife, Jehanne d'Alcy. The still from this film is taken from a reproduction in Paul Hammond's *Marvelous Méliès* (New York: St. Martins Press, 1975), p. 113. A more recent and thorough study of Méliès is John Frazer's *Artificially Arranged Scenes* (Boston: G. K. Hall, 1974). Frazer's book contains excellent synopses of all Méliès's extant films. Other studies include: Georges Sadoul, *Georges Méliès* (Paris: Seghers, 1961) and Maurice Bessy and Lo Duca, *Georges Méliès Magicien* (Paris: Pauvert, 1961).

9. Nor does it seem entirely accidental that Muybridge concludes the male section with what could be taken as a complimentary metaphor of male ejaculation: a man with rifle falling prone on the ground and firing. The point, however, is that while the activity with the rifle reveals the male body in movement, the activity with the bed both conceals and reveals the female body in an erotically charged state of relative stasis.

10. See Lucy Fischer's analysis of a similarly masculine use of a cigarette in the Edison 1905 short *A Pipe Dream.* This film shows a woman who smokes playing with a miniature man in her hand. "The Lady Vanishes: Women, Magic and the Movies," *Film Quarterly* (Fall: 1979), pp. 32–33.

11. Claire Johnston, writing with reference to an earlier article by Laura Mulvey, has proclaimed the basic feminist criticism of the representation of women in film: "woman as woman" is never present. She simply comes to represent the male phallus. "Women's Cinema as Counter Cinema." *Notes on Women's Cinema,* edited by Claire Johnston, *Screen Pamphlet* 2 (London: SEFT, 1977).

12. Robert Taft, "An Introduction: Eadweard Muybridge and His Work," in *The Human Figure in Motion,* p. x.

13. *The Pleasure of the Text,* translated by Richard Miller (New York: Hill and Wang, 1975), p. 10.

14. Sigmund Freud, "Fetishism," *Standard Edition of the Complete Psychological Works,* vol. 21 (London: Hogarth Press, 1968).

15. Octave Manoni, in his book, *Clefs pour l'imaginaire ou l'autre scène* (Paris: Seuil, 1969), pp. 9–34, has emphasized the contradictory nature of this form of belief that knows itself to be false, calling it the process of "je sais bien, mais quand meme . . ." (I know very well, but all the same . . .).

16. Foucault, p. 81.

17. Metz, "The Imaginary Signifier." Translated by Ben Brewster; *Screen* 16 (Summer 1975), p. 72.

18. According to a letter from Méliès published in Georges Sadoul's *Georges Méliès,* p. 127.

19. Sadoul, p. 127.

20. In his *Film Biographies* (Berkeley: Turtle Island, 1977), Stan Brakhage has much to say about Méliès's trauma of dismemberment: "Young George . . . completely overwhelmed, torn to pieces before what-we-would-call his 'birth'—begins as a child to invent a spirit-of-himself which will revenge him . . . a hero who will free the wickedly enchanted—or otherwise destroyed—pieces of his actual being, cause the monsters to dis-gorge the parts of his actuality; and young George, perhaps later then, begins to imagine a heroine who will restore him, a woman who will sew together or otherwise re-member his actual being" (p. 17). Although I cannot agree with this attribution of dismemberment to "young George's" fetus, or to the supposition that a woman would "remember" his being—quite the reverse seems to be the case in both instances—Brakhage does correctly identify the primary concerns of much of Méliès's cinema.

21. Frazer lists this as the correct title of the film, p. 127. There are, however, some Super 8 prints bearing the title *The Magic Box.*

22. An even more threatening version of this same drama occurs in the 1902 film, *Up-To-Date Surgery,* in which a doctor diagnoses indigestion in a patient, performs an operation that cuts the patient up into many pieces, reassembles these pieces in the wrong order, then finally in the right order.

23. Fischer, p. 30.

24. This apprehension of a female "lack" does not mean that such a lack really exists. It is a male fantasy which has been instrumental in the implantation of perversion within the cinema.

25. Sigmund Freud, *Beyond the Pleasure Principle* (New York: Bantam, 1959), pp. 32–35.

26. It is interesting to compare, in this connection, the enormous differentiation in the costumes of the male characters in all Méliès's films to the near uniformity of dress among the females: e.g., the scant sailor suits of the women who help the scientists board the rocket ship in *A Trip to the Moon,* or the similar uniforms of the women in *The Kingdom of the Fairies.*

27. Freud, "Fetishism," *Standard Edition of the Complete Psychological Works,* p. 153.

28. See John Berger, *Ways of Seeing* (New York: Penguin Books and the British Broadcasting Corporation, 1973).

29. I would like to thank Patricia Mellencamp and Stephen Heath for suggesting the "Film Body" portion of this title and the general topic of the presence of the human figure in film. I am also indebted to Virgil Grillo and Betty Theoteokatos of the University of Colorado for helping me to reproduce the Muybridge plates from *The Human Figure in Motion,* and to Andrew Lovinescu of the University of Wisconsin, Milwaukee, for "transforming" the slides into photographs.

V

IMAGES AND PORNOGRAPHY

Claire Pajaczkowska

The London Rape Crisis Centre monitors the press, and keeps newspaper clippings showing instances where a rape story is placed alongside a page three pinup. There are several hundred examples. Each time this happens they write to the newspaper protesting that this kind of layout parallels the titillation of the rape story. The newspapers consistently deny that the image and the story are in any way connected, pointing out the hairline that separates each from the other.[1]

Despite the denials of the newspaper editors, the contiguity of image and text is significant, although to characterize it as a casual relationship is too simple. The story provides the reader with a brief fantasy of committing rape, strictly defined as a mere fantasy by means of the inevitable narrative resolution, its moment of closure, which is the news of the punishment of the rapist, who is thus constructed as a criminal, who is not the he of the reader. In this the Law holds firm, rape is forbidden, rapists are criminals, and it is precisely as the forbidden that it can be enjoyed as a fantasy.

Another group working on the relation between pornography and rape is the most recent and militant campaign within the American Women's Liberation Movement, the new "Women against Pornography" group, whose constituency runs into thousands including both feminists and the far-right anti-obscenity moral reformers. Their doxa: pornography causes rape. Susan Brownmiller, the main organizer of the movement, describes pornography as "the undiluted essence of anti-female propaganda" and claims that "rape, wife battering, incest and street violence are stimulated and in fact taught by pornography. To the rapist or the sadistic wife beater a hard core porn magazine is a do-it-yourself manual for violence."[2] There is obviously a political problem here in that this feminist position on pornography is completely compatible with and complementary to certain mainstream moralities. This problem is repetitive: compare the campaign in the 1830s and 40s in Britain where the Moralist Feminists, ostensibly fighting for continence laws in order to reduce the incidence of wife beating by drunken husbands, became the sight for recuperation into the erotophobic morality of dominant ideology.[3] Again, the 1840s Natural Rights reformers ended up by passing the antihomosexuality legislation which meant that until 1967 homosexuality was a criminal offense. Later in the

1860s, the Ladies National Association for the Repeal of the Contagious Diseases Acts, campaigning against the institution of Morals Police and for a Criminal Law Amendment Bill which was intended to make quite radical changes in the definition of and culpability within prostitution, was similarly transformed into a crusade for purity and the preservation of the family. The present campaign also holds certain clear if unspoken assumptions about the rightful place of sexual practice, the most liberal of which is close to the post sixties "sexual liberation" whereby "anything goes provided it takes place in a natural meaningful relationship" and doesn't involve violence. This set of assumptions reconfirms the marginality of sexual behavior such as sado-masochism, transvestism, transexualism, paedophilia, homosexuality and lesbianism, and prostitution.

In a conference on pornography in New York in October 1979, women spoke at what is called a Speakout about the way in which pornography affects our sexual practice. The term interference came up repeatedly as they described scenes of natural libidinal flows directed toward their sexual partner (usually 'non-sexist' men) which were brusquely interrupted by a memory of an obscene image which succeeded in turning desire into a self-conscious and sordid revulsion. Here again there is a problem for me as, unlike a clinical analyst, I cannot read feminist speech as purely symptomatic, as psychotic. Feminism is correct in identifying a particularly crucial knot of violence and sadism in the articulation of masculinity/femininity in the core of these representations, and Susan Brownmiller is correct, not in her present campaign, but in her earlier differentiation[4] between, for instance, women's rape fantasies and the experience of being raped, insisting that the fantasy should not be misunderstood as a desire to be raped. This differentiation is useful in looking at the way in which pornography functions.

If pornographic images (especially in film) work within the same register as fantasy—predominantly the register of the Imaginary—then pornography is more likely to cause masturbation than rape. Brownmiller echoes psychoanalytic theory in the same way that feminist practice has often paralleled the preoccupations of psychoanalytic theory—in denying the veracity of logical relations and in interpreting these as fantasies. It is in this context that it would be useful to look at the psychoanalytic concepts of the function of the image both in terms of the status of the image in the formation of the subject, and in terms of the production of imagistic representation by the subject. In understanding how it is that our sexualities are constructed in pornography, in imagery, through language, and even in theory, we can then examine how resistance to those representations is articulated. Recently the disparate voices of feminism and psychoanalysis have converged and we can now turn to the work of these women analysts, Luce Irigaray, Michèle Montrelay and Eugénie Lemoine-Luccioni.

Scenes of ejaculation are crucial to the narrative structure of pornographic film due to their function as signifying the truthfulness of the sexual act represented—as proof—and are placed in a narrative structure that is founded on repetition alone. Irigaray claims that *repetition,* the mechanism fundamental to pornographic representation is not in tune with feminine sexuality which is, she claims, constructed in a temporality which is a continuum, where every new time is lived as a first time.

While men for the most part structure their sexuality as a scene, their scene, and repeat it indefinitely.

Irigaray writes on the function of ejaculation in a porn film: "This disgust that women have spoken of experiencing during these scenes doesn't seem to me to be a spontaneous reaction. Unless, and it is often the case, men use their ejaculation/ semen as an instrument of domination setting it up in rivalry with milk."[5] Irigaray goes on to say that maybe it is men who have a problematic relationship to their semen, not knowing how to "situate themselves" in relation to it, often experiencing ejaculation as a loss of their "vital substance," a liquification of their solidity as the emission of semen often accompanies or precedes detumescence (subsidence of the erection). The fact that semen leaves traces of the orgasm, it stains, for many men evokes the prohibition of masturbation. She suggests that the acute anxiety men feel at the thought that their semen might remain unproductive is a fear they project onto women, expecting women to feel dissatisfied if it is deprived of its signification of fecundity, if it is deviated from its final goal of introjection into the female body, if it is misspent through perversion of the sexual act. But Irigaray suggests that this is not a problem that belongs to women, that this is simply the mechanism of attributing to women the patterns of masculine desire; women, she suggests, do not need to have children. It is men who need to have them because they can't make them, and must prove to themselves their ability to father. Their culture is founded on the father-son relation which alone guarantees the continuation of the Name, of property, of Capital both economic and symbolic. This said, pornographic film is useful; it allows us to look at these projections on a screen, then to analyze them with some distance as we are no longer functioning as screens ourselves.

The problem with this argument, apart from the almost caricatural identification of gender difference, and a positing of some essential femininity that could remain alien to and outside of masculine desire and its repetition, is that for Irigaray, as for Brownmiller, film is assumed to work by selecting parts of our sexualities. But what form of sexuality is it that remains outside of representation, of signifying practice? Is this exemption of women from the perversion of repetition simply another kind of purism—(a purism which echoes not only the voices of the women at the Speakout but also the recuperation of nineteenth century feminism)—whereby women, as virginal, experience everything anew for the first time? The criteria we use to examine film must not be of another order than those we bring to bear on political practice.

Apart from privileged scenes like ejaculation, how does film produce and construct certain prescribed sexualities, marginalize others? How is the sexual pleasure of the scopic drive articulated with the identical content of these images where the depiction is of a sexual act? Does this increase scopic pleasure? Or is it the excitation of another register altogether?[6]

To understand the formation of scopophilia as a sexual drive, and its relation to the instinct belonging to sight, we have to examine the relation of these to signification itself. Jean Laplanche suggests that the vital instincts (e.g. sight) are not reducible to signification although the ensuing drives, which are sexual in the proper sense (e.g. scopophilia) are certainly constructed through a metaphoric and metonymic process of derivation—that is through language.[7] If the metaphoric and metonymic systems of slippage from the vital instinct to sexual drive are recognizable as homologous to Jakobson's two axes of language, or of speech, what are the equivalent axes in the register of the visual? Or is metonymy intrinsic to imagery in the same way that metaphor is characteristic of speech? Is the equation one of repression?

Lacan proposes that the image is to the imago what *parole* is to *langue:*

> If the transient images determine such individual inflexions of the tendencies it is as variations of the matrices that those other specific images which we refer to by the ancient term imago, are constituted for the instincts themselves. Among these imagos are some that represent the elective vectors of aggressive intentions, which they provide with an efficacity that might be called magical. These are the images of castration, mutilation, dismemberment, dislocation, devouring, bursting open of the body, in short the imagos I have grouped together under the apparently structural term of imagos of the fragmented body.[8]

It should be noted that a characteristic of the imago is its imbrication in the aggressive instincts and its representation by fragmentation, the divided subject. However, from this formulation in 1948, Lacan moves to the later formulation of the gaze as object petit "a",[9] which involves a very different conception of the divided subject, closer to Laplanche's conception. I will return to this later. But Lacan is not the place to look for an understanding of the image—his insistence is on the Letter.

There are, however, two further inquiries into the specificity of visual signification and its relation to language. Firstly, Barthes in *The Rhetoric of the Image* points out that images are rarely used without some form of written text, the latter having two functions, anchorage and relay. Anchorage is denominative: it fixes the signification of the image by selecting possible identifications and interpretations from the polysemy that is supposed to be characteristic of images, polysemy having an unfixity that is "terrorizing." Relay is specific to diegesis and, although rare in fixed images, is central to film—in the form of dialogue for instance, which not only selects the signification of the image but also advances the action by setting out meanings that are not found in the image itself. This 'image itself' for Barthes is composed of two types of visual message: iconic denotation, the literal image, and iconic connotation, the symbolic image, although the distinction is academic for, as he points out, "The first is in some part imprinted on the second; the literal message appears as the support of the symbolic (coded iconic) message."[10] The distinction between the coded and noncoded message, and the use of the category, message, is a derivation of the linguistic paradigm; there is little in Barthes's theorization of the image that differentiates language from image as a form of signification. However, it is interesting that he uses a Peircian notion of the three part sign for the analysis of pictorial representation as opposed to the Saussurean sign for the earlier work on the language of mythologies.

The three levels of signification according to Peirce are the icon, the index, and the symbol. The icon, insofar as it is a diagram, reflects the internal relation of the signified in the signifier; and insofar as it is an image, reproduces the factual qualities of the signified in the signifier. It is this level of the iconic that is Barthes's concept of iconic denotation. The index infers the presence of the signified by a relation of connection between signifier and signified, implying contiguity. The symbol is closer to being a learned and imposed rule according to which a certain signifier is linked with a certain signified. A slight modification of the latter definition (expedient to Lacan) does, however, allow signifiers having some metaphoric similarity with their signifieds to be assimilated to symbols. What is important here is that the icon is lowest in this hierarchy of increasingly abstract relations of signification, and functions in a sort of sublinguistic capacity. Before going on to suggest what kind of position vis-à-vis unconscious representation this sublinguistic operation accords the image, we should note a difference between two kinds of symbolizations, differentiating between the linguistic sign, which is the conceptual signified in the classic realist text, for example, and the psychoanalytic sign which is a manifestation of a complex or wish.

According to Lacan and Laplanche, the iconic sign, the image, is positioned on the top level of the unconscious, close to the preconscious in which the transposition is very weak, meaning that identical images can occur in both the conscious and unconscious simultaneously.[11] A problem here is that none of these topological models really coincides with the various diagrammatic models of the unconscious and it is impossible to superimpose them and thereby posit analogous systems or representations. Is this due to what Derrida calls the "congenital Phonologism" of the psychoanalytic methodology?[12] Must we reduce the picture to a series of rhetorical figures, decoding the picture surface as if it were a literary text? Jean Paris argues that the recent structuralist attempts to annex the visual arts has not effected sufficient change in the foundation of the semiotic methodology. He quotes Umberto Eco: "One can doubt the linguistic nature of these phenomena."[13] Jean-Louis Schefer states: "Painting is not a language."[14] Christian Metz writes: "It is natural that any semiological reflection about images must *begin* by stressing the concept of analogy." But this beginning which would block further steps is rejected as soon as it arises: "There is in fact an intellectual attitude that could be called a fixation to iconicity."[15] By emphasizing the difference between images and words, this attitude systematically downgrades the latter; it frustrates the imperialistic claims of these theoreticians: "A semiology of images will not develop outside of a general semiology."[16] Since this mathematically definitive science exists mainly in the imaginations of its promoters, to which methods is it going to resort but to the very ones it pretended to get rid of? Which concepts will that "science" use? Syntagms, paradigms, generative linguistics, the duality of competence/performance, the notion of form and its relationship to substance, the "idea" of the distinctive unit and so on. From Saussure to Hjelmslev, from Martinet to Barthes, the elements of the most orthodox linguistics are used: "Linguistics is not a part, not even a privileged one, of a general science of signs, but on the contrary it is semiology that is part of linguistics."[17] "The image is but what we can read in it."[18] Jean Paris identifies a counter-imperialism which starts with Merleau-Ponty's *Primacy of Perception* and continues up to Lyotard's *Desirevolution derivé a partir de Marx et Freud*—a new mysticism is reinstated, the eye organ, of all the senses, is given a power which makes what it sees so primary, Bergson's "immediate data" or as Lyotard has put it, "before any order."[19] But how do "configurations" exist prior to any "construction"? (The irony is that Paris points angrily to the structuralist linguistic hegemony for these very reasons and yet concludes by culling a Chomskyian methodology for the analysis of Renaissance paintings.) The attempt to trace the specificity of the image through semiotic methodology alone seems to finish with either Barthes or Paris, each of whom finally places and locates the analysis of the image within the field of linguistics.

Another inquiry into the specificity of the image comes from Julia Kristeva in *Ellipsis on Fear and Specular Seduction,* where she claims an important differentiation between the two different kinds of looks at work in the spectator subject. In constructing a concept of the specular image which is more comprehensive than simply the mirror image, she posits a relation between the ideational content of imagery and its tendency to be specularized by the subject, to become an image which fascinates.[20] Again following Laplanche's explanation of the scopic drive and its origin in the self preservation instincts in which looking at objects has a necessary function for purely pragmatic reasons, the pleasure in viewing is fully constituted as a sexual drive only when its object finally becomes a sexual object, which according to him, must be the phallus. Thus scopophilia is imbricated in the castration complex, the double process of acknowledgement and disavowal, and the ensuing signifying chains of fetishism. Laura Mulvey, in her article on visual pleasure, has described the way in which this construction of the image "woman" acts both as castrated Other and as fetish or phallic substitute simultaneously. This accounts for the often violent and sadistic treatment of women in the narrative structure of the classic realist film, particularly Hollywood films. As signifier of castration "woman" comes to be punished or killed, even in some cases where she is also fetishized.[21]

Pornographic film raises difficulties for Mulvey's schema of the deployment of the castration anxiety in film. One of the most frequent images in the visual vocabulary of pornography is that of the vulva, female genitalia. Given the dualist logic according to which gender difference is represented in the Symbolic, such images signifying lack should theoretically produce anxiety and not as is empirically known, produce erections and masturbation in the male spectator. According to Mulvey, the particular fetishes which are provided in (filmic) representation are those of certain cyclic narrative forms, replaying scenarios of desire; the figure of the woman as a whole becomes the phallus. The massive diffusion of vaginal imagery might lead us to search these images for other traces of fetishism; we know from Freud that the fetishist can substitute such ephemeral and insubstantial signifiers as "a shine on the nose" for a penis. Thus we find stiletto heels, fur bedspreads, riding crops, varnished fingernails all acting as substitutes. John Ellis even suggests that female sexual pleasure itself can become the fetish. He argues that woman's pleasure has been promoted to the status of a fetish. "Female sexual pleasure has become perhaps the dominant fetish within current public pornographic representation as a result of the expansion of the very restricted and clandestine 'hardcore' representations into the more public arena of 'soft-core'."[22] It is difficult to assess whether he is speaking of an empirical moment or a symbolic representation—but either way I don't think that he is right. In psychoanalytic theory perhaps jouissance as a neologism has come to be fetishized, but in pornography I don't think that it is women's pleasure that is at stake. Maybe the articulation of the castration anxiety in porn films can be understood only in shifting our area of study away from the film text, from studying its "smallest unit of signification" and toward the conditions of its reception. Examining the kinds of active spectatorship which are involved in the viewer's unconscious pleasure in viewing, the scopic satisfaction of primary identification, we also encounter the more conscious activities—masturbation for example.

While we know that fetishism entails a chain of substitution of phallic significa-tion *and* the disavowal of sexual difference, and that certain images of women can come to take on that signification, there is also the possibility that pornographic representation—especially vaginal imagery—might be a way of allowing the sub-ject to fetishize his own penis, through masturbation especially; the penis is also capable of taking on the signification of the phallus. In this way the subject confirms that he is *not* castrated, which is what the fetishism hinges on, the denial of castration, not necessarily concern whether women have penises or not.

Although the castration anxiety can be, and in the case of porn film obviously *is*, played out in relation to symbolised sexual difference and the denial of empirical gender difference, this is not its exclusive or even fundamental terrain. Scopophiiia, according to Freud, comes to be constituted as a search for the maternal phallus by way of the *primal scene* in which there is nothing empirically to characterize the female genitalia as an absence or lack.[23]

This opens up two directions for inquiry into the question of sexual difference in castration. The first is the examination of how symbolic castration is articulated in female sexuality. Can women be fetishists? What is the little girl's relationship to the Oedipal instance and what is her 'negative' entry into subjectivity? Eugénie Lemoine-Luccioni's writing works through this direction, and I will return to her work more fully later. The second direction is to reread any specific case of scopophilia (in the cinema for example), taking into account the other elements involved; once we have shifted the object of the scopophilic drive from being the phallus alone to being the primal scene (as mythic instance), we can consider the importance of movement, sexual *activity*. Kristeva reevaluates the element of movement, of activity as a central constituent of visual pleasure, especially in film. Within her reading of the perceptual register, Kristeva reclassifies the propping of the sexual on the instinctual by reintroducing the term "lektonic traces" originally from pre-Socratic philosophy. These are said to exist in the image in excess of its denotative functions. Thus there is a difference between the legibility of an image and its potential fascination, which could constitute the specifically sexual pleasure involved in viewing, over and above that pleasure produced by the drive to make the image legible.[24] Both the legibility and the fascination of the image, the two gazes identified earlier, are combined in an act of identification. This turns upon Lacan's description of the mirror phase as the earliest instance of the recognition of the image, binding Kristeva's argument to the rigid definition of the image in the mirror phase. She questions the literalization of the mirror apparatus in order to broach the complex process of identification, to give the act a meaning outside of clinical-ontological development. She does not question the Lacanian assumption that the mirror moment is somehow a first moment, a founding moment from which there will be subsequent repetitions which constitute symbolic identification.

Once again this raises the problem of how this initiation into the double, the self/other logic of imaginary division comes to be a passage into full symbolic subjectivity. Michèle Montrelay suggests that this passage is overdetermined as feminine due to women's sexuality being organized in narcissistic modes, and argues that the mirror moment itself must not be seen as a founding moment, but as a recurrence of an earlier loss that begins to construct the ego. In *L'ombre et le nom* she defines the process of the visual register in identification in the following way: "The mirror stage is the reflection of, and veil over, the trace of the separation from the Other, the mother. Lacan's analyses show that the specular image only functions as a reference point when it is a signifier, that is one element of the chain where the desire of the other is articulated."[25]

For Montrelay the mirror image, then, repeats and conceals this first trace. What can we know of this trace? Nothing, as long as reality—that construct of the Imaginary—screens the Real: "The first trace continues to exist, to insist. It is repeated: the unconscious which is substantially measured by this trace can only be so in a traumatic mode. Which is why Freud's concern for a long time was to trace repetition in order to conquer it."[26]

Montrelay's suggestion that the mirror phase is itself a repetition of an earlier experience of differentiation between self and other, and the importance of repetition for the act of identification bears several references to Freud: the play of recognition in the fort/da game, and more specifically to the image, the formulation in the essay "On Negation" of 1925:

> All images, representation *(Vorstellung)* originate from perceptions and are repetitions of them. So that originally the mere existence of the image serves as a guarantee of the reality of what is imagined. The contrast between what is subjective and what is objective does not exist from the outset. It only arises from the faculty which thought possesses for reviving a thing that has once been perceived by reproducing it as an image.[27]

This formulation "works" within Freud's 1917 model of the conscious, preconscious, unconscious, topological system which is in turn taken up by Laplanche in his dissent from the Lacanian unconscious understood as being entirely the effects of speech. While agreeing that the unconscious is composed of signifiers, Laplanche goes on to say: "These signifiers do not however, have the status of our verbal language and are reduced to the dimension of the Imaginary—notably the visual imaginary. These are imagos."[28] It seems that a necessary precondition of any work on imagistic representation that might displace the present structural linguistic hegemony is a historical account of the transformations of Freud's formulation of the unconscious—from the neurological to the mechanistic, through to the topographical and with this, their equivalent forms of representation (in the way that Laplanche traces the transformations of the formulation of the ego).[29] As they stand these various isomorphic models do not superimpose. In this way, without conceptualizing the register of the visual as a homogeneous field, we might discover how, as a *montage,* the imagos are positioned in relation to the drives: the gaze as 'objet a' of the scopic drive. If we abandon the dream of integral lucidity as being also a flight into the opacity of the Imaginary, we begin to encounter the Real problems.

The paradigmatic accounts of subjectivity produced in psychoanalytic theory are ahistorical. That is, both politically paralyzing and inherently phallocentric, as they take existing language structures as the givens of the inquiry. Eugénie Lemoine-Luccioni tries to redefine the formalizations of the subject's passage into full symbolic activity by tracing the trajectories of female sexuality through its insufficient theorization in existing clinical analysis. The underlying thesis of her book *Le partage des femmes*[30] is that woman lives according to an order of Imaginary partition (separation)—which precipitates her into a convalescent narcissism.

First of all, let me explain the content of this notion of partition/separation. We have to locate it as an organization from which the subject passes into symbolic castration through identification; an identification which has no effect until, as Montrelay pointed out, a symbolic division has intervened via a process of symbolization that is inherently female, right from the mirror stage. A number of instances are sufficient to establish the female Imaginary from the model of separation: The woman has two sexual organs which are not alike, the vagina and the clitoris; and she is of the same gender as the parent who gives birth to her. This doubling, this order of the double, is underscored by the instances of pregnancy and childbirth. The woman in becoming a mother is no longer one but two. From her point of view it is she who doubles and redoubles, not the father. These givens are as much imaginary as real, but will always confound the arithmetic of identification constituted by an oscillation between zero and one.

Imaginary partition is organized around the transition from the double to the loss—and from this to the loss of the phallus. But symbolic castration in the ontogenesis of femininity must be seen in terms of the overlooked and yet fundamental events of a woman's organic or physiological life: first her periods (called *pertes* or losses in French) and second, chronologically, childbirth or the separation from that part of herself that had imaginarily come to complete her, during pregnancy, when her menstrual loss, her periods had themselves stopped (loss of period being the first sign of pregnancy). "When she falls pregnant this part of herself is no longer periodically visible."[31] These events and all of the losses in a woman's life, although not constituted as a category capable of scientific use, are sufficient to circumscribe a phenomenon of the Imaginary partition as the psychic organization which is properly female. Woman lives in fear of losing part of herself. A husband may come to be that half that is always lost, and although this fear of losing might be explained as an inverted aggressivity or anxiety, Lemoine-Luccioni doesn't explain it that way. "It is important simply, to stress that she lives the slightest, most legitimate absence as a definitive separation—'it's absurd, she says, but I can't help it.' Rather than castration anxiety women we maintain, experience the anxiety of division, partition."[32]

To repeat the loss of part of herself is not to be assimilated into the fear of losing the penis in a man—the loss of an organ—a loss which will never actually happen. "Even when she says that if her husband were to leave her she would feel amputated, she would in any case be amputated of an organ that is not hers."[33] So can we use the term castration when it comes to women? The question is formulated by the term itself which posits that the lacking thing, the fundamental lack, must be taken on by the sexual organ and its signification, without which we cannot, properly speaking, use the term castration. If we try to analyse the precedents, we remember that in order for there to be a real symbolic chain there must be a lack which engenders a demand. For the woman there is a real loss or imaginarily experienced division as part of herself, herself insofar as she is the one. Her demand is to be given back to herself.

In coitus, the detumescence and the withdrawal of the penis are inevitably significant and take on (prior to childbirth) all of these other losses. They are marked retroactively from the sign and the phallus. What remains clear is that in coitus that part from which she is separated and which will always conceal or reveal an earlier loss, has never been part of her. She passes then from the real loss of an imaginary half of herself to the imaginary loss of an organ which comes to be superimposed upon her partial losses. Later, at the moment of childbirth, the real deprivation of part of the self will become Imaginary frustration, in reevoking the older loss of that other part of herself, her mother, from a fantasized wholeness. This can become symbolic castration if it enters into a symbolic chain of signification.

The woman, herself, lacks nothing, in the sense that no organ can come to be missing from her. On the contrary, it seems that she has an organ too many, the clitoris; how then does she come to see herself as lacking a penis? (Leaving aside, for a minute, the fact that men experience her as lacking and transmit, or in Irigaray's terms, project, this feeling to her although this fact is far from negligible.) Lemoine-Luccioni argues that the expulsion of the baby during childbirth and the withdrawal of the penis during coitus constitute real separations. These are also informed by the scotomization of the anal drive, inasmuch as being a partial drive it is directed toward the Other from whom she waits a reply. The woman separates herself from something in exchange for something else; she asks of the other, the man, to be taken—she gives herself—but as always in this exchange of gifts it is hard to tell whose gain it is: "As a child the girl wanted a baby from her father as a gift, as a consolation of some sort after acknowledging that her mother was occupied elsewhere: with the father again."[34] If the woman lacks nothing, what is the object of her demand? And how does she pass from imaginary partition to symbolic causation? And how does she move from narcissism to objectal libido?

The passage, according to Lemoine-Luccioni, is effected through an act of identification. There is the problem of the dilemma in the choice of identification: whether to identify with a man as the alternative to identification with a woman, or the female (to be seen) position which, given the existing structures of signification, would result in masochism.

But the choice is never posited as an either/or and the woman is always to some extent a hysteric. In identifying with the man, the woman imagines herself to be lacking a penis (which is lacking in the male on the empirical level) and in this way she makes symbolic the lack that all of the phenomena of partition, loss have constituted. She passes from the imaginary loss of part of herself to the imaginary loss of the male sexual organ, and then to the symbolizable loss of a sexual organ, the phallus, which might be any number of things. In the other alternative, that of feminine identification, the woman takes herself as lost object (mother), and the symbol of the lost unity would be the body as complete, without gaps.

To explain the way in which the mirror image can only be either an opening onto the symbolic (male identification) or else a narcissistic containment (female identification) for the woman, we have to go back to the scopic drive and examine the way in which it is also marked as privileged in the construction of female subjectivity. With the mirror image, the girl who is already divided, not simply the *hommelette* of Lacan—scrambled—but who is divided, would hesitate to risk a new schism, one which projects the ego into a distance. For the girl, this distancing is a difficult experience. She tends to oscillate in the image that she believes to guarantee her the equally containing, limiting gaze of her mother, originally, and that comes to be the omniscient gaze of the father. She prefers to believe in this image and believes it to be herself. She confuses herself with this complete figure, without gaps, which would conserve the limitations and security of parental power. So the object of the fort/da game, the mother, is replaced in this reenactment of separation by her own persona, represented by her body as it is in the mirror image.

But in offering herself to the gaze, giving herself to be seen, according to the sequence—seeing, seeing herself, offering herself to be seen, being seen—the girl provokes in the Other, the man, a reply that gives him pleasure. "Every partial drive is evocative, here we are talking of the same thing when we say provocative."[35] An evocation or provocation which is addressed to the look of the Other can only come about if the look of the same, the mother's gaze, has failed the child, so that the look of the Other can occupy that space. It is in this space that the symbolic articulation is introduced. In order to follow the symbolic articulation of the gaze as *petit objet 'a'* Lemoine-Luccioni uses one of Lacan's schemas.[36] This is the first link of the Symbolic chain.

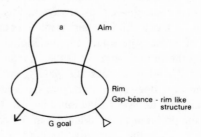

The Aim and the Goal (that would be the satisfaction of the drive) do not coincide; if they did the arrow would go straight on. It is this circumscription of the object 'a', and its introjection, that is the aim. If the drive does not double back on itself, something has happened This something is known as the incursion into the field of the other, where a response or a reply has been procured (provoked).

This schema also holds true for the scopic drive, after the mirror phase has been broached. When the narcissistic resistance of the woman succeeds in deflecting the 'arrow' of the drive, to the extent of making it double back on itself, we get what is called "alienated identification." This replaces an act of discovering the other (albeit through the interpretation of the object 'a', the signifier). It is this deflection that occurs in voyeurism, where the scopic drive, stopping short of the object, doubles back on itself thus making the gaze itself the object 'a'.[37]

Alienated identification occurs if the Other, the mother, fixes the girl's image, as if it were her own image; and it is escaped only when it is the father who has the function of interrupting the reflective gaze, in which case the girl can lose her image of misidentification and can gain her desire. It is the other of the mother that becomes her object of desire, and it is to him, the father, that she offers herself to be seen. The severing of the 'arrow' (the trajectory of the scopic drive that had formerly ordered or structured the girl) operates from the moment the girl offers herself to be seen instead of losing herself in the mirror.

It is in this "giving up to be seen" that the scopic drive proper to woman makes her find her status as Subject, as it is through this partial drive that she manifests and displays her desire for the Other. This then is the choice for the female subject: either to become the object of her father's desire, or to identify with him and incorporate the paternal phallus. This, then, is the hysteria that is not only Dora's but all women attempting to constitute themselves in phallocentric languages.

For many women Lemoine-Luccioni's work seems to confirm rather than alter the discourse of psychoanalytic theory, and in so doing to confirm the phallocentrism of that discourse. Yet the specific displacements that her work is effecting are politically significant. To question the primacy of the castration anxiety at the moment of entry into the Symbolic is to demand a radical reconsideration of pre-Oedipal sexuality in terms other than that of the "dialectic of the imaginary." If the terms of the triangulation whereby subjectivity is mapped can no longer function as unproblematic referents, it is because the positions of fixity of the Imaginary, Symbolic and Real, were in themselves an imaginary fixity. Through the theorization of the function of the Mother as first Other from which all others, objects 'a', are derivations, a displacement is effected; the Oedipal instance can no longer be seen as the source and solution to symptom formation; the castration complex itself can be understood as symptomatic.

With Lemoine-Luccioni as with Irigaray, Montrelay, and Kristeva, the theory changes its status from that of being a science to that of being a practice, whether clinical, textual, or political. And when we are examining specific signifying systems such as pornography, that practice entails that the existing analyses of visual pleasure and fetishism have to be rethought to be able to account for structures of spectatorship that are not simply undifferentiatedly masculine and 'individual'. More importantly this practice means that we have to examine the premise that in fetishism the instance of the threat (of castration) and the instance of perception of the vulva are the same.

An adequate theory of fetishism has to displace the premise of the primacy of the Oedipal moment by examining the territory delineated as pre-Oedipal and by accounting for the further complexities incurred by the original bisexuality of the subject. All of these problems are raised in the simple fact of considering a female subject (Lemoine-Luccioni), which calls into question the psychoanalytic premise of the homologous structuration in male and female subjectivity. Then we can begin to trace the specific ontogenetic trajectory of female subjectivity, through which an inevitable displacement of the primacy of symbolic castration can be made, which is in turn a displacement of the phallocentrism of dominant ideology. Nevertheless it is tempting to ascribe this work and immediate effectivity outside of the parameters of the discourse, to 'psychologize' the contradictions that feminism is faced with on economic, legal and institutional levels, or to 'interpret' the campaigns and slogans that we continue to need as a provisional form of political change.

But it is not in this immediate sense that psychoanalysis is consonant with feminist practice. What we can do is examine the representations through which we are constructed, within which we are given identity, and which constitute the material of discourses such as pornography. Psychoanalytic theory can open up the space within which we can begin to speak about our sexualities, their representations, with a voice other than that of censorship. Not simply to refuse these representations in a mental anorexia but to use them in order to ask ourselves: What are our sexualities, our desires? And 'What do we want'?

NOTES

1. London Rape Crisis Centre (P.O. Box 42, London N65BU). Thanks to Hannah Kanter for her discussion on rape.

2. Susan Brownmiller in a broadcast from the *Women Against Pornography Conference,* New York, September 1979. W.A.P. 579 Ninth Ave., NYC 10036.

3. Ellen Dubois—discussion at a workshop on sexuality at the *Simone de Beauvoir Conference,* August 1979, NYU, Washington.

4. Susan Brownmiller, *Against Our Will—Men, Women and Rape* (Secker & Warburg, 1975), pp. 309–22.

5. Luce Irigaray, "Un autre art de jouir," in *Les Femmes, la Pornographie, L'Erotisme,* ed. M. F. Hans & Lapouge (Seuil, 1978), pp. 43 and 302.

6. The film based on Sigmund Freud's *Dora: A Case of Mistaken Identity,* Jay Street Film Project, NYC 1979.

7. Jean Laplanche, *Life and Death in Psychoanalysis* (Johns Hopkins University Press, 1976), p. 8.

8. Jacques Lacan, "Aggressivity in Psychoanalysis," *Écrits* (Norton, 1977), p. 11.

9. Jacques Lacan, *The Four Fundamental Concepts of Psychoanalysis* (Norton, 1978), p. 67.

10. Roland Barthes, "The Rhetoric of the Image," *Image, Music, Text* (Hill & Wang, 1977), p. 37.

11. Jean Laplanche and Serge Leclaire, "The Unconscious: A Psychoanalytic Study," *Yale French Studies*, no. 48. See also the critical study of the article by Anika Lemaire (Routledge & Kegan Paul, 1979), p. 113.

12. Jacques Derrida, "Freud et la scène de l'écriture," *L'Écriture et la Différence* (Seuil, 1967), p. 111, first published in *Tel Quel no. 26.*

13. Umberto Eco, "L'analyse des images," *Communications,* no. 15 (1970), p. 11.

14. J. L. Schefer, "L'image: le sens 'investi'," *Communications,* no. 15 (1970) p. 214.

15. Christian Metz, "Images et Pédagogie," *Communications,* no. 15 (1970) p. 164.

16. Ibid., p. 166.

17. Roland Barthes, *Elements of Semiology* (Cape, 1967), p. 11.

18. J. L. Schefer, as quoted by Christian Metz in *Communications,* no. 15, p. 9.

19. J. F. Lyotard, *Discours/Figure* (Klincksieck, 1972), p. 41; see also Jean Paris, *Painting and Linguistics* (Carnegie, Mellon, 1977).

20. Julia Kristeva, "Ellipse sur la frayer et la seduction speculaire," *Polylogue* (Seuil, 1977), p. 374.

21. Laura Mulvey, "Visual Pleasure and Narrative Cinema," *Screen,* vol. 16, no. 3 (1975), pp. 6–18.

22. John Ellis, "On Pornography," *Screen,* vol. 21, no. 1 (1980), p. 103.

23. See Sigmund Freud, "Instincts and Their Vicissitudes," *The Standard Edition of the Complete Psychological Works,* vol. 14, Trans. James Strachey (London: Hogarth Press, 1953), p. 130.

24. Julia Kristeva, p. 378.

25. Michèle Montrelay, *L'ombre et le nom* (Paris: Editions de Minuit, 1977), p. 50.

26. Ibid., p. 50.

27. Sigmund Freud, "On Negation" in *Standard Edition,* vol. 19, p. 237.

28. Jean Laplanche and Serge Leclaire, "The Unconscious: A Psychoanalytic Study," *Yale French Studies,* no. 48 (1972) p. 120.

29. Jean Laplanche, *Life and Death in Psychoanalysis,* trans. Jeffrey Mehlman (Baltimore: Johns Hopkins University Press, 1976).

30. Eugénie Lemoine-Luccioni, *Le partage des femmes* (Paris: Seuil, 1976).

31. Ibid., pp. 80–81.

32. Ibid., p. 81.

33. Ibid., p. 82.

34. Ibid., p. 83.

35. Ibid., p. 85.

36. See *The Four Fundamental Concepts of Psychoanalysis,* p. 178; see also Lemoine-Luccioni, p. 86, and Montrelay, p. 115.

37. Jacques Lacan, pp. 182–83.

VI

PRIMARY IDENTIFICATION AND THE HISTORICAL SUBJECT
FASSBINDER AND GERMANY

Thomas Elsaesser

> The entire cinematographic apparatus is aimed at provoking . . . a subject-effect and not a reality-effect.
>
> J. L. Baudry

Film Studies returns to the question of identification[1] in the cinema, which used to be one of the main concerns of mass-media studies in the '40s and '50s, with a symptomatic ambivalence. American social psychologists like Martha Wolfenstein and Nathan Leites[2]—indebted to Siegfried Kracauer and, at one remove, The Institute for Social Research—represented the very type of approach from which film theory dissociated itself in order to establish a "theory of the visible." And yet, by a completely different route, Baudry and Metz seem to confirm a fundamental insight of media-psychology: the cinema as an institution confines the spectator in an illusory identity, by a play of self-images, but whereas media-psychology sees these self-images as social roles, for Baudry they are structures of cognition.

Two kinds of determinism seem to be implied in the perspectives opened up by Baudry's description of the 'apparatus': a historical one, where the development of optics and the technology of mechanical reproduction produce the cinema, as a specific visual organization of the subject, and an ontogenetic one, where the cinema imitates the very structure of the human psyche and the formation of the ego. The 'apparatus' seems to be locked into a kind of teleology, in which the illusionist cinema, the viewing situation and the spectator's psyche combine in the concrete realization of a fantasy that characterizes "Western man" and his philosophical efforts toward self-cognition.

While in Baudry's writing, one can still make out a historical argument which, however remotely, underpins his ideas about the condition of a contemporary epistemology, Metz has used Baudry in *The Imaginary Signifier* in order to establish a classification system rather than an ambivalently evolutionary ontology. With this, the historical determinants seem to be entirely displaced toward other parts of the 'institution-cinema', and the question of identification—in the concept of primary identification—is recast significantly, so as to make as clear a distinction as possible between his work and work concerned with role definition, stereotyping and role-projection.

Metz's and Baudry's arguments have several important implications for film studies. For instance, part of the aim of auteur or genre studies and close textual analysis has been to identify levels of coherence in a film or a body of film or a body of films. In the light of *The Imaginary Signifier* one might be better advised to speak of a 'coherence-effect', and to call the very attempt to establish coherence a displaced subject-effect. The task of analysis or interpretation comes to an end at precisely the point where the spectator-critic has objectified his or her subjectivity, by fantasmatizing an author, a genre, or any other category, to act as a substitute for the 'transcendental subject' that Baudry talks about. The perversity of this conclusion can only be mitigated, it seems, if one reminds oneself that Metz's distinction between primary and secondary identification is a procedural one, defining a certain logic operation. Or as Alan Williams put it: "The first and most fundamental level of meaning in cinema is (. . .) that of the coherence of each film's overall surrogate 'subject'."[3] This leaves open the possibility that the surrogate subject is differently constituted from film to film.

The more immediately apparent consequence of accepting Metz's position affects independent or avant-garde filmmaking practice.[4] Baudry's argument implicitly and explicitly designates the cinema as 'idealist' in the philosophical sense, not because of a specific historical or ideological practice, such as Hollywood classical narrative, but by its "basic cinematographic apparatus." An unbridgeable subject/object division renders the object forever unknowable, and consciousness grasps the outer world only in terms of its own unconscious/linguistic structure. The cinema, in this respect, is an apparatus constructed by a Kantian epistemologist. Metz's distinction of primary identification amplifies this point. The filmic signifier is an imaginary one because perception between spectator and image in the cinema always involves the presence of a third term which is hidden: the camera. It is the repression of this absence and deferment in the act of perception that turns the subject/object relation into an imaginary one. Primary identification designates the unperceived and unrecognized mirroring effect that such a constellation produces for the viewer, with the consequence that all possible identifications with the characters in particular are modelled on and circumscribed by a structure of narcissism which inflects the viewer-screen relationship at any given moment.

Perception in the cinema is voyeuristic not because of any particular kinds of representations or points of view. It is not the implied hidden spectator which a scene sometimes addresses, but the always hidden camera which the scene cannot exist without that turns all object-relations in the cinema into fetishistic ones. They hold the subject in a position of miscognition or self-estrangement, regardless of whether the film in question is representational or not, avant-garde or narrative-illusionist. A film either fetishizes the characters or it fetishizes the apparatus.

According to Metz, there is no escape from this closed circle.[5] In this respect, the cinema is indeed an "invention without a future" because it systematically ties the spectator to a regressive state, in an endless circuit of substitution and fetishization.

Such pessimism has been questioned, not least because it seems to invalidate the political and cognitive aims of radical avant-garde filmmaking. Suspecting a logical flaw, Geoffrey Nowell-Smith[6] has challenged Metz's distinction, by arguing that it is difficult to see how one can talk about primary and secondary identification, if one means by this an anteriority, in a process that is essentially simultaneous and dynamic. Consequently, Nowell-Smith wants to argue that "pure specularity" the transformation of Freud's secondary narcissism into the imaginary reintegration of the subject's self-image, is an abstraction, and no more than a misleading theoretical construct. In any concrete act of viewing, the spectator is involved in identifications which are 'primary' and 'secondary' at the same time (if only by the metonymization of shots), and every fragmentation, be it montage, point of view shots, or any other principle of alternation, breaks down primary identification.

> The very fact that something is posited as primary should make us instantly suspicious. To say something is primary is simply to locate it further back in the psychic apparatus. It does not, or should not, invite any conclusions about its efficacy. I would argue, therefore, that the so-called secondary identifications do tend to break down the pure specularity of the screen-spectator relation in itself and to displace it onto relations which are more properly intra-textual, relations to the spectator posited from within the image and in the movement from shot to shot.[7]

Metz might well reply that he is not talking about a perceptual anteriority, but a conceptual a priori, and that he is not interested in concrete acts of viewing as much as in a classification of distinct categories. However, much of Metz's argument is buttressed by Baudry's essays, whose Platonic ontology of the cinema is historicized only at the price of turning it into a negative teleology. At times, it appears that Metz accepts or is indifferent to the suggestion that the cinema is inescapably idealist. Confronted with the question whether 'primary identification' is coextensive with the cinematic apparatus as analyzed by Baudry and to that extent, unaffected by textual or historical production, Metz conceded, without much enthusiasm or conviction, that conceivably, if the nature of the family were to change radically, so might the cinematic apparatus.[8]

Film Studies has responded to these problems not only by a renewed interest in theory. Equally significant is the attention given to alternative or deviating practices in the history of cinema regarding the relationship of spectator to film, and the kind of 'materialism' or 'specularization' which it undergoes. The Japanese cinema (Ozu, Oshima, Mizoguchi) has become a privileged area for such investigations, in terms of narrative space, point of view shots, or culturally different codes of representation and identification.[9] This paper is an attempt to isolate another deviating practice, within the European context, which has developed as closely as the Japanese cinema in a reciprocity and rivalry with the 'dominant' practice of classical narrative. The recent German cinema seems to me to represent both a confirmation of Baudry's and Metz's arguments, and at the same time offers a textual practice which might make apparent a dimension elided or repressed in *The Imaginary Signifier*. In particular, I am wondering whether the mirroring effect of cinema, the specularization of all subject/object relations, their rigid division (which is the 'other scene' of primary identification), and the return of a transcendental subject may not point to internalized social relations whose dynamic has been blocked, a blockage that Metz and Baudry have theorized and systematized.

In choosing the films of Fassbinder, I am guided by the fact that his work has given rise to the most widespread discussions about spectator-positioning and types of identification/distanciation. Thus, a certain familiarity can be assumed for the terms of the argument and the examples cited.

Most of Fassbinder's films are centered on interpersonal relationships and problems of sexual and social identity, in a way that is recognizable from classical Hollywood cinema; and yet, even on casual inspection, his work seems to confirm quite strongly a heavy investment in vision itself, and a concentration on glance/ glance, point of view shots and seemingly unmotivated camera-movements that foreground the processes of filmic signification. Accordingly, one finds two Fassbinders in the critical literature: (a) the German director who wants to make Hollywood pictures and whose audience-effects keep a balance between recognition and identification through genre-formulae and the use of stars, while at the same time distancing the spectator, placing him/her elsewhere through stylization and artifice. Tony Rayns, for instance, sums up some of these points when he argues that "Sirk taught Fassbinder how to handle genre, which became an important facet of his audience-getting strategies."[10] (b) the modernist in Fassbinder, whose cinema is self-reflexive to the point of formalism, and whose deconstruction of narrative involves him in fetishizing the apparatus. Cathy Johnson writes:

> Fassbinder's highly visible cinematic signifier points to a fetishization of cinematic technique. Because all fetishism is an attempt to return to the unity of the mirror stage, one suspects Fassbinder of indulging in the very pleasure he withholds from his audience. Fassbinder is finally a director who approaches the Imaginary by means of a powerful attachment to and manipulation of cinematic technique as technique, while simultaneously barring entry to those of his audience who seek the Imaginary in the invisible cinematic signifier.[11]

I think one needs to argue that these positions contradict each other only insofar as they see audience-getting and audience-frustrating as opposite aspects of a basically unproblematic category, namely the spectator. It seems to me that Fassbinder's highly systematic textuality is not so much a fetishization of technique as the result of inscribing in his films and addressing a historical subject and a subjectivity formed by specific social relations. What is historical, for instance, in films like *Despair, The Marriage of Maria Braun,* or *Germany in Autumn* is the subject—as much as the subject-matter.

In West Germany, the 'spectator' is a problematic category first of all in a sociological sense. Given that most film production is state and television financed, the audience does not recruit itself through box-office mechanisms but via diverse cultural and institutional mediations. And yet, filmmakers want to create an audience for themselves, not only by being active in restructuring the distribution and exhibition machine of cinema, but also by trying to bind potential audiences to the pleasure and habit of "going to the cinema." Paradoxically, however, the most common form of binding in the commercial cinema, through character identification, is almost completely and consistently avoided by directors like Fassbinder, Herzog, Wenders, Syberberg, or Kluge as if somehow in the absence of a genre tradition, or an indigenous commercial cinema, audiences needed to be addressed at a different level.

It has been argued that the German cinema, and Fassbinder in particular, show in this respect the influence of Brecht: characters do not embody their parts but enact roles. But it seems to me that the viewer/film relation and the relation of the characters to the fiction which they enact is considerably more complex. In one sense, the two structures mirror each other infinitely and indefinitely; yet, as I shall argue there is built into them an asymmetry, an instability that brings the relations constantly into crisis. Where Fassbinder seems to differ from both classical narrative and from modernist, deconstructive cinema is in his attitude to voyeurism and fascination. It is rarely fetishized in the form of action or spectacle, and does not seem to derive from primal scene or castration fantasies, as in the suspense or horror-genre. Yet neither is it ascetically banished, not even in the long frontal takes of the early films. Instead, the awareness of watching marks both the entry-point of the spectator into the text, and the manner in which characters interact and experience social reality. One is tempted to say that in Fassbinder's films all human relations, all bodily contact, all power-structures and social hierarchies, all forms of communication and action manifest themselves and ultimately regulate themselves along the single axis of seeing and being seen. It is a cinema in which all possible subject-matter seems to suffer the movement between fascination and exhibitionism, of who controls, contains, places whom through the gaze or the willingness to become the object of the gaze. It is as if all secondary identifications were collapsed into primary identification, and the act of seeing itself the center of the narrative.

Faithful to a persistent Romantic tradition, German directors seem to be preoccupied with questions of identity, subjectivity, estrangement. Foundlings, orphans, abandoned children, social and sexual outsiders wherever one looks. Yet narrativization of these quests for identity are almost never coded in the classical tradition of conflict, enigma, complication, resolution. Instead of (Oedipal) drama, there is discontinuity, tableau, apparent randomness and fortuity in the sequence of events. One might say that in Fassbinder, but it is also true of Wenders and Herzog, there is a preference for paratactic sequencing, with little interest in action-montage. Identity is a movement, an unstable structure of vanishing points, encounters, vistas, and absences. It appears negatively, as nostalgia, deprivation, lack of motivation, loss. Characters only know they exist by the negative emotion of anxiety—the word that in the German cinema has become a cliché: *Angst vor der Angst,* the title of one of Fassbinder's films, and also an important line in both *Alice in the Cities* and *The American Friend.* As in *Die Angst des Tormann's beim Elfmeter,* it almost graphically marks the place, the position where the ego, the self, ought to be, or used to be, but isn't. It is the empty center, the intermittent, negative reference point which primarily affects the protagonists, but which in another movement is also the empty place of the spectator; and one of the most striking characteristics of the films of Wenders, Fassbinder, and Herzog is the ingenious strategies employed to render the position of the camera both unlocalizable and omnipresent, decentered and palpably absent.

"I would like to be what someone else once was" is the sentence uttered by Kaspar Hauser, the foundling, when he was first discovered standing in the town square. The historical phrase appears in Herzog's *Enigma of Kaspar Hauser* as "I want to be a horseman like my father once was." As an attempt to formulate one's identity, such a project is symptomatic in its contradiction and impossibility. It tries to inscribe an Oedipal supercession in a temporal-historical succession: I/someone else, I/my father is the unthinkable equation, immersed in the Heraclitean flux of identity, difference, deferment. In Wim Wenders's *Alice in the Cities,* the same impossibility articulates itself in terms peculiar to the cinema. Travelling through America in search of himself, the hero takes pictures with his Polaroid. But by the time he looks at them, they never show what he saw when he saw it. Delay and difference as functions of an identity mediated by the presence/absence of the camera. Visiting a former girlfriend in New York, the hero has to agree with her when she says: "You only take pictures so you can prove to yourself that you exist at all." The cinema as mirror confirming an illusory identity, in the form of a double matrix of estrangement. Film and subjectivity find a common denominator in the German word *Einstellung,* whose polysemic etymology is often drawn on by Wenders in his writings. In filmmaking, the term applies both to the type of shot (i.e., the distance of camera from object) and the take itself (e.g. a long take). But outside filmmaking it means "attitude, perspective, moral point of view," and is literally derived from "finding oneself or putting oneself in a particular place." Language here anticipates the image of a spatial and specular relation, which only the cinema can fully realize.

In Fassbinder's *Merchant of Four Seasons,* Hans, the hero—another outcast seeking an identity by trying to take the place where someone else once was— explains how he lost his job: "The police had to sack me from the force for what I did. If I couldn't see that, then I wouldn't have been a good policeman. And I was a good policeman. So they had to fire me." Such double-binds, where identity is coextensive with its simultaneous denial, fatally flaw all attempts at reintegration in Fassbinder, and they form the basis for a structure of self-estrangement that in other films appears as a social problem before it becomes a definition of cinema. In Margareta von Trotta's film, *Sisters, or The Balance of Happiness,* one finds the line: "It's not me that needs you, it's you who needs me needing you." The story concerns a woman who systematically tries to turn her younger sister into a double and idealized self-image of herself, until the weaker one commits suicide in order to punish the stronger one. As a symptom of the split subject, the configuration described here has much in common with recent trends in the commercial cinema, especially as reflected in sci-fi and horror thrillers. To find the same material in the German cinema reminds one of its origins in German Romanticism and Expressionist cinema. The situation where a character seeks out or encounters an

Other, only to put himself in their place and from that place (that *Einstellung*) turn them into an idealized, loved and hated self-image, is of course the constellation of the Double, analyzed by Freud in terms of castration—anxiety and secondary narcissism. If one can agree that, especially in the light of Metz's and Baudry's use of Lacan's mirror-phase, the problematic of Other and Double has emerged as the cinematic structure par excellence of German films this seems to demand further exploration. In classical narrative, the double and the split subject make up the repressed structure of primary identification. It appears that in the German films, because this structure is actually represented on screen, it points to a repression elsewhere, which in turn might serve to 'deconstruct' primary identification.

Fassbinder's filmic output is instructive in that a certain line of development becomes clear in retrospect. What gives the impression of continuity despite the change of genres—gangster parody, melodrama, international art-film—is that an obsession with mirroring, doubling, illusory self-images evolves from being a generalized cinematic theme to becoming a specifically German theme, or at any rate, the occasion for historicizing the obsession.

In the early gangster films *(Gods of the Plague, American Soldier)* the heroes' desire revolves not around the acquisition of money or women, but is a completely narcissistic desire to play their roles 'correctly'. Both men and women have a conception of themselves where their behavior is defined by how they wish to appear in the eyes of others: as gangster, pimps, tough guys, prostitutes, femmes fatales. They play the roles with such deadly seriousness because it is the only way they know how of imposing an identity on aimless, impermanent lives. What authenticates these roles is the cinema itself, because it provides a reality more real, but it is a reality only because it implies spectators. The characters in *Katzelmacher* are passive not because they are marginals, and spectators of life. Their endless waiting wants to attract someone to play the spectator, who would confirm them as subjects, by displaying the sort of behavior that would conform to the reactions they expect to elicit. The audience is inscribed as voyeurs, but only because the characters are so manifestly exhibitionist. Substantiality is denied to both characters and audience; they de-realize each other, as all relations polarize themselves in terms of seeing and being seen. Except that to this negative sense of identity corresponds an idealism as radical as that of Baudry's 'apparatus': to be, in Fassbinder, is to be perceived, *esse est percipi*. To the imaginary plenitude of classical narrative, Fassbinder answers by showing the imaginary always constructing itself anew.

The sociological name for this imaginary is conformism. The melodramas seem to offer a social critique of pressures to conform and the narrow roles that prejudice tolerates. But what if conformism was merely the moral abstraction applied to certain object-relations under the regime of the gaze? An example from *Fear Eats the Soul* might illustrate the problem. Ali and Emmi suffer from social ostracism because of a liaison that is considered a breach of decorum. But the way it presents itself is as a contradiction: the couple cannot be "seen together", because there is no social space (work, leisure, family) in which they are not objects of extremely aggressive, hostile, disapproving gazes (neighbors, shopkeepers, bartenders). Yet conversely, they discover that they cannot exist without being seen by others, for when they are alone, the mutually sustaining gaze is not enough to confer or confirm a sense of identity. Love at home or even sex is incapable of providing the pleasure that being looked at by others gives.

The final scene resolves the contradiction. At the hospital where Ali is recovering from an ulcer, a doctor keeps a benevolent eye on the happily reunited Couple. It is a look which only we, as spectators can see, in a mirror placed on a parallel plane to the camera. The need which is also an impossibility of being perceived by others and nonetheless remain a subject—produces both the sickness and the cure (in this case, a wishfulfilling regression to a mother-son, nurse-invalid relationship under the eyes of an institutionally benevolent, sanitized father figure). Only the spectator, however, can read it as such, because the mirror inscribes the audience as another—this time, "knowing" gaze.

It is a configuration strongly reminiscent of *Petra von Kant*. As the drama of double and Other unfolds between Petra and Karin, the spectator becomes ever more aware of Marlene as his/her double within the film. Instead of adopting the classical narrative system of delegating, circulating, and exchanging the spectator's look, via camera position, characters' points of view and glance-off, Fassbinder here 'embodies' the spectator's gaze and thus locates it, fixes it. Marlene's shadowy presence in the background seems to give her secret knowledge and powers of mastery. Yet this other character, virtually outside or at the edge of the fiction, is offered to the spectator not as a figure of projection, but merely as an increasingly uncanny awareness of a double. But to perceive this means also to perceive that Marlene only appears to be the puppeteer who holds the strings to the mechanism called Petra von Kant. As soon as we recognize our double, we become aware of the camera, and in an attempt to gain control over the film, fantasmatize an author, a coherent point of view, a transcendental subject. We are plunged into the abyss of the *en abyme* construction: Marlene is inscribed in another structure, that of the camera and its point of view, which in turn stands apart from the structure in which the spectator tries to find an imaginary identity. Petra von Kant is dedicated to "him who here becomes Marlene": who, among the audience, realizing that the dedication addresses them, would want to become Marlene?

Fassbinder's characters endlessly try to place themselves or arrange others in a configuration that allows them to reexperience the mirror phase, but precisely because the characters enact this ritual of miscognition and displacement, the spectator is not permitted to participate in it. Explicitly, this is the subject of *Despair,* in which the central character, attempting to escape from a particular sexual, economic and political identity, chooses as his double a perfect stranger, projecting on him the idealized nonself, the Other he wishes to be. When this surrogate structure collapses, the hero addresses the audience by a look into the camera, saying: "Don't look at the camera—I am coming out." If in Metz's term, the screen becomes a mirror without reflection, in Fassbinder's films we see characters act before a mirror, but this mirror is not the screen, except insofar as it coincides with the place where the camera once was. A dimension of time, of delay and absence is inscribed, in such an insistent way as to make it impossible for the spectators to use the screen as the mirror of primary cinematic identification.

Instead, one constantly tries to imagine as filled the absence that provokes the characters' self-display. The paradox which I have been trying to describe is that in Fassbinder's films the protagonists' exhibitionism is only partly motivated by the action, however theatrical, and does not mesh with the spectators' voyeurism, because another, more urgent gaze is already negatively present in the film. Another Fassbinder film, in which this absent gaze is both named and erased is *The Marriage of Maria Braun*. Hermann, Maria's husband, has a role similar to that of Marlene in *Petra von Kant*. His disappearance, coinciding with the fall of Hitler, becomes a necessary condition for the fiction to continue. The *ideé fixe* of true love, on which Maria bases her career, is only disturbed by the periodic return of the husband, from the war, from prison, from making his fortune in Canada. It is for him that she does what she does, but only on condition that his place remains empty—reduced to the sign where someone once was. Absence turns her object-choice into an infatuation, which—expelled and fantasmatized into an *ideé fixe*— becomes a transcendental but alienated self-image. Maria represses the return of the source of idealization, thereby also repressing the knowledge of the source of her economic wealth. Her life and identity appear under the sign of a marriage whose consummation is forever postponed and deferred.

The apparent perfunctoriness and lack of plausibility that strikes one so disagree-ably about motive and motivation in characters like Maria or the hero of *Despair* render palpable the feeling that not only is the visual space centered elsewhere, but so is the narrative. The characters, motivated by attracting a confirming gaze and simultaneously repressing it, display a symptomatically 'paranoid' behavior. An ambiguity arises from the fact that the split corresponds to a repressed desire, where the anxiety of knowing oneself to be observed or under surveillance is overlaid by the pleasure of knowing that one is being looked at and looked after: Fassbinder's cinema focuses on the pleasure of exhibitionism, not voyeurism.

Increasingly, and explicitly, this exhibitionism is identified with German fas-cism. In *Despair,* for instance, Nazism appears as both the reverse side and the complementary aspect of the protagonist's dilemma: to escape the sexual and social demands made on him, Hermann's personality splits—into a paranoid and a nar-cissistic self, and he dresses up in someone else's clothes. Meanwhile, in the subplot, the personality split is metonymically related to economics, the change from small-enterprise capitalism to monopoly capitalism, and the proletarianization of the middle classes, who believe in the world-Jewish-Bolshevik conspiracy as a way of relieving anxiety about the future. The white-collar supervisor Muller, who works in Hermann's family firm, resolves his identity crisis also by dressing up: one morning he appears at the office wearing the brownshirt uniform of the SA. The exhibitionist-narcissist of practically all of Fassbinder's films here assumes a par-ticular historical subjectivity: that of the German petit-bourgeois, identifying him-self with the State, and making a public spectacle of his good behavior and conformism. Compared to Muller, Hermann's paranoia is sanity itself and to narcissism as repressed paranoia in Hermann corresponds exhibitionist aggression in Muller. Conformism appears as the social side of the Imaginary which breaks down and constructs itself always anew in Fassbinder's films. To vary Brecht's poem "The Mask of Evil," one might say that Fassbinder's films, optimistically, show how painful and difficult it is to fit in, to conform.

The structures of self-estrangement, of mirroring and miscognition, of positionality and identification with the Other, the double binds, structures that have habitually been interpreted as coinciding with the construction of the basic cinematic apparatus: might they not here be equally amenable to a historical reading? For instance, in terms of fascism, or more generally, as the need even today of binding a petit-bourgeois audience in the 'social imaginary' of secondary narcissism. What, Fassbinder seems to ask, was fascism for the German middle class and working class which supported Hitler? We know what it was for Jews, for those actively persecuted by the regime, for the exiles. But for the apolitical Germans who stayed behind? Might not the pleasure of fascism, its fascination, have been less the sadism and brutality of SS-officers, but the pleasure of being seen, of placing oneself in view of the all-seeing eye of the State. Fascism in its Imaginary encouraged a moral exhibitionism, as it encouraged denunciation and mutual surveillance. Hitler appealed to the Volk but always by picturing the German nation, standing there, observed by "the eyes of the world." The massive specularization of public and private life, diagnosed perhaps too cryptically by Walter Benjamin as the "aestheticisation of politics": might it not have helped to institutionalize the structure of "to be is to be perceived" that Fassbinder's cinema problematizes? But what produces this social imaginary, once one conceives of the Imaginary outside of cinema or the individual psyche? And conversely, what or whom does the cinema serve by reproducing in its apparatus socially paranoid and narcissist behavior?

Such questions raise the political context in which Fassbinder works, what is usually referred to as the 'repressive climate', the 'counter-revolution' that has taken over in West Germany. As the government perfected its law-and-order state in over-reaction to terrorist acts and political kidnapping, the experience of the semi-politicized student movement and many of the intellectuals was a massive flight into paranoia. In the face of a bureaucratic surveillance system ever more ubiquitous, Fassbinder toys with another response: an act of terrorist exhibitionism which turns the machinery of surveillance—including the cinema—into an occasion for self-display. For in his contribution to the omnibus-film *Germany in Autumn,* he quite explicitly enacts the breakdown of authority, the paranoid narcissistic split which he sees as the subjective dimension of an objectively fascist society. In this film—structured around the question of the right to mourn and to bury one's dead, of letters sent by dead fathers to their sons, of sons of the Fatherland forced by the state to commit suicide, so their bodies can return home for a hero's funeral, of children who kill father-figures and father-substitutes, and then commit suicide inside state prisons—Fassbinder concentrates single-mindedly on himself. Naked, in frontal view, close to the camera, he shows himself falling to pieces under the pressure of police-sirens, house searches, and a virtual news blackout in the media. During the days of Mogadishu, when German soldiers carried out an Entebbe style raid to recapture a hijacked plane, he enacts a spectacle of seedy, flamboyant paranoia: that of a left-wing, homosexual, drug-taking artist and film-maker (the Jew of the 70s?) hiding out in his apartment, while his mother explains to him the virtues of conformism in times of political crisis and why she wishes the state was ruled by a benevolent dictator whom everyone could love. Fassbinder makes the connection between paranoia and narcissistic object choice by a double mataphor, boldly cutting from his mother saying that she wishes Hitler back, to himself helplessly embracing his homosexual lover, as they roll on the floor, just as in *Despair* the employee Muller puts on a Nazi uniform while Hermann goes off in search of a double.

What becomes problematic for Fassbinder is ultimately the question of sexual and social roles, and the impossibility of deriving stable role-models from a 'normal' Oedipal development. In the absence of constructing identity within the family (Fassbinder always demonstrates the violence and double binds that families impose on their members), the need to be perceived, to be confirmed, becomes paramount as the structure that regulates and at the same time disturbs the articulations of subjectivity. This means that the cinema, spectacle, the street, as places where the look is symbolically traced, become privileged spaces that actually structure identity outside the family, and in effect replace the family as an identity-generating institution. A film like *The Marriage of Maria Braun* on one level depicts a socialization process that enforces identity not through Oedipal conflict, substituting an object choice to escape the threat of castration, but through a structure modelled on the reaction formation to the loss of a particularly extreme substitution of the ego by an object. And under these conditions, the individual's most satisfying experience of subjectivity may be paradoxically as an exhibitionist, a conformist, in the experience of the self as object, not for anyone in particular, but under the gaze of the Other—be it history, destiny, the moral imperative, the community, peer-groups: anyone who can be imagined as a spectator. What may once have been the place of the Father, the Law, Authority and its castrating gaze,[12] here manifests itself as the desire to identify with a lost object, the benevolent eye of the 'mother' as we know it from the mirror-phase. It would therefore be wrong to say that the palpable absence of the camera marks necessarily the place of the Father.

Conformism used to be the big subject of American schools of sociology and ego-psychology. David Riesman's idea of 'inner-directed—other-directed' *(The Lonely Crowd)*, Erik Erikson's "approval/disapproval by a significant other", Melanie Klein's "good/bad object" in various ways all used Freud's papers on narcissism or his *Mass Psychology and the Ego* to conceptualize changes in social behavior in the face of a weakening family structure. In Germany, two books by the director of the Sigmund Freud Institute in Frankfurt, Alexander Mitscherlich, discuss the social psychology of German fascism and the post-WW II reconstruction period. In *Society without the Father,* for instance, Mitscherlich argues that fascism, in its appeal to Germans of all classes, represents a regressive solution to the "fatherlessness (. . .) in a world in which the division of labour has been extended to the exercise of authority."[13] Instead of assuming that Hitler figured as the Father, one has to imagine him fulfilling the role of a substitute for the primary love-object.

(The mass leader), surprising as it may seem, (. . .) is much more like the image of a primitive mother-goddess. He acts as if he were superior to conscience, and demands a regressive obedience and the begging behaviour that belongs to the behaviour pattern of a child in the pre-Oedipal stage. (. . .) The ties to the Fuhrer, in spite of all the protestations of eternal loyalty, never reached the level (i.e., Oedipal) so rich in conflict, where the conscience is formed and ties with it are established.[14]

According to Mitscherlich, this helps to explain why Hitler vanished so quickly from the minds of Germans after 1945 and why the collapse of the Third Reich did not provoke the kinds of reactions of conscience, of guilt and remorse that 'the world' had expected. In *The Inability to Mourn* he writes:

Thus, the choice of Hitler as the love object took place on a narcissistic basis; that is to say, on a basis of self-love (. . .) The possibility of any dissociation from the object is lost; the person is in the truest sense of the term utterly under alien control (. . .), the millions of subjects released from its spell will remember it all the less clearly because they never assimilated the leader into their ego as one does the model of an admired teacher, for instance, but instead surrendered their own ego in favour of the object. (. . .) Thus, the inability to mourn was preceded by a way of living that was less intent on sharing in the feelings of the other person than on confirming one's own self-esteem. Susceptibility to this form of love is one of the German people's collective character traits. The structure of the love-relation of the Germans to their ideals, or the various human incarnations of those ideals, seems to us to underlie a long history of misfortune. (. . .) Germans vacillate all too often between arrogance and self-abasement. But their self-abasement bears the marks not so much of humility, as of melancholy (. . .).[15]

The West German economic miracle was sustained psychologically by defense mechanisms. The work-ethic, ideologies of effort, and the performance principle took on such ferocious proportions because of the "self-hatred of melancholia."[16] Why did West Germans rebuild such a conservative and conformist society? Democracy came to them imposed from without, and once again "under alien control," they reconstructed their Imaginary in the image of American consumer-capitalism. In parabolic fashion, this is the story of *The Marriage of Maria Braun,* whose heroine's ambiguous strength lies precisely in her "inability to mourn." Benevolent eyes, such as those of Chancellors Adenauer or Schmidt, gaze in ghostly fashion out of portraits whose frame once contained that of Hitler.

To support a film-analysis, however cursory, with such metapsychological observations courts many risks: can complex social and historical developments be reduced to and modelled on psychoanalytical concepts derived from clinical practice with individuals? Are generalizations about the national character not bound to remain at best abstractions, at worst mystifications that involve a mysteriously collective unconscious? Implicitly analogizing capitalism and the family structure as Mitscherlich does runs counter to the work, say, of R. D. Laing, or Bateson, where it is the family that becomes the place of contradictions specifically produced by capitalism. More serious still is the danger of collapsing a particular form of textual production such as the cinema, with a naive reflection theory, so favored by sociologists of film or literature.

What is different between the Freud of Riesman, Erikson, Klein on the one hand, and that of Lacan, Metz, or Baudry on the other, is that the latter emphasize over and over again, the specularity of relations which for the former are somehow substantial, physical, like the symptoms displayed by Freud's hysterical patients. Lacan's insistence on the image, the eye, in the deformation of the self—however incomplete this would be without his notion of textuality—shows the extent to which he has in fact read Freud in the light of concrete historical and social changes. Conversely, what separates Fassbinder from Mitscherlich, and what makes me risk speaking of a 'social imaginary' without fear of getting it confused with some 'collective unconscious' is Fassbinder's commitment to the primacy of vision and the representation of interaction and action in terms of fascination and specular relations.

If fascism is then only the historical name given to the specularization of social, sexual, and political life, then the concepts of Freudian psychoanalysis can indeed be pertinent, once Lacan has taught us how to read them. But by the same token, it suggests itself that Metz's primary identification partakes, as a theoretical construct or a descriptive category, in a historical development—call it, for the sake of the argument, the specularization of consciousness and social production—which his categories do not adequately reflect. In particular, to talk about primary and secondary identification as if it were a closed system risks conflating important distinctions and, in the case of Fassbinder, and other 'deviant' cinematic practices, tends to institutionalize a deconstructive, overly theoretical reading, where a historical reading might also be essential.

This said, it can be argued that in the case of the *New German Cinema,* we may actually have an interesting example of a productive misreading. One of the problems of the *New German Cinema* is that it is only slowly and against much resistance finding the audience inscribed in its texts—German intellectuals and the middle-class. The major successes have been in the capitals of Western Europe and on American university campuses, i.e., with an audience who, ignoring the peculiar historical inscriptions that the texts might carry, have been happy to appropriate the films on the basis precisely of a familiarity with models of narrative deconstruction, modernist self-reflexivity, whether of the kind typical for certain European films, or of the critical readings that film scholars have produced for the classical Hollywood narrative. In turn, the popularity which the films of Fassbinder, Herzog, Wenders have achieved abroad, and above all the critical attention given to them by magazines, at conferences, or in seminars, have, in a considerable way, strengthened their directors' chances of gaining more financial support in their own country from the government. This repeats the structure (on the level of production) which I tried to indicate is present in the texts themselves: the Germans are beginning to love their own cinema because it has been endorsed, confirmed, and benevolently looked at by someone else: for the German cinema to exist, it first had to be seen by non-Germans. It enacts, as a national cinema, now in explicitly economic and cultural terms, yet another form of self-estranged exhibitionism.

NOTES

1. The reader is asked to forgive a rather large assumption made here. In the context of this essay it was necessary to presuppose the reader's familiarity with two essays that discuss (primary/secondary) identification, the 'apparatus' and 'subject-effect': Jean Louis Baudry, "Ideological Effects of the Basic Cinematographic Apparatus," *Film Quarterly* 28, no. 2 (Winter 1974-75); "The Apparatus," *Camera Obscura*, vol. 1, no. 1 (1976).

2. Martha Wolfenstein/Nathan Leites, *Movies—A Psychological Study* (New York: Atheneum, 1970).

3. Alan Williams, *Max Ophuls and the Cinema of Desire* (New York, 1980).

4. See Constance Penley, "The Avant-garde and Its Imaginary," *Camera Obscura*, vol. 1, no. 2 (1977).

5. See interview with Christian Metz, *Discourse*, no. 1 (1979).

6. Geoffrey Nowell-Smith, "A Note on History—Discourse," *Edinburgh Magazine*, no. 1 (1976), pp. 25–32.

7. Ibid., p. 31.

8. Interview, *Discourse*, no. 1 (1979).

9. See, for instance, Kristin Thomson and David Bordwell, "Space and Narrative in the Films of Ozu," *Screen*, vol. 17, no. 2 (1976); Edward Branigan, "Formal Permutations of the Point of View Shot," *Screen*, vol. 16, no. 3 (1975); Stephen Heath, "Narrative Space," *Screen*, vol. 17, no. 3 (1976); Noel Burch, *To the Distant Observer* (London, 1979).

10. Tony Rayns, ed. *Fassbinder*, British Film Institute (London, 1980), p. 4.

11. Cathy Johnson, "The Bitter Tears of Petra von Kant," *Wide Angle*, vol. 3, no. 4 (1989), p. 25.

12. See Cahiers du Cinema's reading of "Young Mr. Lincoln," *Screen*, vol. 13, no. 3 (1972).

13. Alexander Mitscherlich, *Society Without the Father* (1969), p. 283.

14. Ibid., p. 284.

15. Alexander Mitscherlich, *The Inability to Mourn* (1975), pp. 60–61, 63–64.

16. Ibid., p. 63.

II

The Documentary Cinema

Realism and Representation

VII

SELF-REFLEXIVITY IN DOCUMENTARY

Jeanne Allen

Documentary justifies itself as a category of film on the grounds of its ability to replicate reality not primarily for the purposes of entertainment or diversity, but for evidence and argument. Verisimilitude for the documentary rests on the film's ability to supply a visual record of events which transpired before the camera (its photographic component), minimizing the impact of the filming process to motivate or direct those events (the component most traditionally used to distinguish it from the fictional film), and adopting a filmic style associated with minimal manipulation of the pro-filmic event by the camera and editing process (a style sometimes shared with the fictional or directed film). Hence, documentary is quickly drawn into the ongoing debate among theorists as to the nature of filmic representation and art: whether film is artifice as Arnheim, Munsterberg, and Eisenstein would argue, or whether it is more completely a reproduction of reality as Bazin and Kracauer would have us believe. A paper of this length cannot address this larger issue except insofar as the debate over documentary has become a subset of this pivotal question. Yet the larger theoretical question is an extremely pertinent one given that verisimilitude constitutes documentary's very reason for being.

The second part of the definition of documentary as category of film involves the sense of function or justification: to supply evidence or proof in an argument. Because documentary is a very engaged type of cinema, it brings considerable pressure to bear on its claim of verisimilitude. And this is the perspective from which the use of self-reflexive techniques in documentary filmmaking must be viewed. Self-reflexivity is defined here as any aspect of a film which points toward its own processes of production: the conceptualization of a film, the procedures necessary to make the technology available, the process of filming itself, editing to construct a single presentation from separate segments of image and sound, the desires and demands of marketing the film, the circumstances of exhibition. These processes constitute film's manipulative nature. By presenting them self-reflexively, a documentary film can make an audience aware of the processes of production as a limitation on the film's neutral stance, its ability to document objectively. In doing so the film draws attention to the process of selecting and reconstructing events to convey meaning. Self-reflexivity becomes then a reaction against or a way of countering the traditional mode of the documentary which emphasizes verisimilitude.[1]

One would not then expect to see documentary self-reflexivity in areas which claim to be free of ideological conditioning and for which audiences accept professional authority and expertise in the absence of their own. Several kinds of observation make the claim of objectivity as the basis for professional authority and audience credibility. The anthropological documentary seeks to record evidence of a cultural life style gained from naturalistic or scientific observation. As cultural scientist, the anthropological filmmaker tends to find counterproductive any relativization of his/her perspective and to resist the notion that film incorporates a spectrum of decisions informed by the filmmaker's cultural values. Like other documentarists the anthropological filmmaker uses film to state a truth, this time scientific, i.e. assumed to be outside the boundaries of ideology or cultural conditioning. As recently as 1974, Roger Sandall argued for the objective veracity of the filmic record for anthropological documentation.

> Realism in the cinema has been steadily modified by technical developments which have all tended to enlarge the possibility of observation, to bring the capabilities of cameras and sound recorders ever closer to the human eye and ear. The result is not just that the effect is more 'naturalistic'. It is that fact can be distinguished from fiction and true from false . . . an audience can never tell what happened, in camera or cutting room, when one part of the scene ended and the next began. The inclusiveness of a scene shot with a zoom lens removes all doubt. Watching it on the screen an audience shares with the cameraman one continuous observation which coheres. In such a scene the relation of elements is not merely suggested or implied: it is proved.[2]

Sandall's faith in film technology's ability to increasingly approximate an event may result in further obscuring the ideological functions of film grammar. What Roland Barthes has suggested about the use of the photographic image in advertising might also apply to the increasing naturalism of the documentary mode of filmmaking: "This is without a doubt a historically important paradox: the more technology develops the diffusion of information (and especially of images), the more it provides the means of disguising the constructed meaning under the appearance of a given meaning."[3] It seems clear that the technology and aesthetic of film naturalism may also conceal the operation of manipulative processes.

A second prominent quarter from which the claim for documentary verisimilitude can be heard is that of television journalists who use documentary film as reportage. As Nicholas Garnham points out in *Screen,* "the impartial broadcasting institutions claim to 'reflect' the world. It is therefore essential for their ideology that they adopt the aesthetic mode which claims to do the same, i.e. naturalism."[4] Garnham argues that film technique is not neutral because of the ideological significance of film grammar. But when an audience accepts the objective or scientific claims of professionals the informing power of ideology is not acknowledged, nor need it be.

Consequently, the film spectator apprehends the "reality" presented by the film as the only one actually there for the filmmaker to show. That is why, as Michael

Silverman has recently argued,[5] one cannot dispute the fact that the early films of Rossellini are politically revolutionary. Using a style which Bazin described as framing and containing reality rather than impinging upon it—long takes, depth of field, long shots— confers on the profilmic event the quality of a given whole, in its totality. A world so presented is securely constituted and apparently authentic; existing structures of reality appear to be valid and validated through such styles of filmic representation.[6]

One can see from the discussion above that the claim of objectivity and the credibility that ensues from it can rest on various combinations of the component parts of documentary verisimilitude: the technology of the photographic record, the integrity of the filmmaker's refusal to "influence" the profilmic event, a film style which minimizes manipulation, and the implicit authority of the professional who claims to "stand back" and neutrally observe. It is with this position in mind as the normative posture of the documentarist that we now turn to a discussion of the context in which documentary self-reflexivity appears. There are a variety of ways used to challenge the documentary's traditional mode, but they all share a desire to counter the claim of verisimilitude as a neutral posture. In varying degrees, the following uses of self-reflexivity in documentary film take a skeptical view of the dominant mode and of its assumptions with regard to the reality it seeks to document.

Self-reflexivity is used as a kind of decompression chamber in Jean Rouch's *Chronique d'un été* (1961), a film engaged in what Erik Barnouw called a "kind of hometown anthropology, a study of this strange tribe living in Paris."[7] Not only does the film use the cinéma vérité principle of avowed participation by not hiding the machinery of film interviewing, but it ends with a segment which features the participants in the interviews discussing their reactions to the film. In a sense the participants are given the opportunity to restructure the previous reality with a commentary of their own and hence exert a measure of control previously reserved for the filmmaker. Rouch's experience in anthropological filmmaking had exposed him to criticisms for imposing on his footage tendentious narrations which contained interpreted significance without at the same time revealing the ways in which the film created significance. The addendum for *Chronique d'un été* is presented in contradistinction to the self-effaced style of the anthropological film, which disguises the fact that the filmmaker is the organizing consciousness.

The subjectivity of cinéma vérité, employing such features as the handheld camera which reminds the viewer of the specific, hence limited, perspective of the camera, does suggest a limitation or challenge to neutral omniscience. But these subjective qualities are not synonymous, I think, with self-reflexivity unless they comment on themselves within the scope of the film. One way of commenting upon a subjective film style as a particular and therefore relative one is to contrast it with film which is not congruent with such a style. Alain Resnais's celebrated short documentary *Night and Fog* (1955), alternates contemporary color images of what used to be a Nazi concentration camp (accompanied by a highly personal voice-over meditation on the theme of the present's ability to bury the past) with stark black and white footage of the camp's atrocities during war-time. Resnais also alternates a continually tracking camera ferreting out details about the camps in present time with still shots of the victims of the camps. The black and white footage resists any attempt to be included in Resnais's personal narration. It seems to have a different ontological status; it belongs to historical record. The resistance of the black and white still footage conveys Resnais's message—that the past cannot be buried—at the same time that, by contrast, it points to the ways in which the filmmaker can manipulate his materials to express his own personal truth.

One of the clearest examples of documentary self-reflexivity used to demystify the traditional mode of documentary representation is Dziga-Vertov's *Man with a Movie Camera* (1929). On one level the film operates as a kind of explanation of magic tricks, not only tricks of the cameraman and of the editor, but also the implicit "trickiness" that is built into film viewing. Vertov continually presents us with the superhuman qualities of the camera followed by the human manipulation which yields them. As his explication of editing shows the viewer how the film is constructed, his own pattern of editing, which makes formal comparisons between the film crew and other types of workers, argues that filmmaking is also work rather than magical or "artistic" performance. Vertov's film most clearly stands against an attitude which places film in a transcendent realm impervious to the spectator. Instead Vertov *explains* how film works, how it is organized, and that its sleight-of-hand is the result of human labor. Vertov matches his opposition between everyday common reality and the glamorous, romantic world of the fiction film with an opposition between filmmaking as the result of careful human manipulation and work and filmmaking as a seamless magical world, the mysterious creation of the Artist.

The compilation documentary's approach to self-reflexivity is not limited to the post-filming processes of assembling a film, but might also include its preliminary steps—selecting a topic, searching archives, assembling a unifying structure usually dominated by the soundtrack—thus including sonic elements and aspects of the production process. A compilation documentary might be self-reflexive in indicating the sources for and its use of stock footage, a practice which has bedeviled Jay Leyda, Raymond Fielding, and the United States Information Service for different reasons.[8]

A compilation documentary which makes interesting forays in this direction is Jerry Kuehl's *The Siege of Leningrad* from the BBC's "The World at War" series. Kuehl would appear to be introducing a degree of self-reflexivity into this film by labelling the source of some of his footage, thus pointing to the fact that his film is an assemblage of disparate footage. The impulse to do so stems from a reaction against historical compilation films which are not so careful about combining footage of spontaneous historical events with footage of reconstructed events. By labelling his shots of the reunion of the Russian army after the siege of Leningrad as a reenactment done after the war for propaganda purposes, Kuehl at one level demonstrates a mode of manipulation that can be introduced into the documentary. Kuehl's labelling places that footage in the following context: this is a visual support but it is not historically accurate.

The effect of the disclaimer, however, is not to condition the audience's regard for the historical veracity of the film by suggesting a way in which the camera can affect the presentation of an event. Rather, it is intended to disavow the possibility of such a limitation in the rest of the film. Within the category of reenactment as suspect manipulation, the distinction is valid according to the filmmaker's best knowledge. But the only other case of labelling or indicating the status or origin of the film footage blurs the distinction between "neutral" and "committed" sequences. Kuehl uses some *March of Time* footage accompanied by its narration and music with the implication not that the footage is historically suspect but that it was shot and used within the ideological context of the *March of Time* series. This segment may signal to the audience the way in which documentary footage is used at different historical points for ideological purposes, just as the archival footage Kuehl has assembled for his film is being used at times to illustrate the narration of a particular revisionist historian reflecting upon World War II in the 1970s.

The interesting difference between these two examples of labelling footage is that the first serves to underscore the veracity of all the historical footage not labelled "reenactment" and suggests that it is free from the taint of manipulation; while the second instance calls into question, if only momentarily, the neutral stance of the compilation documentary as historical record. The *March of Time /World at War* analogy is intriguing despite the fact that Kuehl nowhere else seems to be aware or makes explicit the conditioning of his own footage—the selectivity and length of his shots, the manner in which they are edited together, the historian's structuring narration, the highly dramatic music, the muted but eloquent voice of Laurence Olivier. The *March of Time* clip gives the viewer a glimpse of how self-reflexivity might operate in a compilation film, but its exceptional status leaves us with a film which is definitely not self-reflexive. The quality of neutral omniscience of the traditional documentary dominates. And that it does so more forcefully in the voice of Olivier, whom we do not see, is a phenomenon which merits considerable examination.[9]

The important relationship between sound and visuals in the compilation film discussed above is of crucial importance in the last example I will discuss here. Indeed, Chris Marker's *Letter from Siberia* (1958) picks up the implications of potential manipulation between visuals and linguistic anchorage touched on in *The Siege of Leningrad* and makes them of focal concern.[10]

Letter from Siberia might be regarded as a meta-travelogue. While many of the patterns of the film resemble this sub-genre of the documentary, the film is simultaneously an essay-critique of the travelogue and its means of conveying meaning. Marker adopts methods of self-reflexivity, like other documentarists, for the purpose of critiquing a dominant tradition: documentaries which feature the quasi-anthropological and geographical scientist stance, unaware or unwilling to admit that their perspective is structured by ideology and cultural conditioning. Marker's primary mode of challenge is to present a series of discrepancies or contradictions which make the viewer aware that the documentaries disguise the separateness of sound and visual elements to emphasize the naturalness of the film's content.

Marker's film centers around the documentarist's use of the soundtrack to structure the meaning of the visuals. By placing his visuals at odds with the soundtrack, Marker indicates the film's capacity for making arbitrary connections or associations appear natural. For example, the film opens with the announcement that the speaker is writing the listener a letter. The soundtrack then becomes the letter and the visuals implicitly become the illustration of that letter. "As I am writing you this letter, my eyes wander along the edge of a grove of birch trees . . ." While the voice-over describes what he sees, the camera pans in long shot the edge of a grove of birch trees. The viewer is locked into this mode of illustration when later in the film, during a presentation of the activities of the Low Temperature Institute's underground labs, the voice-over remarks, "We see André Gide in person, as well preserved as the 'flower.' " The fur-capped Mongolian-featured face in the foreground which "illustrates" this sentence reminds us as viewers that we are easily caught up in a process of accepting highly discriminatory processes as factual givens.

Another example of the soundtrack/visuals discrepancy in this film hinges on one of the central motifs of the documentary and, indeed, of many travelogue documentaries: the contrast between the past and the present. The voice-over announces: "And now here's the shot I've been waiting for, the shot you've all been waiting for, the shot no worthwhile film about a country in the process of transformation could possibly leave out: the contrast between the old and the new . . . look closely because I will not show them to you again." But Marker does show them to us again and again, the first instance not thirty seconds after this announcement: a cart passing a heavy-duty truck, and later, a flying duck becoming an airplane through editing, an arrow in an historical drama becoming a rocket; the camera continually pans from new to old, power plant to birch trees, city buildings to the forest.

The above excerpt from the narration illustrates the parodic quality of the soundtrack and its challenge to the travelogues whose methods of structuring significance Marker illuminates. At another point Marker offers a textbook lesson in what is meant by linguistic anchorage by presenting an almost identical sequence of shots three consecutive times but accompanied by highly varied interpretive narrations. The narrations are pro-Communist, anti-Communist and "objective," the latter being rapidly followed with a disclaimer on the impossibility of objectivity. Besides this Marker takes occasional verbal pot-shots at cultural provincialism: ". . . and now for the Siberian version of 'diamonds are a girl's best friend'" or "now don't get the idea that they are distant cousins of *Nanook of the North*" or the heavily ironic "the arctic world suffers from a serious lack of Woolworth stores" which is itself critiqued by "and yet our irony may be more naive than their enthusiasm."

While the soundtrack humorously reflects upon the cultural smugness of the travelogue tradition, Marker's exposure of the ways in which most travelogues conceal their ideological perspective emerges from the interplay of soundtrack and visuals. The tensions between these components help to make the viewer aware of how the documentary structures reality through language and how the images are made to illustrate the conceptual reality defined by the voice, so that the viewer experiences not so much a visual truth (the filmic document) as a verbal and conceptual one. Similarly the narration instructs us as to the means of manipulating film material through camera movement and editing. We sense how selecting footage structures a personal vision of the subject Siberia in the phrase, "here's the shot I've been waiting for" which also tells us "this is why I have chosen this shot."

Like *Man with a Movie Camera, Letter from Siberia*'s primary thrust is to counter a dominant mode—the traditional travelogue—by revealing the naturalizing operations of the genre and its implicit ideological position. The other films discussed here explore other means and degrees of self-reflexivity. Certainly many more variations could and should be explored, as well as the subtle differences among them. But this analysis argues for one aspect of the self-reflexive documentary which all of these examples share: the function of challenging a type of documentary which has maximized the claim to verisimilitude and therefore succeeded in effacing the documentary's ideological position. Even Resnais's *Night and Fog*, which seems to counter a specific tradition the least, is so overly a personal statement confronting a historical fact that it makes the viewer aware that a film is always a *statement* by a historical person. This is in itself a strong statement against the tradition of factualness and objectivity.

Documentaries can say to us "this did happen," these women and children were gassed to death and shovelled into mass graves, or these students were fleeing when the soldiers turned and fired upon them. But documentaries rarely confine themselves to pointing. They create meaning with sequence, shot context, soundtrack and so forth. If the dominant mode of the documentary conceals its processes of producing meaning and seeks to present a historical, scientific, or cultural given, self-reflexivity, as exemplified in the preceding discussion, repeatedly argues against the givenness of documentary reality and for its constructedness, thereby documenting the very limitations of verisimilitude.

NOTES

1. I am indebted to the editors of *Ciné-Tracts*, and to Teresa de Lauretis, David Allen, and Bob Dickey for the intelligent criticism and suggestion which has shaped much of this discussion. It has been a pleasure to receive and respond to their careful scrutiny and clear thinking.

2. Roger Sandall, "Observation and Identity," *Sight and Sound*, vol. 41, no. 4 (Autumn 1972), pp. 192–93.

3. Roland Barthes, "The Rhetoric of the Image," *Working Papers in Cultural Studies*, vol. 1 (Spring, 1971), pp. 37–50.

4. Nicholas Garnham, "TV Documentary and Ideology," *Screen*, vol. 13, no. 2 (Summer, 1972), p.111.

5. Michael Silverman, "Rossellini and Leon Battista Alberti: The Center Power of Perspective," *Yale Italian Studies*, vol. 1, no. 1 (Winter, 1977), pp. 128–42.

6. Silverman, p. 131.

7. Erik Barnouw, *Documentary: A History of the Non-Fiction Film* (New York: Oxford University Press, 1974), p. 254.

8. Jay Leyda, *Films Beget Films* (New York: Hill and Wang, 1964). Raymond Fielding, *The American Newsreel: 1911–1967* (Norman: University of Oklahoma Press, 1972). "History and All That Jazz," *Film Comment,* vol. 3, no. 2 (Spring, 1965), pp. 64–66.

9. Bill Nichols, "Documentary Theory and Practice," *Screen,* vol. 17, no. 4 (Winter 76–77), pp. 34–48. See his discussion of modes of address.

10. For the notion of linguistic anchorage, see Barthes, p. 43.

VIII

THE CRISIS OF THE DOCUMENTARY FILM IN QUEBEC

Ron Burnett

At a meeting of Quebec filmmakers which I attended in the spring of 1981 at the Cinémathèque Québecoise in Montreal, Gilles Groulx (one of the most innovative of Quebec's cinéastes) stood up and made the following declaration which, for purposes of brevity I will paraphrase. He said that Quebec cinema was in crisis, not only because it had lost sight of its roots, and its political concerns, but because even its fiction films were derived from the documentary film genre, inhabited by, and instilled with, the ethos of the National Film Board. To an outsider it may seem heretical to state this, because the NFB has an extraordinary world-wide reputation. But in Quebec, the NFB has drawn upon and supported the pool of filmmakers who are active in the culture of the province to a degree that would be unimaginable in any other country. Most of Quebec's best filmmakers have at one time or another been employed there, or have received financial aid to do a project from the NFB. An independent or even alternative film industry does not exist, and it isn't as a result of a lack of effort.

The National Film Board's mastery of the low to medium priced documentary film makes it a very attractive place to work, not only because of the extraordinary facilities which the board has, but because the NFB is truly a filmmakers' dream, a laboratory for the exploration of the medium, a testing ground for ideas which would otherwise not see the light of day. It is precisely its dedication to the documentary cinema, its history as a developer if not one of the main progenitors of the genre, and its clear concern for social issues that Groulx reacted to. The board's relationship to the documentary cinema has been a creative and innovative one, ranging from the documentaries of the fifties to cinéma vérité in the 1960s to *Challenge for Change* which still today stands as a model for what can be done with the cinema when enough energy is put into its potential use as a pedagogical tool. (*Challenge for Change* was a community based project which provided film and video equipment to ordinary people upon request and which also facilitated the projects of independent filmmakers trying to examine the daily lives of the disenfranchised, those least likely to find a voice in the mainstream media. Many films grew out of the program, and it has often been cited as a model not only for the documentary cinema but for video as well.)

Paradoxically, the board's self-professed desire to educate through film fits in with the dominant tradition of didactic films made in Quebec. Its concern with preserving the Canadian heritage and conserving the pictures of an evolving Canadian identity, parallels the concern in Quebec with building an archive of images to record a culture and a way of life which is unique in North America. But, as we shall see, there are some serious problems with the social and supposedly progressive thrust of the NFB. It is these problems which Groulx tried, in a very subjective way, to address and which the following article enlarges upon.

The Board's effects upon film culture in this province can best be understood through an examination of the various debates which suffused the institution during some of its most creative and difficult periods. Groulx worked with the French Unit at the Board which was concerned with using the camera as a tool to depict the social reality of Quebec. In this sense, the Board satisfied a desire on the part of filmmakers like Groulx to see their work as political, as part of the growing awareness that Quebec was developing (1958–64) of its social, economic and cultural history. The filmmakers implicated themselves in the crucial debates of the day. Their cinema was viewed as a "prise de conscience," as the focal point for keeping alive, via images, all that was threatened by English and North American culture. Their cinema would not only educate; it would act as a transformative tool. The documentary would become a window onto history, onto the slippages created by a society in transition, all of this with the aim of finally rescuing Quebec from the influences of English Canada. (Editor's Note: In 1989, the fiftieth anniversary of the NFB, Colin Low, the founder of *Challenge for Change* and one of the most important documentary filmmakers at the board, met his French counterpart Pierre Perrault essentially for the first time though they had shared the same building for over twenty-five years. This extraordinary meeting typifies the way in which the NFB as an institution mirrors the internal conflicts of Canada as a country and the way in which those conflicts have essentially remained unresolved.) This rescue, that is, the promotion of Quebec nationalism through film, would be undertaken even though the NFB was a federal institution financed by the taxpayers of Canada as a whole.

Some of these desires, to speak to Quebeckers about Quebec were not really different from the aims of the NFB in relation to Canada and it was perhaps simplistic of the board's bureaucracy to assume that the institution could rise above the political conflicts of the day in the country as a whole. But, what *was* different, and would lead to later conflicts between the Board and its filmmakers, was the strength of the nationalistic impulse in Quebec. Quebec, a colonized country in the eyes of its nationalist filmmakers, needed the cinema as a vehicle to recover its own identity. In many ways the NFB was not, and has never been, ready to accept the depth and commitment of that impulse. But at the same time it could not reject what the filmmakers had to offer. In the gap created by these contradictions slipped a whole generation of cinéastes. They made films which explored their own psyches and the psyches of the people they assumed they represented, but as their films became more complex, more nationalistic, they discovered that the NFB was not as hospitable as they had first thought and rather than perhaps evolving beyond those contradictions many of the filmmakers, including Groulx, became bitter and resentful about the board's direction, leading in large measure to the comments by Groulx mentioned above.

There is a profound difference between Canadian and Quebec nationalism. The former is not perceived as much of a threat either within or outside of Canada, politically or economically, except to foreign capital. The latter, however, is seen as a threat to the very fabric of the *binational* identity of Canada as a society. The NFB was and is an institution that has tried to unify these differences. Here then are the roots of an irreconcilable conflict between federalism, the NFB, and Québécois filmmakers. Most political institutions in Canada have not been able to mediate or reconcile these or similar differences, and it was perhaps naive to expect the NFB to succeed where others haven't.

The Quebec based NFB filmmakers, (including Groulx, Pierre Perrault, Jacques Godbout, Michel Brault, Claude Jutra, Jean Dansereau) did not attack the Film Board's hold over them at the institutional level. Rather, they cloistered themselves into a very tight group with a particular identity within the NFB. They developed that identity even further by the manner in which they used cinéma-vérité. Here is Gilles Groulx describing this development. "We said to ourselves: The English have a very rigid outlook on the cinema. They don't in essence capture the reality that they film. When they make documentaries they take five shots of a guy walking in the streets. That has no relationship with a document, or even with a documentary! It is fictional cinema made under the guise of the documentary."[1] Or Claude Jutra: "The Québécois quickly took over the philosophy and direction of cinéma vérité. We turned it into something distinctively Québécois. It was very personal: we were more emotional and expressive than the English and we didn't play any of the games with objectivity that the Anglo-Saxons at the NFB did."[2]

The frustration of these filmmakers grew out of the institutional practice of which they were a part. It was the acceptable limits of the National Film Board that they were working within, not only, or in any strict sense, the documentary as a genre. This is not to suggest a monolithic NFB directing and controlling all of the work done by its filmmakers, but the institution subtly defines the parameters of its own practice. It supplies permanent employment to a pool of filmmakers, and in one sense that seems to be an act of support and encouragement. It can be seen however, as a very direct way of legitimizing the role and power of the state in the production of culture. Protesting this is difficult, since an outcry may lead to the destruction of the institution, and consequently to the loss of one of the few contexts where the production of documentary films is actually legitimate and financially feasible. The circularity of this problem, the anguish of being in effect the *Voice of Canada* (one of the most important features of the NFB's charter) to the world, when all that you wanted was to speak on behalf of Quebec *to* the Québécois, that anguish and that circularity defined a large part of the content of the documentary window which Québécois filmmakers opened up.

The NFB is not only about film, but about a concept of Canada. It, in itself, is a medium for the transmission of Canadian national aspirations, in almost direct contradiction to the deeply felt Quebec nationalism of the early sixties. How did the filmmakers deal with this? They began, in effect, by cataloguing the society around them through the cinema, inventorizing the activities of the people, and thereby transforming history into a vast encyclopedia, replete with images which froze forever that which seemed to be slipping away. The archive which they tried to create was by no means neutral, though it partook of one of the problems of the archival: the contradictory layers and levels of history, debates bound up with context and time, are difficult to maintain within the context of an archive. The result is not a denial of heterogeneity but a regularization of historical phenomena into a series of categories which can become rules for seeing and understanding the world. Thus it can be said that the Québécois documentarians who worked for the NFB were desperately stripping away one illusion to create a far more complex one. They were slowly creating the cultural and institutional infrastructure which made the documentary and the gathering of documents the main feature of their political activity. The elevation of the documentary film from *one* of many possible genres that could reflect the particular reality of Quebec, to the *only* style that accurately reproduced "notre caractère national," made the relationship between the NFB and Quebec's filmmakers a symbiotic yet contradictory one. However, the desire to capture the real and make the everyday life of the people the 'subject' of their films was inspired by their politics. The images they wanted, the people they wanted to film, the careful crafting through editing of what the people said, was supposed to stand *for* what the filmmakers themselves *could not* say within the limitations of the institution for which they worked. Thus they delegated their authority away from themselves to the people they interviewed and depicted. This was a convenient way of adapting to the exigencies of an institution which could not condone (even within a relatively liberal framework) the more serious oppositional tendencies represented by the turmoil in Quebec.

Almost from the beginning, the members of the French Unit at the NFB fought with the institution. One of the most notorious censorships took place around the film, *On est au coton* (1970). But the stage for this censorship, which I will discuss in a moment, was set many years earlier. As an example, consider what happened to Arthur Lamothe's film, *Les bucherons de la manouane*. "Even though they (the Film Board's producers) demanded that I cut a number of shots, they did not realize that I had practiced a form of auto-censorship anyway. In terms of information I wanted to go much further than they would let me. I'm aware of the fact that when you work for a federal institution, you have to be ready to censor yourself and to be careful about what you say. Ironically, the text for *Les Bucherons* had been accepted by the Board. In the first version of the film I said: 'Our earth belongs to a foreign monarchy. The capital that runs our companies is American. Our managers are Anglo-Saxons. English is the language of our masters.' They made me cut, English is the language of our masters and they also made me cut that our managers are anglophone."[3]

There is, in what Lamothe says, only a partial recognition of how the institution affected him. Could he expect those he categorized as colonizers to allow an anticolonialist statement to be made? Surely not. Was he fighting the institution from within? Yes, but for what purpose? Though to some extent, the struggle of a Lamothe, or a Brault, or a Groulx challenged the institution, it could not change its fundamental direction. Though the French Unit managed to separate itself from the English side, it was never completely autonomous. In effect, the filmmakers had to give in to some degree. I would suggest that their obsession with the candid eye type of film was an attempt to subvert the censorship since, if all that the camera and crew did was "come upon" a scene, and if those scenes in Quebec were *inherently* political, then the phenomenological moment would represent *truth* without looking like a distortion or even looking as if it had been purposely put there. This was a brilliant strategy until some of the filmmakers, in particular Denys Arcand, began to add the type of voice-over which revealed a far more developed political sensibility at work than in earlier films.

His film, *On est au coton,* was at one and the same time the clearest expression of this crisis and an attempt to break with it. Denys Arcand took a strong political stand and in so doing shifted away from cinéma-vérité. Consequently he made no attempt to hide the very loud voice of his nationalism. The film was also anti-capitalist and a severe critique of the textile industry in Quebec. It took its politics seriously enough to make them a determining factor in not only the representations that it chose, but in the general approach it took to the documentary form. The NFB responded to the film by declaring it to be "unrepresentative" of the problems in the textile industry, and not "objective" in its presentation of the facts. The filmmaker was branded as being insufficiently neutral in his approach. When the then commissioner of the Board, Sydney Newman, was attacked for censorship and for being anti-working class, he defended his position by pointing to the many NFB films which depict working class life and which defended the rights of the workers. He was correct that the NFB had a large inventory of so-called 'working class' films, but he mis-understood the criticism. For Newman, and for the NFB, a working class film was one which partook of a distant phenomenology; a film which showed exploitation but was careful in revealing any causes; a film which, like many of the Candid Eye series, had more of an archival intent than a political one.

The NFB has a catalogue full of voyeuristic looks at the depressing and inevitably hopeless task faced by the poor and by workers in their struggle for dignity and proper pay and improved working conditions. The desire in these films is to depict the real as if reality were not mediated by the representational process. The filmmakers try to enter a reality that they can only experience as voyeurs, a moment in time when the representation of defeat and defeatism seems to fit with their own guilt at being unable to effectively change the story that they are transporting out from the slums to their audiences. Obviously the NFB could not allow films to be made that *challenged* the middle of the road position that *everyone,* the whole populace of the country, was responsible for the economic, social, and political mess which the films documented. This is the error of a narrowly focused cultural nationalism, one that elevates *identity* beyond the actual context to which it is referring. The NFB films on workers all reveal a variety of tensions in our society—we *are* given pictures of daily life—but only to the degree and extent that contradiction and contradictory forces are muted, silenced, by a representational process that screams for change, but that must defend itself against the possible consequences of the outrage. Conflict must coexist with harmony and possible solutions to the problems must always be in sight. *On est au coton* proposes precisely no solution and simply foregrounds conflict and contradiction with a call to action. This polemical use of film is what ultimately angered Newman. It is after all the function of a polemic to stir up the neatly embroidered patterns of conventional discourse, and to shake up the carefully structured lethargy of institutions.

As we can see, there is within Québécois filmmakers a deep desire to break with the Board and a contradictory desire to be supported by it. *On est au coton* highlights these contradictions. *On est au coton* compares the life of a worker with that of his boss in the textile industry through a parallel structure that looks at their daily lives. There is at one and the same time a kind of inevitability to the thematic structure of the film. The oppressors are worse than we think, and the workers face an almost impossible situation which will only be improved through struggle. This is all closely linked to the oppression of the Québécois as a people so that the factory floor becomes a metaphor for the broader battle which must be waged by all Quebeckers against the denial of their economic and national aspirations.

Sydney Newman saw the film as an immediate threat, yet the film itself was ambiguous about the direction which the workers should take. It was an ambiguity born of the problems that the militant cinema of the kind practiced by Arcand had not in a self-reflexive way commented upon. It was an ambiguity partially related to the difficulty that the cinema has in effectively changing the very contradictions that it depicts. It is much like the problem faced by a teacher who may try to speak clearly about a particular political reality and be confronted with an audience, students, who only recognize in a partial and fragmented way what he/she is trying to say. Often rather than trying to take this process into account the teacher will move to a level of greater emphasis and intensity, become even more didactic, rather than less, and attempt to perfect the presentation of the material. A bind results. As the material becomes more and more hermetic, and complete, the audience's fragmentation increases. Communication, rather than improving, continues to break down.

In film, ambiguity is built into every representation and into every message. To enunciate in film is to enunciate ambiguously. In an attempt to fill these gaps, *On est au coton* overstated its case. It did not break the permissible boundaries of the documentary film, it simply extended *the direct* into the didactic and it was the implications of the film as a pedagogical device which scared Newman. He of course partook of the same viewpoint as Arcand as regards the power of film to affect its audiences. For Newman all documentary films had to be careful with their material because they were educational tools. So, though they both came to film with differing points of view they both overstated film's effectivity or at least overinvested in its presumed power. Newman saw the truth distorted and assumed the mirroring of that distortion in the mind of his audience. Arcand structured the film in the hope that the truth he was depicting would also be mirrored in the audience. Ironically, their shared assumption about the power of the medium led them to an almost irresolvable dilemma about the content of the film.

At the meeting which I mentioned earlier in this article Arcand said the following: "What the workers understand, in reality, is their weakness. And there is very good reason for this. Worker power is actually diminishing in our society. This is one of the major problems that traditional Marxist thinking now faces. In absolute numbers, in relation to the rest of the population, the traditional power of the working class is less and less important." This in itself is not a position that the NFB would be uncomfortable with. However, Arcand went on to propose a more radical position. "We are dealing here, with the problem of ideology and not simply one of worker organization. There are a lot of institutional structures within which the working class operates (unions, local organizing committees etc.); creating an organization that would bring all of these forces together, into an autonomous political group would not be too hard. But I don't think that this is the essence of the problem, the crux of this whole thing is ideology. Practice must come from theory which must then be verified again in practice. What is missing in our situation right now is theory, revolutionary theory."

It would not be a generalization to suggest that part of the problem that Arcand faced in working at the NFB was the absence of theory, in an ironic parallel to what he suggested about the Quebec working class and its militant organizations. By absence of theory I mean an absence of debate about how filmmaking is never simply an expression of the personal interests of the filmmaker, but is an activity which operates within historically bound institutional frameworks. As such, a theory is needed to explain the cultural and political conjuncture that made a particular film genre, for example, dominant at the NFB. Furthermore, we need to explain *why* the documentary—direct cinema—became a vehicle for the expression of the perceived interests of the Quebec people. Arcand's attempt to focus in on ideology was a start towards this theorization. But he essentially saw film as an adjunct to political action and as an educational tool. He privileged what he felt were the *content-areas* that needed examination by the cinema. Those content-areas reflected an essential pessimism about working class struggle (and it would be of interest to reopen the debate around *On est au coton,* which is a film that ostensibly proposes a militant line, but, removed from the context of the NFB appears to be quite harmless, almost tentative in its exploration of worker oppression), not only and singularly because of Arcand's outlook, but in part, as a result of the many contradictions that come with the documentary film as a genre.

The "site" of my argument is therefore twofold. In the first place it is not an accident that the NFB made the documentary and cinéma-vérité the privileged style for film production. Secondly, the dependence of Quebec filmmakers like Arcand upon the direct cinema (and there is a need to examine why the term "direct" is a contradiction in terms) is linked to their desire to politicize their audiences, a desire, the theory of which they never examined in very great detail.

Another film by Arcand entitled *Le confort et l'indifférence* (1981), also made at the NFB, reflects all of the above contradictions in an even more emphatic way. It is essentially the story of the failure by Quebec nationalists to win a referendum on the future separation of Quebec from Canada. The film is brilliantly edited, mixing together a variety of images that build into a pyramid of statements about the essential conservatism of the 'people' and their inability to understand the future, their inability to risk the present *for* the future. It uses all of the elements of cinéma-vérité and joins those with the more traditional documentary style. The film pivots around an actor who plays Machiavelli. These "fictional" moments are philosophical interludes, meant to contexualize and explain the preceding footage. The film's critique of the 'ordinary' desires of ordinary people is profoundly cynical and relentless. For our purposes the film reveals and displays many of the problems which I have been discussing. It submerges itself in the national question as if class is unimportant. It bemoans the loss of innocence that Quebec went through and tries to tear away the veil of illusions that the Québécois have about Canada. It uses the documentary as a transparent device for 'showing' what really went on during the referendum. It presumes that the window which it opens will change those who view the film.

In a sense Arcand is struggling with precisely the same things that the filmmakers in the early sixties did. Except that this time his film *is* an archival collection because so much of it is a pastiche of the events of the last twenty years in Quebec. For example, we see the Queen inspecting an honor guard, and this is carefully cut to fit not only its location in the film but also to be preserved as *the* example of the national oppression of the Québécois. Using the Queen as a symbol of oppression is equivalent to the trademark that a company uses to identify itself. Arcand is not trying to set the record straight; he is simply making sure that the record will never be forgotten. He reduces the complexity of both political action and political understanding to a simple moral formulation of right and wrong. What is interesting is that this condemnation of the federal state survived at the NFB. Arcand succeeded where none of the early filmmakers (himself included) could, at least that is the way that it seems on the surface.

As image after image passes by of silly politicians making frivolous promises and arguments about the future of Quebec, and as Machiavelli intervenes to point out the grand stupidity of it all, the film becomes more of a condemnation of the working class as a whole than it does of their politics. It begins to situate itself very much in the mold of many NFB films. Its critique hardly glances at the root causes of fear, the unsettling worry which many Québécois had about the problems of trying to create a new country. In one scene the camera tracks into a van being displayed in a show. The van is outfitted and furnished in the most garish way with a false fireplace, false shelves, false everything. For Arcand this is a synoptic image of those who voted against Quebec. But is it? Can the private pleasure of this man reveal something about workers as a whole? I think not. Arcand instead has taken the very traditional view of the worker as a representative of false consciousness. And precisely, in this way, he duplicates the thrust of many NFB films. As they wander through the desert deprived of knowledge, the workers become victims of their own lacks. Their false consciousness is a simple mirror reflection of the ideological desires of the federal state. This simple determinism is conveniently reenforced by Machiavelli, who plays the role of the all-powerful paternal figure ruling over the cynical mess, providing the grammar as it were, for the cynicism. There is a pathetic scene in which a petit-bourgeois intellectual cries about the loss; one almost hopes that the film is self-reflexively critiquing his position, until we realize that he in one sense represents the film's position. The most devastating criticism is laid at the feet of Prime Minister Trudeau, who is not only a traitor because he is French and a federalist, but because, for Arcand he is the fullest incarnation of the paternalism of anglophone culture.

How did this film pass through the NFB? It is in part a sign of the change that the institution has undergone, responding to the ascendency of a pro-separatist party in Quebec. More importantly, the film is not really a threat. It is made for a very narrow audience. Its constituency is not the workers that it laughs at. Its constituency is precisely those people who it is *not* critiquing. Its cry of pain at the way that history has unfolded, paradoxically says more about the institution from which it is coming than it does about the society to which it is directed.

What must be recognized here is that the NFB is, to all intents and purposes, one of the few institutions in Canada where a film like this could be made. The film's journalistic look and tone is a result of its news clip format, a conventional NFB collage-montage of events that are not analyzed in any great detail. Its determinism reflects its isolation, coming from an institution that must be isolated in order to function. The NFB is like a think-tank. We rarely gain an insight into how it works. No films have really been made about it. Authority is conferred upon those who produce films at the board, though the actual research which makes many of the films possible is never foregrounded so that we may understand its ideological premises more clearly.

Thus it is not an accident that the nationalist drama should play itself out within the confines of the institution. As a preserver of history and culture the Film Board's role is ultimately a pedagogical one. While Arcand's film does not fit into the 'direct', it certainly mixes cinéma-vérité with an intense didacticism that would only be threatening if it could transcend its cynicism. Though it might be brutal to say this, the film is the equivalent of a Sunday morning show on television that looks with a pitiful eye upon the handicapped, trying to overwhelm the audience with guilt, filling them with easy categories of what is true and false, moralizing, endlessly . . .

It does not examine the social or economic relations which gave rise to separatism. It skirts the issues of its own nationalism and thus does not work out the more profound questions surrounding national identity. What we are dealing with here is nationalism as it has always been understood and practiced by the NFB in relation to Canada but taken to its extreme by Arcand in relation to Quebec. "Nationalism in the sense of chauvinism tends to exhibit the same Imaginary values as individualism does: atomism, divisiveness, unconstrained competition, *paranoia* about others and associated forms of pathological behaviour. Chauvinism is moreover predominantly an 'either/or' relationship to other nations just as individualism is to other individuals."[4]

On est au coton was censored because it aggressively examined economic relations between Quebec and Canada but also because it spoke with a voice which threatened the institution of which it was a part. *Le confort et l'indifférence* was not censored because it transformed the complex problems facing Quebec into a morality play, obscuring the very reality it was so desperately trying to depict. The film lays down a challenge that no institution would find threatening. We are all, irrespective of our class interests, lost, and now with the referendum over, there is very little left for us to do but shrug and bear it. Though the very ideology that Arcand decries also emanates from the institution which employs him, he is unable to recognize his own collusion with the interests of the NFB. The paradox here is that the argument over how to depict Quebec and its nationalist aspirations has been repeated but in an acceptable and rather conventional manner. Ultimately the documentary as a form, as a genre points the audience toward a window which viewers themselves must open. In their desire to both represent and reveal the reality of Quebec, Arcand and many of the filmmakers at the French Unit of the board forgot or denied this fundamental reality of the viewing process. In this sense they were equal partners with their English counterparts, a paradox which, to this day, would be denied by both parties.

NOTES

1. Gilles Marsolais, *Cinéma D'Ici* (Leméac, 1973), pp. 77–78.
2. Ibid., p. 78.
3. Ibid., p. 89.
4. Tony Wilden, *The Imaginary Canadian* (Vancouver: Pulp Press, 1980), p. 114.

IX

REALISM, NATURALISM, AND THEIR ALTERNATIVES

Raymond Williams

Some very important questions about television drama are currently being discussed around the focal terms 'realism' and 'naturalism.' In trying to follow the discussion what has most struck me is the extraordinary looseness and shallowness with which these terms are commonly used. They are both, in any case, very difficult and complicated terms, and each has a long and complex history. The problems at which they are directed are also, obviously, complicated and difficult. But the first intervention that I can usefully make is on the terms themselves. And before this is diagnosed as the pedantry of a professor who is also a writer, may I say that it is not only the confused and myopic terminology that has provoked me, but that through and past this, some of the crucial creative and productive issues are being missed or displaced: the issues that interest me practically, as a writer who also happens to be a professor.

I will state some propositions about the terms realism and naturalism and refer those who wish to see them more fully argued to some things that I have written previously which are noted in the appendix.[1]

1. The terms realism and naturalism did not originally refer to conventions and technical methods in art, literature, and drama, but to changed attitudes toward 'reality' itself, toward man and society and toward the character of all relationships. Thus naturalism was a conscious alternative to supernaturalism and proposed the conscious presentation of human actions in exclusively human and secular terms, as distinct from earlier kinds of drama, fiction, and art which had included, as a commanding or at least referential dimension, a superhuman or extra-human power. Realism is more complicated but in its decisive modern development made the same emphasis, and at this level was often interchangeable with naturalism and with materialism.

2. This is not a separate philosophical development, but was the basis for the making of new conventions and methods in art, fiction, and drama. Thus naturalism, specifically associated with the new scientific natural history, proposed as a matter of principle that it is necessary to describe (present, embody, realize) an environment if we wish to understand a character, since character and environment

are indissolubly linked. Thus naturalist dramatists did not include detailed physical and social settings because it was technically possible with new theatrical technology and resources, or because it was one kind of formal method as against others, but because they insisted that it was impossible to understand character and action unless the full physical and social environment which shaped character and action was directly presented, indeed as a kind of character and action in itself.

3. Realism in its nineteenth century artistic sense was similarly an emphasis on the 'real world' as against the characteristic presentation of the world in romance and myth—seen as including extra-human, supernatural and in these terms irrational (noncomprehensible) forces. It was also an emphasis against theatricality and fictionality and against the presentation of substitute worlds. These substitute worlds were seen as based on earlier writings and on the past; on the separation of 'fancy' from 'fact'; and crucially on the interests and evasions of a bourgeoisie which wanted to avoid looking at the social and human world which it had created and now controlled.

4. Naturalism certainly, and realism to a lesser extent, became confined to certain particular conventions and methods, which, in effect, became separated from the original impulse which had provoked them. There is then a necessary distinction between 'high naturalism' and the 'naturalist habit'.[2] It is the established confidence of the naturalist habit—a naturalized assumption of an immediately negotiable everyday world, presented through conventions which are not seen as conventions—which has since been so powerfully attacked, but usually under the loose title of realism. At the same time in reaction against the naturalist habit conventions have been developed to take more account of reality, to include psychological as well as external reality, and to show the social and physical world as a dynamic rather than a merely passive and determining environment. These innovations are often described as moves beyond realism and naturalism, but the confusing irony is that most of them are attempts to realize more deeply and adequately the original impulses of the realist and naturalist movements. They must for this reason be distinguished from those other methods and conventions which are based on attempts to restore the world views which realism and naturalism had attacked: the deliberate reintroduction of supernatural or metaphysical forces and dimensions controlling or influencing human action and character; and the less easily recognizable introduction of forces above and beyond human history in timeless archetypes and myths. For these later methods see the plays of Eliot, Yeats, some Beckett. For the former, see the expressionists and Brecht.

5. In drama, realism is inextricable from new social forces and new versions of social relationships. The crucial moment is the development of realism as a whole form; this must be distinguished from earlier realistic scenes, episodes, and insertions. The break to the new whole form is in eighteenth century bourgeois drama, which made three innovations: that the actions of drama should be contemporary (almost all earlier drama, by convention, had been set in a historical or legendary past); that the actions and resolutions of drama should be secular (conceived and worked through in solely human terms, without reference to a supernatural or

metaphysical dimension); and that the actions of drama should move beyond their conventional social exclusiveness (tragedy as confined to princes) and include the lives of all men ("let not your equals move your pity less"). This movement was not completed until the late nineteenth century; it is still predominant. Whatever immediate conventions and methods of presentation are employed, the great majority of plays have become, within the terms of this movement, contemporary, secular, and socially extended (inclusive).

6. This movement was begun by the bourgeoisie, but in these critical respects—contemporaneity, secularity, social inclusiveness—was at once shared and taken further by the new opponents of the bourgeoisie in the working-class and socialist movements. At this level the diagnosis of 'realism' as a bourgeois form is cant. It makes sense backwards, as a diagnosis of bourgeois realism against feudal and artistocratic forms and assumptions. But in its forward reference, to the crisis within bourgeois culture—that crisis which has produced, as bourgeois forms, many of the anti-realist experiments, as the same time that it has produced anti-bourgeois forms which make the emphasis of contemporaneity, scolarity, and social extension more radical and more critical—the diagnosis of 'realism' as simply and epochally 'bourgeois' merely begs the question.

7. Central to all these developments in world view and form is the actual extension and eventually qualitative change, in audiences. Drama had moved out of dependence on court, church, or state to post-commercial and commercial institutions which in their essential social composition were also contemporary, secular, and socially extended. At the same time there were many contradictions between this general process and particular class affiliations and exclusions in certain institutions (cf. the split between 'West End' and 'popular' theaters in the nineteenth century; the social breaks involved in the new 'free' and 'independent' theaters, all over Europe, in the 1890s, or in the post-1930 'community' theaters and travelling companies). This process with its contradictions is very evident in theater history. Broadcasting, first in radio (but with internal specialisations; compare, in Britain, Saturday Night Theater and the old Third Programme drama) and then decisively in television, transformed even this general transforming change. Drama was for the first time ever regularly available to a total audience, and was in fact used at a much higher level of frequency than had ever been previously imagined.[3]

Application to Problems of Television Drama

What then are the main issues in creation and production, in relation to this historical perspective, and to the actual complexity, as distinct from the short term repetitions, of the terms we use to try and interpret it?

(a) The most important general fact about television drama is that it is in qualitatively new social relations with its audiences. It includes, potentially and actually, an incomparably wider social range than any earlier medieval drama, and by comparison with medieval and earlier drama it has moved the popular audience out of drama as structured occasion and into everyday access. As a social movement this is the culmination of a process historically associated with realism.[4]

(b) This qualitative change has occurred within class societies with contradictory results. Access has been negotiated as exposure; and spectacle the new popular audience as a 'mass market'. Yet compare literacy. This was propagated as a way of enabling working people to read the scriptures and simple instructions. But there was, fortunately, no way of teaching people to read the Bible and official notices which did not also enable them to read the radical press or anything else that they chose. The problems shifted to questions of ownership of the means of production and of control at the point of production. Many contemporary arguments about form are displaced versions of these arguments (compare the last part of John McGrath's *The Case Against Naturalism*).

(c) Within the shifting complexities of the institutions the battle for popular drama has been and still is being unevenly and confusingly fought. As in the press, the popular tendency cannot be avoided; there is an imperative to produce popular work including reproduction of wide areas of majority life in one or other mode. This has included every kind of reproductive evasion or displacement, and these forms of the naturalist habit usually tied to a class reproduction ideology, need to be constantly analyzed and demystified. At the same time, and perhaps especially in Britain, the popular tendency has included (usually with internal struggles) dramatization, in several different ways, of areas of working class life and history which had never before come into any comparably distributed production and which also (quite apart from the size of the audiences) had never in such numbers been previously produced in any cultural form. This important current work has then first to be seen in the historical perspective of the development of realism as a phase of developing class consciousness (the demand to include hitherto excluded experience).

(d) The problems of immediate form have always to be considered in relation to content and to the nature of the audience. Form, theoretically, is always the fusion of specific methods of presentation, specifically selected experience, and specific relations between producer and audience. It is misleading to abstract 'form' (methods of presentation) from these mutually determining relations. That, strictly, is formalism, which assumes that the choice of a method of presentation is purely technical. Formalism in this sense has been reinforced by a fetishism of the medium. The actual production process is a complex of material properties; of processes of signification within these; of social relations between producers and between producers and audiences; and then the inherent and consequent selection of content. To reduce this complex to the 'medium,' with supposed objective properties governing all these processes and relations is strictly a fetishism.

(e) Form must then not be deduced from the 'medium' but from the production process as a whole. In this difficult kind of analysis we must avoid the importation of terms which attempt to cover the problems of the whole process but which are at best shorthand, at worst simple expletives. Moreover, since the production process is specific, we should avoid the unthinking repetition of terms from another specific process, which short circuit the argument. (cf. Troy Kennedy Martin, quoted by John McGrath: "the common denominator in all naturalist plays is that they tell a story by means of dialogue." To the extent that this is true of all naturalist plays it is true of all written plays from Aeschylus onward. To call all theater drama naturalist is absurd. The recurrent and variably solved problem, in all drama, including television drama, is the relation between speech and other forms of signification. Naturalism actually used speech less than most other dramatic forms, because it relied, as a matter of principle, on including physical environment as signifying. If we are to get on with the argument, we have to drop use of relatively meaningful historical descriptions as catchwords for all the varying things that we are against. The other supposed specifying factor of naturalism—natural time—is in fact a well known dogma of the neo-classical theater.)

(f) In the actual historical development there was eventually a distinction between 'naturalism' and 'realism', which may still be relevant. Naturalism as a doctrine of character formed by environment could emerge—in part of the movement did emerge—as a passive form: people were stuck where they were; compare "the room as trap" within the late bourgeois version of "the stage as room." A counter sense of realism, mainly with Marxism, insisted on the dynamic quality of all 'environments', and on the possibility of intervention to change them, within the forms of this inherent movement. In this sense many of the new 'non-naturalist' conventions—showing character and environment not as fixed forms but as processes of formation, crisis, breakdown, and re-formation—have to be seen not as formal 'anti-realist' innovations but as attempts to signify and realize this new sense of dynamic reality. In the period of the invention and application of the motion-picture camera (e.g., in late Strindberg) attempts were already being made to signify mobility, discontinuity, and alternation on the stage. Obviously the technical possibilities of all these new kinds of signification were radically extended by the double (photographed and photographing) mobility of the camera and by processes of film and videotape cutting and editing. Thus television, like film, can, in the simple terms of technical possibility move comparatively easily into this 'post-naturalist' world.

(g) Yet mobility, discontinuity, and alternation were, in any case of the significant new drama, tied, consciously, to the perspectives on reality which formed them. If they are abstracted as technicalities, they can be used, or apparently used, in quite different perspectives. Ironically they are now within bourgeois culture, most frequently used to communicate unconnected and inconsequent impressions of a mind or a world that is mobile and dynamic at its surface only, the larger world view which contains them being again and again the static properties of the "human condition" or the symbolic or archetypal permanences of a universalist psychology or a permanently alienated civilization. Just as we could distinguish 'high naturalism' from a naturalist or nonrealist habit: the mere assumption, as isolated conventions and techniques, of a confused or disinterpreted as distinct from a moving world. Yet formalist analysis cannot normally distinguish between these radically different uses of the same apparent techniques.

(h) The general opportunities for realism in television drama would then seem to be:

(1) altered, potentially altered and alterable relations between dramatic creators and audiences;

(2) inclusion, within the contradictions of a necessarily "popular" medium, of historically excluded or subordinated areas of social experience, at many different levels from the reproductive (because it has hitherto been excluded) to the disruptive and the reconstitutive;

(3) access, within the production process, to actions of the most public kind beyond the scale of the stage or set as room;

(4) access, within the immediate signifying process to procedures of mobility, discontinuity, alternation of viewpoint, within the terms of altered social relations, and thus the deliberate innovation of dramatic processes of formation, crisis, breakdown and re-formation, within a consciously contemporary, secular, and socially transforming perspective. This will include in our own terms radical opposition to the contemporary forms, naturalist and non-naturalist alike, of 'theatricality' and 'fictionality'; a conscious adhesion to a contemporary, secular, and socially transforming world-view; and, crucially, political affiliation to majority experience and its accessible futures.

Within an expanding culture, all kinds of work tend to expand. I think the most interesting new work will be in the area of public actions and mobility and alternation of signification and viewpoint. But given the continuing and massive reproduction of a resigned, displaced and self-cancelling version of majority experience (the naturalist habit deprived of the most significant naturalist intentions, and miscalled realism) there is plenty of room also for the mobility and alternation of viewpoint which is simply the positive insertion, even by the most direct reproductive methods, of a hitherto excluded or subordinated experience. The battles which even this now so often provokes are part of the whole process of changing the culture, which is the only possible perspective for changing its forms.

NOTES

1. For the terms "naturalism" and "realism" see *Keywords* (1976), 181–84 and 216–21.

2. For "high naturalism" and the "naturalist habit" see *Drama from Ibsen to Brecht* (1968), 332–46. See also *The Case of English Naturalism, in English Drama: Forms and Development* (ed. Axton and Williams; 1977).

3. For drama and its contemporary audiences and uses see *Drama in a Dramatised Society* (1975).

4. For television drama see "Television: Technology and Cultural Form" (1975), 55–61, and "A Lecture on Realism," in *Screen*, vol. 18, no. 1; 61–75.

X

FILM AS WORD

QUESTIONS OF LANGUAGE AND DOCUMENTARY REALISM

Peter Ohlin

Revolutionary art is a contradiction in terms, for the artist committed to the formal disciplines of his art finds himself led in directions that alienate him from a pure engagement in the revolutionary cause. And the artist who subordinates his art to the cause of the revolution discovers, sooner or later, that the need for a clear and persuasive rhetoric ceases to revitalize him and becomes a strait-jacket. Such at least seems to be the situation in a society in which there is no necessary relationship between revolutionary art and its effects, between the idea of revolution and its possible incorporation into artistic practice.

Godard was always aware of the difficulties involved in this situation. And his need for a breakthrough, for a direct communication with the actions of the political revolutionary cause led him to break down traditional preoccupations in the cinema with classical aesthetic forms. Godard's later films can be seen as experiments within the larger context of film and agitation or continuing education. They try to have a much more direct relationship to political action, and this brings Godard closer to the impulses of the documentary cinema than the feature film. In this sense he links up with filmmakers like Pierre Perrault in a quest for both revolutionary content and form. This essay will examine Pierre Perrault's efforts to shift the documentary cinema away from its usual concerns and to revolutionize the aesthetics of the documentary as part of an effort to transform Quebec society.

For a filmmaker like Pierre Perrault, the film experience begins as something very simple: the camera and the tape recorder are tools documenting and recording an external reality. But that very simple process suddenly acquires very complex dimensions when you try to invest the mechanical record with a primarily human energy. To Perrault, this fact became explicitly clear when he was making a series of radio programs about the sounds of Quebec: music, songs, fog horns, glockenspiels, furnaces, trains; only to discover that what his own Uncle was telling him about the sound of his mill was much more beautiful than the sound itself: "Isn't that what you would call poetry: to make things, gestures, and circumstances in general, human through language? To go beyond the immediately visual to reach the significant."[1] That is, the human record of a natural fact, memory enacted in a medium like, say, the spoken language, is what creates significance.

The insight had two very important consequences for Perrault. The first of these is that, in sharp contrast to contemporary trends, he was led to distrust the visual image:

> Nowadays people worry a great deal about the influence of the image. People have discovered that they live in the era of the image. One would have to be blind to say something that idiotic. The image has no more significance for our age than the surface of the water has for the sea. It's a mirror. A Mirage. It's what all those see who only use their eyes . . . but what's important is somewhere else, below the surface.

The attempt to break through the mirror, to go below the surface, takes Perrault, instead, into the spoken language as a record of reality experienced. The spoken word may be the most basic medium of communication among human beings (disregarding now such bodily communication systems as dance and gestures which never become individualized personal communication in the same way as the word). The word is not more true than the image; but the difference, in Perrault's terms, is that the image is that of the filmmaker and the word that of the subject filmed; and thus, people speaking from the screen direct themselves. You get to know them and their masks through their words. Consequently, the sound film meant a real advance over the silent film. "Even in an admirable film like *Nanook,* what do we know about Nanook? He is all Eskimos, but is he really Nanook? A little, but only a little."

If Perrault moves then toward a cinema of the spoken language, this is because it is through language that people communicate and define themselves in the minds of others. And all people have something to say: "It is totally inconceivable that a human being would not have anything to say. It doesn't happen. It all just depends on the questions that you ask him, on the space that you make available to him, *(du terrain qu'on lui impose).* And if you find a favourable space, you will get, in reply, his words, his spoken language." Thus the camera produces not only a documentary record of an event but establishes a kind of liberated territory within which the individual is free to express and develop himself. What will be heard in that space is the language of experience, *la parole vécue.* (The importance that Perrault attaches to experience, to the lived life, has made it natural that his films have been categorized as cinéma vécu.) And if the individual expresses himself badly, this is because he has been placed or situated badly and thus will give a false impression.

Superficially at least, views such as these lead to uncomfortably radical conceptions of what film is and can do. When Perrault says that "nothing is more real than an old man telling about something that he has experienced," the result seems quite reminiscent of Godard's statement (after making *La chinoise*) that he could very well imagine himself filming a literary masterpiece by photographing a man, in his chair, reading the book aloud; and that this would be a valid way of going about it.

Such a film need not necessarily be static or uncinematic; nor would it have to be said about it that the images simply illustrate the words. And the justification for it is the second important consequence of Perrault's central insight. For when the filmmaker reproduces the images and sounds of a person speaking, this is a way of reviving an experienced event; and just as the spoken language is a kind of memory, consisting of a lexicon of words and phrases with different associations grappling with an experience of the past, so the language of film is a similar memory. And that action which consists of photographing a speaking person can be experienced by both filmmaker and spectator as an attempt to rediscover the language—maybe just those words, or that aspect of language, which rationally or emotionally defines your relation to history or society, for instance through the linguistic tradition. To rediscover language in this way is to unite the past with the present, linguistically and historically. This union can be made concrete in different ways, but above all it belongs to the basic situation of the filmmaker and his work, that is, that reorganization of the material which occurs when he cuts into the celluloid strip and decides what to include and what to exclude. This is not a matter of objectivity, but rather of that creative mystery which makes it possible for one human being simply to respond in language to another human being; and when Perrault talks about editing, he sounds very much like, say, Chomsky's main argument about the continuous creativity of every individual's daily use of language:

> How is it that out of all the words available to me I can make those that make up this phrase get ready in a certain order to produce a sentence? . . . You can describe the number of manual operations in the editing process. But what happens in the brain . . . all this remains a mystery like language itself or writing or like any kind of writing with a finite number of words given in advance.

Thus to edit a film is not primarily a way of ordering recalcitrant elements but a way of rediscovering their own inherent significance; and this rediscovery, this recovery of the possibilities of language is in itself a new creation which unites the past and the present: the linguistic conventions of the past with the experience of the present, the memory of an event with its creative expression in the present.

When Perrault met and listened to the inhabitants of Ile-aux-Coudres in the St. Lawrence River, he experienced it, he says, as a rediscovery of himself: he found himself not searching for an identity to set against the other identities in the world (Eskimos, Patagonians, Indians) but experiencing himself and those around him as simply people "on an island, an island on the world's atlas . . . all with a language, with sounds, gestures, stories, songs, temperaments . . . Here I thought I could see the beginnings of a future i.e., an inhabitable time, a favorable present . . . I could become my own contemporary."

All of Perrault's films deal, in some form, with this recovery, this homecoming. This is nowhere more evident than in the first film of his remarkably beautiful trilogy about the people of Ile-aux-Coudres, *Pour la suite du monde* (1963). The film take its origin in a note written by Jacques Cartier when he came to Quebec and Ile-aux-Coudres in the 16th century: he writes that he saw a great many beluga whales in the river. The islanders tell Perrault that the whales seem to have disappeared; or at least nobody has seen them since they were caught forty years earlier. For the benefit of Perrault and the film crew they decide to try reviving the old method of trapping the whales (pushing slender poles into the beach into a complex pattern designed to trap the whales that come too close to the shore to get out when the tidal waves recede), using for guidance only the old legends and the childhood memories of old men. After many and lengthy debates about the old traditions, about time that seems to have passed them by, and about the future, interspersed with songs and dances and anecdotes, they catch a beautiful whale which is sold to an aquarium in New York.

Part of the undeniable beauty of the film resides in the extraordinary sensitivity of the photography (by Bernard Gosselin and Michel Brault) which records the whole range of greys between black and white with a gentle and delicate crispness and precision and a knowledgeable respect for the properties of natural light. Beyond that, however, there is an even more remarkable respect for anything in front of the camera, which is equivalent to the sense that while it is desirable to see certain things as clearly and accurately as possible, there is a certain distance beyond which the camera must not go in order not to encroach on the free space the individual must dispose in order to express himself. In terms of the theory of personal space or proxemics, that Edward Hall has suggested,[2] this means that the camera almost never penetrates space beyond personal distance, never attempts to discover a fake revelation in the distortions afforded by the close-up at an "intimate distance."

Above all, one senses that throughout the film Perrault is using his control of imagery and theme as an attempt to recover the past. At a key moment in the film an old man watches the whale and says, "It's been thirty-eight years since I saw one of you." And the film unites a whole series of contradictions: the Renaissance French of Jacques Cartier, preserved in letters and journals, collides with the French language as spoken in Paris and "educated" circles in Québec, and both are at a considerable distance from the French spoken by the islanders (frequently so different that the film has to be subtitled for the benefit of French audiences); and the old traditions, preserved only through legend and anecdote, suddenly become concrete reality, a reality at the same time heroic and anachronistic. This seems to be the intuitive sense of the simple image where we see a lyric pastoral close-up of dew drops on a leaf, until a simple focal change of the lens blurs the image and we see instead the river far away with a modern freighter working its way to Montreal and inland. In its own way, then, the film shows an encounter of the present with an heroic-epic past, and like all epic poems it deals with something that is lost at the same time that a new, perhaps still undefined, culture is born. And in wanting to preserve all this for posterity, *Pour la suite du monde,* the film, no less than the islanders, also creates the beginning of a future for itself, the possibility of a cinema used not simply to document reality but to discover, or recover, a language of images commensurate with the task of formulating possible attitudes toward that past and the present.

That task widens in the following film, *Le regne du jour* (1966), in which two of the main characters of the previous film travel to France to try to trace their ancestors. It is, then, a journey in space and time, an attempt to clarify genealogical and cultural relationships. And Perrault's method of editing together similar ritual events on both sides of the Atlantic, such as the butchering of the pig, the harvesting, the festivals, makes it clear that it is impossible to go home again: we see an old man who with genuine emotion searches for his ancestor in the heroic past, just as Perrault himself seems to follow the old man in a search for his mythic ancestor, knowing however full well that the task he is engaged in is the definition of the new culture, not the resurrection of the old.

In both these films, then, the image functions in a linguistic-cultural-historical context: on one level it allows a human linguistic phenomenon to occur which in turn has wider cultural and historical implications; on another level, the image ceases to be merely a document and becomes a record of the filmmaker's attempts through the editing devices at his command, to make the images assume their role in an entirely contemporary language that would somehow bridge the alienation from the past. Perrault's intense concern with the islanders is not a search for a Québécois identity that would be rooted in a more or less rural-pastoral past; it becomes an attempt to discover in that experience an alienation as central as the alienation of the filmmaker from his subject matter. In fact, Perrault has always insisted on this kind of equation: in the same way that he describes editing as a way of reliving reality, he also describes shooting film footage as a way of life *(le vécu du tournage et le vécu de la vie ne font qu'un)*. While in one sense this is simply the justification for a kind of cinéma-vérité procedure, Perrault seems to take it further when he suggests that "what is important is to live the film on both sides of the lens. It is a joint adventure." But for all its expression of solidarity, that statement also codifies the experience of alienation and locates its source in one element of the very process of film itself: in the glass lens. Indeed, it seems to be one of Perrault's intuitive perceptions that the possibility of grappling with the alienation that defines Quebec only exists in films (in the same sense that Jean-Pierre Lefebvre points out that Quebec borrows its capital from the United States, and its culture from France, Perrault once suggested that a true Quebec liberation could only occur through films which inherently combine those two elements: to be a Québécois is to be a filmmaker, as he put it somewhat extravagantly).

The alienation at the heart of this experience becomes even more evident in the third and final of Perrault's films about the islanders, *Les voitures d'eau* (1969), in which the language of Quebec, its past and present, is placed in a socio-economic context. This means that the film moves closer to a study of the possibility of a practical solution, the possibility of action. In cinematic terms, of course, Perrault's vision of the function of film does not invest action in front of the camera with any particular value in and for itself. Actions can, however, be described as a kind of physical and concrete language; Perrault talks about *"paroles en actes."* And those actions that interest him most are those that express, or can be made to express, something significant: they can be said to be the physical culmination of the linguistic expression *(le geste culmine les paroles);* and in fact it is by fulfilling the language act that a physical action avoids rigid codification and assumes instead the richly creative individuality of human speech.

In *Les voitures d'eau* the islanders dock their old fashioned ships with which they freight lumber for the winter, and construct during long debates about their situation a sail boat in the old way, that is, without blueprints but only with a scale model as a guide. When spring comes, the sail boat is finished, a small, sturdy, graceful little craft, but the situation of the islanders has deteriorated: strikes, competition with giant modern freighters, taxes and insurance, make it more impossible than ever for them to survive. In the last sequence we see an old deteriorating sail ship being burned on the river; Alexis Tremblay, the old man that we have gotten to know so well in the earlier films, a man who more than anyone else gave a heroic power to the traditions of the past, says, "Yes, my friend, that's the way it is with us too. The ship is old. The ship is finished." (In fact, Alexis himself died a few days later.)

The working ship captains know quite well that an old man's concerns with the past, his almost reverent ability to quote the diary entries of Jacques Cartier, are practically irrelevant in everyday terms, since cultural traditions are not enough to feed the stomach. The crisis of their daily life cannot be resolved by the ties with the past; it must get a practical, political solution. But for all their understanding of the situation of Quebec they find themselves largely unable to act positively. The only action that is performed in the film, after all, is the building of the sailboat; and the film performs a meditative hymn of praise to the old crafts involved in this undertaking which stands in sharp contrast to the present realities, economic and political, of the world of the St. Lawrence River. That contrast is also, implicitly, a measure of Perrault's perception that his vision of the documentary film must move beyond its commitment to a language founded primarily on memory in order to uncover a language in which the elements of the past enter new and creative relationships to form the substance of a language which might depict not only the alienation imposed by the perception of the past, but the possibilities of the future as well. And it is clearly that intuition that made Perrault realize that *Les voitures d'eau* had to be the final film devoted exclusively to the islanders on Ile-aux-Coudres; any practical solution to the problem of Quebec would have to take into account the complexity of a present now defined by confrontation, at both economic and cultural levels. In order to record on film, then, what is happening in Quebec, it would not be enough for Perrault to simply engage in the kind of local patriotism characterized by a passionate celebration of picturesque details; for clothes, food, and vehicles may all be an expression of the conceptual world of the inhabitants, but they only express such differences that tourists might find picturesque; they do not express that essential individuality which is embodied not only in words but in the relationship of words to the reality that they describe. What Perrault is led to look for, finally, are those gestures and those words that can be said to mean his country *(les actes et les paroles qui signifient un pays)*. This meaning is in itself not political but rather what precedes the political act, that is, the necessary analysis of a condition.

Un pays sans bon sens (1970) is an enormously difficult and ambitious film, an almost virtuoso tour de force demonstration of Perrault's vision of film. What Perrault has tried to film here is quite simply an idea, the idea of Quebec, by filming those words and actions that have the country for their meaning; and there is no easily available dramatic symbolism or other basic cinematic device that will do this task readily. In fact, the film consists almost entirely of long conversations with various people about this experience of Quebec, which would hardly seem cinematic. Perrault's ambition, of course, is exactly to avoid the cinematic, but to perform with his camera and editor those gestures and actions which make the idea of Quebec take root with the spectators. Having introduced the film with Cartier's description of the first winter in Quebec, in 1535, the rest is an attempt to discover what happened when Cartier went home again. There are no central myths or dramatic metaphors to express that; the only images that are clearly metaphorical or expressive in relation to the film's purpose seem entirely negative: a biology professor from Montreal talks about the typical Québécois Catholics as the white mice he keeps for experiments in his laboratory, and that image keeps recurring, in pictures and in heavily metaphoric graphic chapter headings, and in fact seems suggestive, in its aimlessness, of the organization of the film. Likewise, the image of the caribou running free in the snow to be snared in nets turns into a metaphor for the way a nation can be betrayed. These images describe a loss, an absence, a void, and the desperation of the film lies in its practical and human as well as cinematic sense that this void must somehow be filled. One of the most moving moments, in fact, occurs when a young literature student, born and raised in Western Canada and the US by French speaking parents, explains that he feels at home nowhere. He has never been to Montreal, yet he comes to understand that his journey from Canada to the US and on to Paris must eventually lead to Quebec, a homeland that he has never seen: that is a conviction he arrives at, partly from listening to René Lévesque speaking to a university audience on separatism and partly from trying to understand himself in the act of speaking to and being filmed by Perrault. From having been a French Canadian in exile he becomes a Québécois.

The film reaches no formal conclusions, of course. But out of the spoken words and their relationship to, say, something as simple as the landscape, there begins to grow an intuitive visceral feeling for a country and a culture that is something more than picturesque artifacts and a problem of language. That continuing process is what may become the new Quebec. In this sense, it can be argued that Perrault is making a film in some kind of future tense, narrating the way a nation is born; and if the birth has not yet occurred, the film may help it occur.

As a filmmaker Perrault knows that he cannot impose his solution on the images of living people: it must spring forth directly out of them, their language and their gestures. To that extent, *Un pays san bons sens* remains an open work which appeals to the audience to join the debate. And that is a debate not about political solutions but about the necessary realization of commonly accepted linguistic and practical situations. These realizations, then, are not concerned with socialism or capitalism but with alienation and integrity, oppression and liberation, exile and homecoming.

In leaving his works open, perceiving them in fact in such negative terms as loss, absence, search, and in assuming the radical separation of filmmaker from audience through the power of the medium, Perrault cannot be described as an orthodox revolutionary artist like some other young Quebec filmmakers (although it has been suggested that *Les voitures d'eau* is one of the first really revolutionary films from

Quebec). Yet, Perrault himself has said that he experienced his films as acts of liberation: he felt he had come to finally *"vivre en québécois."* To live or as he learned from the islanders on Ile-aux-Coudres, to learn while living, is more important than writing or making films or theater. "In a cultural revolution it is less important that your film be a masterpiece than that you follow closely the event in a given cultural situation."

Thus, finally, for Perrault as for a revolutionary filmmaker like Fernando Solanas, the film disappears as a distinct phenomenon when it subordinates itself, as it must, to a revolutionary situation. For both filmmakers, a socially aware analysis of film in relation to the social reality leads to the insight that the medium is dead: what remains is revolution, action, life itself. And that death seems somehow built into the alienating character of the medium itself.

To make films, if it is legitimate at all, is a way of life. For Perrault, feature films and documentaries have to be discussed in the same terms. All differences disappear. To make films is a way of life; and to be a filmmaker is to be a Québécois. Nevertheless, within the limits of such an aesthetic, it is possible to maintain different attitudes toward the status of the image and its relationship to the reality that it mirrors, or opens up to, or sets a boundary to. To Solanas, the image is itself of only relative worth; it acquires value only when used in a film act which he describes in very specific terms. That is, whether the image is to be seen as appearance or reality, as drama, documentary, propaganda, or escapism, is ultimately a trivial question that disappears at the moment when the film itself is seen as pretext, as the setting for the kind of theater that Solanas defines as revolutionary activity. And this means that the breakthrough to reality, through the world of the looking glass, is achieved only by leaving the film behind. Ultimately, the quest to take the medium as far as possible in the direction of absolute realism that the medium in its youth seemed to hold up as an attainable prospect ends up with the dissolution of the medium with the environment and no longer commands a particular narrative allegiance. Any other film, available on the market place, might, in theory at least, do just as well. For the filmmaker there is nothing to say: the saying is done by the people, and the task of the filmmaker is to organize the environment in such a way that the narrative of the people will be as fruitful as possible. That activity, then, could either take the form of a politically mature and sophisticated product like *La hora de los hornos,* or, for example, the form of a Doris Day movie exhibiting all the consumer goods characteristic of a capitalist society, to be analyzed by the audience. Thus, whether he knows it or not, Solanas too finds himself moving into the area of specialized adult education, with particular attention given, as is natural, to local problems.

Perrault's basic impulse, too, is local. (In fact, his films may be extremely difficult to absorb for one not familiar with the particular problems of Quebec society.) To him, whether the image is to be seen as appearance or reality is not a trivial question, but a rather simple one, since he relates the function of the image to the linguistic act, as perceived, recalled, or spoken. At the moment of shooting, the image is simply an incomplete record, limited and arbitrary perhaps, but a record nonetheless. At the moment of editing, it becomes a linguistic element whose relative value is defined by memory and which can be used in different ways, not to recapture the original experience (which is impossible) but to recover the expressive content of the original moment. At the level of perception, during the screening, the image exists much less as a record of a concrete experience than as the perceptual expression of the possibility of a language which is cinematic, personal, and experiential, at the same time. This is to say that the narrative task of the filmmaker disappears: it is not a matter of saying something, but of discovering something; and the criteria of success in this undertaking are not found in the medium or its relationship to reality but in the experience. In saying that what matters is not that the film be a masterpiece but that it attach itself to the event, as expressive act (physical or linguistic), Perrault clearly seems to recognize the existence of contradictory standards—and, equally clearly, rejects those related to the formal properties of the medium, in favor of subordinating the film to the event (whether filmed or not). Faced with a choice, then, Perrault might well abandon film, having discovered that film is not his medium.[3] That, of course, is the moment at which the narrative drive towards a pervasive realism annihilates itself.

NOTES

1. Quotations in this essay derive either from conversations with Perrault during his visit to Stockholm in September 1970, or from a monograph published by the *Conseil québécoise pour la diffusion du cinéma,* entitled *Cinéastes du Québec 5: Pierre Perrault,* this contains an introduction by Alain Berson and a long taped interview with Perrault from 1970. Cf. also numerous articles by and about Perrault in *Cahiers du Cinéma,* e.g. nos. 146, 165, 194, 212. At least two of his films, *Le regne du jour* and *Les voitures d'eau,* have been issued as illustrated books—incidentally making quite clear how Perrault sees the everyday spoken word as approaching the qualities of genuine poetry—by Éditions Lidec in Montréal, 1968 and 1969. Cf. also the account of Perrault in Louis Marcorelles, *Living Cinema* (New York: Praeger, 1973), 65–85.

2. Edward T. Hall, *The Hidden Dimension* (Garden City, N.Y.: Doubleday, 1969), particularly chapter 10, 113–29.

3. See, for example, the reverential National Film Board production about Perrault, made by Jean-Daniel Lafond, *Les traces du rêve* (1986), in which Perrault, as filmmaker and Québécois artist, almost explicitly becomes a landscape, a dream, a myth.

XI

MAN WITH A MOVIE CAMERA AND WOMAN'S WORK

Judith Mayne

Dziga Vertov's remarkable film, *Man with a Movie Camera* (1929), with its stunning uses of montage, establishes complex analogies between production, collectivity, and filmmaking.[1] Compared to *Man with a Movie Camera,* what might appear to be significant differences between other films and filmmakers of the 1920s in the Soviet Union diminish; indeed, Vertov's film has become something of a paradigm of the radical possibilities of cinematic experimentation and, more significantly, of the common ground between "production" understood in both a cinematic and a social and economic sense. The narrative structures of Eisenstein's films may be more complex and far-reaching than those found in Pudovkin's films, for instance, but when compared to *Man with a Movie Camera,* these differences appear to be less significant, and rather like differences on a narrative continuum. In contrast, Dziga Vertov was opposed to any attempts to modify or appropriate artistic forms which, in his view, were better discarded. Hence while other Soviet filmmakers of the 1920s would pursue a dialectics of appropriation—whereby it was assumed that however influenced by capitalist and middle-class ideals, narrative forms can be adapted to socialist ends—Vertov's view is better described as a dialectics of emancipation—whereby any vestiges of narrative tradition hopelessly compromise radical cinematic aspirations. In this essay I will argue that the desire to emancipate the production of cinematic meaning in *Man with a Movie Camera* relies crucially on a gender component.[2] The "woman question" is posed differently in *Man with a Movie Camera* than in other films of the 1920s, but it informs just as persistently and ubiquitously the utopian vision of socialism and of filmmaking present in Vertov's film. It has been an implicit assumption of much feminist criticism that only an avant-garde cinema which challenges and questions the hierarchical relations of the look and of narrative structure can provide a truly alternative form of visual pleasure.[3] Such cases have been made, with varying degrees of success, for avant-garde films informed by the theoretical insights of feminism.[4] However, avant-garde films which are not thus informed remain in a kind of critical limbo, and I would argue that *Man with a Movie Camera* is just such a film—a film whose radical and innovative structure and style have not been adequately addressed in terms of the questions of gender that they raise. I am aware that for many critics, gender and the woman question remain suspiciously evocative of what Roland Barthes calls the readerly *(le lisible);* that is, symptoms of an allegiance to a coherent political signified, and to the moralism of the attendant assumption that texts can be readily divided into the categories of "good" and "bad."[5] In other words, a common critical wisdom would have it that the radical process of signification developed in Vertov's film transcends, refuses, or otherwise departs from the universe of binary opposition supposedly inhabited by questions of gender and sexual politics. Now I do not doubt that such critical gestures of transcendence, refusal, or departure are often, and perhaps usually, defenses against feminist inquiry, and in particular against the feminist insight that most notions of transcendence (or refusal, or departure) assume or disguise, rather than challenge, the centrality of the male subject. Having said this, I would nonetheless agree that *Man with a Movie Camera* raises many more complex questions concerning cinema, narrative, and gender than do other films of the period. But I take this as an indication, not that Vertov's film stands somehow above and apart from other films in which the woman question functions so centrally, but rather that the woman question is posed in extremely complex and far-reaching ways in this film.

Put another way, I suspect that to many contemporary viewers, *Man with a Movie Camera* would appear to be a film most resistant to feminist considerations, not only because of its formal complexity, but also because of its legendary and critical status as a paragon of cinematic *écriture*. However, I do not think it possible, in Soviet film of the 1920s, to relegate questions of gender and sexual opposition to secondary or purely "referential" status. I am arguing, then, that *Man with a Movie Camera* is a film which demonstrates, along with other films of the period, the relationship between cinema, narrative, and the woman question; and, simultaneously, that Vertov's film raises different questions than do other films of the period about that relationship.[6]

If the majority of Soviet films of the 1920s develop narrative strategies to represent issues central to socialist culture, *Man with a Movie Camera* appears to be at odds with any such reshaping or redefinition of film narrative. For different reasons, Vertov is the *enfant terrible* of revolutionary Soviet cinema in his own time as well as in our own. While the charge of "formalism" was levelled against many filmmakers, Vertov was particularly susceptible to it, given his determined stance on the politics of socialist filmmaking. And for Eisenstein, of course, *Man with a Movie Camera* consisted of "formalist jackstraws and unmotivated camera mischief."[7] Vertov's position within film history reflects the complex intertwining of political and aesthetic concerns that shaped his own career, and *Man with a Movie Camera,* described by Annette Michelson as "the synthetic articulation of the Marxist project, concretized in every detail of an unprecedented complexity of cinematic design," is the single film that has come to best represent Vertov's radical explorations in socialist cinema.[8] Michelson's exploration of the work of filmmaking in *Man with a Movie Camera,* ranging from magic to epistemology, makes a convincing case for the necessary links between avant-garde practice and Marxist analysis in Vertov's film.[9] And from another perspective, Vertov's importance in the formulation of a relationship between politics and cinematic form is suggested by the interest which his work inspired in the aftermath of the events of May '68 in France. Indeed, Jean-Luc Godard's adoption of the name "Groupe Dziga Vertov" for the collective responsible for films such as *Luttes en Italie* (1969) and *Pravda* (1971) suggests that however enduring the lessons of Eisenstein and other Soviet filmmakers of the silent era, the work of Vertov is more consistently and persistently radical in its insistence on the crucial role of filmmaking in the construction of a socialist view of the world. Indeed, if the emergence of the "Groupe Dziga Vertov" in France is symptomatic at all, it is in terms of the revalorization of the emancipatory view of the role of the cinema, with the attendant devalorization of Eisenstein as a director compromised by an essentially bourgeois view of the world.[10] In the post-1968 French context, however, Vertov's emblematic status had less to do with the opposition of proletarian and bourgeois—even the most circuitous political logic would be hard pressed to define a film like *British Sounds* (1969) as a proletarian film—than with the opposition between cinema understood as a vehicle for revolutionary change, and cinema understood as a political apparatus in its own right.

Vertov went further, perhaps, than his colleagues in examining the place of filmmaking in relationship to the productive labor of socialist society. Central to *Man with a Movie Camera* is the relationship, not only between filmmaking and labor, but also between the different gendered spaces of Soviet society. In some ways, *Man with a Movie Camera* seems to center on women as the privileged signifiers of Soviet culture's celebration of work, community, and technology. The figure of the cameraman, whether cranking the camera or peering through its lens, appears at some points in the film to affirm sexual polarity (for instance, by examining the female body in ways coded for voyeurism and sexual display), at other points to put difference into question, and at still other points to suggest a utopian, almost androgynous fusion of male and female as characteristic of Soviet society. The purpose of my analysis, then, is to explore both whether Vertov's differences from his fellow filmmakers of the silent era extend to a difference in representation concerning sexuality and gender, and how the radical process which so many critics have claimed for Vertov extends to the dynamics of gender. I will begin my analysis of *Man with a Movie Camera* with a consideration of the organization of the film, particularly insofar as the film explores the relationships between cinematic production and the productivity of Soviet society, and between perception and representation. At this initial level of analysis, the relevance of the woman question will not be immediately apparent, but the structure of the film raises further questions which require a consideration of gender and sexual opposition. I begin with an analysis of the formal structure of the film in order to demonstrate, in other words, the insufficiency of an analysis of *Man with a Movie Camera* in which questions of gender are not taken into account.

Man with a Movie Camera is above all an analysis of movement. We follow the cameraman's movements as he films a population which awakens, goes to work, goes to the beach, engages in sports, listens to music; the movements of the film editor as she cuts and organizes the film strips; the movements of spectators who watch a film, and watch themselves being filmed and watching a film. The orchestration of movement is complex to the point that it is difficult to determine where one movement begins and another leaves off. Each movement is inscribed and defined within the context of another, so that a constant flux is created. The analysis of movement as central to cinematic production is thus inextricably linked to the analysis of social production as labor and as ideology.

Man with a Movie Camera can be divided into five major sections, each structured by relationships central to the process of cinematic production. The opening shot of *Man with a Movie Camera* depicts the instruments of film production. The cameraman climbs to the top of a gigantic camera behind which are clouds and a small hill. He sets up his camera and aims. The second image, a building with clouds moving by rapidly in the background, is, we assume, the image filmed by the cameraman. The "how" precedes the "what"; the image is designated as a product of the cinematic process, and not as a reflection of a world outside that of the film. The following two shots repeat a similar pattern with slight differences. In shot 3 we see the cameraman at an increased distance; and the angle of shot 4, a lamppost, is slightly different from the angle of shot 2. A puzzling reversal occurs as well: the off-center but nonetheless continuous match between shots 1 and 2 is impossible between shots 3 and 4, since in shot 3 the cameraman picks up his equipment and moves off-screen. Thus a sense of continuity is established and violated at the same time.

Effects of discontinuity aside, however, the organization of the opening four shots follows a pattern of alternating images. The film as a whole is built on an identical pattern. The first four shots described above depict the instruments of film production and the resulting images. A shift in emphasis occurs in shot 5, where the cameraman walks through a curtain. Subsequent shots suggest that this is a stage curtain in a movie theater. We then see a movie theater preparing for a film screening. Spectators enter and take their seats, the projectionist sets up, and musicians prepare to begin their accompaniment. Here, there is a relationship established between the spectator and the means by which images are perceived: the projector and the movie screen, most obviously, but also the accoutrements of film viewing such as music and the accommodations of the theater. Hence, from the outset, *Man with a Movie Camera* sets up a series of opposing terms: filmmaker and image, on the one hand; and viewer and film on the other.

With the appearance of the number "1" on the screen, the film within the film (seen by the spectators in the theater) coincides with the film that has already begun. The emphasis then shifts to the underlying relationship of the first section of the film, between images and the instruments of film production. This relationship undergoes a number of reversals, pauses, and visual parentheses, but a fundamental organization link is maintained between the chronology of a day in the life of a Soviet city, and the activities of the filmmaker as he produces this chronology. The extension of the first part of the film constitutes the largest portion of *Man with a Movie Camera*.

A vertiginous sequence of superpositions, rapid editing, and split images depicting Soviet citizens listening to and making music marks the final segment of this part of the film. Music defines the transition from the second section of the film, concerned with the conditions of watching a film, to the third, concerned, as is the first section, with the conditions of producing a film. Music also defines the transition from the third to the fourth section of the film, in which the relationship between spectator and film is central. The film-within-the-film continues and is shot from alternating angles. Images of the film-within-the-film (coinciding with our vision of the screen), of the group of spectators watching the film, and of isolated spectators reacting to it, are constantly interchanged.

Approximately half-way through the fourth section of the film, we suddenly see the movie theater in preparation for another film to begin. The lights go down, musicians begin playing, and the curtain opens. From this point on, nearly all of the images are repetitions or variations of images that have already been seen in the film. The final segment of the film presents, then, a reassemblage of the principal elements that form the oppositions between and within previous sections of the film. The final moments of *Man with a Movie Camera* are characterized by a dizzying pace of technical virtuosity, in which the film appears to dissect and, to some extent, to undermine, its own structure. In the last image of the film, a human eye in extreme close-up is reflected in a camera lens, marking a fusion of human perception and cinematic technique. If *Man with a Movie Camera* ends, as any film must, it nonetheless refuses closure in the traditional sense, for the end of the film implies the beginning of another process, a new way of seeing. The conclusion recalls the close-up of the eye at the end of Eisenstein's *Strike*. But whereas the conclusion of Eisenstein's film serves as a reminder of the connection between historical and cinematic vision, the conclusion of Vertov's film marks, rather, the fusion of the human and the technological.

Man with a Movie Camera does not lend itself to the kind of breakdown of narrative structure of the films discussed previously. Indeed, there is something deceptive about the five-part structure of the film that I've described, for *Man with a Movie Camera* resists such linear logic. While the film does begin by representing a series of relationships concerning different aspects of the filmmaking process, there is never a question of film production and film viewing, for instance, retaining their qualities as separate and distinct moments. Rather, film production and film spectatorship become identified as part of the same process. Alan Williams refers, in this context, to the various "narrative perversions" in *Man with a Movie Camera,* stressing the refusal of the film to preserve the oppositions it establishes. "Vertov's text," writes Williams, "will decompose and pervert cause-and-effect narrativity to rely on formal, logical structures which, rather than support the classic metonymy of the fiction film, will create their own progressions based on difference and juxtaposition."[11]

If *Man with a Movie Camera* does not function as a narrative in the classical sense of the term, one might then consider the film as a meta-narrative, i.e., a film that tells a story about itself, about the activities of the cameraman rather than about a fictional character. Perhaps the extreme reflexivity and self-consciousness of Vertov's film is reason enough to distinguish him from his contemporaries. From the very beginning of the film, however, the centrality of the cameraman's vision is put into question, since he moves out of frame in the third shot of the film. In other words, the cameraman cannot be equated with a central character, or even the central narrating intelligence of a narrative film, since visual perspective is not localized in a single figure, but rather dispersed through multiple perspectives. Rather, there is another, more central relationship that structures the entire film, and that is the relationship between perception and representation, with representation understood throughout the film as a process of construction.

Early in the film, when spectators enter the movie theater, two series of images alternate over a brief time span: shots of seats in the theater which "magically" unfold by themselves, and shots of spectators who enter the theater, find their seats, and sit down (folding down the seat themselves). As in the opening four shots of the film, an obvious manipulation of the image contrasts with shots that are more realistic—more "natural." This alternation ends with a shot of one seat unfolding by itself; a woman and small child enter the frame and sit down. Two different modes of representation are condensed in the same image. One emphasizes representation as overt manipulation of the image; the other, as less mediated perception, realistic in its focus. While this event does indeed fit into an ongoing narrative structure, that structure is constantly interrupted by an exploration of how individual events might be dissected and analyzed. Similarly, while there certainly is a narrative chronology in the film ("a day in the life of a Soviet city"), it is a chronology that seems to function more as a vehicle for the analysis of movement than as a center of narrative interest in its own right.

However, it is a mistake, I think, to assume that all traces of narrative are banished from *Man with a Movie Camera*. Rather, the film is characterized by a tension between narration, understood as an illusory ordering of space and time, and production, understood as a laying-bare of that illusion. This is not to say that Vertov's film is therefore a narrative in the same way as the other films of the 1920s. What marks the difference in *Man with a Movie Camera*, when seen in relationship to other films of the 1920s, is its emphasis on a principle of production. At the same time, *Man with a Movie Camera* is distinctive within the context of the 1920s, not because it is a non-narrative film but because it is a different kind of narrative film. For while virtually all of the films of the 1920s are structured by the narrative opposition of "us" and "them," of proletariat and bourgeois, *Man with a Movie Camera* assumes that opposition, and moves into the presumably new signifying territory made possible by socialism. *Man with a Movie Camera* is characterized by a distinctly utopian vision of the cinema as well as of socialist society, a vision of supreme harmony and integration.

Annette Michelson describes the structural center of *Man with a Movie Camera* as the alternation between images of the components of a textile factory and the image of the cameraman who films a hydroelectric plant and mines, the sources of power for the factory. The alternation builds to a superimposition of the cameraman over an image of a woman tending to a machine in the textile factory. Of the relationship thus articulated between filmmaking and textile production, Michelson writes:

> This juxtaposition and subsequent superimposition of filmmaking and textile man-
> ufacture are to be read as articulating that unity within which the 'natural' inequalities
> and contradictions formerly generated by a system of division of labor have been
> suspended. The full range of analogical and metaphorical readings thereby generated
> signify a general and organic unity, a common implication within the movement of
> industry, the euphoric and intensified sense of a shared end: the supercession of
> private property in the young socialist state under construction.[12]

Implicit in Michelson's analysis of the sequence in question is, perhaps, yet another unity, although she does not address it per se. This is, of course, the unity of male and female, drawn here as a configuration of equals, with the classic status of woman as *image* broken in favor of woman identified as agent of production. Although Alan Williams characterizes *Man with a Movie Camera* in terms different than Michelson, he also suggests that the film is utopian in another, related sense, as it militates against the trappings of bourgeois narrative. In defense of his claim that *Man with a Movie Camera* "is to be read not as narrative but as conflict," Williams cites the film's use of point-of-view structures. "Nowhere in the film," writes Williams, "is there an unambiguous use of this common alternation: the seer is never in the same textual space as the seen." Williams cites the example of the athletic sequences in the film, "where slow motion athletes are 'seen' by spectators shot at normal speed and who furthermore look in the 'wrong' direction for good matching."[13] It is by now a truism of film theory and film analysis that the organization of the look through shot counter-shot and point-of-view shots is structured by gender difference.[14] While most analyses of the male gaze and its attendant implications for the representation of the female body take as their point of departure the classical Hollywood film, the cinema was structured by the hierarchy of sexual difference long before the development of the Hollywood film, and in other national contexts.[15] Williams's claims for the use of point-of-view structures in the film might be taken a bit further. For even though Vertov's cinematic innovations and explorations have not been widely read in terms of the issues of gender that they raise, Williams's designation of the "ambiguous" use of the point-of-view structure suggests, especially when seen in the light of how that structure has been analyzed by feminist critics, that *Man with a Movie Camera* is as engaged with the notion of process in sexual terms as it is in ideological, social, and technological terms.

In other words, the central question I wish to ask of *Man with a Movie Camera* is how the relationships of gender—of man and woman in a socialist context, certain-ly, but also of those qualities which, whether through cultural association or through textual production, are designated "male" and "female"—inform the radical vision of process, conflict, and production. The examples cited above from Michelson and Williams are both suggestive, in different ways, of a radical vision of sexual politics that informs Vertov's exploration of the "communist decoding of the world."[16] If indeed this is the case, then Vertov would appear to have achieved something that eluded his contemporaries, the conscious and deliberate articulation of a necessary connection between gender and social formation.

In order to examine in detail how a gender dynamic functions in *Man with a Movie Camera,* I will look at a crucial sequence in the film where two different moments in the process of filmmaking are set up in relationship to each other. Not coincidentally, the principals in this sequence are the cameraman (portrayed in the film by Dziga Vertov's brother), and the editor, portrayed by Vertov's real-life wife, editor, and collaborator, Elizaveta Svilova. This sequence occurs approximately one-third of the way into the film. In the midst of a sequence in which the cameraman films carriages in motion, the movement of the carriages is suspended in a series of frozen shots, and is later resumed after other frozen or motionless images, drawn from different points of reference in the film, become illustrations for the stages of film editing.

There are four moments of cinematic production depicted in *Man with a Movie Camera:* the cameraman and the shooting of film footage; the camera itself, which is seen at crucial moments in the film as a perceptual apparatus detached from the cameraman's control; editing; and the act of viewing a film. These moments are not depicted chronologically, suggesting that they constitute relationships that inform the entirety of the cinematic experience. These different aspects of cinematic production also become metaphoric points of departure. Cinema is labor, hence similar to the work of machines in the numerous factory segments of the film. In more general terms, cinema is linked to the structural patterns of the games and sports Soviets play and watch, and the music they listen to. Cinema is like these activities, but cinema is also given a special function as the medium that alone is capable of producing the representation of analogy, of the similarity of motion and of structure. This view of the cognitive capacity of cinema assumes that as technological form, cinema is capable of changing significantly the nature of human perception. Such an assumption cuts across two contexts: cinema as a representational form that simultaneously demystifies, and cinema as part of a social whole, the context in which any change—perceptual or otherwise—is ultimately defined.

Like other Soviet filmmakers of his time, Vertov considered montage both the essence of cinematic form and the foundation of cinema as a dialectical medium. Thus it is not surprising that a demonstration of editing occupies a special position in *Man with a Movie Camera.* The camera, the act of filming, and film-viewing are all depicted in the film from the outset. It is not until somewhat later, however, that editing is demonstrated, and in a sequence that is set off from the rest of the film (that is, "set off" to the limited extent that anything is set off in Vertov's film). Hence, given this special role assigned to editing, the four major aspects of cinematic production appear initially to be separated according to an opposition between perception (the camera, the filmmaker, the film spectator) and construction (the film editor).

The editing sequence consists of five segments, each of which demonstrates a specific function of montage. The first segment consists of nine stills, the first four of which are repetitions from the carriage sequence immediately preceding.

Although movement is frozen, linear continuity is preserved. Shot five, a frozen long shot of a city street full of people, has not been seen in the film. However, similar shots of city streets are used in *Man with a Movie Camera* as a means of indicating the progression of a day's activities, with the amount of activity and the number of people present indicating the time of day. This is the first image of this kind to signify a city at the peak of activity. Just as the basic element in the representation of motion and movement in film is a single motionless frame, so the height of a city's activity is represented by a still shot.

The four images which follow repeat the familiar pattern of alternating montage. Two shots of peasant women, their heads in scarves and facing screen right, alternate with two shots of little girls wearing bows in their hair and facing screen left. The first peasant woman appeared earlier in the film. However, recognition of the image is not as immediate as recognition of images of the carriages or of the city street, for the image appeared relatively quickly, and does not have the same foregrounded function. The second peasant woman appears in this sequence for the first time, as do the children who reappear much later in the film as spectators at a magic show on the beach. While these four images have different points of reference (the past, present, and future tenses of the film), they are linked here by a repetition of the central structuring device of the film, the alternating montage pattern. Thus we perceive continuity of movement as both presence and as illusion. The demonstration of illusion is taken yet another step further, beyond simple frozen motion: the images of the little girls are filmstrips, with sprocket-holes clearly visible. Cinematic time is the function of cinematic space, itself broken down into two separate components, the space of the screen and the space of the filmstrip. The first segment of the sequence, consisting of these nine shots, is informed by a principle of laying-bare cinematic space and time. Cinematic space is reduced to the boundaries of the filmstrip, and cinematic time, to the individual photogram.

The second segment of the sequence consists of two images of rolls of film classified on shelves. These images recall the rolls of film shown when, early in the film, the projectionist loads the projector to begin the film-within-the-film. In that scene, attention is drawn as well to the isolated image on the filmstrip, a window which later appears immediately after the number "1" appears on screen. A chronology of the status of the image is sketched, from the reel of film to the single photogram to the image in movement on the screen. Here, in the editing sequence, the same principle occurs in reverse, from image in motion, to single image on the filmstrip, to rolls of film. The reversal is important on other levels as well. The earlier scene suggests at the very least the kind of voyeuristic fascination that has been central to the cinema since its earliest years of development, for what else is an image of a window, if not an invitation to explore what lies within its frame. That the projectionist is male, and the person whose waking rituals (within what we assume to be the same room) are witnessed is female, suggests the classic structure of the man who looks and the woman who is looked at. However, what is more difficult and more crucial to assess is the perspective from which such a voyeuristic structure is put into place. The relationship is in no way naturalized; that is, the projectionist may well be a figure of mastery and control, but control is directed towards the technology of cinema. But it surely is no coincidence that technology and the female body function as subject and object, respectively. However distanced and demystified, the structure presented still maintains the traditional contours of the man who controls the image, and the woman who *is* the image. When the relationship between filmstrip, film reel, and moving image is again articulated in the editing room sequence, it appears as though the voyeuristic configurations of the previous scene are being thrown into question. A woman's gaze replaces a man's, and instead of the frame within the frame of the window on the filmstrip, we see the filmstrips of the little girls. There is still an association between inert material and female identity, but the association is complicated by the fact that the active agent in the editing sequence is also a woman.

Between the isolated, frozen images that occur at the beginning of the editing sequence and the rolls of film classified on shelves, ready to be edited into a film, some type of work occurs, like the threading of the projector which allows the transformation of the film strip into the image in motion. The third segment of the sequence demonstrates this work, which is a bridge between the images inscribed by the cameraman and the images that the editor classifies, and between those images and the ways in which they are organized in the film. In segment three, a series of images depicts the basic materials with which the editor works: a motionless take-up reel, photograms of a plump peasant woman, and the film strip being wound onto the reel. We see the editor operating the take-up reel and, in close-up, cutting the film. Finally, the film strip is transformed. An eyeline direction match unites the image of the peasant woman and the editor as she examines the film strip. The film strip then "comes alive," its boundaries redefined as identical to those of the screen. Three aspects of cinematic production are separated, and each is identified as part of yet another process. The illustration of the editor's materials gives indications of the method used; and the illustration of cutting indicates, through the eyeline direction match, what the product will be. Such a fusion of method and material suggests a constant process, and not a resolution in the form of a final product.

The fourth segment of the sequence reiterates the work of editing in shorthand form, showing editor, film strip, and image in motion. The images transformed are those of children who, like the little girls seen earlier as photograms, reappear later in the film. Thus the work of editing, previously demonstrated on an image which appears nowhere else in the film, here becomes defined more immediately within the narrative of the film. This integration of editing into the text of the film continues in segment five. Two frozen images of the old woman and a city street are the same images seen in segment one. These frozen images alternate with the same images in motion, and the editor appears less frequently. These images return us to the narrative context of the film, yet they function simultaneously as objects, as pieces of raw material that are transformed. Hence, representation is defined as the process of transformation rather than as reflection. Finally, the carriage sequence recommences, briefly interrupted three times. In extreme light and dark contrast, the editor's hand moves over a film strip, on which the image is unreadable. Hence, the re-establishment of so-called normal continuity is accompanied by intense abstraction, for this image could be any image, and the moment of transformation, any moment. The continuation of the carriage sequence is interrupted again by an image of the take-up reel, now moving rapidly and bearing a full roll of film. The reel defines the duration of the editing sequence, like the shots of city streets that function as temporal markers in the film. Thus the take-up reel marks the time of the projection of the film that we are watching. Finally, we see the cameraman walking down a street. The sequence continues as he moves on to other activities.

It is significant that in the editing sequence film strips are cut, looked at, and classified, but never fused together. Montage is Vertov's principle of construction, understood both as putting things together and as taking them apart. Elements may be brought together in one direction, only to be taken apart in another. Thus montage cannot be equated with a single technique. Vertov's writings on the function of montage might appear to be simple ecstasizing on the virtues of the "pure cinematic language" the filmmaker sought to elaborate. Seen in the context of the editing sequence, however, this statement clarifies to what degree montage, for Vertov, cannot be focused on one particular technique: "Every kino-eye production is subject to montage from the moment the theme is chosen until the film's release in its completed form. In other words, it is edited during the entire process of film production."[17]

There are elements in the editing sequence that are shared by the activities of the camera, the filmmaker, and the spectators. The camera aligns itself with human perception to reveal different structural properties of the objects before it, and the work of the editor functions similarly to clarify and analyze movement. Also, the editor's relationship to the film is analogous to the relationship between the cameraman and what he films in the preceding carriage sequence. And the ways in which the editor views the images are not unlike the ways spectators look at the film screen. The initial separation between perception and construction which marks off the editing sequence serves, then, to redefine more clearly the interdependence of the two terms as inseparable moments of cinematic production. Production is defined in *Man with a Movie Camera* as a multidirectional flow, implying a refusal both to ground the image in one-dimensional reality and to assign it a set of closed meanings.

Yet for all of Vertov's preoccupation with the circulation of images, and with patterns of continuity that disrupt rather than contain, the editing sequence has surprisingly familiar contours. We see a woman in a room, who works exclusively with images of women and children. Outside that room is the public sphere of filmmaking—the (male) cameraman and street activity. While the editing room can hardly be described as a "private" space, there is a spatial tension generated on the basis of interior versus exterior space, female versus male activity. To be sure, it could be argued that *Man with a Movie Camera* poses the opposition only to demolish it. It certainly is true of the film that collectivity reigns supreme, so that what we see is the redefinition of the private, isolated space of women in capitalist society into the collective, socialized sphere of women and men in socialist society. Given the constant flow that permeates all levels of *Man with a Movie Camera*, it is tempting to argue that the difference between male and female—between, here, the cameraman and the film editor—becomes a point of departure and a form of differentiation, rather than a fixed reference point of active versus passive, of subject versus object.

I referred earlier to the parallels between the editing sequence and the previous scene in the film where the projector is loaded, and the film within the film begins after the appearance of a "1" on the screen. We see a young woman awakening in a room. This is virtually the only "private" sphere represented in the film, as if the increasing momentum of *Man with a Movie Camera* creates a collective cinematic space in which these vestiges of traditional narrative are done away with.[18] In this scene, close-ups of the camera alternate with images of the woman's eyes. Her foggy vision is clarified as the scene outside her window moves into crisp focus. Thus the camera begins to function as a substitute for (imperfect) human perception. The camera has, at the very least, a two-fold function here, for it is both a point-of-view within the film, and a substitute for the woman's own vision. Such a fusion of subject and object—through the camera, the woman becomes both the object seen and the perceiving subject—is perhaps the most utopian vision in the film. Now one could argue that it is symptomatic of a duality of activity versus passivity, and its attendant sexual implications, that it be the woman who must be fused, as it were. Yet at the same time one could argue that because the figure of woman exemplifies objectification, the fusion of the kino-eye with the woman's perception is a radical demonstration of *Man with a Movie Camera's* challenge to cinematic and cultural convention. While it is true that Vertov's film brings questions of gender to the forefront of cinematic signification, the fusion of human and cinematic perception in this particular scene is nonetheless characterized by the woman's function as other—she is an isolated, apparently bourgeois figure in a private space, in a film that celebrates proletarian collectivity.[19]

A more obvious function of the camera in the film is in terms of what Seth Feldman calls a "barometer of social involvement."[20] When the cameraman films Soviets who awaken and go to work, close-ups of the camera lens alternate with shots of a young man who awakens from a night spent on a park bench. The boy mugs for the camera, conspicuously amused. Immediately following the last image of the boy is a shot of a woman cleaning a city street. The only other conscious mugging for the camera occurs during the carriage sequence. A variety of social classes are represented. An obviously middle-class woman passenger in one of the carriages giggles as she imitates the movements of the cameraman's hands. The camera differentiates between those committed to the work of Soviet society and those extraneous to it. The symmetry here is striking, for one person who is aware of the camera is male and presumably sub-proletarian, while the other is female and middle-class. While the attempt at equality is admirable, the social function of the camera here is different from the perceptual function discussed above. For in the previous case, the camera embodies a desire to incorporate the poles of male and female subjectivity, whereas here sexual division becomes a support for the commentary on class differences.

But the progression of *Man with a Movie Camera* suggests that the desire to incorporate male and female difference within the camera constitutes the larger movement of the film. The filmmaker is often portrayed in a social context, and whatever other cinematic reasons there may be to designate initially the work of film editing as more isolated or "privatized," the signifying effect is to create a separation between male and female realms of activity. Film editing initially appears in a way marked off from the social arena defining filmmaking and the life of socialist society as a whole. However, the work of the film editor reappears approximately half-way through the film. Through a series of rapidly-edited shots, montage is equated quite literally with the productive work of Soviet society. Different forms of labor are shown, including that of the cinema. Alternating images depict two kinds of labor. People beautify themselves, and it surely is significant that men and women both are depicted in this context. One woman has her hair washed, another has makeup applied, a man gets a shave, a woman has her hair cut and styled, and another gets a manicure. Alternating with these images is another kind of labor. Clothes are washed, an axe is sharpened, shoes are shined, and mud is thrown on a building. Each juxtaposition of images is determined by movement and direction matches. The formal continuity is disrupted by the opposition between productive labor and the pains taken for the purpose of beautification. Shots of the camera and the filmmaker begin to replace the images of productive labor, equating the two and implying that filmmaking is also antithetical to the work of superfluous decoration. A similar opposition underlies an alternation between a manicure session and the film editor as she, in movements formally similar to those of the manicurist's hands, prepares to join pieces of film together.

I would not disagree with Alan Williams when he writes:

> The motions of a beauty parlor are compared with the cranking of a movie camera, to various machines in a factory, to a lower-class woman washing a wall. But the similarity of these actions and their placement at the same time of day in the (pseudo-) narrative continuity serve to underline a difference between the productive work of the working classes and useless expenditure of energy by the bourgeoisie.[21]

I take Williams's remarks as a reminder that however tempting it might be to evaluate *Man with a Movie Camera* in terms purely of cinematic *écriture*, of the dizzying free play of signifiers, this is a film which exists within a political context. I would argue that the structural similarities between beauty parlors and filmmaking are certainly meant to be undercut by the enormous differences that separate them, but that the process of differentiation is not completely convincing. For an image of a man getting a shave notwithstanding, the term of comparison here is first and foremost the feminine—a world of closed spaces, of self-absorption and of preoccupation with decoration and display. To be sure, this is a world designated as bourgeois, and throughout the film there has been a differentiation between proletarian and bourgeois primarily through the representation of women. As Stephen Crofts and Olivia Rose point out, for instance, there is a contrast between "the perfunctory hair-combing of the women leaving work" and "the satire's constant return to cosmetics, manicuring, etc., an industry whose targets are women."[22]

My point is not that Vertov's film relies on sexual duality in its attempt to articulate a vision of the collective strength of socialist society, and that the vision of collectivity in the film is therefore compromised by a resurrection of sexual hierarchy. Nor am I arguing that this sexual opposition somehow "undermines" *Man with a Movie Camera*. Indeed, one could argue that the strength of the film lies precisely in its recognition and articulation of the difficulty presented by "woman" in any social discourse—whether it be capitalist or socialist. What I wish to stress, rather, is that in articulating a vision of the intertwining elements of socialist society, the points of difficulty, of tension, are virtually always associated with women. True, the opposition between proletarian and subproletarian occurs primarily through the representation of men, but this opposition occupies relatively little screen time. *Man with a Movie Camera* presents a utopian view of collectivity, in which the forthright analogies between cinema and labor are accompanied by other analogies that are far more ambivalent. The film distinguishes between women on the basis of class, and enthusiastically represents women workers as the very embodiments of socialism. In the continuation of the "beauty versus labor" scene described above, a series of images of a young female worker sewing portrays labor in a more organic, less fragmented way. Unlike previous shots, where workers were portrayed in more partial fashion, here the focus is on the worker in more complete terms. The focus on the individual worker shifts to images of collective work in the textile factory. Finally, images of the textile factory alternate with shots of the editor; movement and direction matches unite the two series of images. Film editing is thus equated with social practice, and in the series of images that follow, machines, the camera, and the film editor are interwoven in a dizzying montage that conveys the height of the day's production.

In another section of the film, however, the traits of femininity are not so easily integrated into the flow of socialist production. Approximately half-way through the film, couples are filmed in an administrative office filing for marriage and divorce, and declarations of birth. Suddenly the emphasis shifts to become much broader, and the human life cycle is represented in condensed form: a woman cries over a grave, a funeral proceeds down a street, a newly-married couple steps into a carriage, a woman gives birth. The theme of the human life cycle is introduced in a cut from a couple in the office, filling out a birth declaration form, to an old woman crying over a grave. The woman in the first shot is wearing a white scarf, and out of shyness (we assume), she covers her face with her hand. The elderly woman in the second shot also wears a scarf, and covers her face in exactly the same manner. Hence the headdress provides the match to connect two different emotions, timidity and grief. But there is also a more obvious connection between the shots, and that is the display of emotional responses. The scarf motif is carried throughout the series of images, so that when a bride and groom descend from a carriage it is the woman who becomes foregrounded as the principle of continuity, and when a woman gives birth, the towel draped across her head places childbirth within a formal, cinematic pattern of production and reproduction. The accoutrements of female identity— clothing, gesture, the expression of emotion—become the signs upon which the representation of the human life cycle is based. Woman in *Man with a Movie Camera* functions on one level as a kind of figural excess, most frequently associated with class distinctions, but also—as in the representation of the human life cycle—in terms that are irreducible to class determinations. The film creates a vision of socialist society where men and women, and male and female positions, are as interconnected as the camera lens and the process of editing. Yet while *Man with a Movie Camera* puts forth this utopian vision, it complicates it at the same time by exploring the very foundations—ideological as well as formal—of cinematic representation. Woman functions in a more complex way in *Man with a Movie Camera* than in other films of the 1920s, whether those explicitly concerned with the position of woman, like Pudovkin's *Mother,* or those in which a preoccupation with questions of gender complicates the overt class allegiances, like Eisenstein's *Strike* and *October.* Yet the relationship between subject and object in *Man with a Movie Camera* retains the familiar contours of gender polarity. On-the-street filming may well reveal the class divisions that persist in Soviet society, whereby some Soviet citizens—captured as they awake from a night spent on a park bench—do not have the comforts of a home. When the citizen in question is a woman, however, the class commentary is submerged by sexual objectification, with the woman's body fragmented by the distinctly and eagerly male point-of-view of the camera. Certainly *Man with a Movie Camera* celebrates an ostensibly new eroticism of the fusion of human perception and the cinematic machine, but one cannot help but remark upon the persistence with which the woman's body remains the object of that perception. And the woman in the white scarf, shielding her face from the camera while her male companion chuckles, suggests, if not a resistance to being filmed, then at the very least a discomfort with the social and technological function of the cinema so enthusiastically embraced in *Man with a Movie Camera.*

NOTES

1. This essay is excerpted by permission from Judith Mayne, *Kino and the Woman Question: Feminism and Soviet Silent Film* (Columbus: Ohio State University Press, 1989) and first appeared in *Ciné-Tracts,* vol. 1, no. 2, Summer, 1977.

2. After I had completed the book from which this essay is drawn, I discovered Lynne Kirby's excellent essay on *Man with a Movie Camera,* which argues "that *Man with a Movie Camera* is a film about women, and that the point of view on women is a divided one—a division not only between a critical and an affirmative perspective, but also between a feminine and a masculine voyeurism" (p. 309). See "From Marinetti to Vertov: Woman on the Track of Avant-Garde Representation," *Quarterly Review of Film Studies* 10, no. 4 (1989), 309–23.

3. The classic statement of the position is Laura Mulvey, "Visual Pleasure and Narrative Cinema," *Screen* 16, no. 3 (Autumn 1975), 6–18.

4. See, for example, E. Ann Kaplan's discussion of the "Avant-garde Theory Film" in *Women and Film: Both Sides of the Camera* (New York: Methuen, 1983), 142–70.

5. Roland Barthes, *S/Z* (1970; New York: Hill & Wang, 1974), trans. Richard Miller, pp. 3–4.

6. For a discussion of other Soviet films of the 1920s in relationship to the woman question, see my *Kino and the Woman Question: Feminism and Soviet Silent Film.*

7. Sergei Eisenstein, "The Cinematographic Principle and the Ideogram," in *Film Form* (1949; rpt. Cleveland: World Publishing Company, 1957), trans. Jay Leyda, p. 43.

8. Annette Michelson, "Introduction," *Kino-Eye: The Writings of Dziga Vertov* (Berkeley: University of California Press, 1984), p. xxxvii.

9. See Annette Michelson, *"The Man with a Movie Camera:* From Magician to Epistemologist," *Artforum* 10, no. 7 (March 1972), 60–72.

10. See, for example, Gérard Leblanc, "Quelle avant-garde? Notes sur une pratique actuelle du cinéma militant," *Cinéthique,* no. 7–8 (n.d.), 72–92.

11. Alan Williams, "The Camera-Eye and the Film: Notes on Vertov's 'Formalism,' " *Wide Angle* 3, no 3. (1979), p. 16.

12. Annette Michelson, "Introduction," *Kino-Eye: The Writings of Dziga Vertov,* pp. xxxviv, xl.

13. Alan Williams, "The Camera-Eye and the Film," p. 17.

14. The classic account is Laura Mulvey's "Visual Pleasure and Narrative Cinema."

15. See, for example, Lucy Fischer, "The Lady Vanishes: Women, Magic, and the Movies," *Film Quarterly* 33, no. 1 (Fall 1979), 30–40; Judith Mayne, "Der primitiv Erzähler," *Frauen und Film,* no. 41 (1986), 4–16; and Linda Williams, "Film Body: An Implantation of Perversions," *Ciné-tracts* 3, no. 4 (Winter, 1981).

16. Dziga Vertov, "The Birth of Kino-Eye (1924)," in *Kino-Eye: The Writings of Dziga Vertov* (Berkeley and Los Angeles: University of California Press, 1984), ed. Annette Michelson, trans. Kevin O'Brien, p. 42.

17. Dziga Vertov, "From Kino-Eye to Radio-Eye (1929)," in *Kino-Eye: The Writings of Dziga Vertov,* p. 88.

18. As Youri Tsyviane points out, a film poster is intercut with the initial images of the woman in the room, and the film being advertised is later revealed to be an "artistic drama," entitled *The Awakening of a Woman,* thus, says Tsyviane, *Man with a Movie Camera* is a similar awakening from "the bad dream of artistic cinema." See *L'Homme à la caméra* de Dziga Vertov en tant que texte constructiviste," *Revue du cinéma,* no. 351 (June 1980), pp. 124–25.

19. Stephen Crofts and Olivia Rose suggest that it is *only* the woman's class status that is significant; hence, they write that "her class position is defined . . . by her wearing styled lingerie (hence the montage's stress on her bra and slip). . . ." See "An Essay towards *Man with a Movie Camera,"* *Screen* 18, no. 1 (Spring 1977), p. 36. The authors emphasize throughout their essay that the film's "open-ended structure neither dictates a single reading nor proposes indiscriminate choices with a range of possible readings, but rather directs the spectator towards readings promoting ideological awareness" (p. 34). The authors' notion of ideological awareness does not seem to extend to gender, except as a simple reflection of class.

20. Seth Feldman, "Cinema Weekly and Cinema Truth: Dziga Vertov and the Leninist Proportion," *Sight and Sound* 43 (Winter 1973–1974), p. 35.

21. Alan Williams, "The Camera-Eye and the Film," p. 17.

22. Stephen Crofts and Olivia Rose, "An Essay towards *Man with a Movie Camera,"* p. 38.

III

Signs of Meaning
The Image in Question

XII

PARADOXES OF REALISM

THE RISE OF FILM
IN THE TRAIN OF THE NOVEL

Margaret Morse

The commonplace assumption that the cinema is a 19th-century form, a continuation of narrative modes and melodramatic contents pioneered and naturalized in the novel, will find some support in Ian Watt's *The Rise of the Novel: Studies in Defoe, Richardson and Fielding* (Berkeley: University of California Press, 1957). The novel may have risen, then, but film as a great narrative fiction machine and socializing agent would simply have stepped into the traces of its predecessor, the novel, a social and cultural construction of the 18th century. Both cultural forms can indeed be subsumed under a generalized interest in depicting reality, the authentic record of everyday human experience in narrative fiction. However, a serious application of Watt's methodology to film makes possible some refreshing ways of differentiating novel/film, and raises other questions that a strictly semiotic, psychoanalytic, or Marxist approach would not.

The Rise of the Novel: Reception and Methodology

After its American publication in 1957, simultaneously with its appearance in London, *The Rise of the Novel* garnered a position as the college text of the 1960s on the subject matter, a combination literary history and critical evaluation of the influential novels of Defoe, Richardson, and Fielding. While the scholarship may have been superseded by subsequent research and new data, and perhaps other texts may now be preferred (judging by the moderate slump in sales in the 1970s), Watt's work remains unique as an approach, an audacious union of the sociological and the philosophical, of the empirical and the theoretical, presented in a both scholarly and personal mode. While one can point to many parallels in film theory and criticism, there isn't one approach which makes the link between a history of changing social relations and cultural institutions, the mode of production and reception of film texts and the analysis of the texts themselves in their historical context.

That Watt's now classic book has not ceased to be of interest to literary scholars and theoreticians either in the United States or in Europe is indicated by the plenary address and panel discussion by and with Ian Watt in 1978 on the book at the Southeastern American Society for Eighteenth Century Studies, and by the recent translations into German and Polish in 1974 and Italian in 1976.[1] What interests me and perhaps other scholars of the 1980s about Watt's approach is its scale of relevance, for what is at stake is not any particular novels or even the novel as a discrete genre with specific properties, but what a Watt translator has termed "the conditions of production of cultural models."[2] My own previous research has also taken courage from *The Rise of the Novel* in an attempt of similar scale, to show the failure or growing irrelevance of particular cultural models in turn-of-the-century Vienna.[3]

The variety of approaches needed to work at Watt's scale of relevance is somewhat intimidating and the epistemological problems are truly hair-raising. The exact mix of methodological traditions in *Rise of the Novel* can probably not be duplicated since they are a largely intuitive product of the cross-currents in Watt's own intellectual history, a unique and perhaps inimitable person expression. Nor should that mix of empirical, sociological, and phenomenological approaches be replicated exactly, because in the meantime we have obtained some of the tools needed to work analytically where Watt was working intuitively. (More on this later.) What allows Watt to negotiate the shaky epistemological grounds inherent in his project with some grace is his lack of interest in the novel as a discrete theoretical construct. He also does not set about devising a narrative of its history, the manner in which the novel has risen or fallen. He does insist on analysis of concrete novels and draws on demographic data with aplomb, but these are not the crux of the matter either. What matters is the link between these realities and the conditions which made them possible, as theoretically reconstructed. Such linkage is hardly empirical; it is admittedly hypothetical and its virtue lies in its explanatory power.

How does Watt proceed with this montage of what Christian Metz, for example, describes in regard to the cinema as two different kinds of history; external and internal, i.e., the history of the cinema as a social, cultural, and economic institution and the history of film in its own autonomous development as a meaningful form? How does Watt keep separate yet show correspondences between social norms and particular linguistic performances? between material and ideological preconditions for the novel and novels? His solution is to work the link in two directions, from a general premise about social and cultural norms and patterns of life to its illustration in particular novels (i.e., individualism in Defoe's *Robinson Crusoe),* and from constellations of relationships in the novel to their social, cultural, and material preconditions (i.e., from the sado-masochistic relationship between Lovelace and Clarissa to the division of labor and sex-roles in 18th-century English society).

Anyone familiar with the Kuleshov effect will recognize that these links are ultimately made in our mind, but Watt's correspondences are quite convincing to me and underline the value of heterogeneous approaches. However, I would recast the project in other terms, for what he is doing in the critical currency of today is reconstructing positions of enunciation and the context that made them possible. The concept of language as enunciation emphasizes speaking (and other linguistic acts) as a performance by a subject to an addressee in a particular space and time. One useful distinction which the idea of enunciation makes possible is that between an act of enunciation and an utterance: the "I" who speaks is different from the "I" who is the subject of a sentence. The position of enunciation implies a place in the social order as well as a temporal and spatial position. The subject of an enunciative act does not have an infinite number of possibilities available to him or her; rather they are distributed unevenly according to material conditions and ideological factors (and I would include gender, race, class, age, sexual preference, etc. under the category of ideology). It is possible to reconstruct the position of enunciation from the utterance because every utterance is marked to some degree or other by the attitudes and values of the subject position from which it was enunciated.

Watt posits preconditions for enunciating and receiving particular kinds of utterances (novels) and locates positions of enunciation and reception in English society (authorship, readership, marketplace, etc.). He then sets these positions, from which a certain kind of literary performance is possible (middle class, relations to print medium, literacy, privacy), in relation to the positions from which particular utterances in specific novels appear to be made, primarily in terms of the relation of the author to the utterance. In the process Watt conflates the actual author (Defoe, Richardson, Fielding) and the subject of enunciation, but I am not sure it harms his conclusions. The "position of the subject" so often encountered in film theory is actually that of five different subjects: actual author in a social context; subject of the enunciation; subject of the utterance; subject of address, which can also be reconstructed from the utterance; and, the actual viewer. These "five subjects" are worth keeping in mind, because they may diverge. Psychoanalysis also reminds us that the subject is split into conscious and unconscious as well.

After establishing the dominance or at least the importance of women in the 18th-century reading public (with leisure, literacy, privacy, and upwardly mobile aspirations by means of personal relationships) and having already established the relation between the novel and the private sphere where women have been relegated, Watt goes on to make some interesting assertions about the relation between Defoe and Richardson and their female characters. Defoe's Moll Flanders speaks with a "male voice," a voice which is in fact identical to Defoe's. Moll's astonishing unselfconscious egotism and the gulf between her moral beliefs and self-serving values are not irony on Defoe's part, but represent his own inner contradictions and those of a society undergoing secularization. Richardson, on the other hand, has a strong identification with women of his circle and his female readership, allowing his Pamela a "female voice," ultimately transformed, however, into a very authoritative "male voice." These assertions about the amount of identification between author and character and the sex of his voice are intuitive conclusions on Watt's part. It is possible to be sensitive to modulations of the text and to sense the gender and social location from which an utterance could possibly come—and I prefer that way of looking at it to the idea of a "female voice" in the text. But at this point in discourse on literature it is possible and productive to use a more precise semiotic tool and to demonstrate (through the use of shifters, relatives, performatives, tenses and evaluative and emotive terms) the "imprint of the process of enunciation in the utterance."[4]

There is another issue involved in the linkage of preconditions for enunciations and the actual reconstruction of positions of enunciation from the (novelistic or filmic) utterance: What kind of link is it? The relation established is not necessarily homologous; nor does this two-way vector of linkage imply that social and historical conditions determine the text or vice versa. The relation between socio-historical context and imaginative literature which I have extrapolated from Watt's analysis is one where imagination supplies an identity founded on continuous spatial and temporal experience, the possibilities for which were increasingly absent in 18th-century middle-class society.

I have alluded here to another critical vocabulary lacking in Watt's book—not Freudian psychoanalysis, for that is in evidence, especially in his interpretation of Richardson, but a Lacanian approach. Watt manages to describe the fiction-effect, identification and the split-subject without any recourse to Lacan. Watt's thinking precedes and parallels that of Christian Metz in "The Imaginary Signifier,"[5] which does depend on the Lacanian notions of mirror-stage and the imaginary. The ahistorical and anti-contextual bias of Lacan is, of course, not assimilable to Watt's approach, concerned as it is with socio-historical context and with an instance of cultural change which seems to presume the changing psyche as well. And where one wishes to compare cultural models for their commonalities and differences, Watt's approach is the more productive one, vis-à-vis Lacan.

One possibility of linkage between our two kinds of histories seemingly unaccounted for is that of noncorrespondence. What if a cultural model were autonomous, without social function, or atavistic and residual, having outlived its relation to changing society? The possibility exists, especially if we consider film a product of the 19th century in a late 20th-century world. A specific case of noncorrespondence, it would seem, is between the possibilities for enunciation by women in today's society and the dearth of utterances which could be made from female positions in film. To what do we owe this puzzling lack in film of female subjects? There is another possibility besides anachronism, one to which Watt's analysis of the sadistic relationship in *Clarissa* is a precursor—that of cultural model as an ideological weapon, a tool to maximize or minimize the possibilities located in positions marked by gender, class, age, and so on. If the novel is a female-sympathetic model, as Watt implicitly claims, it may be possible to show how and why film is a male-sympathetic model. The linkage then becomes available to more than a sociological or psychoanalytic approach—it becomes part of a conflict theory of cultural models, ideologically and positionally marked.[6]

Major Premises: The Paradoxes of Realism

A major feature of the novel, according to Watt, is its valuation both of the detailed presentation of everyday life in all its particularity with "optical accuracy," and concern with the individual life in all its singularity against that background. Hence characters in novels have proper names. This preoccupation with realism, defined in this manner, marks a change in values and patterns of awareness in English society, distinguished first by a diminishment in scale from broad public concerns to private life and personal relations, and then by valuation of the autonomous individual as opposed to the social order and its hierarchy. Watt mentions the social changes of urbanization and development of a market economy which makes such things as specialization, money and bookkeeping, print and the literacy needed to circulate it, postal and highway systems, possible and necessary. Paradoxically, besides massing human beings, these social changes also isolated them from each other. Privacy and leisure are creations of the period as well, not yet commodities but by-products to which middle-class women, servants, and apprentices had greater access than other groups. (Current social histories may revise Watt's conclusions about the leisurely life of women of the period.)

Another paradox implicit in Watt's analysis is that the very factors which split experience into partial events—the division of labor and the separation of private life from social and economic activity—are supported by an ideology of individualism and identity founded on memory, temporality experienced as causal succession of events in continuous space unified in a single consciousness. Identity founded on narrativity seems to be something new; Watt cites medieval definitions of realism and the abstract relation between scenes in Shakespeare (among other things) as evidence for a prior sense of reality and identity.

What had changed in the meantime? In Adam Smith's pin factory in *The Wealth of Nations,* each worker rather than making a whole pin undertook a part of the process, the head for example. Smith imagined that the workers would cooperatively put the pins together, part of a larger cooperation between entrepreneurs, landowners, and workers. However, it became clear in Marx's analysis of alienation that workers may lose contact with the final product and with the meaning of the work process. One of the attractions of Robinson Crusoe, in Watt's analysis, is that he overcomes the specialization of his age and becomes the dream of the absolute individual, an island entire unto himself, able to supply every need, replete with stock, bookkeeping, and an utterly selfish relation to other human beings. And this selfishness was also a part of Adam Smith's cooperative model, for each worker, entrepreneur, and landowner in pursuit of his own benefit would ultimately serve the social welfare, regulated only by an invisible hand, the only site where the whole came together. Robinson Crusoe has an exceptional whole command of everyday life in his hands; he knows where his bread comes from, from wheat to table. And Crusoe is not only a whole individual in ideology, but in a continuous narrative available in one possessable item at a reasonable cost.

In Richardson's novels, the female experience of isolation and lack of control over her own fate is given direction. Richardson had written a manual for seduction as well as manuals for letter-writing and burial in *Pamela* and *Clarissa,* and he prepared women for the two possible outcomes of the only strategy available to those given no place of their own to speak from, marriage or death. These options achieve recognition and fix identity in a male-oriented society, where women were increasingly dependent on marriage at the same time that marriage grew increasingly difficult to achieve. Unfortunately the invisible hand had not provided English society with a cooperative sexual division of labor, and the sexual codes of male and female could be diametrically opposed in their aims and interests. The massive epistolary exchange in the many volumes of Richardson's novels gives an overview of·what was going on in the consciousness of correspondents on both sides of the closet.

It is interesting that the novels of Defoe and Richardson both mimic not life directly, but the literature of unified experience, the autobiographical memoir and correspondence by letter. Both novelists base their claim to a depiction of reality on the authenticity of these personal records of experience. Of course these would have been unique and singular objects, written in everyday language by hand in a situation of privacy and leisure. The novel, however it may be written, is produced under quite other conditions: printed replication en masse for a market in the public sphere. Consumption is again private, in the closet or a room of one's own, which makes possible the performance of novels as silent reading, with consequent lowering of censorship and increasing ability to identify with the fictional world. The realism of the novel, the sense of unmediated access to unified space and time, is achieved by making both the prose and the print as transparent as possible. Prose is the poetic language most analogous to the language of everyday life, hence invisible and universally accessible to the literate. The enunciative stance of the witness in a court of law giving circumstantial evidence is the one adopted by an author, who like the court seeks to keep his/her own subjectivity invisible. The uniformity of the print medium makes literacy as automatic reading possible; its very impersonality authenticates the reality of the personal expression of experience. The visibility of print in a tangible object, a book, makes the inner and outer life of an individual equally real. What these formal means ultimately make possible is the illusion of reality, the vicarious enjoyment of the experience of others as a continuous whole, and the adoption by the reader of the position of a voyeur with a paradoxical point of view, invisible oneself yet able to see even into the consciousness of others.

In relation to the cinema, anyone who thought that the camera was the first to institute this psychic regime of voyeuristic identification with pure seeing will be reminded that the novel is also a mechanically reproduced visual medium and a recording art; this fact plays an important part in its fiction-effect on the reader. The ultimate result of what Watt terms "formal realism" is that the novel is "capable of a more thorough subversion of psychological and social reality than any previous (literary genre)."[7]

Watt goes on, however, to distinguish a second kind of realism, different from the formal or presentational realism already described (and hence not restricted to novels). This is a "realism of assessment." In Fielding's works, the author's presence and values are felt in explicit commentary and in "words and phrases (which) intentionally invoke not only the actual narrative event, but the whole literary, historical, and philosophical perspective in which character or action should be placed by the reader."[8] This variation of the novel is characterized by obtrusive patterning of plot and by figurative language which draws attention to itself. In the process the novel itself and the attitude of its narrator to it comes into view in order to become "real." The aim of realism is to bring the novel "into contact with the whole tradition of civilized values," and the ordering of social groups rather than the sovereign individual. At the cost of the pleasures of identification with the illusion of reality, this kind of realism, the novel as discourse, brings with it detachment and the possibility of conscious assessment by the reader.[9]

Another paradox of realism is that the social orientation of the novel of assessment is expressed at the price of its popularity, and its self-conscious form, less accessible and comprehensible than transparent prose, and is ultimately more elitist. This configuration has been a recurring dilemma in the cultural models of theater and film, for each has a similar "formal realism" and a "realism of assessment." The politically progressive filmmaker, for example, has a choice of producing a Hollywood-type of film in hopes of reaching a larger audience—at the cost of hypnotizing it rather than changing its conscious conviction; or, of producing a film which is also real as discourse and therefore of sacrificing the larger audience unprepared to understand the film or take pleasure from it.

Watt's analysis has the merit of setting these two realisms in their social and historical context. The solution to the dilemma, then, would seem to lie in the matrix of relations which are the preconditions for the dilemma rather than in the valorization of either pole. As long as sovereign individuality is the mythic foundation of the social order, such a dilemma seems inevitable. The remarkable achievement of the novel as a cultural model is to have harnessed the forces of psychic regression to an ideology of individualism. Dionysian communion, founded upon dropping the barriers between self and other, had a socializing function of furthering identification and cooperation with the social order: the novel socializes into individualism the "selfishness" which was the motivating force of Adam Smith's cooperative social and economic order. At the same time, the novel made possible a reassessment and change of personal identity on the basis of narrative reflection; that is, it offered the possibility of changing one's position of enunciation from that assigned by the social order, a change of identity not as conversion but as moral choice.

It is possible to recast Watt's two contrasting realisms in terms of modes of enunciation. Emile Benveniste has made a distinction which would be useful in a Wattian-type project. This is the differentiation between utterances which are openly the product of a particular enunciative situation located in time and space between a speaker and an addressee (discourse), and those utterances which efface or mask the enunciative process (history or story). Both film and novel belong to the second type (story), as shown in the application of the distinction to literature by Gerard Genette[10] and to film by Christian Metz.[11]

However, is the distinction story/discourse a matter of degree or of differences in kind? Subsequent thinking on genre theory by Genette and others maintains that a genre such as the novel is a matter of consensus and convention, an arbitrary and historical concatenation of elements. A mode of enunciation (inclusion or exclusion of interlocutors and enunciative situation, i.e., discourse/story) can be distributed differently within a text and among the texts assigned to a genre. Evaluating presence in a novel is clearly a matter of degree; in the end the reader surmises even without explicit guidance the position of author-enunciator through points of view which reflect the enunciator as well as mirror "reality as the novelist saw it."[12] The difference between open discourse and masked discourse or story is an important one, especially in ascertaining the relation of a text to its reader as well as to its writer, a difference which must be ascertained case by case rather than globally. The recasting of Watt's two realisms in terms of enunciation allows them to be set into relation to other cultural models such as film.

Novel/Film: The Great Hollywood Commutation Test

Thus far the numerous commonalities between novel and film have been underlined by reviewing Watt's analysis. His book seems a harbinger; his conclusions antecede those of film theory of the next two decades. But what if we were to substitute film for novel in Watt's approach, rather than merely appropriating his conclusions on the novel to film? Do any differences come to the fore when the invisible hand is replaced with the likewise invisible and omniscient eye? Are realism, individualism, literacy, and privacy the keywords of film?

If the fragmentation of experience was a prime factor in the need to create an identity from narrative, the changes in economic and social life of the 19th and early 20th century augmented and extended that fragmentation until it pervaded every aspect of life. The division of labor was extended so that labor was divided into head work and hand work, and control was exercised over the hands and the order of completion of tasks, by dividing the tasks into tiny bits and by regulating the execution and rhythm of work. These changes are known globally as "Taylorism" and they improved efficiency of factory production by taking what was essentially a whole worker with a partial task in Adam Smith's conception and dividing the worker into convenient pieces (mind, hand, leg, etc.). The assembly line is the embodiment of this organization of work with an additional feature—a car can be made in many different places and at different times and assembled in a convenient rather than logical order of parts.

Now all of these features which hold true of labor itself are also true of film. Film reassembles fragments into an identity in place and time which is imaginary in its wholeness and continuity. Furthermore, the assembled whole may never have existed referentially or in pro-filmic reality. It was a true revelation to Kuleshov's workshop to discover, for example, that one could make a place which never existed by putting together bits of landscape into "creative geography." His workshop also made a "woman" out of bits and pieces of film of different women. (How revealing it is that these two bodies-in-pieces assembled into objects of desire were a landscape and a woman—and not a man.)

The pair decoupage/montage (cutting up the story, selecting out the pro-filmic reality and cutting it out with the frame into bits/creating a succession which evokes a whole) is the order of the assembly line itself—but it is the spectator who assembles the final product, the imaginary space or identity. The cultural model film evokes is a factory world: it is collectively made, capital-intensive, comsumed publicly in specially designated places, and like a laborer's time, it is a commodity which is not tangible, nothing more than the right to rent a seat for a specified time. The Hollywood factory system with its hierarchical and minute division of labor is just the most obvious and consequent embodiment of intrinsic properties of film as a cultural model.

Post-revolutionary Soviet filmmakers like Dziga Vertov recognized that the division of labor in film production and reception is a very important and regressive aspect of its form; Vertov has been accused of "implicit Taylorism"[13] but that accusation is readily applied to film as a whole—Vertov had the insight to make it explicit. Like the worker, film marches the spectator along at a pace determined by the machine.[14] Vertov's critic suggests a "slow-down" as the answer to the "speed-up" of the machine of narrative. But evidently something more fundamental would have to be changed in the division of labor in film to overcome the features of the model itself.

The model of film is also the product of the "male" side of the division of labor. It presumes (no matter what sex actually occupies a "male" position) a primacy of the public sphere while the private sphere is a support system charged with reproducing the social order. That films appear to address women as spectators obliquely, through a male-charged point of view, corresponds to the larger social context where women also accept and translate address from the male position to their own. To occupy male positions in cinematic production or to produce better "images" of women (the very idea of which shows how naturalized the image of woman as commodity has become) does not in and of itself make women subjects of enunciation. In the larger social context, as long as the basic division of labor (work presuming a supportive private sphere) remains the same, every gain made for women in occupying positions in the social order is a loss for men and an additional burden to women (the double load). Considering the interests within the social order, it would be remarkable if a cultural model produced and consumed in a male-oriented sector did not serve the ideological interests of that sphere. (In Richardson's day, the aspirations of women coincided with the interests of the rising middle-class.)

With this in mind, it is possible to interpret the resourcefulness of Griffith's *Lonedale Operator* (1911), that virtue in women which used to be known as "pluck," as a mistake similar to the mismatching eyelines and mixed-up screen direction in the same film. The telegraph operator besieged by thieves telegraphs for her own rescue and then faints. She proceeds to hold her attackers at bay with a wrench which looks like a gun. In the remake of the film in 1912, Griffith has the heroine shoot through a keyhole at her attacker with a gun, repeating a motif of *The Lonely Villa,* where the evil housemaid shoots wildly through a hole in the wall. The woman is without an overview, unable to handle the tools of a male world.

Other forms of fragmentation experienced in the 19th century can contribute to our understanding of film as cultural model. The railroad, feature of the first wave of industrialization, united distant places along a track sequentially—but at the cost of making space discontinuous. What is in between stations loses its meaning as real space and becomes visually-appreciated landscape. It was the railroad which also brought to consciousness the separate nature of light and sound; at the speed of train travel, the image of the train is separate from the sound of the whistle. (And the discovery of the Doppler effect is attributed to observation of the changing pitch of a train whistle.) The automobile has an effect similar to a train on space, except that one has more points of departure and destination in its traces. The telegraph and telephone also separate the interlocutors of discourse from the limits of spatial continuity—except that of a wire. The electric light freed human activity from its temporal regulation by daylight; energy freed the sphere of labor from private life even further. The phonograph frees sound from its place, time and subjectivity of origin; the camera abolishes time by fixing the image, and abolishes spatial continuity by bringing life-like images of distant places to the viewer. Eyes and ears of nineteenth-century spectators were displaced along wires, tracks, roads, and filaments of diverging places and times.

The task of creating a sense of unified experience and an identity in the 19th and early 20th century—considering also that spectators themselves were from a far more heterogeneous group in terms of class, national, and cultural traditions—was a far more prodigious one than that faced by the cultural model of the novel. The developing primacy of the image over the printed and spoken word in public life is a feature of the period. The image is a socializing force in a different way than the word, more conducive to the task at hand. The desire for continuity which would make sense of the fragmented and discontinuous experiences of everyday life is understandable. The now so disparaged continuity of editing was a formal and ideological achievement which we in the present can perhaps dismiss, given that it is fully naturalized. Besides developing its own logical formal relations (eye-line matches, direction matches, 30 degree and 180 degree rules, etc.), early films often employed an array of other machines to motivate relationships between shots which were discontinuous in the visual field of the diegesis (the world evoked by the narrative). Distant spaces in simultaneous time are evoked and connected by railroad and telegraph as well as by formal alternations between them in *The Londale Operator;* by automobile and telephone in *The Lonely Villa;* and by a relay of automobile, train, telephone, and hand-delivered note to the final destination of the rope in the last modern sequence of *Intolerance.* It is true that the gathering of the clans in *Birth of a Nation* lacks such mechanistic motivating links, but it is more than compensated for by the impressive visual scene of lines of men on horseback who are at once relays and rescuers. The look is a powerful tool of linkage, but it is limited to the visually or subjectively accessible. Some exceptions prove the rule: consider the impossible look of Marie de Medici and son on a cut to an event which happened earlier and elsewhere, a Huguenot uprising in *Intolerance*. Or the look between Dracula and Elizabeth, in Transylvania and Bremen respectively—such hypnotic telepathy has become one of the powers of every film viewer. The habits of the present day viewer have become so different, that it is startling to follow the link between two alternating spaces, be it the pneumatic tube system of Paris, the telephone system of London, a Belgian train, or Roman highway system, all of which have been featured in commercial (formal realist) and avant-garde (realist films of assessment) in recent years.

But to return to an earlier period when a new organization of space and time had yet to lose its strangeness, the major theme of comedy was precisely the machine—train, automobile, factory, and the cinema. The very assumptions and devices of linkage upon which the cultural model of film is based were put into question: cars wove wildly, unrestricted to any path, pies were substituted for looks, and impossible matches aided improbable rescues. The double-take of the Buster Keaton character in *The General* at the missing box-car uncouples the link between seeing, knowing, and controlling reality.

It is important to remember that the look Buster Keaton gives the missing box-car is actually directed out at us, the subject of the camera-spectator position. It is we who put the fragments together, who assemble the machine into a whole which never existed. And we do it retrospectively.

The whole we assemble is accessible to very little conscious, but much unconscious revision; unlike the novel, the film disappears to anyone who doesn't have access to a machine. When we do have access to a film, we can retrieve it only along a line or filament, whereas the book and the library are a remarkable tree-like ordering system. The book exists in real space, the film exists only in memory, except for those few who have depreciated capital stock, actual film, in their possession. Our means of reassessment are drastically curtailed in comparison to the novel. Furthermore, film gives us access to the perceptual consciousness of the subject, but the conceptual and introspective consciousness of the novel is virtually lacking. It is time to ask whether or not the substitution of images for the printed word in the narrative does not make possible an utterly different means of constituting a subject. And furthermore, would it not be productive to see whether or not the processes of substitution and the legitimation of the image can be followed formally and thematically in film history?

Rather than assuming that the cultural model of the film filled a need (which began with Plato or with the Renaissance or with industrialization) for increasing realism, the question is whether there wasn't something uncanny about these life-like moving images and sounds which was only gradually deconstructed. Suppose that the increasing realism of film (sound, color, wide-screen) was slowly made possible by the suppression of the power of images to invoke reality. The relation of images to effigy magic is widely known; the invocatory power of images to create rather than represent a world still plays an important part in our enjoyment of them. Our modern visual culture, including not only film but advertising, television, design, etc. would seem to have been made possible by the mass suggestion that images do not have the power to invoke reality.

A legitimating function of titles and allusions to books can be easily recognized in the early films of D. W. Griffith and others. The image track is like an overgrown book illustration securely anchored by the printed word. It strikes me as quaint that in the German film *Uncanny Stories* (1919), three portrait paintings on a wall come to life at the stroke of midnight, leaf through all the books, and find the stories in which they then play the main parts.

Anxiety over loss of conscious control of events and over the seductive power of the filmic and the female image are an overriding theme in Expressionist film. In a late contribution to the discourse on cinematic seduction, Fritz Lang's *M* (1931), there is the visual premise that two parallel societies exist, a lower criminal world based on the visual and the aural with a hermeneutics of total observation, and a society of the law based on the hermeneutic principles of the letter, archives, and the trace. If the printed word has social primacy, the formal relationships in the film equate the two societies of image and sound/word as interdependent, equivalent and equally subject to the law. The irrationality ascribed to the visual-aural is displaced onto an outsider-madman and onto every man.

Early Soviet cinema displayed an implicitly ambiguous attitude toward the cultural model of film. Lenin's promotion of Soviet film can be seen as an attempt to capture a dangerous power for the Party rather than as a positive or appreciative aesthetic attitude. In Eisenstein's *October,* the progressive revolution is in the hands of those who use the printed word and the map for the rational control of the crowd; the provisional government is motivated by effigies and images. In Vertov's *Man with a Movie Camera,* the aggression of the camera, the sedentary spectators, the ad juxtaposed with the consumption of beer, the speed-up of the assembly worker, and many other moments display a relation to film ranging from ambiguous to critical. This uneasiness with film seems impossible to recapture in a world of the fully naturalized image.

Have realism and an identity founded on narrative become something which we can afford to get rid of? The proper name of the character in the novel has been replaced by the star with a role. The "image" has largely replaced the concept of identity as correspondence between reality and consciousness. Those who sell only their labor power as time need no image; wherever some element of personality (presence, charisma, sexual attractiveness, executive ability) is a commodity, the image is indispensable. The demand for authenticity in the image of the politician is still there, but it is validated by shaping private life to the image and publicizing it. What can be ascertained in popular culture is a growing demand for the simulated rather than for the realistic, for the sign of an experience rather than the experience (as if it were real). The 1919 promise, threat, or command: "Du musst Caligari werden!" seems so outdated, because on the one hand, as we have produced and naturalized the cultural model of film, we have become Caligari; on the other hand, in greater numbers we'd rather "love to hate" a low-down, two-timing, ranch-stealing scoundrel on television.

Fiction is suspended disbelief in the world evoked by the narrative, but now the accent has shifted. Our imaginary bodies are dispersed in networks over space and in time; our living bodies are often immobilized at a desk, a console or in the dead-space in between. The average American family daily spends almost the equivalent of another working day watching television. In such a social context, the claim of realism to imitate the experience of everyday life faithfully has lost both its power and credibility.

NOTES

1. I would like to express my thanks to Ian Watt for his generosity in making background information available, including his own article, "Serious Reflections on The Rise of the Novel," (1968), pp. 205–16, reprinted in *Towards a Poetics of Fiction,* ed. Mark Spilka (Bloomington and London: 1977), which provided many of the insights into his work in evidence here. This does not suggest that he would support my premises or conclusions, for, of course, the overall interpretation of his work and any further additions, applications, speculations, and mistakes are my own.

2. Grosso Destreri in his introductory essay to *Le Origini del Romanzo Borghese,* Italian translation of *The Rise of the Novel,* brought to my attention by Watt.

3. "The Works of Arthur Schnitzler as an Index of Cultural Change: Relations between the Sexes in Social Reality, Ideology and the Imagination." Dissertation, University of California at Berkeley, 1977.

4. "Enunciation," *Encyclopedic Dictionary of the Sciences of Language,* by Oswald Ducrot and Tzvetan Todorov (Baltimore: Johns Hopkins, 1979), 324.

5. In: *Screen* 16:2 (Summer 1975), 14-76, a translation of "Le signifiant imaginaire," *Communications* 23 (1975) 3–55. Metz's approach is more worked out and precise, however, than Watt's; Metz does not necessarily share Lacan's biases, just some of his conceptual apparatus. Metz's work has been implicitly assimilated to Watt's in the application of a Wattian approach to film because Metz has done most to define what the cultural model of film is.

6. For an example of such an approach, cf. 3 above.

7. *The Rise of the Novel,* 206.

8. "Serious Reflections," 99.

9. "Serious Reflections," 98 and *Rise,* 288.

10. "Frontières du recit," *Communications* 8, 152–63.

11. "Histoire/Discours," *Langue, Discours, Societe-Pour Emile Benveniste* (Paris: Editions du Seuil, 1975), 301–306.

12. *Rise,* 118.

13. Stanley Aronowitz, "Film—The Art Form of Late Capitalism," *Social Text* 1 (Winter 1979), 110–29.

14. Cf. Thierry Kuntzel, "Le Defilement," *Revue d'Esthetique* 1973, 97–110.

XIII

CULTURE, HISTORY, AND AMBIVALENCE
ON THE SUBJECT OF WALTER BENJAMIN

John Fekete

There are several Walter Benjamins, not one. Put more precisely, his work is emblematic of his affirmed methodological bias toward a multiplex collage of aspects (rather than, say, a powerfully controlled montage): its theoretical parameters intrinsically embody ambivalence (rather than coherence), tension (rather than identity). There is the apocalyptic Benjamin of Talmudic and cabbalistic inspiration; the libertarian Benjamin, claimed by the Frankfurt school, whose thinking juxtaposes micrological insights in defense of particulars against the usurpations of universalizing systems; and the politicizing Benjamin, associated with Bertolt Brecht, whose thought runs in macrological channels and explores orthodox strategies that surface most explicitly in those two essays of the 1930s, "The Work of Art in the Age of Mechanical Reproduction" and "Author as Producer" that are most dear to today's neo-Marxist cultural orthodoxy. Each of these strains facilitates brilliant insights in dimensions ranging from aesthetics to social theory to philosophy of history; each is also caught within the dead ends of its contexts.

After a generation of relative neglect, and on the basis of a growing (if still small) volume of translations,[1] Benjamin's writing is beginning to find its proper international audience, although it is still the case that one has to read German to have access to the main body of discussion that has developed around his work in the last decade. We are only at the beginning of gaining an entry into Benjamin's world; the work and pleasure and reward of appropriation and full scale theoretical inquiry and dialogue lie ahead. What we can sketch is a preliminary map of some of the coordinates, especially from the sides of aesthetic theory and philosophy of history and some central motifs involved with questions of aura, information, film, and a democratic or mass art.

In method, Benjamin sought to become a semiologist of far-ranging exegetical scope who would decipher the coded meanings of objects at all levels of signification and social structure, from times past and present. "All human knowledge must take the form of interpretation," he wrote in 1923,[2] and his devotion to that principle brings him close to the broad circle of modern hermeneutics, the New Critical tradition (including Ezra Pound's ideogrammatic and Marshall McLuhan's paratactic exegetical approaches), and structuralism. At a time when the great realist tradition in art and interpretation lay in ruins and the gap between the individual subject of action or perception and the larger social movement grew wider, and their links more tenuous, Benjamin, like Joyce, was troubled by the increasingly problematic locus of the individual observer and tried to redefine the authorial subjectivity out of existence, to yield the fullness of epistemological space to the presence of the object. Theodor Adorno notes[3] that the epistemological intentions that developed along with Benjamin's massive Arcades project from the 1920s—thousands of pages of which exist as fragments of a plan to decode the nineteenth century historically and philosophically—call for the elimination of all overt commentary from the presentation of disparate materials. Benjamin's dream was to compose his major work, as the culmination of his anti-subjectivism, in the form entirely of citations.

Moreover, his collage was to be protected from the rationalist fiction of unitary cohesion through an adherence to a principle of fragmentariness which Benjamin adopted even as he moved toward the sensory depths of the particular objects of his attention. In one sense, this philosophy of fragments, surely one of the most important features of Benjamin's work, provides a critical challenge to the dominant tendencies of the inter-war period which were totalitarian on both theoretical and practical levels. For emancipatory discourse it may remain a valuable contribution to the attempt to constitute a viable alternative syntax to the totalitarian grammar of our rationalist traditions. In some aspects, in line with Ernest Bloch's search for the utopian dimension of all manifestations, Benjamin's methodological principle points to the ultimate libertarian frame for those manifestations, free of authorial/authoritarian intervention. Yet the position is historically ambivalent (as I shall argue later) and methodologically as well: the aspiration to an objective collage of objective fragments has close points of contact with both a crippling positivism and dogmatic structuralist pretensions to metonymically exhaustive apprehension.

Benjamin never wrote his major work; but the heterogeneous fragments that enter his field of observation are given organization in his own writings by a messianic hope for an end of history. In effect, it has been noted[4] Benjamin adopts a radical critique of the 'belief in progress' in the name of which the ideologues both of administered society and of socialism (which took on the credo of progress as the heritage of the bourgeois Enlightenment) have cravenly legitimated technocratic rule and the sacrifice of the present to an abstract future. Correspondingly the notion of a *radical rupture* (in what he calls messianic time) that would explode the undesirable continuum of history becomes a touchstone of his thought. Again, this philosophy of history hides a problematic doubleness (to which I shall return later). In one respect, it is a powerful antidote to abject craven evolutionism, to the belief in the progression of universal history through homogeneous empty time; yet the antidote is purchased at a high price.

The despair at seeing no way forward is also projected backward. The categorical structure of the enlightenment is projected back from the present to cover the entire terrain of historical time, to exhaust the entire continuity of human history. The consequence of such ontologization of the enlightenment (which was typical of the Frankfurt School's brand of critical theory)[5] is translated into the aspiration at the heart of Benjamin's historical conception to be liberated, not only from a transitional phase of social life but from the very continuum of history. The distortion, necessarily, is pervasive: by correlation with the eruption of homogenized otherness that is expected in an indeterminate 'then' in the future, the 'not then' of present and past homogenized. For example, Benjamin comments: "There is no document of civilization which is not at the same time a document of barbarism. And just as such a document is not free of barbarism, barbarism taints also the manner in which it was transmitted from one owner to the other. A historical materialist therefore disassociates himself from it as far as possible. He regards it as his task to brush history against the grain."[6]

Benjamin's unusual position within Marxism can be seen to have evolved in connection with and out of several different and conflicting ideological patterns. A Jewish mystical strain is generally recognized in the early work and in the 1922 project for a literary journal, *Angelus Novus,* but also in the final "Theses on the Philosophy of History." Later he was strongly drawn to Brecht's Marxism, to his professed "materialist crudity," to the possibility of uniting artistic/political integrity with urgent, concrete political focus. At the same time, Benjamin shared philosophical and sociological interests and approaches with members of the Frankfurt School, for example with respect to the culture industry, and indeed received financial aid from them after 1935.[7] In addition Benjamin's orientation to Marxism in the 1920s and thereafter bears the mark of Georg Lukacs's *History and Class Consciousness,* though not necessarily in terms of Lukacs's most creative aspects. The resultant formulaic confidence in a determinate collective subjectivity (sharply separating Benjamin's outlook from that typical in the Frankfurt School) enters decisively into his provocative and stimulating consideration of films.

A portrait of Benjamin's unique intellectual physiognomy needs to take account, as well, of his unwillingness to attach himself solely to a given identifiable ideological pattern. Some elements of this are now well known. He did not follow his friend Gersholm Scholem to Jerusalem, nor Adorno and Horkheimer to the United States. In Parisian isolation he suffered Scholem's criticism that he was losing himself in a crippling Marxism. Benjamin endured Adorno's skepticism of his friendship with Brecht, and the refusal to publish a section of his work in the journal of The Institute for Social Research on the grounds that the connections he drew between different social levels were too direct and immediate and theoretically incoherent. He put up with Brecht's criticism that his style was too diaristic, and he patiently observed the limitations of Brecht's sensibility and Marxian categories in relation to Kafka and the problems of parable and allegory, of linguistic strategy. And in opposition to Lukacs's stress on continuity, in history and in culture, Benjamin emphasized discontinuity; where Lukacs saw revolution as the consummation of the historical process, and articulated a persisting cultural concern with the preservation of the great bourgeois tradition of critical realism, Benjamin saw revolution as a radical break with the entire development up to the present, and sought to mobilize language to explode reality, not to evoke its totality. He came eventually to abandon the bourgeois tradition altogether as indeed his experience told him that bourgeois society has repressed its own ties with tradition through an excess of topical information.[8]

In seeking to account for this experience, Benjamin began to formulate a historical/political communications theory out of a pool of rich insights. The work is uneven. I shall return to the more enduring aspects later, noting for the moment that what rises to the surface under the Brechtian influence in the two essays that date from the mid-1930s, "The Author as Producer" and "The Work of Art in the Age of Mechanical Reproduction," is a militant attitude addressed directly to the producers of art and calling attention to the practices of workers who write. In this way, Bernd Witte argues, Benjamin takes up the literary practices of the German Union of Proletarian Revolutionary Writers, a group whose members attempted to expand reportage and correspondence into the proletarian novel—as the only examples of the positive transformation of art through a revolution in its production techniques. Lukacs, by contrast, always attacked this kind of position prominent in pre-Stalinist Russian cultural politics, as an aesthetically ineffective type of literary spontaneity, thereby anticipating Adorno's similar criticism of the "Mechanical Reproduction" essay because of what Adorno called the anarchist romanticism of Benjamin's "blind confidence in proletarian spontaneity" which reduces art to political utility.[9]

In and through and perhaps in spite of these controversies and the unsympathetic theoretical climate, Benjamin tenaciously seemed to find in Marxism the promise of a rational poetic of history and mythology of social relations. His writings abound in lyrical comments about print and causality, messages and media, dramatic images and social forms, anticipating work on a terrain that Marshall McLuhan has more recently made his own, and doing so with a scruple and subtlety foreign to McLuhan's purpose and without McLuhan's peculiarly incongenial premises and assumptions. Perhaps Benjamin owes to Marxism his understanding of the work of literature as a determinate product of a given society, and consequently his notion that the modern city is the defining locus of imaginative life, that the industrial city has literally restructured our inner landscape.[10] But his specific type of Marxism seeks to embrace a multiplicity of related structures from diverse spheres of social and cultural life and to apprehend the general principles that connect them together. Benjamin tries to read the landscape of the nineteenth century, including its artistic, economic, political, and other contours, as though it were a language whose appropriation depends on the articulation of its grammar through a collection of specific speech acts. In all this as in the predisposition towards discontinuity, the subordination (even tendential elimination) of subjectivity, and the mythomorphic or poetic rhetorical cast of his writing, Benjamin becomes visible to us as a forerunner of some variations of modern structuralism. Indeed, this methodological point of contact with an ascendent intellectual movement accounts, at least in part, for the attention that his writing has begun to receive in the last decade, a generation after his death.

Unavoidably, his work shares in the weaknesses of structural methodology, most notably the inability to develop an adequate conception of the subject and of the growth of the human substance. (Arguably, it was precisely this inability in the face of the times that prepared his susceptibility to the solicitations of structural method.) In any case, his resonant prose yearns to respond fully to the autonomous body of any specific object of his perception, in its singularity, and in this he differs from the scientific structuralism of our day (and from Lukacs as well). We need to recall here that Benjamin did not aspire to a systematic theory of literature and distrusted systems. His style incorporates the interval; he leaves spaces between one item and another, vacancies providing opportunity for a reflection. Indeed, this form which his writing tends to take, aphoristic fragment, testifies to his methodological hostility to systems period. He recognized and feared the tendency in his time for any observation of systems to become in its turn systematic. The aphoristic fragment, however, as experience shows,[11] sets its own horizons. It does not develop— it is patient, opaque, and mysterious, a pillar of an epistemology of discontinuity. As a way of seeing the world, a way of processing information, the aphorism both implies a greater whole and yet is complete as a fragment.

Indeed, the aphorism became a characteristic literary/philosophical device employed not only by Benjamin but by the Frankfurt School critical theorists generally, in their attempt to resist the spread of totalitarian discourse. The First World War essentially closed the books on entrepreneurial capitalism and equally on its most radical negation, classical Marxism. The inter-war period convulsively produced the frame and the vectors for a global social transition to systems of collective, controlled, and coded bureaucratic domination characterized, *mutatis mutandis* by the extension of the power of collective capital over all facets of life, the politicization of the economy, and the colonization of consciousness. The rise of fascism and the collapse of potential proletarian opposition meant conceptually not only having to lay to rest the fairy tale of an inevitably emancipatory socialist future, but also having to do without the Lukacsian tendential totalizing subject of history, indeed without any totalizing social agency through which could be constituted the Hegelian/Marxian dream of an emancipated collective subjectivity. Totalizing macrological social theory itself had to be ruled out owing to the absence of appropriate collective epistemological grounding.

In this predicament where the dominant transformative tendencies (which Herbert Marcuse accurately characterizes as tendencies of one-dimensionality) sought to destroy all otherness in order to make possible the restructuring of capitalism, Adorno and Frankfurt theorists tried to reconstitute critical theory so as to preserve particularity and nonidentity. In Paul Piccone's reconstruction, in order to salvage revolutionary subjectivity at all (and deprived of a normative mediational function), Adorno's social theory retreated to micrological levels where "analyses of the particular aphorisms provide glimpses of the false totality no longer immediately apprehensible through discredited and traditional conceptual means. The aphorism retains its critical edge by escaping into a poetic mode of discourse."[12] Yet here again we have a problematic response, in Benjamin as in the others. Although the aphoristic defense of nonidentity may have been, under the circumstances, a necessary response, yet it was a necessary evil. The relative protection that the micrological fragment enjoys from the dangers of instrumentalization is also translated in the long run into a relative impotence and incapacity at counter normative mediation. In addition, although the retreat of critical theory into a micrological sanctuary can be seen as an effective counter-move to an allegedly totally administered society, it becomes obsolete and ineffectual once, as in our own time, the merciless transition to advanced capitalism is achieved. Over bureaucratization becomes counterproductive, and the logic of one-dimensionality is slowly reversed in order artificially to generate institutional free spaces for the recreation of the spontaneity/negativity/otherness/nonidentity that administered society needs as internal control mechanisms for stable growth (and which it had destroyed in the transition period).[13] The aphoristic fragments that once carried critical protest (Benjamin) today carry reconciliation (McLuhan).

In Benjamin's case, this problem is only compounded by the unresolved coexistence in his outlook and writings of what can today be regarded as unregenerated macrological junk derived (via Brecht especially) from traditional Marxist doctrine. To "prefer Benjamin's politics to that of the Frankfurt School" is to introduce sectarian premises into an otherwise illuminating discussion.[14] At the same time, through his concern with class politics, Benjamin is prepared to make some of his best known and most valuable contributions in the area of political communications theory, specifically around questions of aesthetic information and aesthetic democratization. Benjamin is one of the very few Marxist intellectuals who have entered perceptively into that realm of cultural media where Marshall McLuhan has gained such commanding stature. His approach, unlike that of either conservative or radical critics of media, is to look on mass communications as new languages whose collectively appropriated grammar may hold great positive potentialities for human culture.

Benjamin's chief aesthetic problem is the impact of the work of art, its effect in the world. Thus at the center of his philosophy stands the question of aesthetic reception, of the function of art. It is this approach that opens the work into the world; and it is the deep ambivalence in the situation of aesthetic reception today in the world that is at the root of a fundamental ambivalence in Benjamin's aesthetic.[15] Benjamin recognizes that aesthetic theory can only give up the principle of a work's autonomy and integrity; yet this is in danger within the frame of contemporary reception. Benjamin attempts two kinds of solution to this dilemma. In the first model, that even problematic (distracted or entertained) reception becomes a formulative principle of art so that the integrity of the work is preserved even with changes in the conditions of reception. It is in this crucial respect that Benjamin's aesthetic theory can be distinguished from conventional sociologies of art. He does not simply inquire into the sociological fate of an achieved work; the effect of the work, its function, the reception it will get, fall, in Benjamin's view, among the deepest and most basic formative principles in the very composition of the work of art. In the case of Beaudelaire, Benjamin cites the inattentive audience that the poet can expect as one of the fundamental formal problems of his art, and he demonstrates that precisely this unfavorable atmosphere for poetic creation becomes the material basis for great poetry.[16] In other words, Benjamin deals with the conflict between integrity and reception by incorporating the end point of aesthetic communication with the starting point of aesthetic intention.

Benjamin's second model follows the inverse strategy; here he finds aesthetic integrity exhausted within the novelties of reception. In the case of film, regarded as a new art form that has no tradition and is totally at the mercy of modern forms of reception and autonomy, as traditionally conceived, Benjamin does not try at all to inquire into the possibilities and conditions of artistically great films. In this sense, strictly speaking, he is not developing a film aesthetic at all—he is not conceiving of film as an aesthetic form. On the contrary he explicitly argues that, in the period of mechanical reproduction of works of art, "the work of art becomes a creation of entirely new functions, among which the one we are conscious of, the artistic function, later be recognized as incidental."[17] In this process the work of art is relativized.

In a derivation from Lukacs's conception, art may be said to function as humanity's time-consciousness, an independent sphere of life crucial to the species' sense of identity. It is both memory and future/hypothesis, the kind of consciousness of self that recalls and refers to mankind's most important values and intentions. At the same time, art always speaks for those small communities (not the whole of society) that feel the radical need for such aesthetic function; and consequently art is always a demand for an extended consensus, for a community that will assert validity.

In Benjamin's conception, art no longer functions as such an autonomous sphere of life. It is said to lose its autonomy, its aura; it becomes naked information available for political appropriation. Adorno had said that the deaestheticization of art may be a sign of its development, in that it may conquer new territories, but only provided that it genuinely creates form. Benjamin takes a different route. He gives up on aesthetic form, in favor of a preoccupation with the utilization of aesthetic content. Put differently, he shifts levels and turns his attention to the technical medium as a political form in a social arena. In this context, the two points he raises, concerning cinematic technique designed for mass reception, and the effect of this technique on masses of people, both become very important.

Now, the reason that film is important for Benjamin is precisely because of its democratic character—in the sense of his claim that film is universally accessible and sensorially direct, that everyone is an expert, and that criticism of film is one with enjoyment of film. Today we know that the art film and the mass entertainment film have separated into different categories and although the art film remains to an extent popular, it is no longer a democratic genre. Nevertheless Benjamin's question can be said to remain just and significant: how is a democratic, collective reception of art possible? Benjamin's hopes are pinned on mass agitational film, and his answer is formulated in terms of reception tied to entertainment. He discovers a fundamental characteristic of modern reception: distracted appreciation. Concentration would lead into the work of art; the distracted mass consumes, absorbs, assimilates the work of art.

Architecture is the art that Benjamin offers as the prototype for this kind of reception. The analogy is revealing and opens Benjamin to the Adorno type criticism that he reduces art to a political utility. For architecture is uniquely that form of art whose practical utility is completely independent and separable from the aesthetic. Aesthetic formation, by contrast, cannot break away from the practical point of view. This principle remains creative in architecture, but it is destructive of form in every other art. But Benjamin, having chosen the effect of art, often interpreted as direct and immediate, as the key problem in his aesthetic, stylizes this effect into pure utility and instrumentality as far as his history of film is concerned. As it happens, contrary to the utopian hopes of the film and aesthetic avant-garde it was precisely the manipulative film industry with its offerings of pseudo-, or substitute art, that was able to make the most of this characteristic of film; namely that film is able to have an immediate, useable, instrumental impact on everyday life.

The whole question of aura hangs in the balance on this problem of utility and immediacy. It may be said, in any case, that Benjamin develops his point of view of modern media too narrowly out of the visual arts where aura may be tied to the material uniqueness of the object. More importantly, Benjamin fails to consider the forms of mass communication to be aesthetic forms and consequently surrenders them to his naive political assumption that the mass movement which he expects to mobilize (with the help of film) to defeat fascism will also mean the end of the bourgeois world and hence open up a world of higher creative immediacy. But the world of domination has remained, while even the former audiences of the Brechtian epic theater are gone. In such a context, it would seem to be disastrous to embrace the disintegration of all aesthetic distance and plenitude and aura, and to permit the reduction of all autonomous aesthetic transcendence to the topical immediacies of politically manipulable information.

But the paradoxes of the problematic of aura cut even deeper than that in the new world of advanced capitalism a generation after Benjamin. Aura is now reproduced systematically at the level of social code. Benjamin speaks of changes in aesthetics since the appearance of the new photo-mechanical procedures for transmitting cultural messages. He argues that the loss of aura, of that distance which guaranteed originality and authenticity, alters aesthetic meaning—indeed that through the camera and the cinema, art becomes information de-ritualized, manipulable, and accessible to all. We have to add that the volume of information increases dramatically to the point where the production, movement, and appropriation of information become our dominant social preoccupation. The proliferation through our new cultural media of a virtual infinity of signs constitutes a multiplex information environment that becomes internalized as our primary social experience. One thing that this situation is not accessible to in any creative fashion is an intervention conceived simply on the level of the political mass—such homogenized collectivist fictions are best left to the hallucinations of political orthodoxy.

Three kinds of comments can be made here. Firstly, we are not at all in adequate touch with this process and are very poorly oriented with respect to its creative possibilities; in fact, we may decay in face of the challenge, owing to the malignancy of our favored social forms and mythologies. Secondly, in the multi-dimensional symbolic universes that we have come to inhabit, there exist vast possibilities for artists; moreover, all of us are willy-nilly bound to live as (more or less talented) artists. In other words, with the aid of our new technologies we may achieve richer freedoms, provided we create adequate forms.

Thirdly (and this is the socio-cultural center of gravity of our contemporary auratic problematic), in symbolic space-time the interface of art and information creates a systematic code of signifiers, separated from what each might signify on the basis of a one-to-one correspondence, and endowed with a tremendous social power attached (more or less) to the basic logic of the continuum of domination. The very meaning of an object—as we have recently begun to thematize[18]—is no longer in relation to a need (a utility) to be satisfied; it has become arbitrary, indifferent to this need. Its meaning resides in its abstract and systematic relation with all other object-signs. It can then be consumed in its specificity along with all other object-signs in the framework of the systematic code that is formed by the system of abstract relations that the object-signs entertain among themselves. Aura is reborn on a system wide level, in the distance between the phenomenological level of individual need and desire and the epistemological level of the codification of the signs. The solid "reality" of nineteenth-century rationalizing yields to the hyperreality of the code and of simulations, models and facsimiles. Significance congeals into the false aura of the false structural totality of the generalized code. Autonomous subjectivity retreats and declines.

No structural or technical view can help us see our way clear of this dilemma: the prolonged cybernetic coordination of information, in and of itself, can only contribute to an over bureaucratized stagnation, or drift, or decay. As everything is absorbed into the code, like light into a black hole, the resultant closed system becomes entropic and enters into crisis. (I have already described the process in other terms above, in connection with the Frankfurt School's response to the one-dimensional transitional period between entrepreneurial and state regulated capitalism.) Free spaces must open up, crevices in the falsely auratic code, necessary for the survival and recreation of the code itself. The false aura that grew, sustained and objectified itself by a usurpation of collective subjectivity may begin to yield—not to collective instrumental utility—but to the spontaneity of autonomous (inter)subjective power. We are now on uncharted land though it is recognizable as the terrain of philosophy of history. And here we can return to Benjamin and conclude with a final sweep along this ground.

John Berger suggests that the awakened interest in Benjamin coincides with the current period of reexamination of Marxism occurring all over the world. Concerning this interregnum, he writes: "The interregnum is anti-deterministic, both as regards the present being determined by the past and the future by the present. It is skeptical of so-called historical laws, as it is also skeptical of a supra-historical value implied by the notion of overall Progress or Civilization. It is aware that excessive personal political power always depends for its survival upon appeals to an impersonal destiny: that every true revolutionary act must derive from a personal hope of being able to contest in that act, the world as it is. The interregnum exists in an indivisible world, where time is short, and where the immorality of the conviction that ends justify means lies in the arrogance of the assumption that time is always on one's side and that, therefore, the present moment—the time of the Now as Walter Benjamin called it—can be compromised or forgotten or denied."[19]

Berger is undoubtedly right to identify these dimensions as relevant to Benjamin's importance and growing reputation. At the same time, as I have earlier suggested, Benjamin's philosophy of history is problematic, as is most evident from the "Theses on the Philosophy of History." In rejecting the homogeneous empty time of social democratic evolutionary theory, Benjamin has recourse to the revolutionary explosion of Messianic time that ruptures the fabric of history. "For every second of time (is) the strait gate through which the Messiah might enter."[20] This conception carries two thoughts: unpredictably and at any-time/any-place, the great event may occur; and thereupon everything will be instantly different from before, transfigured and redeemed.

This indeed appears to be nondeterministic in its first aspect. But in order to protect the future from the syllogisms of rationalist deductivism, and the Now from the imposition of the sterile claims of abstractly deduced future, the future is closed off from any scrutiny at all, indeed from any projected, intended, or speculated connection with Now. This attempt to sustain the future as pure Negativity, as a radical value alternative whose further determination is denied in order to keep it free, unsoiled by the past, and un-instrumentalized, produces ultimately too radical a discontinuity and becomes a transcendent conception that altogether occludes the question of historical subjectivity. For no future can be a human future, our future, if it is not conceived in the form of a "from now to the not-yet-now," that is in a form that includes a transition, some moments of continuity, some links between memory and intention. Thus in backing away from immanent determinism, in the end the conception falls through the trap door into the unknowns of transcendent determinations.

The second aspect, likewise, in the allusion to instantaneous correlation and transformation of all aspects of human life (if only to blow everything out of the continuum of history) in the image of messianic redemption, reintroduces at the transcendent level that supra-historical logic of homogeneity that was to be cast out. The event magnetizes the entire human field.

Curiously, Benjamin's critique of the transparent, homogeneous, empty time of rationalism arrives at its mirror image, the opaque, homogeneous, saturated time of irrationalism. This, too, is part of its appeal for a certain audience. Both conceptions are tendentially equally totalitarian in their references to both future and past. What they share is a belief in the rationality of the present system of domination, whose continuation they either affirm or deny. Both permit the actual to usurp and exhaust the notion of the rational. To cut it off, to end the continuum, then, Benjamin abandons the dialogue with the future (in the sense of 'from now to the not-yet-now') and points only to an apocalyptic future (eschatological rupture).

Correspondingly he abandons dialogue with the past; the future is to be an absolute *novuum*. It is this same dynamic that we found on the micrological level in his libertarian/objectivist conception of a composition of citations that denied the authority of the present (that present that has no continuable future) to dialogue with the past and interrogate it according to its own rationality (structure of needs, desires, codes) and sense of continuity. The method here indicates a wish to withdraw into particulars that are not dominated by the concept, that are not rational. On the level of the philosophy of history and on the level of epistemology, an inability to experience and conceive of the prevailing totalitarian social rationality as only transitionally one-dimensional and not in permanent exhaustive command of the entire field of reason entices the theorist into the mysticism of unreason.

There is no easy solution to this; as long as the structures of the capitalist domination occupy most of the social field, its antinomies will have continuing play. The drama of rationalism and irrationalism that Lukacs explored in *History and Class Consciousness* evidently proceeds to unfold.

Walter Benjamin could not so totally transcend his time—the most barbaric of this century—as to leave us with a complete viable cultural model. Yet precisely because he responded fully to his time—and because we have the option to dialogue with his work in terms of a value continuity that we can choose between past, present, and future—the reconstruction and appropriation of his work in the course of a full inquiry into its parameters promises to yield valuable notes toward a conception of reason and culture that may be coextensive with a sense of both limits and possibilities, and may mediate our new historical present toward a self-emancipating future that is—as Benjamin would have it—never deducible from the immediate givens.

NOTES

1. *Charles Beaudelaire: A Lyric Poet in the Era of High Capitalism*, trans. Harry Zohn (London: NLB, 1973); *Illuminations*, edited and introduced by Hannah Arendt, trans. Harry Zohn (New York: Harcourt, Brace and World, 1968); *Understanding Brecht*, introduced by Stanley Mitchell, trans. Anna Bostock (London: NLB, 1973).

2. Letter to F. C. Rang, December 9, 1923.

3. *Prisms*, trans. Samuel and Shierry Weber (London: Neville Spearman, 1967), p. 239.

4. See Bernd Witte, "Benjamin and Lukacs, Historical Notes on the Relationship between Their Political and Aesthetic Theories," *New German Critique 5* (Spring 1975), pp. 16–17.

5. See Paul Piccone, "Introduction," in *The Frankfurt Reader*, ed. Andrew Arato and Eike Gebhardt (New York: Urizen, 1977).

6. "Theses on the Philosophy of History," no. 7 *Illuminations*, p. 258.

7. See Martin Jay, *The Dialectical Imagination: A History of the Frankfurt School and the Institute of Social Research, 1923–1950* (Boston, 1973), passim.

8. See Bernd Witte, "Benjamin and Lukacs," pp. 16–17.

9. See "Correspondence with Benjamin," *New Left Review* 81 (Sept.–Oct 1973), pp. 55–80.

10. "Walter Benjamin: Towards a Philosophy of Language," *Times Literary Supplement* (22 August 1968), p. 887.

11. Maurice Blanchot, "Walter Benjamin: Reprises," *La Nouvelle Revue Française*, no. 93 (1960), pp. 475–83.

12. Piccone, "Introduction," *The Frankfurt Reader*.

13. Ibid.

14. Frederic Jamieson, "Benjamin as Historian, or How to Write a Marxist Literary History," *Minnesota Review* 3 (Fall 1974), p. 116.

15. Sandor Radnoti, in an excellent Hungarian article entitled "A Filmhatas Ertelmezése Walter Benjamin Esztétikajaban" ("On the Interpretation of the Impact of Film in Walter Benjamin's Aesthetic Theory"), has stressed this point. My comments below on Benjamin's film aesthetic follow closely a part of Radnoti's argument.

16. See "On Some Motifs in Baudelaire," *Illuminations*, pp. 157–202.

17. "The Work of Art in the Age of Mechanical Reproduction," *Illuminations*, p. 227.

18. See especially, Jean Baudrillard, *La société de consommation* (Paris: S.G.P.P., 1970); *Pour un critique de l'économie politique du signe* (Paris: Gallimard, 1972); *L'échange symbolique et la mort* (Paris: Gallimard, 1976).

19. "Antiquarian and Revolutionary," *New Society* (June 18, 1970), p. 1067.

20. "Theses on the Philosophy of History," no. 18, *Illuminations*, p. 266.

XIV

QUESTIONS OF PROPERTY
FILM AND NATIONHOOD

Stephen Heath

The context of this first Martin Walsh lecture is the Film Studies Association of Canada conference on "Cinema and Nationhood"; its intention is to honor the memory of Martin Walsh in a way that he would have thought appropriate—raising and attempting to develop a little some current issues in film theory that would be part of a critical discussion of the idea of a "national cinema." What follows is thus turned toward the conference and its theme but stands prior to it: the aim, remembering how much Martin Walsh's own work was concerned with a certain political-theoretical avant-garde represented in practice by the films of Godard and Straub-Huillet, is to indicate a series of questions of property in cinema, to suggest something of their importance for us today.

That the conference theme involves a necessary reflection on cinema is not as simply obvious as it appears. The cinematic relation of nationhood, at least if this latter is conceived politically, a site not of given unity but of contradiction and present struggle, must problematize the cinematic, the institution *of cinema*, which is nevertheless the very condition of its existence, with 'nevertheless' the term of contradiction and present struggle in cinema. One version of this is provided by four Canadian filmmakers (Betty Ferguson, Garonce Mapleton, Judy Steed, Joyce Wieland): "What has filmmaking got to do with Canadian identity and Canadian independence? How do you avoid American ownership in your own film?"[1] The question of ownership goes further than the directly economic (which is not to say that that at any particular moment it is not the most direct concern), extends into the difficulties with regard to film and cinema of such expressions as 'identity', 'independence', 'your own film'. How are films owned? What are the incidences of proprietorship in cinema? It is these questions of property that will be envisaged here, bringing them round to consideration of the fact—the operations, the effects—of the cinematic institution that any political undertaking in national cinema has to face. The questions fall under the following headings: *image, sound and language, representation and sexual difference, ideology and representing, film as historical present use-value.*

The film image is given first and foremost as the property of the reality from which by the accepted conventions of photographic reproduction it is seen to derive (inaugurating that play of copy and origin that is a constant point of exploited pleasure in film). Achieved within the photographic industry, the industry in which the Lumière brothers and Edison are inventors and businessmen, the cinema is caught up in a founding ideology of the visible, reality there to be seen. That presence, however, is equally the property of the subject as spectator, the subject-relation of the vision of 'reality' (the play of copy and origin is precisely a play of *an image for a subject*). From the start, and necessarily, it is not simply 'reality' that is proposed on the screen but the subject of that reality too, its completion: in fact, the subject in reality produced by cinema—which cinema really produces, for which it assigns the 'reality'. Cinema is not a vision but a circuit of vision, the overlay in which the look of the camera and the look of the eye come together, complete, make each other's turn, realize in that movement the subject in place. The circuit is effectively a shift of relation to the real, is effectively a new construction of position: the camera displaces the eye, assumes its power, sees for it, and returns that power on the terms of the institution of cinema, the terms of a standard vision, a standard of vision, remade from film to film and then becoming, as previously and continuously the photograph itself the currency of reality, subject, their relation—in the way that determines both the enthusiasm for what is then regarded as the new 'medium', the attainment of the 'universal language' acclaimed by the first Lumière spectators, "*la langue universelle est trouvée!*"[2] and the disdain with which it is viewed by the guardians of national tradition as minority culture, as witness Leavis for whom "the motion picture, by virtue of its intrinsic nature, is a species of amusing and informational Esperanto."[1]

The stake of the film image is in its relation, its force of enunciation. Notions of an immediately unifying language do not come by chance in connection with a cinema that is established exactly in respect of those same notions, for the universalized 'mass', held to the one image, to that identity (after all, as Straub puts it, "Esperanto is a bourgeois dream"[4]); a cinema that elides the possibilities of disjunction that formed the project of Vertov's kino-eye—disalign camera-eye and human-eye in the interests of the redefinition of the subject-eye of the individual into an operative, transforming relation to reality—or those of that dialectical development of forms posed by Bataille after a lecture by Eisenstein—"the determination of a dialectical development of facts as *concrete* as visible forms would be literally shattering."[5] From its early history on, the idea of cinema as language is symptomatically general and vague, so much analogical gesturing—images as equivalent to words and so on (that whole 'metaphor' of language that Metz's initial semiology rigorously explored and displaced); with the generality and vagueness being the very stance of the establishment, cinema playing between articulation and reproduction (a play summed up in expressions of the kind "the language of reality itself") to offer a form of justification by seeing, meanings sanctioned in and by the seen.

The force of the enunciation of the image in cinema is something akin to a veritable terrorism: image and succession of images are regulated, an accomplished fact, the enunciation as though over, absent, but with that absence filled by the given presence on the screen, without fissure, impossible to interrupt. In one of his first essays, Metz insists on a correspondence between the filmic image and the sentence—as opposed to the word—in natural language; the image is always actualized: "a close-up of a revolver does not mean 'revolver' (a purely virtual lexical unit) but at the very least, and without speaking of the connotations, it signifies 'Here is a revolver!' "[6] What Metz is pointing to is the existence of a shot as utterance, its being-there-for, its address: every image is the compulsion of an event, not some simple entry of a word. That compulsion, however, comes with a certain 'innocence' (the ideological potential of the photographic-filmic image, the play mentioned above), the marks of the enunciation are relatively unspecified in the image (there are not equivalents, for instance, to the pronouns in language); we know how to contradict a linguistic utterance, we are much less sure with an image, are confronted with its apparent completeness *as image* (hence the falseness of which Godard often speaks: the image false inasmuch exactly as it brings with it an effacement of the act of its proposition; truth is to be grasped not simply in the enounced but equally in the enunciation, in the distances, gaps, contradictions of the two). Which completeness, coming back round once more to the image as utterance, is precisely, only apparent: the image is never complete in itself—if it were, there would be no place for any viewer and so, finally, no place for any image—and its limit is its enunciation, its address—the limit where it enters the circuit of vision, completes with the subject it thus entertains.

The image completes on the subject as *its* spectator, term of a constant appropriation. How to resist an image, to refuse its belonging? "It is with the images that captivate its eros of living individual that the subject comes to deal with its implication in the sequence of signifiers," writes Lacan,[7] almost as though describing cinema with its succession of images, the subject implicated there, ceaselessly, as the 'there' of the image. Cinema works to the utmost that regime of the privilege of the subject that has it that the image cannot but be *mine*, by *my* seeing,[8] even when nevertheless it is seen—a seen—*for* me; which is the problem of belonging, the difficulty of contradicting 'my' image. The succession is then, of course, exploited to compound this closing—this closeness—of the image on the subject: articulation of images as continuity, narrativization of that continuous articulation as the steady assignment of a developing view, a stable memory, something for someone, someone for that something, these meanings, this vision. The desire for images is maintained and fulfilled in the very time of the succession, mapped by the realized film into the time of that desire, of the process of captivation: perpetual balancing of seeing-seen, identification with camera—identification with person or object, from shot to shot and within the single shot itself via movement of human figures or camera creating new planes of fascination, a kind of extreme rendering of the scopic drive. Which is the necessity in Godard or Straub-Huillet of the attempt to disappropriate the subject of the image: images divided, crossed out, written over, multiplied in the single frame, returned to a television screen in Godard; images interrupted by black leader or, more interestingly, drawn out into an excessive time of vision and movement, something of a long chance of realities— the car sequence of *History Lessons,* the pans of *Fortini/Cani*—in Straub-Huillet.

The film image, then, cannot be accepted without questions as a simple point of departure for a political practice of cinema. Linked to a production of 'the visual', the illusion of a direct vision and the subject position-desire, the imaginary, of that illusion, it must be posed as false. The visual in this sense does not exist: the image and its subject completion are produced in codes which include, among others, the codes of the specific machination—the operation—of the image in cinema, the codes of the constructed reality represented, and the codes of language itself—the whole problem, to go no further, of the nomination of visible object, of their linguistic visibility. The image is never pure, never 'an image'; strictly, indeed, the image is not an order of the visible but of the invisible, a speculation that adjoins real, symbolic, imaginary, the subject against difference, transformation, the history of the subject in process (symptom: the degree to which the coming of photograph and cinema has undermined the critical production of history, henceforth fixed as simply past, as spectacle). The problem cited by the Groupe Dziga Vertov in *Pravda*—"sounds which are already right on images which are still false"—or Vent d'est—"this is not a just image, just an image"—is always contemporary.

That quotation from *Pravda* raises the question of sound in cinema, more particularly of the relation of spoken language and image. It is very evident, of course, that sound is quite directly bound up with issues of property in the history of cinema: the coming of sound ensures Hollywood domination of the film industry at home and abroad and the banks' domination of Hollywood; equally, it sustains certain class definitions of cinema, confirming a normalization of the audience in terms of the generalizing of middle-class ideology; equally again, it provides the point of reference for the elaboration of the legal status of ownership in connection with creative contribution in film, the property rights of individuals involved predicated on the traditional categories of literary expression, the whole ideology of the word, and the ownership by producers, production companies, predicated in turn on the buying of those alienable rights.[9]

Beyond those issues, but constantly participating in them, the question of sound is the question of language and of property in and through language. Comolli, in his series of essays on cinema technology, stresses a relative lack of reflection during the time of the development toward sound as to the use to which the new possibility could and would be put: "the talking picture would talk, that was that."[10] Which meant, once the variety-feature aspect of cinema performance important in the initial stages of sound had been displaced by the power of the word, the triumph of the aesthetic forms of linguistic organization of the middle-class—the forms of bourgeois theater, support, and source of that 'theatrical cinema' foreseen in its ascendency and so loathed by Vertov would be established. The sound track is given as hierarchically subservient to the image track and its pivot is the voice as the presence of the character in frame, a supplement to the dramatization of space, along with accompanying 'sound effects', with the narrative modes of cinema established in respect of that theatricality. The emphasis is everywhere on the unity of sound and image across the voice (locus of synthronization), the latter at once subservient to the image (literally conceived as in the perspective of the image which in return it 'deepens'; hence the whole discussion of 'sound perspective' in the technical journals of the nineteen-thirties)[11] and entirely dominant in the dramatic space it opens within it (precisely the 'deepening'), setting the limits of scenes, casting little narrative parts readily available for the easy dubbing required by the international marketing of the industrial product. Marginal in the Hollywood industry, the documentary, duly categorized, receives a complementary standard of sound and image relation: the document of the speaking subject, the topic of the film; the control of the commentary, the ruling enunciation, the unlocated, unquestionable voice-over, preponderantly male, that is there with the images, declares their meaning, assigns the truth that the image must express. Whether in feature film or documentary (and the division-categorization would itself need to be grasped in its ideological functioning), language owns the images, determining their space, their time, their sense, monopolizes them, making them one.

Obviously, the very choice of which language can be crucial in a given social-cultural situation, as between English and French, for example. It is important to remember, however, that choices are made, conflicts engaged just as much within the particular language, a single unified system only under the abstraction of linguistics in most of its current versions. The articulation between language and ideology is complex[12] and the former can in no way be subsumed into the latter, which would be to ignore its productivity, its process of meaning and subject, yet it remains nevertheless that language is never encountered other than as discourse, within a discursive formation productive of subject relations in ideology, and that there is no such thing as a simply national language. Benjamin was right, and right for us today despite Stalin's subsequent correct rectification of the unproblematic location of language as a superstructural category, to hold to the stress made in the following passage which he quotes from the Russian linguist Marr in his 1935 article on the sociology of language: "One leaves the realm of science and of every real field of investigation when one envisages such and such a language of a supposedly national civilization as though it were a matter of a mother tongue employed by the whole mass of the population: national language as a phenomenon independent of states and classes is from the very start a fiction."[13] Language is a site of struggle, and a site of struggle in film: imagine a cinema that would show what was at stake in its language and make heard what was invisible in its images. Examples? *Differently, Othon,* or *Ici et ailleurs.*

There is an area of political concern within which questions of property with regard to the images and sounds of cinema are acute, an area which intersects with and comes back on any discussion of cinema and nationhood, that of representation and sexual difference. In the films of the dominant cinema, the imaginary of the film is 'the woman', the signifier the look as phallus, as order, as the very apparatus of the film—cinema as relay of looks, ensuring play in coherence, the constancy of speculation—which serves endlessly to remake the scene, the theater of the male gaze, the total spectacle; with narrative balancing out, accounting for the movement of the symbolic, taken up in the seen as scene: the object lost and gained, a whole scenario of fantasy. That scenario can be grasped most readily, outside of its flat assumption, it is exasperation in the classic tensions—the work of an Ophuls, for example—of auteur-art/industry-standard: fascinated return on the woman as center, the imaginary as masquerade become the very surface of the text, laid out, *exposed:* the masquerade of 'the woman' (the luxurious feminine of jewelry, furs, mirrors . . .), the masquerade of 'woman in film', cimema's object of desire, its pursuit-and-goal (ceaseless tracking of the woman for the gaze, the look, of her spectacle, of the desire to come there in a ceaseless momentum of appropriation at its extreme in a film like *Madame De . . .*). The sole imaginary? The sole signifier? 'Sole' in the sense that any difference is caught up in that structured disposition, that fixed relation in which the film is centered and held, to which the times and rhythms and excesses of its symbolic tissue and its narrative drama of vision are bound. The crucial issue in this context is then that of the place of women in that relation, the place of the look for women, an issue that has frequently been considered in terms of an emphasis on a lack of investment in the look by women; as Luce Irigaray puts it: "Investment in the look is not privileged in women as in men. More than the other senses, the eye objectifies and masters. It sets at a distance, maintains the distance. In our culture, the predominance of the look over smell, taste, touch, hearing has brought an impoverishment of bodily relations. It has contributed to disembodying sexuality. The moment the look dominates, the body loses in materiality. It is perceived above all externally and the sexual becomes much more a matter of organs that are highly circumscribed and separable from the site of their assembly in a living whole. The male sex becomes *the* sex because it is very visible."[14]

For a woman to take place in a film, in the films of cinema, is for her to represent male desire: to stand as the term of a social representation of desire determined by and redetermining a structure of division—the social operation of 'male'/'female', 'man'/'woman'—and oppression on the basis of that division—the difference assigned functioning as the inevitability, the right, of the domination of the one category by the other. This is clearer than ever today when images of women as woman's image are a deliberate focus of ideological concern in dorninant cinema, from *Three Women* to *The Turning Point,* from *The Goodbye Girl* to *Coma,* in differing degrees of abjection (strategy of a film like *Coma:* produce a 'strong' woman's image to weaken it, and her, back into place: she refuses to fix him a beer but to allow the film to fix the woman in the shower; she leaves but, alone, her hand stretches out too late to the ringing phone in a pathetically held shot; and so on, in a perpetual process of admission and erasure, and anyway always a bind of *images*). The question is finally that of the fact of cinema, of this late nineteenth-century machine (contemporary with psychoanalysis, itself worrying over what Freud calls "the riddle of the nature of femininity") and its intrication in a specific representing function, a specific construction of a male desire (so too psychoanalysis? is the nature of those decisive encounters in its history—Breuer and Anna O, Freud and Dora, . . . Lacan and Aimée—quite by chance?). Yes, of course, the question is crude, simplistic (as is that parenthetically addressed to psychoanalysis), not allowing for the historical diversity of cinematic practices, but it remains nevertheless important, must inform any consequent alternative practice, whether attempting to evict all scene and realize film in the process of its material effects (the 'structural/

materialist' emphasis of Peter Gidal[15]) or to produce a different scene, a new relation for women to film (the 'new language' demanded as an urgent task by the Musidora group, for example).[16]

Which is to return to the look, the question of cinema for women there in that relation. The whole problem is raised acutely by Oshima Nagisa's *In the Realm of the Senses,* a film that seems to come close in its difficulty to a passage in which Irigaray develops the idea of women's non-investment in the look: "the possibility that a nothing seen, that a not masterable by the look, by specula(riza)tion, may have some reality would indeed be intolerable to man, since threatening his theory and practice of representation . . ."[17] Oshima's film is crossed by that possibility, which is its very trouble of representation: the look in the film sees everything and sees nothing, and that nothing seen is woman present and negated and present again in the edge of that negation, that nothingness, according to a contradiction indicated by Oshima, in directly symptomatic fashion, in a comment on the film: "when I write a script, I depict women, but when it comes to the filming, I end up centrally depicting men."[18] But this is to say that the possibility, a nothing seen, is not posed, as it were, from some outside; on the contrary, it is produced as a contradiction within the given system of representation, the given machine. The problem is one of a specific institution of positions and relations of meaning, not one of an essence to be recovered, and the 'nothing seen' is grasped as such from within that institution, as a point of and against its particular structure of repression, its particular construction (just as the 'invisibility' of the sex of the woman described by Irigaray is only a figure of an order that defines woman from man and sets her as the scene of his representation and power). Thus cinema divides not in any immediate sense on men and women but on these positions and relations of 'man' and 'woman' in its representations and its production of those representations, the subjectivity it engages; with the lack of investment in the look by women realized *there,* ideologically, not from something originally wanting in women, women then being turned back to a kind of archaic sensuality (a place in which they have been historically accommodated by men).

Any political discussion of cinema and nationhood has to involve discussion of sexual difference but that in no sense, or in a reactionary sense only, can be conceived of as the 'addition' of some 'further problem': the latter discussion is there in the very terms of the former as point of contradiction and struggle in representation, in the institutions of representing, in the property of images and sounds in the relations of men and women, their constructions.

Representation: images, argumentation, deputation; the turn together—representing—of these different elements is important. The history of the individual as subject and as subject in and for a social formation is never finished. Its constant termination, the stable relation of subject in constructed meaning, a specific subject-construction, is the effect of representation, and an ideological effect: any social formation depends for its existence not simply on the economic and political instances but also on a reasoning of the individual as subject, reproduced in images, identities of meaning, finding his or her delegation there. The term of this process is suture: the join of the subject as unity of the recognition of sense, ground of

intelligibility. Cinema is an institution of representing, a machine for the fabrica-
tion-maintenance of representation; it is as such that it is a crucial investment, as
such that it is developed and exploited, for a narration of the subject in a narrative
that is its mapping—again and again, the constant termination—within the limits of
existing representations and their determining social relations. The category of this
mapping can be called the novelistic:[19] the location of the spectator subject of
cinema in a unity which encompasses, from apparatus to final narrative image, the
individual *as* individual view within given social orders of meaning that are returned
as his or her place and action; with family relations taken as the arena of the
social-individual construction-placing and of the necessary containment—
possibility and limitation in one—of action; cinema as family machine (after and
concurrent with the novel, prior to and concurrent with television, according to that
pattern of taking over in which one machine is replaced by another that includes it
and thus allows it a certain displacement into margins of excess to be newly
exploited and delimited, commercially and ideologically; as with cinema today, for
example, turned to a violence and pornography not available to television as the
current central machine), all tension of change articulated within the drama of the
films produced and within the very function of the producing, the very institution of
representing.

What is now being realized, in fact, with regard to the history of the cinema,
though its writing has not as yet shifted in consequence, is that history is not to be
understood via the concept of 'realism', ideas of "progress towards realism," and so
on, but, first and foremost, in respect of terms of subjectivity, of the contract of the
subject in representation, exactly the representing operation of cinema. Something
of this can be fairly readily grasped, moreover, in the contradictions of property and
expense to which the various technological innovations-elaborations forming part of
that history give rise. Family machine in its representing not in its ownership,
cinema weights expense massively on the side of production, an area of capitalist
(and/or national, state) investment, with reception inexpensive, the price of the
ticket, of one's 'place'; innovations-elaborations greatly reinforce this expense,
hence inaccessibility, of production (sound and color are the obvious examples),
creating indeed conditions of *national* inaccessibility, the collapse, weakening or
sheer impossibility of even beginning to exist of many national film industries in the
face of the monopoly capitalist expansion of Hollywood. At the same time,
however, the wider implications of that expansion both in industries having interests
that go beyond the sole market of cinema—the photographic industry, for instance—and in the general ideological stake in representing for which cinema is
only one factor allow a crossing of cinema with technological developments—small
gages are the obvious example—that recast it in different versions of family
machine, notably that of the home movie. What remains constant is the very fact of
the production of the machines and the force of standardization achieved therein:
standardization of the technological base, the actual machinery; standardization of
the product, the film; standardization of the subject, the relations-positions of
meaning. The relatively inexpensive product is as standardized—and above all in
that 'variety' that is now sometimes acclaimed in it—as the expensive industrial one

capitalist industry): the 'personal' is simply, as it were, restandardized, the Super 8 home movie is a fully functioning *social* representing. The possibility, nevertheless, is that in the recasting necessarily involving as it does new availabilities of property for family individuals, certain loosenings are there to be used, certain dis-appropriations-rerelations can be made—16mm, Super 8 as terms for groups, of a struggle exactly against the available 'national cinema' (anyway usually multi-national, that is, American—"how do you avoid American ownership in your own film?").

History in cinema is nowhere other than in representation, representing, precisely the historical present of any film. Which is to say that the automatic conjunction of film and history-as-theme, as past to be shown today, an attractive strategy for a cinema developed in the perspective of a certain conception of nationhood, is an idealist abstraction, an ideal of film, and an ideal of history. The present of a film is always historical, just as history is always present—a fact of representation not a fact of the past, a production of discourses from the present, a construction, where the present is then equally always already historical, itself the process of that construction, a political reality. Cinema is part of that present process, which is where *its* history, the history of cinema, is crucial to film. To make a film is always at once a problem of film and cinema, a problem of a—of this—signifying practice and its specificity (the latter including the terms of its articulation of the non-specific-to-cinema), its institution. When Michel Foucault comments of the film *Moi Pierre Rivière* by Rene Allio that "it was difficult and truly extraordinary to be able to reduce the whole cinematic apparatus, the whole filmic apparatus to such slenderness,"[20] one has to reply that it is exactly in that supposed 'reduction' that the apparatus is most thick, most ideologically consistent. The history of a film cannot be collapsed into the alibi of the document, the past as referent-guarantee *(Moi Pierre Rivière* is full of 'cinema', not of 'the past'). Any relation of nation and history in cinema, then, is reactionary if not passed through reflection on its current reality, which reality—hence also the reflection—includes the specific institution of representing. Nationhood is not a given, it is always something to be gained; and a political national cinema must assume its history in that struggle.

On that assumption will depend the value for use of the particular cinema developed, the particular films made. In the dominant institution of cinema, films are set as far as possible within the limits of a strictly regulated—economically and ideologically—context of exchange: the film is a mode of exchange of subjects, a universal representative (which universality is its representing operation). "The relation between the film-text and the viewer is the prerequisite for political questions in the cinema."[21] Alternative practices are alternative insofar as they transform the relations of representation *against* representing, against the universal-izing conditions of exchange; representation held to use (a definition of Brechtian distanciation), that is, to division, disunity, disturbance of the (social) contract (of film).

That transformation engages, has to engage, the three instances of the relations of the spectator as subject in a film: *preconstruction, construction,* and *passage. Preconstruction* involves the ready-made positions of meaning that a film may adopt, not simply large categories, definition, political arguments, thematic boundaries, and so on, but equally, for example, the codes and orders of language itself, the existing social conventions of color, the available ideas of film (genre is a major factor of preconstruction). *Construction* is the subject-position related in the film, more or less coherent, more or less a simple finality. *Passage* is the performance of the film, the movement of the spectator making the film, taken up as subject in its multiple process of realization. The ideological achievement of any film is not merely in one or the other of these instances; it is first of all in its hold of the three together: the appropriation of preconstruction in construction (in fact, a reconstruction) and the process of that appropriation—with, in dominant cinema, narrativization, the movement to narrative mapping novelistic, the final term of that hold, catching up the spectator as subject in the image of the narrative, its images, and in the film as narration of that image, those images.

It is in these three instances and their hold that are produced the relations of representation of a film. Debate around films often stumbles over issues of effectivity, "the real effect of a film," deadlocks on notions of either "the text itself," its meaning "in it," or else the text as nonexistent other than "outside itself," in the particular responses it engages from any individual or individual audience—the text 'closed' or 'open'. The reading of a film, however, must be seen as neither constrained absolutely nor free absolutely but historical, and that historicality includes the determinations of the institution cinema, the conditions of the production of meanings, of specific terms of address. The property of a film is not yours or mine, whether makers or spectators, nor its; it is in a conjuncture of questions of property across those three instances of relation, which makes nationhood not a simple criterion that can be used—situation, theme, or whatever—to measure, evaluate, describe this or that film, this or that cinema. For a film, for a cinema, to begin to pose those questions of its property in a political definition of nationhood and to pose nationhood in a political definition of film and cinema is to begin to break exchange for use, universal for struggle, which after all is the real and urgent task.

As did many of you here, as did so many people elsewhere, I knew and loved Martin Walsh. None of you, with direct awareness of his work over five years to help develop Canadian film studies and film culture generally, will doubt that the theme of this conference would have been important to him. Nor can it be doubted, from the interests and emphases of his writings, that he would have wished that theme to involve the issues I have tried to raise in his memory. Let me say finally that I have been honored and moved to do so.

NOTES

1. "Canadian Home Movies," *Women and Film*, vol. 1, no. 5–6, 1974, p. 42.
2. Cf. G. Sadoul, *Histoire génerale du cinéma* (revised edition), vol. I (Paris: 1963), pp. 288–90.

3. F. R. Leavis, *For Continuity* (Cambridge: 1933), p. 28.

4. "Entretien avec J.-M. Straub et D. Huillet," *Cahiers du cinéma,* no. 223, August-September 1970, p. 50.

5. G. Bataille, *Oeuvres complètes,* vol. I (Paris: 1970), p. 230.

6. C. Metz, *Essais sur la signification au cinéma,* I (Paris: 1968), p. 72; trans. as *Film Language* (New York: 1974), p. 67.

7. J. Lacan, *Écrits* (Paris: 1966), p. 710.

8. "The privilege of the subject seems to be established here from that bipolar reflexive relation which has it that, as soon as I perceive, my representations belong to me." J. Lacan, *Le Seminaire livre XI* (Paris: 1973), p. 76.

9. Cf. B. Edelman, *Le Droit saisi par la photographie* (Paris: 1973), pp. 53–54; B. Brewster, "Brecht and the Film Industry," *Screen,* vol. 16, no. 4, Winter 1975, pp. 18–23.

10. J.-L. Comolli, "Technique et idéologie" (6), *Cahiers du cinéma,* no. 241 (September-October 1972), p. 20.

11. Cf. M. A. Doane, "Ideology and the Practices of Sound Editing and Mixing," paper presented to Milwaukee conference on *"The Cinematic Apparatus,"* February 1978.

12. Discussion can be found in S. Health, "Language, Literature, Materialism," *Substance,* no. 17, 1977, pp. 67–74; "Notes on Suture," section III, *Screen,* vol. 18, no. 4, Winter 1977/78, pp. 69–74.

13. W. Benjamin, *Schriften,* vol. III (Frankfurt am Main: 1972), p. 463.

14. Luce Irigaray, *Les femmes, la pornographie, l'érotisme,* ed. L.-H. Hans and G. Lapouge (Paris: 1978), p. 50.

15. Cf. P. Gidal, "Theory and Definition of Structural/Materialist Film," *Studio International,* November 1975, pp. 189–96; S. Heath, "Repetition Time: Notes around 'Structural/Materialist Film,' " *Wide Angle,* vol. 2, no. 3, pp. 4–11.

16. Cf. Musidora, *Paroles . . . elles tournent* (Paris: 1976).

17. L. Irigaray, *Speculum: de l'autre femme* (Paris: 1974), p. 57.

18. Quoted in *Cahiers du cinéma,* no. 285, February 1978, p. 72.

19. Cf. S. Heath, "Film Performance," *Ciné-tracts,* no. 2, 1977, pp. 14–16.

20. "Entretien avec Michel Foucault," *Cahiers du cinéma,* no. 271, November 1976, p. 53.

21. C. Johnston, "Introduction," *Edinburgh 77* Magazine, August 1977, p. 5.

XV

THE FUNDAMENTAL REPROACH
BERTOLT BRECHT AND THE CINEMA

Ben Brewster

I take my title, the "fundamental reproach," from a note in Brecht's *Arbeitsjournal,* the diary he kept from 1938 to his death in 1956. This fundamental reproach of Brecht's was one made to the cinema and film from the standpoint of a man of the theater. Even though he wrote this note in 1942 Brecht was more or less cut off from the theater and was attempting to make a living within the American cinema. My own sympathies are not with the theater, but on the contrary with the cinema, and I might as well admit that I rather dislike the theater, so I am not reproducing this series of criticisms of the cinema in order to imply that the theater and certainly the theater we know, does have enormous advantages over the cinema. On the contrary, my interest is to test Brecht's objections to the cinema and to suggest ways the cinema might be transformed in relation to them.

This diary entry dates from March 27th, 1942, and it was written in Los Angeles:

conversation with wiesengrund-adorno, who is very jumpy because of the curfew,[1] about the peculiarities of the theatre as opposed to the film. The lehrstück, the learning-play, can obviously be excepted for there the actors act for themselves alone. The theatre's first advantage over the film is in *dramatik* that is in the division between play and performance. In principle, of course, one could make as many filmings as one liked of one particular theme, but there hasn't yet been a 'piece' of that type. Of course, with films today controlled by clothes merchants and bankers, an artistic film is hardly conceivable. The USSR in fact already rather produces film which will not be ridiculous in five years time, and Chaplin's work too, is stylised so that the themes appear historicised, and still have flavour after some time. There are technical objections that can be made vis-à-vis music and also apply to speech. "The microphone is monaural, one-eared, and thus is unable to communicate music conceived in binaural terms, with its inherent sound perspective. Moreover there is a legally imposed limit to the number of cycles per second which are transmitted, and finally there is the problem of the hearing stripe."[2] Technical improvements might be made in all these respects, but I don't myself believe that all technical problems are soluble in principle. In particular, I think that the effect of an artistic presentation on its spectators is not independent of the effect of the spectators on the artist. In the theatre, the audience regulates the performance. The film has monstrous weaknesses in detail which seem unavoidable in principle. Here is the delocalisation of the sound; the hearer has first to put every line of dialogue into a character's mouth. Then there is the strict fixation of viewpoint; we only see what one eye, the camera, saw. This means that the actors have to act for this eye alone, and all actions become completely unilinear, and so on. More subtle weaknesses: the mechanical reproduction gives everything the character of a result: unfree and unalterable. Here we come back to the fundamental reproach. The audience no longer have any opportunity to change the artist's performance. They are not assisting at a production, but at a result of a production that took place in their absence.

This quotation contains a whole series of interesting problems which are worth discussing, but I think I should begin by making two caveats. First, the occasion is a discussion with Adorno, and Brecht is clearly paraphrasing him at various points in the note. It might thus seem that Brecht here is adopting Adorno's pessimism vis-à-vis the mass media, going back on the positions he had taken in the *Drei-groschenprozess* in 1931. I think my drawing out of Brecht's points will show that the position they imply is not an Adornoan one. Second, it is a common objection to the cinema, particularly from actors who are primarily stage actors and find acting in the cinema very difficult, that there is an empathy between performer and audience in the theater which is absent in the cinema. I think it is important to stress that Brecht is not making this objection to the cinema, he does not think that it is, as it were, a less empathetic medium than the theater. On the contrary, Brecht's point is that distantiation is precisely possible in the theater because of the co-presence of audience and actors. It is the co-presence that makes it possible to establish a distance from the actions which are portrayed on the stage.

I think this relation can be illuminated by a model for the way in which an epic theater or a progressive form of an art of representation would operate which, although I am not sure that Brecht ever directly refers to it, is implicit in a lot of his work: the model of a dialogue or conversation. In any conversation, there is a moment of identification or empathy *(Einfühlung)* between the two people engaged in conversation. There is the moment in which in hearing what the other conversant says, I identify with that person and simultaneously identify their objects, grasp their drift, what they mean. But there is also always the second moment in conversation where I separate myself from what has been said and reply. This separation from the objects is also a separation from the conversant. The mode of reply can always be one in which the basis of what has been said and the position from which it has been said can be challenged. A conversation is productive when it proceeds by establishing a concurrence in meaning, breaking with that concurrence and establishing (perhaps) a new one. The simplest way in which this occurs is when I challenge in somebody's conversation the use of a term; I say, you can't talk about such and such in those terms. There is a breaking with the set of identities established in common by the conversants and hence of their mutual identification, so that whatever is being talked about can be reconstructed in terms which will enable them to derive some use from the conversation. There is also, of course, something else that may occur in conversation, and that is that the conversants may come to a limit of this operation of redefinition, the limit at which dialogue ceases to be possible. It is at this limit that a political division is produced between the two speakers; a point of fundamental principled difference emerges through the conversation. Thus there is a possibility of a false unity between them being broken down in the process of conversation.

It seems to me that this model of what takes place in a conversation is very illuminating for the way in which Brecht conceives the relation between audience and actors or audience and presentation within the epic theater. One of the most famous examples he uses is in fact based on a kind of conversation intermediate between an ordinary conversation and a play: the example of the street accident. When the witnesses at an accident are called on to say what happened, they will act out what happened to whoever is requesting the information. Here there is an oscillation between presentation and conversation: the speaker goes over to the spot and lies down in the street and says, "She fell down here," and then gets up and says "and the car was over there," and so on. There is not just talk but also the performance of actions which are performed in the way things are discussed in a speech; that is, they are presented both for identification and then distantiation by the other partners in the dialogue.

Now when we turn to formal plays, we have a further series of problems. First there is the problem that Brecht excludes straight away at the beginning of the diary entry, that is the problem of the *Lehrstück,* the learning play, which is not intended to be performed before an audience at all, but only for the members of its cast, and I shall come back much later to talk about the *Lehrstück* in relation to the cinema. When, on the contrary, we are dealing with a play which is pre-written and is being formally produced for an audience, there is the set of problems that Brecht considers in this entry and in general, about the relation between the presentation, that is the performance, and the play.

First of all, there is one which is again very familiar: the problem of the relation between an actor and his or her role in the epic theater. For Brecht it was important that a distinction be maintained throughout the performance between the actors and the parts that they are fictionally playing. What is important here (especially when discussing it in relation to the cinema) is the fact that in the theater the co-presence of actors and audience ensures that there is one level at which the audience is assisting at a performance and can see actors on stage, which is what they have come to see, and at another level, precisely the level of the fiction that is being presented, they see these actors no longer as actors but as their fictional parts. But, given a certain kind of play in a certain kind of production with a certain kind of acting, the presence of the actor allows the distinction to be maintained. One can identify with the actor, which implies a separation from the role, and then identify with the role, and that implies a separation from the actor. To achieve identification with role and actor at one moment is precisely the aim of a theater of catharsis. There is the same oscillation between identification and nonidentification in epic acting as there is in conversation.

A second problem which Brecht discusses in the diary entry is that of the relation between the particular performance and the fact that what is being performed is a particular play, separate and separable from the performance. The word he uses, *Dramatik,* refers to the traditional theatrical text: what is inherited and a relative constant in the theater is the text of the words spoken by the actors, and a particular performance is a performance of that text. Brecht was not interested in a theater of improvisation and insisted on the importance of actors precisely quoting a text, but also, particularly in the last period when he was working with the Berliner Ensemble, he wanted a kind of documentation of the theater which would go beyond the text in this narrow sense into a whole series of other areas: the *Theaterarbeit* and the model books try to present photographic and other methods of documenting decor, grouping, gesture, and so on, which another particular performance will reproduce and adapt as it reproduces and adapts the traditional play text. In this difference between performance and text, which has to be maintained for Brecht and should be a moment of every performance, there is again something which relates to the model of conversation. *Mach Meinem Letzen Umzug,* Hans-Jürgen Syberberg's film which includes footage he shot on 8mm in 1952 of rehearsals for Brecht's Berliner Ensemble production of Goethe's *Urfaust,* contains a remarkable example of this. *Faust* is a classic text, but the Brecht production moves away from a conventional presentation of the text and, while keeping very strictly to Goethe's structure, produces a distance from the play as a classic and in so doing effects a transformation in the German cultural tradition, i.e., makes a political intervention. The production devalues Faust as the central figure until he becomes the type of the German ideologist as characterized by Marx, and the play thus becomes quite different. It remains in a sense very tragic, but the tragedy becomes the tragedy of Gretchen—what kind of ideological subjection must she be a victim of to be vulnerable to such a charlatan? This critique of German ideology operates not only at the level of the content of the play, but also in relation to where the play stands within the German classical tradition. A double operation is performed on the content of the play the the nature of a classical text. This only works because the text is Goethe's *Faust,* because the audience are not coming in to see something completely new. For the first time, they are coming to see a play which is a recognized classic in a production which displaces it in relation to that classical tradition.

It is easy to see that Brecht's objections might hold very strongly vis-à-vis the cinema; the kind of operations I have discussed are very largely obscured or made difficult by what are often quite strictly technical properties of the cinematic medium. I want to examine this fundamental reproach as it were from two sides. Firstly, from within the film text and its performance; and secondly, from the standpoint of the production, distribution, and exhibition of films, that is from the side of the cinema as industry.

Stephen Heath has argued that in the cinema as we know it, that is the cinema as it has developed within capitalist societies (the question as to whether it has developed fundamentally differently in socialist societies is a difficult one which I shall touch on a bit later), that the film has functioned as a machine to produce and reproduce what is outside the cinema as a set of memory images.[3] These images are retrospective, but they are insistently immediate—there is nothing behind this screen, beyond the memory projected on to it. Hence a second viewing of a film abolishes the first, becomes it. The distinction between moment of text and moment of performance is abolished. Brecht himself suggests that it would technically be possible to establish a body of film subjects and then make many films of each of those subjects, but I doubt whether that would make much difference. Within the institutions of the commercial cinema, particularly at periods when it has been dominated by studio production, there have been occasions when it has operated in almost that way—the notorious pile of scripts on Jack Warner's desk, which were made in succession, and when the bottom was reached, the names were changed in the top one and it was remade, and so on down the pile. This is a caricature, but there is a sense in which for a powerful studio system, subjects exist which can be made again and again and again, and yet there is never the relation between a text and its performance that Brecht singles out in the theater: the process of changing the name, and even more the very institutionalized nature of film performance and film-making for that performance convert the film into a new film which is then seen for the first time. If the audience says, that is just the same film as the one we saw last week, it would mark a failure of that adaptation for the institution.

Second there is the question Brecht raises about the unique perspective. As an effect of perspective projection and the way in which the screen is viewed in the cinema, all the audience see the picture from the same place. Acting is as it were directed at that ubiquitous place; there is no oblique view, whereas in the theater there are always as many points of view as there are seats, and some of these points of view can be quite oblique, so the play is not directed at the spectator in the same way. This is the area, also discussed by Stephen Heath, of identification with the camera, which is so central to film viewing. It is particularly important to emphasize this here because identification as it is normally used by Brecht in discussing the theater is identification with characters. In the cinema as we know it identification with the camera is always the ground upon which identification with character takes place. Hence in the structure of the point-of-view shot, to take the simplest example, in the alternation between shots of a character looking and shots of an object from what appears to be the position of the character, the fact that I can identify with the character by adopting his or her viewpoint depends on the fact that in the objective shot I had already vicariously adopted the viewpoint of the camera. In the theater my viewpoint remains my own from a particular place in the auditorium, looking at a performance as well as at a fiction. It is this identification with the camera that Brecht is talking about here, that again makes it difficult to separate the objects being shown from the process by which they are being shown, that is, the particular performance.

Finally, there is as within the theater the problem of the identification of actor and role. As everyone knows, stage acting is different from screen acting; it is often said that the difference stems from the possibility of the close-up producing an exaggerated style which is perfectly acceptable on the stage but unacceptable on the screen. However, there is something more central. In general, the kind of screen acting which has been most successful is that kind which precisely produces an identification between the actor in everyday life and the actor on the screen—John Wayne remains John Wayne whatever he is playing. The kind of acting which works within this system (which is by no means an acting of no skill) is one which obscures the separation between actor and role. The only times when this does come through in the narrative cinema are when the role itself includes that doubling to some degree. In the film in which Brecht himself participated, *Hangmen Also Die,* there are sequences which show torture, police brutality, as an established routine. The presentation of their work as routine is compared to the means employed by the Gestapo. In these sequences there is a break between the actions and the characters performing them, and thus, in a sense, between the actions and the actors. In sequences where the heroes and heroines of the film appear there is no such separation, and it is very hard to see how one could be accommodated to this cinematic form.

However, the traditional narrative cinema does exhibit an area of trouble vis-à-vis actor and role, precisely in the star system. Naturalistic presentation is consistently broken within the commercial cinema in the interests of the star system. This is most obvious in the costume picture, where however much attention goes into authenticity in the decor, the stars' clothes present a kind of compromise between historically authentic costume and the clothes the stars would wear in everyday life. But this trouble is no more than that, because the star functions as one of the images which are part of the establishment of the film memory: rather than the star emerging as an actor, the star emerges as an image; the image is capable of disturbing the development of the narrative, and Laura Mulvey has discussed how the image of Marlene Dietrich functions in this way in Sternberg's films, but the disturbance of the text is contained in the institutions of the star system as an ancillary part, an 'other side' of the cinematic institution itself.

To turn now to the objections from the viewpoint of production, distribution and exhibition, I should like to give as an example a genre which Steve Mamber has studied, the cycle of films on the campus revolt which emerged in the USA in the late 1960s and early 1970s, the most typical of which was probably *The Strawberry Statement.* The commercial cinema speculates on topicality, but in so doing it faces a characteristic set of difficulties. First of all there is the long time between the inception of a production project and the final release of the finished film. Secondly, the predominant aim of production in the USA has always been to produce films which have the widest possible market at home and abroad. (There are certain sectors where the exploitation of a narrow market in depth has been the commercial strategy adopted, but through most of its history this has not been the predominant form.) Hence a topical theme may have ceased to be topical by the time a film attempting to exploit it appears, and there is a potential audience which may have no interest in the topical theme. The original project for *All the President's Men* was simply to exploit the topicality of the Watergate theme, and to use completely anonymous look-alikes for the central parts, increasing the authenticity and hence the topical appeal. But it was impossible to get the film made on those terms. The central parts had to be allotted to major stars, since the distributors (whose guarantees were required to raise the original capital) were not to know whether Watergate was going to be anathema to much of the American public in six months time, or whether anybody in Europe was the slightest bit interested in it, whereas they knew very well that they would all be interested in Robert Redford and Dustin Hoffman. Thus they could gamble on the topicality while covering themselves by insisting on another, more general interest. Now in the campus revolt genre this process had specific political effects. An all-out concentration on the topicality of the theme was avoided by what was called "human interest." The campus revolt incident in the films was usually inserted into a plot in which an apolitical student goes to the university and gets involved in militant activity because of sexual difficulties; he then resolves his personal problems, drops out of militant activity and thereby avoids being caught in its defeat. So the campus revolt is there, but there is the more human story alongside it. It is obvious in this case that, without there necessarily being any direct political censorship or control of the subject matter, the pressures of the distribution problem, precisely the problem mentioned by Brecht of the separation of the moment of the production of the film from the moment of its consumption, have imposed a plot strategy which completely defuses any politically radical potential in the subject matter of the film made. The fact that this strategy is 'human interest' links it with Brecht's critique of the bourgeois theater for substituting for the specific and therefore class dimension of its subject matter one which anyone in the audience can sympathize with, that is the universally human dimension. Political subject matter is completely defused and reduced by being treated as universally human rather than specifically political.

My other example is the Chinese cinema as a whole in the last decade. In his book on the Chinese cinema[4] which was written just at the beginning of the Cultural Revolution, Jay Leyda argues, and I think quite convincingly, that the Policy of the Cultural Revolution meant the death of the cinema as he conceived it, that is, the artistic cinema which Leyda stands for, which informs *Kino* and his other works. He had had hopes of such a cinema in China, but thought it totally impossible under the conditions of the Cultural Revolution. Indeed, the cinema more or less disappeared during the height of the Cultural Revolution, and for a year or so the only productions were documentaries and filmings of Peking Opera productions. Bearing in mind Brecht's objections, one of the reasons why this should have been the case is clear enough. It is extremely difficult to fit the cinema, and certainly any cinema that we know of, into a political movement whose aim is the criticism from the base of all the structures of society, because of the highly centralized nature of its production, and the interval between production and exhibition (especially in remote regions). A travelling theater, on the contrary, can adjust its repertoire to immediate local needs much more easily, and the travelling theater seems to have flourished during the Cultural Revolution. But this is not the whole story, for, as I have said, Peking Opera films and documentaries continued to be produced. In each case, the model character of the productions seems to have been decisive: the Peking Opera films were at least in part designed as models for local opera troupes in the new style of Peking Opera, whose abolition of 'Ghosts and Monsters' served both as one of the initiating sparks and as a general metaphor for the Cultural Revolution. Even for nonspecialized audiences they were emblematic of the general aims of the movement; while the documentaries were usually accounts of the activities of a model worker or cadre, anchored in their own time and place, with the result that a separation between the events filmed and the conjuncture in the place and time of their projection was built in. But for all the reasons already discussed, the fiction film resists this specification, and therefore had to be put into abeyance. When it returned from around 1970, it took off from the reform of the Peking Opera. Before the Cultural Revolution, the traditional sufferings of the heroes and heroines of Peking Opera had simply been given a class origin; during the Cultural Revolution, on the contrary, the suffering hero or heroine was largely replaced (under the slogan of 'revolutionary romanticism') by a representative of the toiling masses triumphant. The new fiction films have followed suit. But the result is a cinema of centralized directives. Revolutionary actions have not been presented as models for critical adaptation to local conditions; however radical the message, it has to find a guarantee in a command from the top (a telegram from Mao Zedong in *Breaking with Old Ideas*) or in nature (youth as such and the Chinese landscape in *Hong Yu*).

Brecht argues that the problems which I have discussed so far may be problems which have no technical solutions in principle. But if there are no technical solutions, can any other solutions be offered? I should like to discuss three.

The first is exemplified by the films of Jean-Marie Straub and Daniele Huillet. Many of their films address themselves to the problem of the text and its performance, to the fact that in general text and performance are fused within a film. Nearly all the Straub-Huillet films are in some way concerned with establishing a distance between the cinematic presentation of a text and that text, and this is the source of much of their success and interest. In films like *Machorka Muff* and *Nicht Versohnt* this is already the case, though less explicitly than later. *Not Reconciled* is an extremely difficult film to cope with as a film in the sense of the standard cinema, because it does not have in itself the power to substitute for and therefore abolish the text of which it is an adaptation. You cannot understand the *story* of *Not Reconciled* in the ordinary way you understand the story of a film, unless you know the novel on which it is based, with the result that there is a tension within the film between the Heinrich Böll novel which is being adapted and the particular filmic presentation. Of course the same thing is much more explicit in films such as *Othon* and *History Lessons,* where a text is recited or presented in a relation which completely contradicts any possibility of that text assuming its simple fictional place. This is one way to reestablish that separation between a text and a film performance which is a presentation of that text, which Brecht insisted was so important a part of the epic theater.

The second solution I want to discuss is to work for different forms of distribution and exhibition which allow audiences a different kind of relation to the film. A simple example is to make the film not the only part of the performance, but to have someone there to make a presentation of the film, producing a distance between the film performance itself and the situation in which the film was made. Obviously there is a quite traditional market for the presentation of a film, where an appearance by the filmmaker is part of the package—he or she is interviewed respectfully or gives a little presentation and the films are shown, and this is already an economically important aspect of distribution in certain areas of independent film. It cannot simply be offered as a recipe without further specification. But in the case of *The Nightcleaners* film, the Berwick Street Collective, who made it, do try and handle the film performance in relation to this Brechtian objection. In making the film, the Collective took aesthetic and political decisions with very little direct consideration of the audience to which the film was to be addressed; that is, they carried out those operations within the text which seemed to them to be necessary to make the points they held had to be made, about the political issue they were dealing with and its representation. Now the film is constantly attacked on the grounds that it cannot have any effect because most audiences simply reject it. The Berwick Street Collective answer to this attack is that if possible they should be present when the film is shown, so that the performance can be challenged by an audience and they can then respond to that challenge, making the mode of presentation of the film the object of discussion in a triangle between the film, the audience, and the filmmakers. Obviously it does not have to be the filmmakers who perform this role; it could be a film critic or a political militant. Thus it is possible to construct a form of exhibition which introduces this third moment and therefore produces the possible effect of difference which Brecht insisted on.

The third of my examples of a possible solution is very speculative. It derives from Brecht's theory of the *Lehrstück*, the learning play. As you know, in the late 1920s and early 1930s, Brecht wrote a number of plays which he gave this name and which were designed to be performed not before an audience but by a group for themselves. Brecht had in mind a variety of specific institutions, notably schools and the Communist Party's ancillary cultural organizations, where these plays could be performed. But they were based on a more general theory that Brecht developed very fragmentarily, which eventually included a kind of utopia or model of a theater of the future, based on the example of the *Lehrstück* (which he insisted throughout his life was the most advanced kind of theater he had ever done, while the parable plays, which present the theme through a story in the more conventional way, represented a necessary political compromise, given his particular situation). The culmination of the idea of the *Lehrstück* was what he called a 'pedagogium', which was to be an institution within a society of the future that would hold in some archived form models of every known and classified form of behavior. Members of the society could go into the pedagogium and draw out a particular action which for some reason concerned them, see it demonstrated and try it out for themselves. This has a double edge to it. At one level it is quite straightforward; if someone wants to make an after-dinner speech, Brecht suggests, they could go to the pedagogium and draw out the model of the after-dinner speech and try it out, with the result that they would be more successful the next time they made an after-dinner speech. Thus the pedagogium has an absolutely direct utility in terms of a particular kind of behavior. But Brecht also thought that its stock should by no means be restricted to socially useful actions (assuming that making after-dinner speeches is a socially useful action), but should also include quite directly anti-social forms of behavior, models of which would be available on exactly the same basis (that is, the pedagogium would make no judgment as to what is or is not a socially useful action).

What is speculatively interesting for the cinema here is that the form of the model that could be drawn out is not specified by Brecht himself. He might well have meant that there would be actors who could be booked to carry out the action first, but it is clear that there is an opportunity here for the use of film. Brecht himself does seem to have had a somewhat similar idea—obviously in a less speculative and utopian form—about parts of *Hangmen Also Die*. According to Fritz Lang, one of his proposals was that, although what Lang had to do was to make a film which would have a sale within the American commercial cinema, the film should be made so that there should be sections in it which would demonstrate various types of social behavior; the sections Brecht was particularly interested in were ones which concerned a group of hostages from all classes of Czech society arrested as a result of the assassination of Heydrich, and their reactions to one another within the prison camp. Brecht proposed to Lang that these parts of the film should be extractable, so that later he could take them out of the fiction film which Lang had made, and use them in post-war Germany to assist reconstruction, assembling them in whatever form was appropriate for demonstrating the nature and effects of German oppression in Czechoslovakia to a post-War German audience who had, of course, been deprived by twelve years of Nazi rule of that knowledge. This suggests a possible type of cinema which breaks away completely from traditional forms of distribution and exhibition and yet is implicitly there in Brecht's own ideas about the cinema, and is one of the ways of trying to deal with his fundamental reproach.

NOTES

1. Imposed on "enemy aliens" (including Adorno and Brecht) at the U.S.A.'s entry into the war.

2. The quotation is in English in the original. The "hear stripe" is presumably the range of audible frequencies—or does Brecht mean the sound strip?

3. Stephen Heath, "Film Performance," *Ciné-Tracts*, no. 2, Summer 1977.

4. Jay Leyda, *Dianying*, (Cambridge: MIT Press, 1972).

XVI

SEMIOTICS, THEORY,
AND SOCIAL PRACTICE
A CRITICAL HISTORY OF
ITALIAN SEMIOTICS

Teresa de Lauretis

In the introduction of a special section on theory of *Jump Cut 12/13*, the editor, Chuck Kleinhans, states that "it would be a lot easier to assess the genuine political significance of semiology in Marxist terms if its proponents were not so coy or reticent." He is referring explicitly to Metz and to Eco in whose *A Theory of Semiotics* "the relation of this theory to Marxism and his political allegiance remains unexplained" (p. 38).

The criticism implicit in these statements, which anyone familiar with Italian or French contemporary culture could easily dismiss as unfounded, must nonetheless be answered, for several reasons. First. Semiotics has come of age in American academia, is becoming recognized as a legitimate critical apparatus in the humanities at large, in the study of mass communications, especially cinema. But for this very reason the objection must be dealt with all the more seriously: there is a real danger in this country that semiotics may be rejected outright and uncritically, by the left, for its bourgeois abstraction if not for its bourgeois extraction—a danger contrary but equal to ideologizing semiotics as an objective "scientific" method of analysis.

Second. All theoretical activity functions within discursive practices (high level of abstraction, conceptual manipulation, specialized terminology, etc.) which engage and require certain social knowledges that were historically the heritage and possession of the bourgeoisie as a class. Knowledge of Marxist theory is no exception, and to the extent that such knowledges become (as they have in Italy) also the possession and the heritage of the working class, one can speak of social progress. To see theoretical discourse as necessarily mystificatory or coy or elitist is not a progressive stance. On the other hand, theories construct their objects according to criteria of pertinence, for purposes, and by cognitive processes which are not natural but social, historical, and not exempt from the complex mechanisms of ideology.

Hence the risk is always there that a theory may identify its theoretical object with the empirical object, material reality, and so naturalize its concepts and assertions; that is to say project them from the universe of discourse into material reality (which thus appears to be itself systematic when it is merely systematized, i.e., organized conceptually, through a set of concepts or discourses) and then claim to be "explaining" precisely that reality. Because, history teaches us, this idealist danger is the horizon of theoretical discourse in Western cultures, criticism of any and all theories is an indispensable part of political practice.

Third. The object of semiotics is a theory of the modes of production of signs and meanings, which constitute the major component of social reproduction after physical reproduction. Semiotics is therefore not spared the old dilemma of any thought that aspires to be systematic: if there is a fundamental, substantial discontinuity between knowledge and the real, how can a theory hope to bridge the gap, given that the theory belongs to the area of discourse? Historical materialism proposes that, while the gap between thought and reality cannot be filled, its terrain can be mapped. I chose the metaphor carefully to reflect the two domains involved, the natural and the social, as well as the cultural operation performed, i.e., model making, a necessarily reductive operation whose significant feature is that of being projected or aimed toward a communicative purpose, a purposeful social practice.[1] The project of semiotic theory is precisely such mapping: how the physical properties of human beings and of the natural world (voice, energy, body, things, etc.) are socially assumed as signs, as vehicles for social meaning; and how these sign vehicles are culturally organized into sign systems subject to historical modes of sign production. And so the relation of semiotics to historical materialism and its political significance are indeed very important issues.

I do not presume to do more than open the discussion here and hope that others will continue it. I will only discuss Italian semiotics, with unavoidable references to France, and focusing on some recent and still open questions. But even with regard to Italy alone, the topic is enormously complex as is the sociohistorical context of a country where one can vote for the Italian Communist Party (PCI) without being a Marxist while certainly not all Marxists vote PCI, and where a Marxian universe of discourse is shared by all intellectuals—right, left, and ultraleft. However limited, my discussion is meant to contextualize semiotic research and theory in the sociocultural reality of Italy and to view it critically—in other words, to historicize it. If any safeguard can be built into theoretical discourse, it should be the possibility for self-criticism and the means to historicize itself.

1. What Semiotics?

Like any other cognitive system, semiotics is subject to historical determinations, or rather over determinations. Not only did it rise fully armed from the mind of Saussure or Peirce, Eco or Kristeva, but it was elaborated somewhat differently in different sociocultural areas according to their specific thought traditions and political realities. The term itself has a well known history: at the beginning of the century Saussure postulated a discipline of semiology to study all sign systems, with linguistics as one of its particular domains; in 1964 Barthes's *Elements of Semiology* reversed the plan and proposed that all sign systems should be studied as an extension of linguistics. Rejecting such dependence on the linguistic model, which wider research in nonverbal sign systems had revealed vastly incorrect, the International Association for Semiotic Studies[2] adopted the term "semiotics," calling attention to an important shift of the theoretical gears from the binary model of Saussure to the earlier triadic models of Peirce and Frege which had largely been ignored in Europe, overshadowed by the success of Saussurian linguistics.

The Peircian notion of interpretant and his theory of unlimited semiosis as social production of meaning offered a way out of the closed universe of Saussure's *langue,* which is homogeneously constituted of concepts (both signifier and signified are entities of a psychic order), and excludes from its conceptual domain not only material reality or the individual subject but—most importantly—the social construction of reality through language. Peirce's semiosis, in which the three terms interpretant, sign, object are not empirical entities but functional positions, endlessly interchangeable, is a process of multidimensional mediation in which the object ("reality") is at any given point inseparable from both the sign and interpretant. Within this triadic framework, the object is qualitively different from the old referent (the object-in-itself) and therefore a legitimate theoretical object of semiotics.[3] Moreover, in concerning itself with both sign and meaning production, semiotics opened up, and had to deal with, another can of worms—the question of ideology, including the ideological effects of its own discourse.

While the term "semiotics" is now fairly consistently used in Italy in reference to the practice of signs and thus to the production, organization, and circulation of meaning, both "semiotics" and "semiology" are still used in France. Since North American readers are more likely to encounter French rather than Italian texts, some clarification may be useful. The most clear-cut distinction between the realm and operations of the two textual practices, *sémiologie,* is given by Julia Kristeva. As Eugen Bär summarizes.

> The perceptual level of the *signifiant* constitutes le sémiotique which is investigated by disciplines collectively called la sémiotique, whereas the conceptual level of Saussure's sign, le signifié, constitutes le symbolique, dealt with by la sémiologie which cover practically the whole range, in a loose sense, of contemporary semiotics. Kristeva's *tetta nuova* is therefore what she calls le sémiotique, the ill-defined and definable presyntactic, presemantic, prelogical space which she baptizes with the Platonic term chora. . . . Roughly, the semiotic chora represents the genesis of semiosis in matter, but a matter ultimately not susceptible to scientific hypothesis and not accessible to scientific investigation, although such methodology may be instrumental along the way.[4]

This is, of course, not merely a terminological difference. It implies both a different conceptualization of the object and a different practice of semiotic research; it prescribes the necessity to go beyond the communicative moment of meaning circulation to the "other scene that is the production of meaning anterior to meaning," the unconscious.[5]

The references to Freud in Kristeva's language are not incidental but programmatic, underscoring the centrality of psychoanalysis in contemporary French theoretical discourse. Several intersecting lines of thought weaving back and forth from Lévi-Strauss's structuralism to Althusserian Marxist theory, from Freud revisited through Lacan to the revision of Nietzsche, are traceable in French semiology and in Kristeva's semiotics, which Bär not innocently defines "a genealogy of signs."[6] Whereas in Italy attention has shifted to the area of the social production of meaning, I have the impression that both sémiologie and sémiotique are primarily focused on the signifier.

2. Structuralism and Early Semiotics

When 1968 happened upon the scene of Europe, most of Italy had not been reading Freud or the phenomenologists for long but had a solid acquaintance with Marx and Hegel. Instead of Bachelard, Bataille, and Breton, Italians had been debating Gramsci, Lukács, and Vittorini. Nietzsche remained highly suspect, like the domestic version of the superman—D'Annunzio—until the last few years.[7] Even the *neoavanguardia* or *neosperimentalismo* would avow a debt to Surrealism sooner than they could admit any linkage to Futurism which was still, in the mid 60s, a skeleton in the national closet.[8] Brecht was certainly preferred to Beckett, and despite the extraordinary bloom of the new cinema around 1963, the mortgage of neorealism long defunct was still ponderous.[9] Through the 60s, the best critical efforts in Italy were devoted to undo the complacent mood of the 50s when the post-war economic boom, the consolidation of Christian Democratic rule, and its reactionary cultural politics had almost succeeded in sweeping under the rug both Fascism and the Resistance.[10]

At the time when structuralism took hold, in the early-to-mid 60s, primarily in the work of linguists and medievalists, art historians and aestheticians, Italy was also re-examining its cultural history within a framework that was more political than philosophical. Marx was not read as a philosopher but as a revolutionary and a political thinker, his words rendered tangible in the praxis of two large Marxist parties. After the bankruptcy of Crocean idealism, the influence of new philosophies like existentialism and neo-positivism had not significantly affected the area of literary studies. In a stifling intellectual climate, structuralism meant first of all a rigorous textual method, a scientific habit of thought, and a new practice of criticism, all the more appealing since Italy had no experience comparable to New Criticism or to Russian Formalism. Understandably, then, structuralism seemed to be exempt from the teleological overtones of either Croceanism or deterministic Marxism. Moreover, its interdisciplinary thrust and sound basis in the social sciences made it possible, theoretically and methodologically, to revise the concepts of high and popular culture and to relate art to the sphere of the mass production and consumption of cultural objects.

It is important to understand the role of structuralism in Italian research because it was the generative force from which and against which, dialectically, semiotics developed: in the first instance, whereas structuralism was developed mainly as an analytical tool for the study of literary textual systems, early semiological studies (as they were called after Saussure and French usage) were mostly concerned with nonliterary and pluricodic systems for which no methodological and critical instruments existed—comic strips, folklore, architecture, cinema, television, and mass media. Umberto Eco's *La struttura assente* (Milano: Bompiani, 1968), certainly the most comprehensive work of early Italian semiotics, consists of five sections representative of the range and vitality of the semiotic project: (A) notions of general semiology; (B) visual signs and codes; (C) architectural signs and codes; (D) a critical discussion of structuralism as both methodological and philosophical construct; and (E) a survey of the semiological field. The last two chapters in particular indicate another important aspect of semiological studies, namely their theoretical component.[11] In the second instance, early semiotic theory and practice were directly involved in the neo-Marxist critique of structuralism.

At the end of the 50s, the new left's literary and cultural debate was led in journals like *Officina, Il verri,* and *Il menabo* (edited by Italo Calvino and Elio Vittorini) by people like Pasolini, Leonetti, Scalia, Roversi, the so-called "critical Marxists." Following Vittorini in his polemic with Palmiro Togliatti and the Soviet invasion of Hungary, the new Marxists assumed a highly critical stance vis-à-vis the Soviet oriented cultural politics of the PCI under Togliatti's leadership. They objected to its instrumentalization of Gramsci's "esthetics" and its normative and historicist view of literary practice along the lines of socialist realism. If it succeeded in reassessing and definitively closing the postwar period, the work of these journals was not able to redefine radically, and thus to bring forth a new conception of, the relationships binding writers and intellectuals to society, art and literature to political action. Romano Luperini argues that, throughout the 60s, the failure of neo-Marxism and of the artistic/literary *neoavanguardia* was their inability to see and define the role of intellectuals in a society which had reached the stage of mature capitalism (in 1958–63).[12] According to Luperini, they failed not to perceive but to analyze the total absorption of bourgeois thought and of all "creative" work by capital, as well as the integration of workers into the system through unions, parties, and the ideological consensus procured via the neocapitalist mass media. By not seeing themselves as part of the capital's apparatus, Luperini states, the artists and intellectuals of the *neoavanguardia* believed in a revolutionary function of art as, essentially, disruption; and while they saw the artist as a disinterested creator of nonideological experimentation, they held an equally incorrect view of neocapitalism as monolithic, all-powerful, in total technological and ideological control of social reality. This was unexpectedly disproven by the events of '68, which brought about very different views of social reality and of political practice, as I will try and show later. But, regardless of these failures, as interpreted by Luperini, the neo-Marxists and the *neoavanguardia* (especial Gruppo '63 to which Balestrini, Sanguineti, and Eco belonged among others) were the most effective voices in Italian cultural theory and the most lucid opponents of structuralism.[13]

Very briefly stated, the neomarxist objections to the "structural method" were:

(1) its idealist premise: positing an apriori structure as immanent in the text; (2) the tautological fallacy of a criticism solely directed at verifying the existence of formal structures already assumed to be in the object; and (3) the ideological stance behind the structuralist approach to the text as a system or totality unrelated to other sociocultural formations. These crucial questions acted as a critical goad for those who, like myself, had realized the valuable aspects of structuralism toward a renovation and de-provincialization of Italian culture. In the changing historical situation that culminated in the political events of 1968, structuralism came to denote a reactionary and narrow view of the critical activity, while its early innovative charge and conceptual tools were assumed, developed, and sharpened by semiotics.

3. The Third Copernican Revolution

Whereas one has the impression that in France, 1968 and its aftermath brought about a reversal, a total denial of structuralism by its very proponents (with the exception of Lévi-Strauss), as witness the editorial history of *Tel quel,* it seems appropriate to say that in Italy structuralism was transformed into semiotics by a conscious political shift. (And this is at least one of the reasons for the obvious differences between French and Italian semiotics in what may be called their politics of enunciation: the discursive practice of Italian semiotics is much less flamboyant or self-reflexive than that of the French heirs of Artaud and Mallarmé; terminology tends to be more stable, its use much less fetishistic. Many Italian semioticians, like Eco, seek wide reception through the newspapers and the media; they analyze mass cultural phenomena and do not disdain the low prestige roles of popularizer and the textbook writer. This is, of course, in line with the Italian left's traditional populist commitment to pedagogy, and has its roots in Gramsci's original analysis of the political importance of cultural hegemony.) In his recent *Produzione del senso e messa in scena,* Gianfranco Bettetini states that the crisis in the traditional concept of the sign, as unitary entity or elementary unit capable of conveying meaning, is at the basis of the transition from early semiotic research, restrictively focused on the formal aspects of signification and sign systems, to its current concerns with the operations of meaning production and their ideological and economic supports. Like psychology and linguistics, semiotics initially sought to establish itself as a scientific discipline, a universal science of signs, in a climate of persisting positivism and under the empiricist banner. Thus the methodological necessity to define levels of analysis and criteria of pertinence, which is a legitimate requirement of all theoretical research, and was confused with so-called "scientific neutrality." Had it remained within the dominant scientific tradition, semiotics too would have come to identify methodological needs with an ontological foundation. Fortunately semiotics was just getting on its way in the late 60s when the problematic of ideology erupted in the human sciences and opened to question all their operations—from the initial choice of hypotheses to the reading of the data and to the social impact, utilization, or manipulation of the findings. This third Copernican revolution (as

Bettetini calls it) placed the subject of ideology squarely at the center of any research into social structures and relations; voiding the claims of scientific neutrality, it stressed the role of ideology in "overdetermining not only the communication models used in infrasocial exchanges, especially in the area of mass communication, but even the instruments used to analyze their structures and their effects."[14]

If the older and more established human sciences continued, for the most part, along a strictly experimental path, without seriously questioning their own practices, semiotics was still relatively unofficial—open territory, as it were. And so it was able to subject its epistemological premises to self-criticism, for example the notion of the sign, the ideological implications of a purely "descriptive" intentionality, the fragmentation of the social sphere into discontinuous systems, etc. By abandoning altogether the hypothesis that a text or a message could be studied in itself and by means of a metalanguage (that is to say that a language could be isomorphic with, and therefore able to translate, either "reality" or a metalanguage), semiotics research ceased to be a kind of linguistics applied to verbal and/or nonverbal messages; from the formal study of signification systems, it turned to examining the modes of sign production and the previously ignored area of meaning (the semantic field). Since the expression "modes of sign production" may sound blasphemous to some readers, I must justify it and explain how it is used by Eco, from whose *A Theory of Semiotics* I lifted it.

Communication and signification, Eco maintains, function in a complex and dialectical relationship. One cannot really conceive of signification systems (the phonemes of a language, road signals, a set of semantic contents like the system of kinship, etc.) outside the social purpose of communication. Vice versa, it is impossible to study communication processes independently of the underlying systems of signification. Which also means that the elements of each system must be, and in fact are, understood by someone, i.e., must be correlated to a culturally assigned content or meaning. The rules that establish the correlation between a physical or material sign vehicle and a content are historically and socially determined, and therefore changeable. These operational rules (and not the sets of elements constituting each system) are what Eco calls codes.

> Properly speaking there are not signs, but only sign-functions. . . . A sign-function is realized when two functives (expression and content) enter into a mutual correlation; the same functive can also enter into another correlation, thus becoming a different functive and therefore giving rise to a new sign-function. Thus signs are the provisional result of coding rules which establish transitory correlations of elements, each of these elements being entitled to enter—under given coded circumstances—into another correlation and thus form a new sign. . . . Therefore the classical notion of "sign" dissolves itself into a highly complex network of changing relationships. (p. 49)[15]

The codes as socially established relationships between signs and meaning change whenever new or different contents are culturally assigned to the same sign vehicle or whenever new sign vehicles are produced. A different interpretation of a text (a sign for Eco can be any significant unit, from a single word to a string of signs, a text or even a macrotext, depending on one's level of analysis) or a new text sets up a new content, a new cultural unit that becomes part of the semantic universe of the society that produces it. So that, in studying the codes, semiotics also studies the production of signs, which requires labor, both physical and intellectual, of different types for different signs. The expenditure of physical or intellectual energy in order to produce signs is, of course, interrelated with the social utilization of the semiosic labor and thus with the social relations of sign production—hence the term "modes of sign production" is not a mere formalistic echo of the Marxian concept. For Eco semiotics is a critical discipline "concerned with signs as social forces" (p. 65).[16]

With the redefinition of its object in view of a materialist but nondeterministic practice, Eco's theory steers clear of the claim to scientific status that other semiotics inherited from structural linguistics and, in Italy, from the dominant Marxist tradition, a claim evident for example in the work of Ferruccio Rossi-Landi. The two scientific frameworks of linguistics and Marxist economism provide the foundation of Rossi-Landi's work. Translator of Charles Morris, on whom he wrote a monograph as early as 1953, Rossi-Landi has been concerned primarily with the relation between sign systems and ideologies. In *Il linguaggio come lavoro e come mercato* (Milano: Bompiani, 1968), he postulates a homology between linguistic production and material production based on the homology between message *(énoncé)* and industrial artifact; if language products can be seen as artifacts and vice versa, material artifacts function as nonverbal systems, his task is to prove that commodities may be interpreted as messages, and messages as commodities. The scope of his work is "a global semiotics of social codes" and, complementarily, the "interpretation of all social codes, including verbal codes, in terms of work and production" (*Semiotica e ideologia*, Milano: Bompiani, 1972, p. 207). In *Linguistics and Economics* (The Hague: Mouton, 1975), he applies deductively the labor theory of value and the Marxian concept of alienation to linguistic production, equating value with meaning. By considering "human language as the principal object of linguistic science" and "economic exchange as the principal object of the science of economics" in a unitary way, Rossi-Landi intends to begin a semiotic elaboration of the two social processes which we can identify provisionally as "the production and circulation of goods (in the form of commodities) and as the production and circulation of sentences (in the form of verbal messages)" (p. 5). A look at the table of contents of *Linguistics and Economics* indicates that the parallelism is worked out in great detail from "Utensils and sentences" and "Use-value and exchange-value, from word to message," to "Linguistic capital" (constant and variable), "Linguistic private property" and "A hint at linguistic alienation." The role of semiotics, concludes Rossi-Landi, is to mediate between the dimension of the modes of production and the dimensions of ideologies:

> With the rise of industrial capitalism in the late eighteenth and nineteenth centuries, there emerged also the means for studying the capitalist mode of production and its relative ideologies, and lastly for projecting scientifically a better society, that is new

programmings destined to substitute the capitalistic ones. This also allowed for the emergence of a general doctrine of man in which the importance of modes of production and of ideologies was for the first time placed in a proper light. All the same neither the first nor the second dimension, even if added together, gives us a complete description of the social programming of human behaviour, if we do not add to them the dimension of the programmings which govern both verbal and non-verbal communication. This third dimension which mediates between the first two, making possible among other things, their reciprocal influence, had also been glimpsed by Marx's genius. It is, however, only with the arise of neo-capitalism that the means have emerged for a frontal study of the models and programs of communication. And since there is no communication without sign systems, this study belongs to semiotics, the general doctrine and science of signs and their systems. Semiotics finds its proper place, its significance, and its foundation alongside the study of the modes of production and of ideologies, within the sphere of the social programming of all behaviour. (pp. 202–203)

Since, according to Rossi-Landi, both the economy (modes of production) and ideologies are to be treated as sign systems and postulated as homologous to language, it seems to me that his semiotics is not a mediation (or a way of mapping) between material reality and the social construction of reality; on the contrary, from his argument semiotics appears as a kind of universal key to the entire spectrum of phenomena, which are thus precisely homologized by semiotics.[17] It is by relinquishing the claim to a scientific knowledge of material reality that semiotics, as formulated by Eco, can provide a critical knowledge of what might be called social reality, i.e., the conditions of production, circulation, and consumption of social discourses (in the broadest sense) from which representations, beliefs, and values are engendered.

4. The Writing on the Walls

How did the theoretical and ideological shift from a semiotics of signification systems (now called "classical semiology") to a semiotics of sign production come about? The re-reading of Peirce, who had been known earlier mostly through the work of Morris, marked a crucial theoretical step forward in this direction, as indicated above. Whatever may have been the influence of Peirce on Anglo-American thought, its recovery by Italian and European semiotics at that historical moment was neither coincidental nor without consequences that must be assessed in the specific socio-historical context. A similar recovery, which may have been under way for some time in the United States, need not proceed in a similar direction or bring similar consequences. For the thrust and the impact of a theory are historically overdetermined, i.e., conditioned by, and in turn conditioning, in a very complex interaction, all kinds of social practices. Thus to claim that the European discovery of Peirce caused "the crisis of the sign" and the demise of structuralism and Saussurian semiology around '68 would be a gross idealist simplification. It was, most likely, the events in the real world that made people look for better models, more useful interpretants of the writing on the walls. Bettetini writes:

> A rightful attention to the problems of meaning and the complementary discourse on neutrality and on the non-innocence of formal structures were not brought about simply by the internal difficulties that the object analyzed kept posing to a structuralist methodology, but were also urged by external events which in turn forced (semioticians) to re-think the problematic of ideology and to study its interconnections with all communication phenomena. (p. 22)

The external events were those of 1968 in Europe, the student movement in the United States, the crisis of all types of bourgeois rationalization, the recall of the values of the imagination and poetic productivity. Such events, he continues, which could not be foreseen by previous semiotic practice, warranted that the contradictions of our social system existed in reality and were evident to many people and groups; they were described not only at the theoretical level by a few prophets, semiotically or otherwise, but at the level of a new social consciousness, in the light of a new idea of possible relations between people and between people and things. The crisis denounced by the cultural revolution could not be reduced to a crisis of the semantic field, where ideology had been conveniently tucked away. It obviously had to affect the entire process of meaning production inclusive of the semiosic activity by which signs and codes are elaborated and transformed—a production, in other words, that continuously intersects both expression and content planes and that is itself historical and ideological.[18]

This notion of production of meaning is not to be understood as Kristeva's "other scene" of a productivity anterior to meaning, i.e. on the level of the Freudian drives, but in a more literal sense, and on the level of consciousness. Historically it seems to be directly related to the political situation of present-day Italy, to the new forms of class composition that have emerged since the early 70s, and to the recent analyses of the role of the cultural worker in the class struggle. Briefly, and with the inevitable simplification of any summary, the question of a contemporary definition of social classes and productive forces is at the heart of a debate between the "ultrared" groups and the PCI. Examining the events surrounding the occupation of the University of Rome in February 1977, *Lotta Continua* states:

> The relationship between mass workers (industrial workers in the old class composition) and tertiary (clerical workers, information workers, students—all with higher education) is a decisive strategic pivot on which turn a) the restructuration project supported by big capital, b) the "new model of mediation" being experimented with by the PCI, and c) the possible class recomposition which may blow up a) and b). It is not by chance therefore, that both the bourgeoisie and the PCI have deployed, in the last few years, a capillary offensive aimed at dividing the industrial work force from the tertiary work force, promoting the corporative ideology of the "worker-producer" against the "parasites" opposing manual to intellectual labour. . . .
> The new level of cooperation and combination of the work force required by mature capitalism both in the factories and in the tertiary activities . . . is the crucial point. Not only does it erase the clear dividing line between productive and unproductive

labour, which an entire tradition of Marxist scholasticism has unsuccessfully tried to hold up; but, above all, it defines a new quality of living labour (intellectual labour incorporated into the capitalist reproductive machine) as the first of the productive forces, the source of the accumulation and valorization of capital (i.e. of exploitation). The extraction of surplus value extends to the entire complex of manual-intellectual activities in which capital combines living labour changing the very content of the workers "toil."[19]

Thus, the article concludes, to insist on the (early capitalist) division of labour for which manufacturing workers are the legitimate productive work force, while students and "intellectuals" can only overcome their "petty bourgeois parasitism" by becoming functionaries of the mediator-state, is an ideological mystification. By insisting that the productive forces are those strictly related to machinery, plants, or things, the PCI is playing along with the counter-offensive of big capital, wholly concentrated on destroying the principal productive force, which is precisely living labour, and the political class composition that unites industrial and cultural workers.

I would suggest that this new concept of living labour, and the qualitative shift in the conception of productive forces that it implies, parallels the current semiotic concept of meaning production. As living labour, defined in relation to a higher level of class composition, comprises both the intellectual and the manual activities of work in industrial as well as cultural/service production, the semiotic concept of sign production refers to the work of producing intellectual meaning through material, physical sign-vehicles. The emphasis is no longer on the sign systems as mechanisms that generate messages (i.e., on the sign systems seen as the "machinery plants" of semiosic processes); instead, semiotic research focuses on the work performed through them, which constitutes and/or transforms the codes, the subjects using the codes (i.e., performing the work), and, however slowly, the systems themselves. Thus, the subject of the semiosic activity is no longer the transcendental subject of structuralism, "the human mind" but a historical subject, and therefore a class subject (at least as long as the theoretical concept of class is a useful interpretant of social reality). In the last chapter of *A Theory of Semiotics*, Eco asks:

> Since it has been said that the labour of sign production also represents a form of social criticism and of social practice . . . what is, in the semiotic framework, the place of the acting subject of every semiosic act? . . . (What is) the role of the "speaking" subject not only as a communicational figment but as a concrete historical, biological, psychic subject, as it is approached by psychoanalysis and related disciplines? (p. 314)

He agrees with Kristeva that the subjective determinants of a text, the bio-psychological processes that Freud labeled drives, are indeed part of the signifying process; but, like ideological and economic motivations, they can be studied by semiotics only insofar as they are expressed through texts, i.e., multiply levelled and relayed interactions of signs and meanings.

> The most reliable grasp that semiotics can have on such a subjective activity
> (Kristeva's le sémiotique) is one provided by a theory of codes: the subject of any
> semiotic enquiry being no more than the semiotic subject of semiosis, that is, the
> historical and social result of the segmentation of the world that a survey on Semantic
> Space makes available. This subject is a way of looking at the world and can only be
> known as a way of segmenting the universe and of coupling semantic units with
> expression-units: by this labour it becomes entitled to continuously destroy and
> restructure its social and historical systematic concretions. (p. 315)

This is a more cautious, perhaps more narrowly bounded, definition of the
subject than is found in Kristeva and in recent film theory, for example Steven
Heath's.[20] Nevertheless, in my opinion, it has the advantage of being solidly
anchored to history and to verifiable social practice—an advantage that becomes
indispensable at the times when social practice is changing, as it now clearly is in
Italy.

5. How Political Is the Private?

The picture painted by the North American liberal press of an Italy en route to social
democracy, with the moral rewards of the historical compromise slightly outweigh-
ing the (endemic?) ills of social violence and economic crisis, is inadequate as well
as condescending. But an overly optimistic view as might be put forward by official
or unofficial left apologists would be at best wishful thinking, at worst, anti-
historical. Since the 1975 and 1976 elections, new or newly avowed issues have
emerged which are not contemplated by the present social system and for which as
yet there seems to be no useful theorization. I am referring to a mosaic of marginal
and heterogeneous groups who enjoy the economic status of unemployed or un-
deremployed but whose needs and demands and private-political practices are vastly
different. Radical women, the workers of *Autonomia Operaia,* the student movement, and other facets of the new left do not merely question the validity and the
operations of all institutional apparati (the family, the educational system, the party,
etc.), but explicitly refuse to function within them. Moving into the wide theoretical
gap to the left of the traditional Marxist left, these groups have brought about a new
polarization of the sociopolitical sphere. At the same time, by virtue of their very
differences and diversity, they have set in motion a process of radical cultural
change that challenges the most established values of Italian culture, both bourgeois
and socialist.

If we take at face value semiotics' claim to be a critical discipline vis-à-vis all
social communication, we must expect it to be prepared to deal with these emerging
needs and the social discourses that express them. If indeed the possibility of
self-criticism and the means to historicize its own discourse have been built into
semiotic theory after 1968, as was suggested earlier, a further political shift may be
due shortly. And I suspect, solely on the basis of a personal bias, that the early signs
of any theoretical reshuffle to come will be found in the personal-political practices
of the semioticians themselves. Let me give two examples.

First, the recent polemic stirred up by Félix Guattari and other French intellectuals who accused the PCI and the Communist mayor of the city of Bologna in particular, of taking totalitarian measures in the repression of dissent. The polemic was set off by the arrest of Francesco Berardi, a prominent member of the Bologna "autonomist" collective *A/traverso* and of the independent Radio Alice; he was arrested last July in Paris on several charges of inciting to riot during the student-police confrontation of March 11, 1977, in Bologna. The French newspaper *Le Monde* of July 12 and 13, 1977, reports that a group of well known French intellectuals, among them Sartre, Foucault, Sollers, Deleuze, Guattari, and Wahl (who is the editor of the Seuil series that is publishing Berardi's book) formed a *Comité contre la répression en Italie* and signed an appeal, which they sent to the Belgrade conference, denouncing the consequences of the historical compromise and the undemocratic measures employed by the Bologna PCI in the repression of far left dissenters. The strong response in *Le Monde* of July 13, by Bologna mayor Renato Zangheri, professor of political economy and member of the central committee of the PCI, set off an avalanche of debate.[21] Although it would be silly to say that Eco speaks for semiotics, his work is to date the most comprehensive formulation of the field and of the reach of its conceptual instruments. Moreover, for the Italian general public and press readership, Eco does represent semiotics as Sartre represented existentialism to North American readers some years ago; therefore, at least in terms of broad cultural practice, Eco's position in the debate with Berardi and the authors of *Anti-Oedipe*, Deleuze and Guattari, is an indication of the relationship of semiotics to current sociopolitical issues. For the politics of semiotics, like the politics of any other cognitive instrument, is to be looked for not only in its theoretical object and analytical method, but certainly as much in its general and specific practice at all levels of discourse, from the concrete or the "technical" to the abstract. To say that Eco's stance is that of a realist between the PCI and the "Amazonian forests" is to say nothing new and, in the present Italian situation, almost nothing at all. But to present his many arguments, semiotic of course, would involve writing another article. So instead I will translate a few passages of his article, "Chatting among Ourselves Barbarians."[22]

> When I received the text of Guattari's appeal, after some hesitation, I did not sign and explained my reasons to my French friends. It was just fine for me to protest against the warrantless search of certain publishing companies and the private homes of the writers who had published the Radio Alice texts. But such protest was preceded, in the French manifesto, by a catastrophic scenario of the Italian reality, dominated by a single party repressive of all dissent. I briefly thought of what use the document might be put to by DeCarolsi and his friends during their coming trip to the United States. Nothing more was needed to invite CIA intervention against the communist coup in Italy, guaranteed by the French intelligentsia. Not only toothpaste salesmen, I believe, must watch out and calculate the effects of their sales pitch on different strata of the population.
>
> I discuss with some movement students. They complain that most of those intellectuals who are always signing appeals for imprisoned South Americans or for every Pole under investigation did not protest the closing down of Radio Alice . . .

The students are right, but I try to explain why the people who could have protested did not do so. They feared that, by defending their independent radio, they would be considered supporters of the sharpshooters. Exactly the students reply, that is precisely Cossiga's and L'Unita's blackmail. I respond: are you sure that you did not contribute to the setting of the premises for their blackmail? Look at the university wall: on one side I read "Mao Dada" and "Free Alice." On the other side I see "Pig policeman we will shoot you in the mouth." Of course I know that two different people did the writing. But . . . you expect public opinion to distinguish them when it hardly sees a distinction between two extra-parliamentary groups? Public opinion does not read according to the rules of avant-garde vertical writing. It reads as it read in the 19th century, as it reads the railroad timetable. How do you expect it to distinguish metaphors from programs, or one type of program from another? You should have made the distinction clear. . . . You have a right to the space for your dissent: but define it more clearly. Now, however, I address this same question to the PCI: how do we define the space for dissension at the moment when the largest force of the Italian left approaches the exercise of power?

Is it true that in Italy people are arrested for crimes of opinion? No, replies the Judge, those who incite to a crime are arrested, and incitement is not an opinion but a criminal act. No problem, if incitement is translated as the expression "Kill So and So!" But if it is manifested as theorization of the armed struggle against the state? And how soon? Now, or in a few years? Or in a distant future? Where is the threshold between inciting to revolt and utopistic fabulation? The affair is very delicate. It had to do not only with public safety or the administering of justice, but also with political science and the administering of the law. Taking the concept of incitement very broadly, one must prohibit the printing and sale of the classics of Marxism. . . . What is the difference between an opinion that produces immediate effects, one that produces long term effects, and one that will never produce any effects? The liberal ethic was very clear if naive: the poet is irresponsible, the philosopher talks and does not act. Even pornography was absolved, so long as it was redeemed by art. But, are we still thinking within the ethics and philosophy of liberalism? Marxism has taught us that there is a very strict nexus between theory and practice, and that ideologies are weapons. What is happening forces us to a redefinition of the theory-practice nexus. But also to a redefinition of the notion of freedom of expression in a society dominated by the rapid circulation of the mass media.

To conclude my first example, there is some evidence that semioticians are willing to take seriously the emerging social issues of group autonomy vs. party organization, subjective needs vs. state controlled productivity demands, the unconscious, please, difference, and so on.

The second example is not so hopeful, I'm afraid: even those semioticians who are prepared to readjust their theoretical aim and to focus on the unchartered territory of the social unconscious (that area that also includes the imaginary) are impotent so to speak to confront the social needs expressed by women. To anyone who observes directly the practice of semiotics, particularly in the semiosic acts and social behavior of the semioticians (as I did last summer at the International Center for Semiotics and Linguistics in Urbino), it is obvious that their inability to deal with feminist critical issues derives from the simple refusal to hear, to see, to take them into consideration. Explanations for this behavior, were anyone interested, could be found in areas of theoretical discourse that semiotics has certainly considered, for example Freud's notion of disavowal *(Verleugnung)* leading to the creation of the fetish, the penis substitute that ensures the permanence and value of the phallus (the phallus as universal equivalent). But despite the self-critical tools developed by male discourse, and despite the new post-1968 political consciousness, women are still regarded through the optics and within the parameters that Lévi-Strauss finds in so-called primitive societies: as commodities, as signs produced in a social discourse by and for men, and therefore excluded from the universe of cultural productions and of discourse itself.[23] This is the original infamy of the title of Lea Melandri's book which lifts the unspoken and the unspeakable (infamy, in-fari) taboo on female sexuality, imposed to hide its original expropriation, its reduction to a biological/economic function.

> When one takes for granted that there is no specific difference between male and female sexuality, and that female sexuality coincides with the male's desire, the equivalence woman-proletariat is quite easy, too easy. The woman's body as it appears on the social scene, is already other, alienated from itself. It is essentially labour power to produce children, housework, and pleasure for men. Male dominance does not begin with private property and the monogamous family, as Engels says, but is located in the origin of the relationship between the sexes by an act of expropriation which only today has surfaced to consciousness. With the dominance of male sexuality, the material and ideological primacy of economic relations over all other social relations is also established. . . . The fusion-confusion between sexuality/ maternity, sexuality/procreation has already taken place. . . . In order to sing triumphantly of the happy love of proletarian women (as Engels does) one must have no doubt about the identity between pleasure and male sexuality; one must refuse to see that women's sexuality, the less it is clothed in material, religious, ideological structures, the more it reveals its violently imposed kinship with childbearing, illness and death.[24]

Although Melandri, author of the passage quoted above, is not a professional semiotician, her analysis of the relation of sexuality to social formations and of the ideological discourses that support and reproduce them is an excellent suggestion as to how semiotics could be used precisely to demystify the dominant semiotic practice. She examines a series of texts, from a worker's letter published in *Il Manifesto* to the first issue of the autonomous revolutionary paper *Rosso* from Freud's analysis of *Dora* to Joseph Goux's *Freud, Marx,* looking for the codes that may explain the paradoxical facts of our historical reality—"a sexuality obeying norms so ancient as to seem entirely outside the present economic laws, an economy that by repressing sexuality has become itself factory of the imaginary" (p. 81). Discussing for example, Goux's proposition that the genesis of the institutions which govern the cultural exchange of values (language, the law, the Father) was already theoretically implicit in the genesis of money,[25] Melandri points out that oppositions such as body/soul, real/ideal, particular/universal, matter/rationality are not to be traced only as far as the oppositions use-value/exchange-value or commodities/money, i.e., to the conceptual distinction between variables and invariant in the logic of exchange. Idealism opposed body to soul and matter to mind by concealing not only labor as producer of commodities but also in the very beginning, the female body. "Woman enters history having already lost her concreteness and singularity: she is the economic machine that produces the species, and she is the mother, an equivalent more universal than money, the most abstract measure invented by patriarchal ideology" (p. 27). While bourgeois economism, in separating the relations of production from all other types of exchange, proclaimed objective, necessary, and historical only the facts of political economy, its critique, Marxism, exposed the social relations of production, the alienated human labor behind production. But historical materialism has stopped its analysis of the material bases of existence short of the sexual order; that is to say, it too, like bourgeois ideology, consistently seeks to reduce the diversity or qualitative jump between two perhaps irreducible material orders, the sexual and the economic. To argue, as Goux does, that the opposition of the sexes was genetically the origin of the class struggle but is structurally its "mirror" in advanced societies, and thus to subsume the man-woman relationship under the class conflict, does not mean simply affirming sexuality as solely male, it also means denying women any possibility of historical existence, while perpetuating man's alienation from a portion of his material sexual existence (the need for love). The old etymological associations mother-matter-mass, which Melandri hears echoing in Goux's writing, point to a risky semiotic pattern, a binarism that opposes matter and rationality, body and mind (if not soul)—in other words, to the old teleological ghost hovering at the end of a materialistic rainbow.

These are some of the historical signs that, in a hopeful mood, I think may further transform semiotic theory and practice; just as a qualitative shift in the sociopolitical conception of productive forces after 1968 may be seen at the base of semiotics' concern with sign production and code operations, a theorization of subjectivity and, crucially, sexual difference in their historical forms and in relation to the cultural apparati of social reproduction will have to become, after 1977, central to the semiotic debate.

Note: Part of the research and the writing of this essay were done under the auspices of a fellowship at the Center for Twentieth Century Studies of the University of Wisconsin at Milwaukee. I also wish to acknowledge my debt and gratitude to my friends Tom Anderson, Samuel R. Delaney, Renny Harrigan, Andreas Huyssen, Judith Mayne, Marcella Tarozzi, and in particular Julia Lesage for their careful readings, critiques, suggestions, and discussions of the manuscript in its several stages.

NOTES

1. See Luis J. Prieto, *Pertinence et pratique* (Paris: Minuit, 1975).

2. Founded in 1969, it held its first congress in June 1974, in Milan. L. Nelson, "Signs of the Times: Semiotics 1974," *The Yale Review* 64 (1975), 296–320.

3. The triadic models of Peirce and Frege are discussed at length by Eliseo Veron in his forthcoming *Production de sens*. He points out how Peirce's notion of semiosis outlines a process of meaning production not only unlimited but also historical (subject to time, to the future) and social (determined by a "community"). See Eliseo Veron, "La semiosis sociale," *Working Papers*, no. 64 (Universita di Urbino: Centro Internazionale di Semiotica e di Linguistica, 1977); Veron cites from *The Collected Papers of Charles Sanders Peirce* (Harvard U., 1931–58).

4. "Psychoanalysis and Semiotics" *Semiotica* 16 (1976), 374. Bär cites *La revolution du langage poetique* (Paris: Seuil, 1974).

5. Julia Kristeva, "Semiotiké," *Recherches pour une sémanalyse* (Paris: Seuil, 1969), pp. 38–39.

6. "Kristeva's theory of a semiotic chora, at face value a genealogy of signs, may hide therefore a semiotic teleology, namely insofar as signs, besides pointing to the intelligible, also return us to the somatic infrastructure of which they are made" (Bär, 375).

7. For example Paolo Valesio, "The Lion and the Ass," *Yale Italian Studies* 1 (Winter), 67–82. And it is not a coincidence that Liliana Cavani's latest film is entitled *Beyond Good and Evil*.

8. For an overview of some current evaluations of Italian Futurism, see Stephen R. Sharkey and Robert S. Dombroski. "Revolution, Myth and Mythical Politics: The Futurist Solution," *Journal of European Studies* VI (1975), 231–47; and my "Futurism, Marinetti and Modernism" in *Appolinaire and Modernism*, ed. Pierre Cauvin (Austin: University of Texas Press, 1978).

9. The debate about (neo) realism still central to Italian film theory, deserves a lengthier discussion than would be possible here, especially in view of the role played by semiotics in it. See, for example, Emilio Garroni, *Progetto di semiotica* (Bari: Laterza, 1972); *L'indice del realismo* (Bompiani, 1971); and Eco's critique of iconism in *A Theory of Semiotics* (Bloomington: Indiana University Press), pp. 191–217. Additionally, studies that must be mentioned here are Martin Walsh, "Re-evaluating Rossellini," *Jump Cut* 15 (1977), 15–17, and Michael Silverman, "Rossellini and Leon Battista Alberti: The Centering Power of Perspective," *Yale Italian Studies*, 1 (Winter 1977), 128–42.

10. I hope not to offend the reader of *Ciné-Tracts,* sometimes viewers of American war movies, if I make the perhaps obvious point that the Resistance was for Italy a successful war of national liberation and as such, gave the country's sociopolitical consciousness an irreversible push to the left. This fact, however, has been suppressed not only in the banalities of the 50s war movies but, with more serious effects, by the ideological mystifications of most Anglo-American historiography. For a concise and well informed account of the Italian resistance see Frederico Chabod, *A History of Italian Fascism* (Fertig reprint, 1975).

11. The difficulties encountered by semiologists dealing with cinema and theater in light of the Saussurian langue/parole model are a good example. See Stephen Heath, "Film/Cinetext/Text," *Screen* 14 (Spring/Summer 1973), 102–27.

12. Romano Luperini, "Traccia Del Dibattitio Teorico-Letterario Nell'Ultimo Decennio In Italia." *Che Fare* 8/9 (1971), 268–88. (*Che Fare,* a journal of the revolutionary left devoted to theoretico-political analysis, was founded in 1967 by R. Di Marco and a dissident wing of Gruppo 63.)

13. See Umberto Eco, "The Death of the Gruppo 63," *20th Century Studies* 5 (September 1971), 60–71. For Luperini's critique of structuralism, see his *Marxismo e letteratura* (Bari: De Donato, 1971) which I reviewed in *Clio* 4 (October 1974), 129–34.

14. Gianfranco Bettetini, *Produzione del senso e messa in scena* (Milano: Bompiani, 1975), p. 13; my translation. An English translation is supposed to be published soon by Mouton.

15. It seems to me that these notions of code and sign function define possibilities of research in, for example, cinema (as industry as well as apparatus) that could not be envisaged by a semiotics of the signifier or by a semiotics of the system (which is what was generally meant by the term code as in Metz). But this must be the topic of another essay.

16. I will not discuss *A Theory of Semiotics* at length because I have already done so in my review article "Semiosis Unlimited," *PTL: A Journal for Descriptive Poetics and Theory of Literature* 2 (1977), 367–83. For additional information on Eco's view of his own work and of semiotics, see my interview recorded in February 1976 in *The Canadian Journal of Research in Semiotics* 4 (Spring-Summer 1977), 107–14.

17. But it may well be that the monumental tautology I perceive in this argument and in Rossi-Landi's entire enterprise is only my failure of understanding. Similar doubts, however, are also expressed by Giorgio Patrizi, "La critica del segno: Appunti per una ipotesi politica della semiologia" in *Marxismo e strutturalismo nella critica letteraria italiana* (Rome: Edizioni Savelli), pp. 211–37. On the question of Marxism as science, see Lucio Colletti, "Marxism: Science of Revolution?" in Robin Blackburn, ed., *Ideology in Social Science* (New York: Vintage, 1973), pp. 369–77.

18. The notion of expression and content are derived from Luis Hjelmslev, whose *Prolegomena to a Theory of Language* (Madison: University of Wisconsin Press, 1969) has had a determining influence on Italian semiotics. Hjelmslevian semiotics is the basis of much of Eco's and Garroni's work in *Filmcritica*.

19. F. D., "Quale unità opera studenti?" *Lotta Continua* (19 February 1977), p. 4. For this new analysis of living labor, LC cites Romano Alquait, "L'università e la formazione. L'incorporamento del sapere sociale nel lavoro vivo," *Aut aut*, 154 (1976).

20. Stephen Heath, "Film Performance," *Ciné-Tracts* 2 (Summer 1977), 7–17.

21. For different views on the left, see Giorgio Amendola's interview with *Paese Sera* of July 17, 1977 and Enrico Deaglio's recap "Allineati e coperti" in *Lotta Continua* of July 16, 1977 (LC was the only ultraleft paper which, supporting Bernardi's views, was not solidly against the French manifesto). In Italy this action was read in the context of the anti-Marxist spiritualist positions of the nouveaux philosophes—see Lucio Colletti's debate with André Glucksman and Bernard Henry Lévy published in *L'espresso* (July 24, 1977), pp. 45–51 and 107–10. For a well informed account of the political action of independent radios, see Suzanne Cowan, "The Unhappy Adventures of 'Alice' in Blunderland," *Radical America* 11/12 (Winter 77–78), 67–77.

22. "Il caso Guattari: Due chiacchiere fra barbari," *L'espresso* (July 31, 1977), but also Eco's "No, perdio, non mi suicido," *L'espresso* (April 1977), pp. 52–63.

23. See Gayle Rubin, "The Traffic in Women: Notes on the Political Economy of Sex," in Rayna R. Reiter, ed., *Toward an Anthropology of Women* (New York: Monthly Review Press, 1975), pp. 157–210; and Elizabeth Cow, "Woman as Sign," *M/F* 1 (1978), 49–63.

24. Lea Melandri, *L'infamia Originaria* (Milano: Edizioni L'Erba Voglio, 1977). This and all other passages quoted are in my translation; the italics are Melandri's.

25. Jean-Joseph Goux, *Freud, Marx: Économie et Symbolique* (Paris: Seuil, 1973), p. 57.

IV
Film Form/Film History

XVII

MEDIA REPRESSION

A PERSONAL STATEMENT

Peter Watkins

Recently, I read two articles on the front page of the Danish newspaper *Politiken*—the first confirmed that there are now at least 10,000 attempts at suicide each year in Denmark; the second article dealt with the arrival in Europe of the new American tactical nuclear missles. Then, this evening, my older son told me by phone from Paris that the French TV has this day been warning of the possibility of nuclear war, following the Soviet invasion of Afghanistan. The Danish report on suicide raises a grim irony, which I will mention later. But the other two media items provoke a worrying thought, which will be the basis for this article—that, if our planet is indeed plunged into nuclear catastrophe—countless millions of those who will suffer, will have had little if any knowledge about the nature and implications of the weapons that have caused the suffering, or about the social and economic and military and political forces and doctrines that have led to the war (i.e., World War III). In other words, though we have heard and read in the media about the possibility of nuclear war, most of us—including those in the media who have produced the words—have only a vague comprehension as to what these words mean, in their full context. We sit, and the words slip past, meaningless. But what is happening here? How can we be so passive about so major a potential disaster? Is there a relationship between our inactivity and the ways in which we receive our "information" on this and other world-subjects? I believe that the answer to this question is unequivocally "yes"—and I would like to offer, through my own personal and professional experience—several connecting points between the current world dilemmas (most specifically, our inability to react to them), and what I see as the present crisis in the mass media, especially TV. We can perhaps understand it, first, as a problem related directly to the withholding of information from the public. Secondly, as related to the yet uncharted effects of the highly structured and repetitive visual language system that TV uses to impart what "information" it does convey.

Let us look at the suppression of information. In 1965 I made *The War Game* for BBC-TV, depicting the outbreak of World War III. The film dealt with the escalating spread of nuclear weapons, and stated that by 1980 the conditions would be ready for a use of these weapons. *The War Game* described the possibility that a nuclear war could start by the use of tactical nuclear weapons in the European/NATO area. In November 1965, the BBC banned *The War Game* from being shown on TV, either in Britain or anywhere else in the world. Further, the BBC have maintained the world-wide embargo on the TV use of the film for 14 years, despite its relevancy to the contemporary world. In 1968, Sudwestfunk (a West German TV company based at Baden-Baden) gave me a signed contract to remake *The War Game* to show the possible results of a nuclear attack on Hamburg. Ten days before I was due to start work, SWF tore up the contract, and I was told that the film was cancelled—one reason being that it was not "aesthetic" to show nuclear war on TV. In 1975 Danmarks Radio (Danish TV) and Norddeutscher Rundfunk TV (based in Hamburg) agreed to co-produce a film with Bo Melander and myself, to show what could happen if the Indian Point reactor 2 north of New York City went into melt-down. At the last moment, the West Germans collapsed the production, claiming that they had been informed by one of their "technical experts" that such a melt-down was impossible. Early this past year, the Canadian Broadcasting Corporation asked me to make a film for them. I proposed to show what could happen if the newly constructed reactor in the Philippines (partly fuelled by Canadian uranium) went into melt-down. The CBC abruptly withdrew its offer of work, and the letter confirming their rejection of the Philippines film was typed two days before the Harrisburg accident in the United States.

In 1976, with Poul Martinsen and Carsten Clante, I made *Evening Land (Aftonlandet)* for the Danish Film Institute. This film shows a strike in a Copenhagen shipyard, prompted by the management's acceptance of a contract to build the hulls for four nuclear missile submarines for the French navy. At the conclusion of the film, a meeting of European Defense Ministers (which we staged ourselves) is shown discussing the need for NATO to acquire the Cruise Missile (an American tactical nuclear missile) as a "balance" against the Soviet arms build-up. *Evening Land*—probably the first political feature film of its kind ever made in Scandinavia—was heavily attacked by the Danish and Swedish press, and withdrawn from its cinema in Stockholm after a few days. More recently, it has become clear that the Danish Film Institute will not permit *Evening Land* to be released to American cinemas or universities, and Danmarks Radio have refused to allow the film to be shown on Danish TV, despite the urgent relevancy of this film to world events (the Danish Parliament is currently debating whether or not to permit the Cruise Missiles onto Danish soil). The Chairman of Danmarks Radio has charged that *Evening Land* does not "reach a standard which DR finds necessary." Given that many Danes I have spoken with find the average program content of DR to be immature, boring, and irrelevant to their lives, one wonders exactly what this "standard" is. I recall watching a recent program on Danish TV, in which most scenes consisted of a crowd of men in grey suits chasing a naked belly dancer down endless corridors. This was an hour long film (I think it was a Hungarian spy drama) and it was shown at peak-hour viewing. To claim that such rubbish has a "standard" and at the same time ban a serious and relevant film such as *Evening Land* is an indecent and hypocritical joke.

One realizes, of course, that the arguments of "standard" and "quality" are being used in a special and highly selective manner which is not normally applied to the vast bulk of TV material which reaches the public. This is a completely untenable paradox. So much of contemporary TV—with its emphasis on physical or moral violence—its tasteless "low common denominator" comedies—its extravagant and empty costume dramas—its absurdly fragmented and often superficial current-affairs programs and news-items—are all a tremendous insult to the integrity and intelligence of the audience. The gap between audience wishes and the transmitted material is now vast—and it is still the TV profession itself which ignores this gap—claiming, as it does, that the average audience is intellectually lazy, and does not want to be bothered or worried by serious or complex programming. As a part of the phenomenon, TV has developed to the point of mania the simplified narrative structure, with its synchronized sounds and images—completely antithetical to the complex experience of life. Any attempt to work with film in a more liberating manner, dislocating time and space, is reacted to with enormous resentment within much of the TV profession. A similar reaction is provoked by the use of amateur actors—especially if they work in a free and improvisational manner. It is almost as if TV is deeply afraid of losing what it sees as its control over the audience—a control which could be threatened by the use of freely associative sounds and images, or by people (and not rigidly organized actors) expressing themselves freely and in a complex way. This fear within TV manifests itself in many ways, and not only with ostensibly political subjects.

After the first showing in Norway of *Edvard Munch* (NRK-TV and SR-TV, 1973–1975) a group of Norwegian TV producers reportedly condemned the film for, among other things, my use of amateur actors. A senior official with Swedish TV, on the radio, attacked me for "developing the cult of the amateur" and another Swedish TV official stated, also on radio, that I did not know what I was doing when I made films. In many quarters within Scandinavian TV, there was obviously a great deal of resentment for the film *Edvard Munch*—for its amateur actors, for its style, and for its complexity. The Norwegian TV (NRK) then censored the sound-track, despite a special Norwegian law which is supposed to protect the integrity of any creative work. The Swedish TV tried to hold back *Edvard Munch* from being shown at the annual Nordisk Film Screenings (they evidently felt that the film was not worth showing to TV delegates from other countries). In the same period, the NRK destroyed all the sound mixing tracks of the film, and all the original quarter inch recordings, just at the time that I needed them to re-mix the cinema version of the film. A few months later, the NRK tried to hold back the film from being shown at the Cannes Film Festival, and did succeed in preventing *Edvard Munch* from representing Norway at the Festival.

It is obvious, in fact, that the "liberal" repression which has been emerging as a phenomenon in TV over the past 15 years, is now fully out in the open, and that what one has to fear—is not only the conservatism and political timidity at the managerial level—but a particular kind of jealousy (of commitment) that cuts in from the ranks of one's own "radical" colleagues. This jealousy links with an increased personal emphasis on ego, ambition, self-fulfillment, and job security.

One can almost see the fear which now drips down the walls of TV-corridors. And, using the names of "quality" and "professionalism" and "objectivity" and "standard" the middle-echelon of Western TV are now exercising a repression which is even more severe than that of the political bosses who they like to claim are responsible, but in fact whose only guilt—often—is that they (the bosses) provide an excuse, or a front, for the middle-echelon to carry out a wave of censorship (and self-censorship) unparalleled since the inception of public TV broadcasting. The result: that personal, subjective, committed, individual program and filmmaking are being openly stamped out, in the name of, and for the sake of, "authoritative" and "objective" programming. In a word, personal propaganda is being eliminated for the sake of corporate propaganda, quite oblivious of the fact that the effect (on the audience) of the highly structured, fragmented and repetitive language-system developed by TV has rendered the concept of "objectivity" both absurd and at the same time, highly dangerous. But, oblivious to this, Western TV is desperately pursuing its goal of safe, noncontroversial "quality" wrapped within a facile, narrative structure and quite ruthlessly eliminating everything which threatens this "ideal."

In 1974 I made *The Seventies People* for Danmarks Radio TV. This film dealt with the complex social causes of suicide within Denmark, including a system which places great stress on young people; the role of the media, and various ambient "external" pressures, such as the nuclear arms race, and world instability. *The Seventies People* stated that—contrary to the official Danish statistics—the rate for attempted suicide in Denmark was at least three times higher than previously made known. The film stated that there were (and are) perhaps as many as 7,000–10,000 attempts at suicide each year in Denmark, with the rate being especially high among young people. Despite the ironical fact that the recent article in *Politiken* now confirms the basis for *The Seventies People*, the film was viciously attacked by the Danish press when it was shown on TV, and since that time, DR-TV have stated that they will not allow the film to be shown again on Danish television; neither will they permit it to be shown in cinemas or schools outside Denmark. I am sure that the embargo now placed on *The Seventies People* has two root causes. Firstly, because the film is deeply critical of the Danish social welfare system. Secondly, because the complex structure of the film does not conform to the prevailing "standard of quality" within TV.

At this point I should mention that both *The Seventies People* and *The Trap* (an anti-nuclear TV play written by Bo Melander, which I directed for the Swedish TV in 1975) have also been refused transmission by the Norwegian TV, on the basis of being, in their opinion, of inferior quality. Danmarks Radio TV has refused to transmit *The Trap*, also, on the same grounds. While on the subject of "quality," I should mention that the BBC in 1965 used a similar logic to justify their banning of *The War Game*. The first paragraph of a mass-produced letter (which the BBC sent out to the public, stating that the film would not be shown on TV) declared that television, by its nature, is an experimental medium (!!) but that the "element of experiment" in *The War Game* was unsuccessful, and a senior officer at the BBC explained to me, in private, that one of the reasons why *The War Game* was not going to be shown on TV was that the film "was less than a masterpiece". ("Such program experiments sometimes fail and have to be put on one side at some stage in the production, even though money has been spent on them.")

There is much more that could be said, but space forbids it. The problems attendant on my work stretch far beyond Scandinavia. My films have been very heavily attacked both in Britain and in the United States. The attitude of the British film establishment toward my work, for over ten years, can be summed up in the recent statement about me made by a London magazine: "His entire oeuvre may be characterised as a progression from polemical hysteria towards formal paranoia." In the States, at least three productions of mine, attempting to depict the suppression of the North American Indians in the last century, have been collapsed, and my only American film (*Punishment Park,* 1970) has been refused a theatrical release, and any TV screening, for over six years in that country.

In Canada, some six or seven years ago, the head of the National Film Board rejected my request for the board to finance a documentary reconstruction of the Louis Riel uprising, on the grounds that he disapproved of *The War Game.* It became obvious that this official arranged the only meeting we had, not to discuss the Riel project, but to relieve himself of his pent up feelings about *The War Game.* "You are a very dangerous man, Mr. Watkins!" he shouted at me, his voice breaking with fury. His further implication was that a film on Riel, made by me, would lead to revolution in Quebec and bloodshed on the streets.

While no one could claim that the commercial cinema is an easy arena in which to practice commitment, at least it is honest (relatively speaking) with regard to its limitations and its censorship. But TV, despite—or perhaps because of—its pretense to 'quality', has, in the past fifteen years, largely corrupted its early promise and degenerated into a brutal, hypocritical, and cynical industry, with an ever-increasing contempt, both for its audience, and for those of its members who try to take the medium seriously. As a working profession, and as a means of expression, TV clearly no longer expresses or has any place for the person with commitment, or passion of feeling, nor for anyone who has a deep concern for and with the social process. One may only look at what is happening in the world around us—complex and serious as it is—and then glance at the trite and simplistic rubbish that is the standard fare of TV—one may only question people in the streets of any major city, to ask them what they know about the events of the world (especially the nuclear arms race)—to understand the hideous disparity between the output of TV, and the realities of the human experience, quite apart from understanding the grim toll of withholding essential information from the public. (One recent and particularly unhappy irony of television was that—before the Harrisburg accident—the TV silence on the subject of nuclear energy and its technology—especially its dangers—was almost as total as the current TV silence on the nuclear arms race, and on the effects of nuclear weapons. One can only hope that the same media "logic"— of waiting until the problem becomes "news"—will not be applied to World War III. . . .)

Most significantly, though, I believe, in relationship to the present world crisis, is that TV has developed its own particular form of language system, which operates within predictable sets of codes, symbols, and time structures, with uniform rhythms and repetitive patterns, all of which are highly dangerous (or suspect, to say the least), as they seriously affect the perceptions, feelings, knowledge, and political opinions of countless millions of people—as well as, and because of, playing a principle role in distorting any particular piece of information which that language system is attempting to convey. Virtually nowhere within contemporary Western television is this language system—and its effects—being studied. All that TV appears to be concerned about now is "style"; money; ratings, and endlessly producing the stuff—totally oblivious to the consequences in human cost.

The phenomenon of TV—in terms of the critical approach adopted towards it—varies greatly, according to what country one is in. Generally speaking, the "New World" countries of America, Canada and Australia appear to be somewhat more critical toward TV—the public tend more to query and even reject the assumed role of TV—than is the case in Europe and Scandinavia, where television appears to have a much more accepted, even "respectable" position, within the social process. One indicator of this is that one can find dozens—hundreds—of courses in the media, in universities and colleges throughout the U.S., Canada and Australia. It should be said that most of these courses are not critical, and are invariably preparing youngsters to re-perpetuate the same media machinery. But there are some courses in these countries which are critical and analytical, and in open discussions on the subject, one can see immediately that the public there has a variety of feelings and reactions to the role of the media (especially toward TV)—ranging from a passive acceptance to an extremely critical position, even of total rejection. This presents a variety of reaction, that simply does not exist in the same way or degree in Europe, and which, particularly, does not exist in Scandinavia, where a number of university courses, critical towards the media, can be counted on the fingers of one hand, and the role of TV appears to have an unprecedented authority among the public and, most disturbingly, an authority among those of university age and those in the younger executive/professional grouping—even, it should be said, among those of a more "radical" incline.

Nonetheless, one factor remains constant no matter what country one speaks of, and that is the undeniable impact of TV upon each culture. Further, the scale of the phenomenon—in terms of the numbers of those watching TV sets every night—remains beyond dispute. In the United States, the daily viewing average per child is at least two and a half hours per day, often higher; in Australia, an estimated twenty percent of children are watching between four and six hours of TV each day of the year. I do not have the European and Scandinavian viewing figures, but I imagine that they run into at least two hours per child, per night. Watching. And listening (sometimes). Watching—what? Well, coming across from that flickering rectangle is a highly rhythmic language system, as I have inferred earlier, whose manner of delivering "information"—no matter what the subject—tends to have certain uniform patterns. Uniform patterns within the time allocated to each scene and to each "shot"; uniform patterns to the combinations and groupings of scenes, "shots" and camera movements, etc. We are here looking at the primary building blocks of a second language system, which we have all been acquiring since we first switched on a TV set, and which more and more is impairing our use of the first language system (words, sentences, paragraphs, etc.) of our native tongue, with which we used to communicate.

If we take, as an example, an average TV evening news-broadcast, running from 7:00 to 7:30 pm, we can immediately see what is occurring, if we lay out the structure, news item by news item, commercial by commercial (if applicable), cut by cut. If we carefully lay out, on paper, the internal building blocks—examining each cut from moving frame to static frame, each cut from visually weighty frame to a relatively empty one, each cut from color-rich frame to pastel one—if we carefully examine each move of the camera, each zoom, each pan, tracking shot—if we examine the use of sound, and the use (or nonuse) of silence—if we analyze the narrative structure of beginning, middle, climax, and termination inherent in each news-item—if we examine the repetitive patterns within the groupings of filmed news-items and studio news-items; the average amount of time allocated to each item, and to the number of words spoken by the narrator—we are thus beginning to examine, block by block, the building structure of the TV language, and we realize, as we must, that what we are looking at is not a casual outflow of random sounds and images, but a tautly organized system of conveying what are presumed to be messages.

Further, it should be understood that this language system does appear to have certain "constancies"—no matter whether it is being used for a feature film such as *Jaws* or for the nightly TV news, and that it is applying the same manner of delivery—the same fragmentation—to all subjects. That is to say, there are direct parallels in structure and rhythm between the kind of television broadcasts in the United States, Sweden, Canada, Denmark, Italy, Australia, France, etc. As well as direct parallels in editorial policies in the "understandings" as to what can or cannot be said on the voice-track, or which subjects are allowed on the screen and which are not, and, above all, parallels in the "understandings" as to what is meant by "objectivity."

In other words, no matter who is using this language system—for no matter what social or political ends—even for the ends of so-called "entertainment"—the results are manipulative. The only difference is in kind. And this mono language-system— via the instant spread of pre-packaged TV satellite programs—is now reaching into every corner of the globe. Editors are cutting film with the same "understood" rhythms, producers are directing programs with identical structures, editorial policies, etc. And perhaps the most worrying factor of all, is not only the universal dimension of this phenomenon, but its equal application over almost all subject matter.

In conclusion, then, the problems for me, as a personal filmmaker, range from the corporate circumstances under which I have had to work, to the forms that I use in conveying my "messages." I have tried to write about both dilemmas in this piece, because both are relevant, but I am certainly aware that—because I do describe the barriers against my own work—some within the TV profession will react by saying that I am being too inward-looking, only concerned with my own misfortunes, etc. Certainly, this reaction may occur, precisely because much of the problem within TV now is that the group or the corporate structure has come to mean everything, and the role of the individual has been reduced to that of an anachronism—either as a program maker, or even as someone uttering an opinion that varies from the group "norm." But I make no excuses that I have dealt here with my own experiences—these personal examples are the best and most valid evidence that I can give, for the repression in the Western media today, and for the variety of forms that it can take—ranging from direct suppression, to a tacitly understood group-censorship. I know, from many conversations with other TV program-makers, and especially after talking with many young filmmakers, that my own evidence of the suppression within television today can be duplicated many hundreds of times over. In brief, I find myself now joining the ranks of others, rendered inoperable within television, because of my concerns and political commitments.

Yet, the need for struggle today is imperative, given the push on all social fronts towards group conformity, quite apart from the extremely dangerous situation that our world is now facing, on the entire economic-political-military front. And that meaningful struggle is now utterly impossible within this profession. Perhaps, yes, 15 years ago, but not now. Almost everything of any consequence is either reduced to banality (partly by policy, partly by the language system) or is suppressed. Of course, part of the personal dilemma could be seen, in some cases, as being that of the "inevitability" of the artist "suffering" in an alien culture (world) etc. There is a certain historical truth to this, and perhaps under other circumstances I might have continued with my film-work, accepting (more or less) the "inevitable" consequences of working in this way. But, my fear of what we in the mass audio-visual media are doing to manipulate the public—and my fear of the unknown consequences of this manipulation, strike deep. I feel that I must try to discover—or at least research—more about what it is we do—I do—when we use these sounds and images, especially in this repetitive way.

In the coming years I intend to study the effects of film and television on our society, and to help stimulate a public awareness of the need for an intensive examination of this very meaningful (and often dangerous) sector of the social process. I have studied the structure of TV evening news broadcasts, in several countries, and I hope to begin a series of discussions in various Western TV organizations, in an attempt to help create a dialogue—a process of self-questioning—as to the nature and the effects of our language system, whether used in news broadcasting, narrative film, or "documentary." In this way, I hope that I can help, with others, to create a healthy and much needed challenge to the overly-centralized role of the mass media in our society.

XVIII

CAMERA MOVEMENT AND CINEMATIC SPACE

David Bordwell

Camera movement in the cinema is one of the most difficult areas for critical analysis. Seen as an alternative to montage, or as a stylistic fingerprint, or the occasion for reverie, camera movement has usually been considered too elusive to be analyzable. This essay is an attempt to examine more closely the functions of camera movement in cinematic representation. While several theoretical frames of reference (the semiological, the psychoanalytic) could help us in this task, I shall try to develop another approach, a perceptual approach, because of my conviction that a recognition of the perceptual features of cinema should be part of any thorough attempt to understand filmic experience.

Let me suggest the value of this approach with reference to a specific issue. It is a commonplace of contemporary film theory that certain cinematic processes seek systematically to station the viewer as subject before an idealized objectified representation. This is a useful hypothesis, but too seldom do theorists analyze the perceptual bases of that subjective stationing. If we consider, for example, perceived depth on the screen, it is certain that pictorial codes function to help efface the image surface and push us toward reading the picture as an imaginary space, a scenography; and it may be fruitful to think of our relation to that scenography as being one whereby, as Baudry puts it, "the imaginary order fulfills its particular function of occultation, of filling the gap, the split, the subject on the order of the signifier."[1] But we should also recognize that the traditional conditions for viewing a film already, at the perceptual level, reduce the number of cues which might help us to locate the picture as a flat surface. For instance, inter-position, the possibility that the presence of other viewers beside and in front of us might let us see the screen as only one surface among a series of surfaces, is minimized by some very habitual theatrical practices—staggered seating and the correct viewing angle so that nothing blocks our view of the screen. Binocular disparity (the fact that the eyes see two slightly different fields and get slightly different information from each field) is ruled out by the "ideal viewing distance," which seeks to minimize the difference between the two eyes view onto the screen. The fixity of the screen itself eliminates the need for the viewer to make efforts of accommodation, those

229

muscular movements that are necessary to focus the eye. Finally, we do not inspect the image on the screen as we might a picture as we stroll through a gallery. Any movement parallax on the part of the spectator is minimized by the fixity of the seat and the limitations put on the spectator's head movements. In sum, then, the viewing situation filters out many cues which would call our attention to the screen as a surface.

Now the above sketch simply sets out some negative conditions for our viewing; a complete analysis would have to consider all the factors of the image and of the viewer's mental processes as well. If I cannot examine all of the perceptual conditions of film-viewing here, still less can I be exhaustive in applying a perceptual analysis to the representational functions of camera movement. Yet we can begin to ask how camera movement asks to be "read" perceptually. Though the temporal and expressive functions of camera movement are extremely important, I shall confine this analysis to some problems of space. What kinds of spatial perception are entailed by camera movement? /

Representing space, depicting an absent space, seems fundamental to camera movement as ordinarily used. Like most of our critical concepts in cinema, however, "camera movement" is not derived from a unified critical theory, but rather has issued from a mixture of technical jargon and critical parlance. The very notion "camera" already situates us not before the cinema screen, but in a film studio, in production surroundings which include a mechanism called a camera. A profilmic event, this account might go, exists in empirical reality and is filmed by the camera. This event is represented, re-played on the screen. On this account, camera movement simply means that the apparatus which films this event moves while filming this event. The word "pan" then names one kind of movement of the apparatus, "tilt" another, "tracking shot" another. And both the camera's movement and the filmed event are recorded by the camera itself, to be re-presented on the screen.

The advantages of the profilmic event account are apparent. The model can be made quite exhaustive. With the aid of spherical geometry, we could plot within a three-dimensional system of coordinates any sort of camera movement in relation to any sort of subject movement. Such a geometrical system would have an advantage over the empirical terminology in revealing deductively many possiblities of camera movements which are seldom used and for which, in fact, we have no names. (What do we call it when the camera spins on its own axis, either horizontally or vertically?) By assuming the empirical existence of an object which can be manipulated in a three-dimensional space, the profilmic event account could yield significant categories. The three-dimensionality implicit in the profilmic event model suggests as well, a basis for the orthodox comparison between the camera and the human body. The head may rotate, that is, pan or tilt, or the entire organism may displace itself, may "locomote" by tracking or craning.

Still, the profilmic event model poses difficulties when we apply it to the problem of camera movement. Because this account repeats the problematic dualism between some innocent "real" event and some transformation of that event by the act of filming, the profilmic event model cannot specify the perceived screen event which we identify as camera movement. Camera movement during filming is neither a necessary nor a sufficient condition for the perception of camera movement in the finished film. Some obvious examples would be process work or backdrops unrolling behind people walking on treadmills. Animated film poses a supreme example of this problem: we may see camera movement in an animated cartoon even though the empirical camera has remained absolutely stationary during production. All such screen events use an immobile camera to present enough correct on screen configurations for us to identify "camera movement." Similarly, the movement of the camera during production does not guarantee that a perceptible camera movement will appear on the screen. Recall how, in the "Lullaby of Broadway" number in *Gold Diggers of 1935,* Winnie Shaw's head, a pinpoint of light at the center of the screen, comes swimming out of the darkness at us. In production, of course, the camera was moved, but on the screen the overriding perceptual fact is that of a face floating out toward us. More elaborately, in Dreyer's film *La Passion de Jeanne d'Arc,* though the camera did move in production, in certain shots, figures walk across the room against blank backgrounds and don't seem to be moving; they seem to jog in place. Similar effects occur in the films of Miklos Jancso and Michael Snow. The conclusion is that we need another model for describing camera movement, one that does not rely on a conception of some profilmic event through which, around which, toward which the camera is moved.

There must be perceptual cues which determine a "camera-movement effect" on screen regardless of whether the camera moved in production or not (since we recognize camera movement without necessarily making any inferences about production circumstances, and since animators have intuitively understood what cues will produce that camera-movement effect). But the cues must be visual ones. (Or in the case of the sound cinema, visual and sonic ones: This essay confines itself to visual cues.) This of course already limits the range of the cues available for us to sense the camera-movement effect. In our normal movement through the world we operate with a host of cues—kinesthetic cues, bodily movement cues, tactile cues, labyrinthine cues, cues for balance and gravity, as well as visual cues. Special screening conditions, of course, sometimes supply those other cues as well, as in "Hale's Tours" or Disney World's "Trip to the Moon" ride. But usually cinema screenings omit such desiderata and make visual and sonic cues do duty for all the other kinds. From the standpoint of the history of the concept of representation, this funnelling of information onto the visual channel would be another symptom of the Post-Renaissance linkage of sight with truth. Perceptually, however, limited cues can still be powerful. For instance, in ordinary situations, nonvisual cues are utilized during active locomotion, when we determine our movement through the world or some movement of our body. But passive locomotion, say, riding on a train or bus, enforces a much greater dependence upon purely visual cues. When we sit in an unmoving train, the sight of a passing train can even mislead us into thinking that we are moving and the other train is stationary. Our dependence on visual cues is more strongly marked in a passive locomotion situation, the situation most analogous to the cinema spectator's viewing situation.

Camera movement, I suggest, presents us with a constricted but effective range of visual cues for subjective movement. The primary cue for recognizing the camera movement effect is what psychologists of perception call "monocular movement parallax," a concept first explained by the psychologist Helmholz. When we walk through a countryside with eyes fixed on the distant horizon, he noted:

> objects that are at rest by the wayside appear to glide past us in our field of view in the opposite direction to that in which we are advancing. More distant objects do the same way, only more slowly, while very remote bodies like the stars remain permanent positions in the field of view. Evidently, under these circumstances, the apparent angular velocities of objects in the field of view will be inversely proportional to their real distances away; and consequently, safe conclusions can be drawn as to the real distance of the body.[2]

In more formal terms, for the impression of subject movement to arise, a differential angular velocity must exist between the line of sight to one object and the line of sight to any other object at a different distance and/or angle within the visual field. Mathematical formulas have been constructed to calculate and predict such differential velocities.[3] In applying this to camera movement, we could on the basis of on screen evidence state mathematically the conditions for, say, a pan shot; that is, a specific set of differential angular velocities that are obtained among objects moving across the frame. For the camera movement effect to occur, monocular movement parallax must be read from the entire visual field. If only a part or item in the visual field yields that differential angular velocity across time, then camera movement will not be specified—only the movement of that object will be specified. Thus camera movement can be described and analyzed perceptually, as a screen phenomenon. A Gestalt psychologist like Rudolph Arnheim could explain that total displacement of the visual field effected by camera movement by using concepts like dependence, enclosedness, variability, size differences, and so on.[4] A psychophysicist like James J. Gibson would hold that perceived subject movement is indicated by changes in the rate of displacement of contours in a visual field; Gibson could analyze that flowing optical array on the screen into features of texture gradient, and then the relationships between those features could be specified to give us an analytical description of camera movement.[5] However different the theoretical frames of reference, camera movement could be described as a system of perceptual relationships.

One of the principal kinds of information that differential angular velocities produce is spatial. I suggested earlier that the conventional viewing situation works to block our perception of the screen as surface. What enters to fill that blocked perception is an extensive system of cues for reading the represented space as possessing depth. Within this system, the moving camera becomes a powerful tool for rendering a static visual array as three-dimensional. A still picture—a photograph, or a painting, or a single frame of film—yields a great number of perceptual cues for the layout of the depicted space—the familiar size of objects, overlap of objects, shadows attached to objects, cast shadows, detail perspective, aerial perspective, linear perspective, color, and others. Experiments have shown, however, that despite such cues a static picture retains a certain fundamental ambiguity about its spatial layout. In 1946, for instance, Adelbert Ames constructed a room which could be viewed only through a peephole, and showed that when a single vantage point forbade the spectators' investigating the object from other positions, a criss-cross of lines and planes could be read from that point as a perfectly legible image (a chair, say). But only from that point. This entails that the perceptual configuration "chair" can be produced by an infinite number of possible arrays. As Gombrich puts it, "Any number of objects can be constructed that will result in the identical aspect from the peephole."[6] Similarly, R. L. Gregory has constructed objects which seem impossible and contradictory when viewed from a single fixed point.[7] The conclusion has been that any pictured scene may be read as an infinite set of possible three-dimensional shapes. The static image does not specify the physical layout of a depicted space. Now the familiarity of objects and the movement of objects (as in cinema) reduce such ambiguity considerably.

But subject movement can virtually eliminate any ambiguity. "In any given configuration," J. J. Gibson writes, "the optical flow [produced when moving from one point to another], the transformation, is specific to that layout of surfaces, and no other."[8] That is, subject movement gives us a sufficient amount of information to define a particular spatial layout. A moving vantage point supplies a dense stream of information about objects' slants, their edges, their corners, their surfaces, their relations with other objects. Julian Hochberg puts it another way: "When the observer moves, the informational economy of seeing only one spatial arrangement in front of him or her becomes overwhelmingly greater then that of any other. In fact, it appears that if he uses all the visual information that is available, there is no way at all of fooling a moving observer once we let him determine his own movements."[9] So in its most usual employment, the moving camera replaces that free binocular movement parallax which we surrender upon settling into our cinema seats and substitutes a monocular movement parallax that can eliminate an enormous amount of ambiguity about the spatial layout of that scenographic space.

The ability of subjective movement to endow static arrays with depth is usually called the "kinetic depth effect." As camera movement, the kinetic depth effect operates to some degree in panning, tilting, and all other rotational movements around the axis of the camera itself. But the kinetic depth effect achieves its greatest power to define space through the traveling shot. Indeed, directors seem to have intuitively understood how traveling shots can produce the kinetic depth effect. Some of the most celebrated early tracking shots, such as in Pastrone's *Cabiria* and Griffith's *Intolerance,* give volume to otherwise static architectural masses, rendering enormous sets legible as depth rather than as a flat construction. "In dollying," says Alan Dwan, "we find it's a good idea to pass things in order to get the effect of movement. We always noticed that if we dollied past a tree, it became solid and round instead of flat."[10]

No sooner have we eliminated the profilmic model, with the camera as a mechanism coasting through a three-dimensional studio, than we find ourselves confronting a set of on screen cues which install the viewer as a subject moving through a fictive scenographic layout. Monocular movement parallax thus defines not only the space of the image but also the perceptual position of the viewing subject. If only one spatial layout corresponds to the trajectory of the movement, it is also true that only one trajectory is specified by the differential angular velocities of the objects. Thus we can hardly resist reading the camera movement effect as a persuasive surrogate for our subjective movement through an objective world. Under normal circumstances it is virtually impossible to perceive those screen events as merely a series of expanding, contracting, labile configurations. The cues overwhelmingly supply a compelling experience of moving through space. The charm of the profilmic event model is that from those plentiful screen cues, the person versed in the ways of cinema can easily extrapolate a dualism of filmed event and a mobile filming mechanism. To use the terms proposed by Stephen Heath, camera movement operates in that zone between the spectator's "look" and the camera's "look," perceptual cues serving to identify the two.[11]

This essay has necessarily limited itself to the perceptual representation of space through camera movement. Obviously the entire question needs more examination. We must study not only space but the temporal and expressive functions of camera movement. Because the camera movement effect depends upon perceiving differential angular velocities, the duration and order of stimuli are also central to its effects. Through time, camera movement can reinforce, modify, or shift expectations and hypotheses about the scenographic space. Moreover, because of the predominant anthropomorphism of our conception of camera movement, we need to look at the concept of the "expressive" features of camera movement (what makes a movement languid or portentous or fluid?). Finally, the whole problem needs to be examined in a historical frame of reference.[12] The most useful conclusion to this essay might be some suggestions about the extent to which a unified spectatorial position may be undermined by camera movement.

If the mobile frame normally yields a strong illusion of a subjective movement through an objective space, a filmmaker can seek to disturb the objectivity of that space or disturb the subjective status of the view of that space. First, it is possible to establish a scenographic space which, in one way or another, becomes difficult to read. In Murnau's *Sunrise,* for example, the country village has been built in false perspective, and the camera movement through the village makes objects which are already unnaturally large or small swell or diminish with excessive speed. Later in *Sunrise,* when the husband goes out to meet the vamp in the swamp, the camera picks him out against the moon, swings left and through some trees to reveal the vamp, standing and waiting for him under a second moon. Disparity is built into the scenographic space itself; the profilmic event becomes contradictory. Or in many films the camera will show us a character in a locale, track or pan away, and reveal the same character elsewhere dressed differently. (Such effects occur with various inflections in films like *Vampyr, Last Year at Marienbad, The Passenger,* and *Partner.*) Obviously, offscreen space always plays a considerable role in camera movement, but most particularly here. What is violated is our expectation that the space outside our traveling vision will be homogeneous with what is within our traveling vision. These examples also indicate that these spaces become inconsistent not through a strictly perceptual interrogation of the camera movement effect, but through narrative systems that establish norms about what could be in a scenographic space.

There is a second, potentially more radical possibility; that of troubling the subjective position defined by camera movement. At first glance, a simple device offers itself: simply stipulate that a camera is producing the image, thus foregrounding the apparatus as mechanism and not organism. But the camera point-of-view is easily read as that of a machine steered by a human subject. A camera implies a cameraperson. Our eye then becomes simply that of the camera, still comfortably moving through an objective array.

More significantly, the viewer's position in camera movement may be made difficult through the creation of inconsistent subject positions. For one thing, there are the possibilities of constructing contradictory or difficult subject positions by fracturing the image so that the camera movement is no longer rendered as the movement of a subjective eye though an objective world. Gance's superimposed tracking shots, the pendular and prismatic movements in Leger/Murphy's *Ballet Mécanique,* and the split-screen effects in Vertov's films explore this possibility. Alternatively, the camera movement can block an anthropomorphic reading, refusing it as an intelligible or likely surrogate for bodily movement. Since camera movement makes kinesthetic cues come to us through the visual channel, it's possible to present kinesthetic cues which violate some normal conceptions of how our body might move. What comes to mind immediately are those unnamed movements forbidden by the dominant narrative and stylistic systems in cinema. The assumption is that since the camera is to its support as the head is to the body, the camera cannot execute those movements that our head cannot or "normally" does not execute. To my knowledge, it is chiefly animated film and avant-garde films which have begun to explore the possibilities of such forbidden movements; Michael Snow's *La Région Centrale* is the major film here.

Finally, there is the possibility of making a subjective-movement position inconsistent at the narrative level as well. This will often involve a playing upon point-of-view shots. At the close of Oshima's *Battle of Tokyo,* the protagonist Motoki, as subject and point-of-view character, splits and so does our position as and with him. At the beginning of a handheld shot, we are posited as seeing what he sees through a movie camera's viewfinder. But in the course of the shot, he runs out from behind the camera, into his/our viewpoint. What were his eyes, his bodily movement, and thus ours, are no longer his, and the idea of "our" position becomes highly problematic. It is a permissible play with convention to have a character enter a shot which has been initially established as her or his point of view, but not when that point of view is defined as that of a camera in his hands. Moreover, Motoki runs into our field of vision carrying the camera through which we are presumably seeing him. Our subjectivity is split, our position impossible.

As most of these examples have suggested, camera movement's impression of reality has chiefly been undermined at the level of narrative, not at the level of perceptual activity. This is probably why camera movement is usually studied as a narrative device. The ways in which the camera movement effect yields certain perceptual cues are rarely contested. Most saliently Michael Snow's films point toward ways of making problematic the sheerly perceptual features of camera movement. Consider only one strategy, that of camera movement velocity (a strategy apparent in a film like "————"). At the highest speeds, or with abrupt and unpredictable stopping and starting, acceleration and deceleration, a pan shot can make it difficult to read a space as scenographic. There is produced a tension between reading the shot as the movement of a body swiveling quickly or that of a series of abstract patterns whizzing across the screen. Such a constant hesitation between readings of the image defines, perhaps, some conditions for working upon the sheerly perceptual features of camera movement. Problematic camera movements, contesting the unity of the scenographic space or the unity of the viewing subject, have impelled us to ask, "What is seen?" or "Who is seeing this?"; theorists and filmmakers must now ask, "What is this mode of seeing?"

NOTES

1. Jean-Louis Baudry, "Ideological Effects of the Basic Cinematographic Apparatus," *Film Quarterly XXVIII*, 2 (Winter 1974–75), 45.

2. Quoted in James J. Gibson, *The Perception of the Visual World* (Cambridge, 1950), p. 119.

3. C. H. Graham, "Visual Space Perception," in Clarence H. Graham, ed., *Vision and Visual Perception* (New York, 1965), pp. 511–16.

4. See Rudolf Arnheim, *Art and Visual Perception*, second edition (Berkeley, 1972), p. 394ff.

5. See Gibson, *Perception, and The Senses Considered as Perceptual Systems* (Boston, 1966), p. 161.

6. The experiment is described in E. H. Gombrich, *Art and Illusion* (Princeton, 1965), p. 248ff.

7. R. L. Gregory, *The Intelligent Eye* (New York, 1970), p. 37ff.

8. Gibson, *Senses,* p. 199.

9. Julian Hochberg, *Perception* (Englewood Cliffs, 1964), p. 94.

10. Quoted in Alan Dwan, *Peter Bogdanovich* (New York, 1973).

11. Stephen Heath, "Anato Mo," *Screen XVII,* 4 (1976).

12. I have suggested a start in this direction in *Camera Movement, The Coming of Sound, and the Classical Hollywood Style,* Purdue Film Studies II (1977).

XIX

THE MYTH OF TOTAL CINEMA HISTORY

Will Straw

> For it is no longer a question of feeble con-
> jecture, hearsay and memory, of dead scrab-
> bling through the inept film criticism of yester-
> year: the authentic raw material for research
> awaits the new expert's eye.[1]

One recurrent feature of film studies literature, particularly in the last half of the 1970s, has been the expression of malaise over the underdeveloped state of film historiography.[2] This has been accounted for in history-of-science terms as neces-sarily following upon an initial phase of collecting and organizing the archival material of historical research prior to its assimilation within a coherent framework.[3] This felt necessity for an increased rigor in the writing of film history, however, may be linked in part to the manner in which Film Studies has emerged institutionally as an academic discipline. The development of film study programs, usually out of English or Mass Media departments (and their academic consolida-tion), has had, as one of its effects, a reaction against the History of Cinema books traditionally used as course texts.[4] The trend toward the centralization or duplication of research material holdings, in (or accessible to) university film departments, making necessary a specialization and localization of historical work, has served to foreground the absence of a methodological and theoretical foundation for the writing of film history.

What I wish to undertake in this article is an examination of the dominant ways in which the historiographical project has recently been conceived in the literature of film studies. I take it as a given that there remains little value in reiterating once again the presuppositional weaknesses of those histories which are the object of critique of this recent work. Rather, I shall attempt an interrogation of the ways in which this dissatisfaction has been posed, the models of history-writing proposed as its resolution, and the implicit conceptualization within such writings of notions such as that of History. This of necessity involves a detour through certain con-siderations of a wider nature on the historiographical project itself as developed with regard to the writing of general history.[5] The manner in which recent writing in Britain, associated in part with the work of Hindess, Hirst, Cutler, and Hussain, has been dealt with by the historiography under discussion will also be discussed, as well as its more general implications for the practice of writing film histories. "Different forms of investigation and practices posit entities and produce results which are in no way to be regarded as partial 'knowledges' of one great whole which are linked by common principles"[6] Conceptualizations of the historian's practice may provisionally be differentiated as to the principles of validation upon which they base themselves. By this I refer not only to the criteria by which the historian's raw material is judged to be true or false, pertinent or irrelevant, but importantly, the manner in which the discourse of history established and orders its objects, as well as the project or imperatives validating such work. To the extent to which auteurism has understood itself as a practice of history-writing, for example, one can see in it the following levels of validation:

1—an initial conception of its project as a necessary rectification of reductionist (i.e., "forest") accounts of Hollywood cinema;[7]

2—a principle of corpus selection based upon an assumed continuity between a group of films bearing the same director's name;

3—an enumeration of such continuities, through analysis, as that which reaffirms the coherence of the corpus; and

4—the wider vision of a larger history which would be an inventory of such continuities, of directorial careers—a mapping across the body of Hollywood cinema of parallel oeuvres.[8]

Methods of history-writing may further be differentiated as to the relationship they posit between "event" and document, the former representing the object of history-writing and the latter the discourses through which it is (variably) known. The fact that the "event" as past is absent from the present of the historian, while documentation survives to confront the historian, is the initial contradiction of historiographies. One, traditional historiographical practice would take the event as given, usually under the evidence of a proper name or categorical label ("The Battle of Waterloo," "The Coming of Sound") and regard the relationship to such an event of existing documentation as a purely transparent, referential one. Another, while acknowledging that entities-as-unities are necessarily constructed or delimited in the historian's discourse, would see this construction as a necessarily provisional step permitting the organization and coherence of archival documentation.[9]

The past thus functions, within historiography, at once as that to which access is presumed given by the archive, and as that which unifies the archive. Principles of archival understanding are thus dependent upon the manner in which the past is conceived: as a series of events of which artifacts are surviving effects; as a field which, presumed unified (in a philosophical conception of time or history), thus guarantees the coherence of disparate documentation. The recognition that the manner in which the past is conceived produces principles of data correlation, and that the inverse is likewise true, makes the reconstruction of the past in the historian's discourse a determinate representation of the past, governed by the imperatives of the present conjuncture, rather than a simple restoration through the access offered by the archive. Edward Buscombe, disputing the implications of this for historiography, writes:

> In particular, in what sense is it true by definition that all which is past does not exist? Only surely in the narrowest sense that would see the present as a kind of geometric point having position but no length, so that the present is always instantly becoming the past. In which case, how do you analyse the current situation? Isn't it always already the past and so non-existent by the time that analyses have been made? And how can it be argued that the past only exists in its representations without arguing the same of the present? What can we know of the current situation except through its representations, in which case how does our knowledge escape ideology any more than our knowledge of the past?[10]

This is misleading above all to the extent to which it represents the work it is disputing (that of Hindess and Hirst) as posing a distinction between the ideological (that is, representations) knowledge of an absent past and the scientific presence to knowledge of the present. The distinction made by Hindess and Hirst between the past and the "current situation" occurs within an argument which suggests that forms of discourse upon the past draw (and not simply "should draw" in a purely prescriptive argument for political relevance) their principles of validation and pertinence from the conjuncture in which they are produced. They share with discourses upon the "current situation" the property of existing as a result of imperatives specific to them: "Theories only exist as discourses—as concepts in definite orders of succession, producing definite effects—(posing, criticising, solving problems)—as a result of that order. Theoretical discourse, like discourse in general, speaking and writing, is an unlimited process."[11]

History-writing which understands itself as defined by properties of its object, or by original theoretical axioms, must seek its validation in properties of that object or from such axioms. Thus, a historiographical practice which works to organize coherently the body of facts existing upon its object will define this work of organization in relationship to the perpetually deferred final assimilation of such data which would constitute a completed history. Practices which begin with a theoretical model thought to correspond to properties of its object will conduct historical work as a process of fleshing out such a model with available data. Regarding this, the primacy of the relationship between "event" and documentation in traditional theorizations of history-writing (including much of the film work referred to more directly below) may enable us to point to a fundamental source of the confusion operative within film historiographies. Film history would in part appear to differ from general history in that, whereas in the latter access to the knowledge of (past and therefore absent) "events" is sought through existing discourses upon them, the object of major strands of film-historical work, the film-text, is perceived as surviving as just such an "event." The distinction between the two problematics history-of-film/history-in-film is in a sense indicative of the manner in which a necessarily inseparable relationship diverges within two approaches to the theorization of history. The latter—"history-in-film," whose pertinence arises either within general history (films as one of a number of documents of a past) or the sociology of cinema (films as representative of aspects of societal situations) is considered, rightly, to pose the "event"—documentation relationship faced by general historiography—the status of referentiality remains problematic. The "history-of-cinema" problem appears to escape this concern by virtue of such documentation, the film-text, being itself the "event" subject to historical explanation; the role of documentation is here shifted to archival, largely written material. The implicit positivism of much writing in film history may be said to stem in part from this assumption that "event" and documentation, film text and archival material (studio records, trade journals, etc.), by co-existing in the present, remove the otherwise necessary work of reconstructing a past which is by definition absent from the present of historical work. To the extent to which this is the case within film historiography, it remains in a pre-theoretical, purely method-ological phase which is twice removed from critiques of philosophical conceptions of the past. The film historian's work, in a majority of cases, is thus conceived of as one of tracing the relationship of archival material to the film-text, this relationship posited as being a direct one. The pertinence of archival material lies in its providing the truth of the film text; the latter, in turn, as historical given, is the pre-condition for the meaningful organization of archival documentation.

Thus, whereas general historiographies attempt to conceive the knowledge process in terms of a relationship between archive and "event," much film historiography distinguishes, within what this general historiography would subsume under "archive between film-text as object and written documentation as the source of knowledge upon that object." One cannot differentiate general and film history on the grounds that film historians are lucky enough to have "The Jazz Singer" still in existence while "The Battle of Waterloo" is not. Writing within the history of the cinema which moves in a circular and unproblematized path from archive to film-text necessarily conceives all points in this circuit as existing in and accessible to the present, through a notion of films as reducible to products. John Ellis writes:

> Contrary to the multiplication of the possible products of cinema, I would venture that the cinema does not really produce anything. This, like most things, is not as extraordinary as it first sounds. To say that the cinema produces films is plainly inadequate: films as strips of celluloid in cans are without great value, certainly not meriting the amounts expended on their production. The formula 'cinema produces films' refuses to ask the question of what a film is.[12]

One of the recurrent recent ways in which this reduction of films to their physical presence is avoided is through a theorization of film as textuality or discursivity. This is a necessary surpassing of the tendency toward hypostatization, but one that is frequently reworked within more traditional varieties of historical explanation. Edward Buscombe remarks that: "Film history, in order to be a science, has to constitute the object which it will study. What the object is can only be determined by a theory of how the film text produces meaning, since it is that meaning which is the object for which history can account."[13] While, as suggested, this is a necessary advance upon empiricist or static accounts of the film text, its status as the "object" of history is, in Buscombe's formulations, contradictory. The film text functions, for Buscombe, as "object" in the sense that it constitutes a theoretically-conceived entity. It is this which historical investigation must explain. However, it is also the "object" of history in the sense that previously constituted, generally linear, histories will be brought to bear on this object in a relationship of explanation to explained:

> But supposing we can establish the object for which film history will account, what kind of explanations for texual history could history offer? At this point it may be useful to make a distinction between two kinds of film history. The first kind would offer an account of the development of cinematic forms; it would trace, for example, the changing conventions and techniques of film lighting or of editing. To put it another way, it would be a history of style in the cinema.[14]

> The first kind of history—of cinematic forms—could explain how it is that some of the features of a single textual system (a film) come to have the meaning they do. Only actual textual analysis can tell us what those meanings are, but this kind of history could explain how those meanings originated.[15]

> Thus the history of cinematic style will, we assume, have a relative autonomy in relation to the industry. . . .[16]

Here, the problem of history-writing is not so much solved by the theorizing of its object, but displaced—the question of the manner in which a "history of style" would differ from the histories Buscombe is reacting against (the very terms in which this is proposed suggest it would not, significantly) is left hanging. The "object" of Buscombe's historiography is not the field of the historian's discourse but rather, the entity upon which that discourse will be brought to bear. The archive—the existing body of documentation on "film style"—is unproblematically thought to provide a history which will serve to explain the "event," the film text. While acknowledging the difficulty of the problem with which Buscombe is grappling, I would suggest that he fails to provide an "object" of film study which does not separate a manner of ordering the past as a field of investigation and the object of such an investigation.

To adopt the concept of the past as necessarily a theoretical mode of coherence is to shift the relationship between archive and film text. The one is not the explanation of the other; both are "the various discourses that the past has thrown up, and that have been accumulated in various forms of archive."[17] What is called the past—the conjunctures and processes which are the conditions of production of such discourses—is necessarily more/other than the sum of the data upon it, or principles of data correlation which enable its cohering within a general framework. What I shall designate as the "archivist" formulation of historiographical problems, and which I see as dominating much recent film historiography, is a tendency to pose such problems in methodological, almost quantitive terms. This may take the form of questions about the relationship of existing, inevitably nonexhaustive data to the ideal totality of such data which would be the basis of a total history of the cinema; or of the relationship of individual work to the elaboration of such a history. The principles of validation of such work lie in its perceived capacity to establish links and sequential relationships between facts; the relevance of existing documentation or individual work is valorized in a part-to-whole relationship with regard to a complete history to which such work is a contribution. Thus fully achieved history of the cinema is posited, in varying degrees of explicitness, as the point at which existing data has been assimilated within a framework which provides its coherence. As Robert Allen suggests: "Because material problems afflict film historical work study so severely, there is the temptation to see the collection of data as the film-historical problem, jumping with both feet into the empiricist camp of historiography and assuming that the more "facts" we gather around ourselves the closer we come to an ultimate solution to our film historical dilemma."[18] In this sense, there is an important continuity between the rejected histories of Knight, Mast, and Jacobs and a good deal of the recent historiographical writing which I would call "archivistic." What is shared is a recognition of the inevitable limitations of individual work in the face of the mass of data with which one is confronted, and a common perception of this as the central problem. (The apologies traditional in film histories as to the practical impossibility of exhaustivity and the regretted necessity in recent historiographical writing of limited objectives are both meaningful only against the larger project of a history of the cinema.) What is disputed is the extent to which this inevitable process of exclusion can serve to justify a retreat into subjective whim. In neither case is the possibility of a complete cinema history considered in anything beyond what might be called logistic terms.

Gerald Mast's "Film History and Film Histories"[19] is symptomatic of work which uses principles of validation while attempting in a contradictory manner to escape them. Mast's discussion of his book *A Short History of the Movies*, and of film history in general is an attempt to restate the inevitability of individual choice within a division of labor that denies the incompatibility of such choice with making a worthwhile contribution to film history—a modest and valid position on its own terms. However, Mast's comments waver between the popular envisioning of a complete history as the retroactive valorization of such individual work and arguments as to the impossibility of such a total history:

> The history of the cinema will never be written; we shall simply have to be satisfied with histories of the cinema. This grand pronouncement contains an assumption not only about the infiniteness of cinema data but about the ability of any single human intelligence to collect it all and set it forth absolutely right. History is not a single entity with a single mind. Different histories will say different things.[20]

> The only way to accomplish the myth of totality—to recapture the totality of cinema history—will be with the total aggregate collection of cinema histories.[21]

Remarks such as "the history of the cinema will never be written" and references to "the myth of totality" take the form of epistemological theses—they at least gesture toward a critique of the notion of written history recapturing "the totality of cinema history" as the truth of the past in its fullness. However, there is a quick elision of the epistemological into the logistic, into what is in many ways simply regret at the brevity of men's lives. The dominant image of the historian's activity in such writing is that of collecting and assimilating data, and the obstacles to a total history (the completion of such processing) rest in the practical limitations of individual capabilities.

Much of the reaction to earlier general histories has taken the form of rejection of all-encompassing historical work in favor of a multiplicity of histories—"Different histories will say different things." While the response of historiographies to the acknowledgement of multiple possible historical accounts may take a variety of forms, characteristic of the film historiography discussed here is a continued effort to recuperate this heterogeneity within the project of a total history.

Mast proposes a number of total histories—"a history of cinema styles," "a history of cinema contributors," "a history of camera technology," of which a total cinema history would be "the aggregate collection."[22] The point is not the extent to which Mast himself forcefully subscribes to the likelihood of such a project, but that it serves to determine the pertinence of local practices of history writing. Such formulations encourage specific models of history writing. A notion of the writing of history as the assimilation of data within one of the "histories" Mast proposes finds as the form of coherence most appropriate to it the linear narrative. Historical explanation is given in the cause-and-effect sequence through which these discourses are ordered.

Charles Altman likewise suggests a smilar inventory of multiple histories as a necessary stage in the writing of film history, preparatory to "a synthetic process whereby general historians build these analyses into a coherent whole, thereby discovering the complex web of generalizations—different in every period—which tie each aspect of film history to the next."[23] Governing such writing, I would suggest, is the implicit metaphor of History-as-Edifice, as essentially cumulative, with specialized research supplying the bricks and intermittent moments of theoretical synthesis the mortar with which to construct the perpetually deferred, but teleologically necessary, goal of a film history. The acknowledged existence of multiple "points-of-view" is regularly reformulated so as to be reducible to the choice made as to individual emphasis within an interdisciplinary division of labor.

Concurrent with the metaphorization of the historian's project as edifice is the thinking of its object in topological terms. In arguing that the self-understanding of much film historiography is one expressed in methodological principles, I mean that it accepts its domain as given in the cohering of discontinuous data under a label such as "American cinema" and seeks, through the establishing of coherent order, to reaffirm the homogeneity of this domain. This unity is presumed by the project of a total cinema history, and the task of history writing is one of reconstituting this unity through the linking of localized work to the larger edifice. The topological image of the object is evident in the manner in which it is divided—a mapping of (however relatively) autonomous regions.

The writing discussed here does not offer an explicit philosophy of history in the sense, for example, of a structural grid or model which empirical work would simply fill in. The task of historiography in these examples is one of dividing the surface of its object, American cinema, for example, into particular areas of investigation, but the nature of these areas, of their relation to the whole, is not given in a model of the object. It is a methodological division, based in part on the obviousness of certain categories (style, genre) rather than on principles of a general model (such as Althusser's "instances").

It might further be suggested that such a conceptualization of the writing of film history has brought about in part the increased predominance of corporate-economic histories in recent writing.[24] Faced with the inevitable lack of internal coherence or desired closure of generic or stylistic histories, the narrativization of economic "events" is perhaps the only mode of historical work having the appearance of a certain finitude. Within the strata of parallel genealogies (stylistic, technological, etc.) conceived by the writers discussed above, it alone appears to possess its own internal, researchable dynamic. If the economic can be narrativized, it is because it is implicitly accepted as the "truth" of film history, within the attendant metaphors of stable base and incoherent effects.[25] The undeniable provisional value of such work is in part undermined by its reliance on linear-causal modes of explanation, and by its displacing of other areas of historical research wherein the ultimate unsuitability of such models has shown itself more quickly (though this displacing, of course, is not the "fault" of those engaged as individuals in economic history).

The above is a tentative attempt at deducing from work in recent film historiography what might be called its imaginary—that is, the larger unity from which individual work derives its pertinence. I present it fully anticipating its being characterized as in some way theoretically nihilist. I remain convinced, however, that the "everyday," "innocent" circulation and reception of historical work distinguishes between such work in terms of its pertinence to current modes and situations of reading and theorizing the cinema-institution-machine. A foregrounding of the manner in which archival materials intervene to produce representations of a past would allow for a necessary recasting of the role of historical work, overcoming the current separation between such work and the theoretically-informed reading of films.

NOTES

1. Iris Barry, "Motion Pictures as a Field of Research," *College Art Journal,* vol. IV, no. 4 (May 1945), p. 209.

2. This is attested to by the number of journals publishing special issues on the writing of film history and by a series of programmatic writings recognizing and attempting to resolve this perceived gap. See, for example, *Cinema Journal,* no. 14 (Winter 1974–75); Charles Altman, "Towards a Historiography of American Film," *Cinema Journal,* no. 17 (Spring 1977); Gerald Mast, "Film History and Film Histories," *Quarterly Review of Film Studies,* vol. 1, no. 3 (August 1976); Edward Buscombe, "A New Approach to Film History," Film: Historical-Theoretical Perspectives, *The 1977 Film Studies Annual: Part Two;* Buscombe, "Introduction: Metahistory of Film," *Film Reader No. 4;* and Robert C. Allen, "Film History: The Narrow Discourse," Film: Historical-Theoretical Perspectives, *The 1977 Film Studies Annual: Part Two.* This article is in general terms a discussion of the above writing.

3. See Buscombe, "A New Approach to Film History"; and Altman, "Towards a Historiography of American Film."

4. Allen mentions Jacobs's *The Rise of the American Film*, Mast's *A Short History of the Movies*, and Knight's *The Liveliest Art*. Mast refers to his own book, to Knight and Jacobs, and to Alan Casty's *Development of the Film*. Altman discusses several dozen titles on a variety of subjects, less with regard to their general methodological principles than to the variety of information they contribute.

5. Throughout, I use "general history" to designate the wider, generally nondiscursive history understood as being the province of History as a discipline. This is a provisional use, adopting the terms of self-understanding of this discipline for convenience. I use "historiography" and its derivatives in a similar way.

6. A. Cutler, A. Hussain, P. Hirst, and B. Hindess, "An Imaginary Orthodoxy—A Reply to Lawrence Harris," *Economy and Society*, vol. 8, no. 3 (August 1979), p. 327.

7. See Andrew Sarris, "Towards a Theory of Film History," *The American Cinema* (New York: Dutton, 1968).

8. This is clearly more characteristic of American auteurism than the French *politique des auteurs*. Nevertheless, the divergence between the former as historiographical axiom and the latter as principle of evaluation is reproduced within American auteur studies—in the tension, in later, more microscopic director analyses, between such work as the elevation of hitherto neglected directors (Joseph H. Lewis, etc.) to a level of acknowledged artistry, and an opposing tendency to develop analyses, through such directors, of the everyday working situations of studio contract directors within a complex of determinations. (This is, in a way, homologous to, within mainstream historiography, the movement from traditional "great men" histories to the *vie quotidienne* work of the Fernand Braudel variety—though I stress the looseness of the analogy.)

9. Régine Robin, *Histoire et Linguistique* (Paris: Armand Collin, 1973), offers a survey of various ways in which the relationship of documentation to a past has been conceived, particularly within historiographical procedures which draw upon methods of discourse analysis. See also her "Discours politique et conjuncture" in Pierre R. Leon and Henri Mitterand, eds., *L'Analyse du discours/Discourse Analysis* (Montreal: CEDEC, 1976). For a more general discussion see in particular: Michel Foucault, *L'Archéologie du savoir* (Paris: Gallimard, 1969), and two books by Michel de Certeau, *L'Absent de l'histoire* (Paris: MAME, 1973), and *L'écriture de l'histoire* (Paris: Gallimard, 1975).

10. "Introduction: Metahistory of Film," p. 13. Buscombe's remarks are directed against a passage he reproduces from Barry Hindess and Paul Hirst, *Pre-Capitalist Modes of Production* (London: RKP, 1975), p. 309.

11. Barry Hindess and Paul Hirst, *Mode of Production and Social Formation* (London: MacMillan, 1977), p. 7. I suggest that their argument is not purely prescriptive partly as a result of the charges of pragmatism which have met their work, though the political role of theoretical work is clearly important to them. Nevertheless, the nonclosure of discourses, their necessary determination within theoretical and institutional settings should be seen as inherent to all theoretical discourses, not only those which work upon their determination to transform its effects.

12. "The Institution of the Cinema," *Edinburgh '77 Magazine*, p. 57.

13. "A New Approach to Film History," p. 5.

14. Ibid., p. 5.

15. Ibid., p. 6.

16. Ibid., p. 6.

17. Mark Nash and Steve Neale, "Film: History/Production/Memory," *Screen*, vol. 18, no. 4 (Winter, 1977/78), p. 77.

18. "Film History: The Narrow Discourse," p. 10.

19. See note 2 above.

20. Mast, "Film History and Film Histories," p. 298.

21. Ibid., p. 313.

22. Ibid., p. 313.

23. Altman, "Towards a Historiography of American Film," p. 24.

24. In part because they are linked to increased accessibility to archives, etc., I should make it clear at this point that my intention is not somehow to suggest that such work should not have been done, or that all of its practitioners consciously suscribe to the conception of history described here. I wish rather to examine the form historical discourses are increasingly taking and the reason why these rather than other modes of history writing meet with very little scrutiny. Douglas Gomery's work stands alone in actively engaging in debates surrounding the writing of economic history.

25. The notorious example of this economism is Gerald Leblanc's "Welles, Bazin et la RKO," *Cinéthique*, no. 6 (though other articles in the same issue are equally representative). I would not accuse any of those writing economic film history in North America of theoretical economism of such excessive and acknowledged proportions. What I am describing suggests a retreat into economic discourses because they give the impression of offering greater coherence and more autonomy than other discourses in film history.

XX

NOTES ON COMMUNICATION AND REPRESENTATION IN THE DEVELOPMENT OF EDUCATIONAL TELEVISION

Phil Vitone

Since the end of World War II research into educational uses of television has constantly increased. It has become the single most studied area of educational inquiry. Hailed as a major advance of the technological age, television appeared to present a wide number of suitable applications to a range of pedagogical and organizational problems facing educational policy-makers.[1] Researchers were, from the beginning, well financed, and they responded quickly with methods and programs for use.[2] The effort was also fueled by the electronics and communications industries, particularly in the United States, creating an atmosphere of optimism that ensured the long term presence of the technology in educational establishments.[3]

Social attitudes toward television, on the other hand, have never been entirely positive, nor have they reflected secure, comprehensive understandings of the medium. Similarly, literature and research existed in the Educational Television field, as well as in other areas of educational study, which took a critical and cautionary position toward the application of television and other technologies, suggesting that there was a general over-optimism and prematurity of approach.[4]

Furthermore, many research studies provided undeniable evidence that there was "no significant difference" between television teaching and "live" teaching. These reports forced even some of the most vigorous early proponents of television education to review claims and methods. From the late fifties to the present, changes have been initiated which attempt to maintain original conceptions and goals through the introduction of more sophisticated productions and variations on hardware use. A variety of literature, from the most eclectic and intuitive handbook to the most serious academic study, has saturated the field with new and supposedly improved methods. On the other hand, certain positions and methods, such as the simple recorded lecture, have been generally discredited or viewed as limited. New impetus for research and development has come from those positions within the Educational Television community which have sought to incorporate theoretical aspects of learning and communication into production and programming. *Sesame Street* is an obvious and striking example of this latter direction of the field.

The development of Educational Television reflects, in large part, a rather functionalist perspective on the medium.[5] The technological ability to produce messages for large or small audiences corresponded very well with two general categories of television use. What became known from the late sixties onward as Educational Television, or "ETV," referred to a "soft" use of the medium to "enrich" or "supplement" a viewer's knowledge, often intended for large, disparate audiences of the type reached through broadcasting. The second category of instructional Television or "ITV" referred to the "hard" use of the medium in order to teach some subject matter "directly."[6] This latter use was most suitable to a situation where a certain control, monitoring, and regulating of results could be obtained; that is, within a small space or grouping, such as those found in a closed-circuit or tape-playback context.

Differences between ETV and ITV in programming, production methods, approaches to subject matter, and definition of audiences represent different degrees of emphasis in the delineation of an instructional strategy. Operational distinctions, however, could not respond to the increasingly apparent complexity of television communication: division between ETV and ITV was based implicitly on the realization that home and school offered two different sets of conditions for the reception of messages. This is to say that home ETV had to compete with other types of television available: school ITV or ETV did not offer the same choice. The popularization and "soft-sell" approach of broadcast ETV was a clear, competitive reaction to commercial television that did not include any real attempt to theoretically analyze the nature of the effect and desirability of the latter type of programming upon audiences.

The entire question of television mediation of communication, though taken up as a central issue in other fields of research, remained marginal through the mid-sixties in ETV research. Only by the end of that decade were theoretical questions regarding potentialities and limitations of television communication raised centrally for educational purposes. Significantly, such questions arose, as formal and central concerns in a separate area of educational study, which has been called "media studies."[7] The desire to provide students with basic "criteria for evaluating"[8] media messages has, within the past decade, promoted the development of critically oriented courses on media analysis and production in the curriculum of educational institutions in various countries.[9] Communication theory, aspects of semiology, psychology, political theory, and aesthetics have provided the basis for insight, investigation, and instruction. Television and its messages, for the purposes of a media studies curriculum, has been understood from a humanist, hermeneutical perspective, in opposition to the predominantly functionalist-behaviorist approach of the major part of ETV research. Educational technologies have only within the last ten years considered factors such as media bias, personal interpretation, social and cultural mediation of television messages as being of any value and significance to the ETV field. Though the work of communication theorists such as Marshall McLuhan and Harold Innis, as well as the semiotic work of Roland Barthes, has existed since the fifties, it has only been since the early seventies that any attempt was made to relate those ideas to ETV theory and practice.[10]

The increasing, but late appeal cognitive and communicational models of perception had for program design necessitated information on the audience. Attempts to obtain the guarantee that a program's concepts and content would be received by the audience meant that its members had to be known and any intervening factors accounted for.

The position of the ETV field in relation to present media and communication research has yet to be fully articulated. It is the purpose of this paper to fill in some of the terms of this relationship, as well as illustrate reasons for its having been neglected in the past. In so doing, with particular reference to the "media studies" project, it becomes possible to evaluate models of ETV practice in terms of communicative practice, thereby illuminating the relationships established between intentions, practices, and actual effect. This last aspect is of significant interest to the ETV field, as it would provide information concerning the terms of methodological success, still an area of contentious debate.

In an effort to expand upon points made above, as well as initially describe the framework for investigating the relationship between communication and ETV, it is worth presenting the following comparison: whereas, the initial interest held by media studies has been the degree of student success in deciphering the validity and acceptability of information transmitted along the various technological communications channels, ETV has reflected, for the most part, a preoccupation with the successful transmission of particular messages revealed through transformations in behavior. The former is concerned with evaluation and contextualization (decoding) of received information; while the latter arranges information and constructs messages (encodes) for its audience, with reference to a particular subject matter. Though these do not reflect opposite positions, a series of problems have arisen when the criteria for evaluating media programs have been compared with the major historical forms of ETV. Media-studies refer the student, for one thing, to the many possibilities for "hidden agendas" being located in transmitted messages.[11] This points to a deeper level of information existing covertly in the television program's codings and seemingly outside the message. Such "coded" information may reflect social, national, and cultural biases.

The vehicle for such "hidden agendas" particularly in the case of television is to be found in, and dependent upon, audio-visual representation understood as verisimilitude. In relation to images, the term refers to an understanding of the image as truthfully duplicating and rendering the constituent elements of an object or exposition.[12] Media studies and communication studies, in general, as well as recent trends in semiology, film theory, literary criticism, and learning theory, would advise a cautious, discriminating attitude in regard to either viewing media or producing films or television from such an approach. However, representation, standing here for the reproduction of the "real," has been, and continues to be, the underlying principle upon which the overwhelming majority of ETV programs are based. These questions, that is, the status and function of audio-visual representation, need to become an important part of the agenda for the ETV research community.

ETV Development

The roles that television has played as an educational technology are heterogeneous, reflecting the multiplicity of pedagogical methodologies which the medium has tried to incorporate into its operations. Educational Television (ETV), and the more specialized variant of Instructional Television (ITV), have had rather unstable histories, demonstrated in inconclusive research findings, indefinite production methods, a variety of failures, and relatively few successes given the aspirations of its community.[13] Many researchers have indicated that the medium was and remains poorly understood, thus corroborating views held by others in the fields of sociology, communications, and Mass-Media Studies.[14] It has been argued that the ETV-ITV project was, in great part, inaccurately conceived and inappropriately operationalized.[15] Yet it remains a field where there is continuing interest in technical applications, in part the result of a continuing belief in the medium's potential, and the demands for accelerated education in a modern technological society.[16] This has been a cause for dismay among a number of ETV researchers who can only view such developments in Educational Television as lacking direction, furthering the unproductivity of the past.[17]

By and large, subsequent, on-going research has progressed along these two general lines: one endeavors to expand television use through the development of production methods which are rigorously evaluated in order to ensure significant instructional impact. The second line of research seeks to understand instructional practice through a further examination of existing and potential forms of television production within a communication theory orientation. The first case involves the development of television techniques which would reproduce the conditions for learning established by psychological and behavioral research. This does not simply demand the adaptation of television to pre-existent pedagogical practices, but also to the evolution of those instructional means, specific to the medium, which would achieve particular educational aims. There has been great interest in research into a possible grammar and symbolic form of television communication, as a means of coding information "natural" to the medium which would enable more consistent reception of the instructional message.[18] The desire for immediate and spontaneous interaction with video material has led researchers to, among other things, examine the psychological basis for image communication, "visual literacy," and a consideration of popular television programming and the techniques employed to generate interest and attention.

The second research direction is concerned not so much with operationalizing the medium towards known goals, but with the possibility that the unknown ramifications of increased television use will necessitate new pedagogical goals. Such a perspective suggests that a re-orientation of social attitudes toward knowledge has occurred as a result of the development of electronic communications technology. Mass communications research which investigates and determines the social and cultural effects of television is of obvious interest to this second approach. Commercial television techniques are not merely appropriated, but critically examined for the information they, in themselves, produce. Mass-media is understood as being a second, alternative information source which enters into subject matter areas that schools have both traditionally explicated and ignored. This suggests that society's educational network is larger than the school and its practices and approaches. Television is not simply a technical aid, but also an object for study and exploration. The two positions of viewing television, either as a technical aid, or as an object for study and expression, reflect different understandings of the communicational functions of the medium. These approaches are based upon certain key assumptions concerning communication and representation in general.

ETV and the Study of Representation

A central concern in film theory has been thinking out ways of conceptualizing representation. Structurally, representation is viewed as a subjective and abstract derivative of the actual subject matter which the former stands for; it is an ideology-laden depiction. A problem, however, is that such incomplete reconstructions are so often perceived as complete duplications. Correcting this misapprehension would depend on a "decoding" of the (audio and visual) image, uncovering its partisan aspects. This view of the nature and function of representation (simplified here for sake of argument) is antithetical to a position which holds that certain types of representation, audio-visual reproductions generated by mechanical and electric technology most centrally, can produce verisimilitude. In other words, these media do actually reproduce and restore the objective essence of whatever subject is under their scrutiny. There is no question of selectivity by the producer of crucial details, properties, contextual, historic, and other aspects of the subject which forms the image, nor of the presumed ontological status placed upon these features. Theories have been advanced which attempt to provide explanations for why the reduction of reality reified in a representation can be perceived as totalizing duplications. Certain reductions either as caricatures or idealizations have such an omnipresent acceptance in culture as to suggest that people are driven (compulsed) to affirm them. Evidence for what seem to be unconscious motivations appears to be suggested in the overwhelming popular indulgence in cinematic narrative representational structures. The critical review of compulsion is thought to occur as a result of decoding, as was said; or through altered representational structurings that force or engender a self-reflexive posture, or at least obstruct simple unconscious acquiescence to dubious pleasures arising in the aftermath of repression.

It is in regard to the above and other theoretical views of how meaning is mediated and formed in representation that the problematic of Educational

Television becomes interesting. Most crucially, it facilitates an opposite approach to the problem of representation by involving interpretive resistance to meaning. Unconscious motivation and the structures which correspond to it notwithstanding, representation in ETV has existed not strictly as an abstract construction providing the receiver or consumer with a desirable concreteness, but also precisely as an artificial totality needing to be cosmeticized and "effectively" communicated. This is done in the simple hope that the message will be positively received. Simply stated, the ETV project involves the viewer not in being awakened from a dream-like stupor, but coaxed into dropping a certain alertness. Historically with ETV, many empirically-based studies and observations have found viewer satisfaction and understanding minimal in relation to the product. ETV producers haven't viewed their programs as ideologically involved, yet they have faced audiences who have rejected programs as if there were this type of conflict.[19] Some ETV developers have felt the need to obtain from their audience specific information concerning those audio-visual representations which meet the latter's approval, in order to adapt favorable images to a program's purpose. An outstanding example of a promoter and developer of this interactive approach to ETV program creation is the Children's Television Workshop, creators of *Sesame Street, 3-2-1-Contact,* and other trend-setting series.

What is suggested by the above, that is, suggested by the history of ETV, is that there is a yet unspecified interactive component to the establishment of meaning in "one-way" audio-visual communication or representation. There is a need to investigate the rudimentary meaning structures and the necessary conditions for their mediation in the building and communicating of representation. Correlatively, the relative ability of any producer to communicate meanings with audio-visual means to a usually anonymous spectator must be ascertained by a fuller examination of all of the variables mentioned in this piece. Questions as to the power of the medium must also be asked in relation to the viewer.

NOTES

1. George N. Gordon, "Instructional Television, Media, and Contemporary Education," *American Education in the Electronic Age,* ed. P. L. Klinge (Englewood Cliffs, N.J.: Educational Technology Publications, 1974), pp. 138–57; T. R. Ide, "The Potential and Limitations of Television as an Educational Medium," *Media and Symbols: The Forms of Expression, Communication, and Education,* the 73rd Yearbook of the National Society for the Study of Education, Part I, ed. David R. Olson (Chicago: University of Chicago Press, 1974), pp. 330–56; Paul Saettler, *A History of Instructional Technology* (New York: McGraw-Hill Inc., 1968), pp. 227–28, 249.

2. Robert R. J. Blakely, *To Serve the Public Interest: Educational Broadcasting in the United States* (Syracuse: Syracuse University Press, 1979), pp. 138–42; Ide, "Potential and Limitations," p. 331; Saettler, *History,* pp. 227–30.

3. Armand Mattelard, *Multinational Corporations and the Control of Cultures* (Sussex/New Jersey: Harvester Press/Humanities Press, 1979), pp. 128–92.

4. See for example: Gilbert Seldes, "Television's Place in Art and Culture," *Educational Television, The Next Ten Years* (Stanford: Institute for Communication Research, Stanford University, 1962), pp. 103–15.

5. The term functionalist refers to the instrumental use of a technology for the achievement of set goals. The technology here is an adjunct or aid to a process usually considered in behavioristic terms. This view is opposed to one which sees television technology as producing its own undetermined effects on behavior. Whereas in the first case video would be investigated as far as certain desired properties or effects, the latter makes no such investment; both positively and negatively understood aspects of technology are viewed as relevant and the technology becomes a central, as opposed to subsidiary, interest.

6. ETV and ITV are the standard abbreviations used by the field of education as a whole for Educational Television and Instructional Television, respectively.

7. For a brief historical sketch, see John Maddison, "Introduction," *Media Studies in Education, Reports and Papers on Mass Communication,* no. 80 (Paris: UNESCO, 1977), pp. 7–11.

8. Sirkka Minkkinen, *A General Curricular Model for Mass Media Education* (Altamira: J. M. Llorca for UNESCO, 1978).

9. *Media Studies in Education.* The report gives a brief outline of a number of media studies programs in various countries.

10. See for example: Roland Barthes, *Mythologies* (Paris: edition du Seuil, 1957); Harold Innis, *The Bias of Communication* (Toronto: University of Toronto Press, 1951); Marshall McLuhan, *The Mechanical Bride: Folklore of Industrial Man* (N. Y.: Vanguard Press, 1951).

11. Minkkinen, pp. 25–31.

12. The term is used in much film theory in this regard. For an example, see Kristin Thomson, "The Concept of Cinematic Excess," *Ciné-Tracts,* no. 2 (Summer 1977), Montreal, pp. 54–63. "The spectator who takes films to be simple copies of reality will probably tend to subsume the physicality of the image under a general category of verisimilitude; that shape on the screen looks as it does because 'those things really look like that' " (pp. 57–58). Verisimilitude can be understood as a formal term for the commonsense notion that "photographs never lie." Minkkinen, p. 73:

> Paintings and drawings are always the artists' personal interpretations of reality or of ideas. The idea and the actual image itself are formed gradually. The case is not the same with photography although it, too, calls for selection and the development of the ideas interpreted through the images selected. The camera operator on films, television productions and still photography selects an object and decides on such factors as lighting, angles, visual framing, timing, the disposition of the object before the camera and the location, and the technical equipment required. From then on, it is the camera that determines the outcome. The external world is recorded in the sequence: object/objective/film, and the resulting photographic record is to be taken to be a proof of what has been recorded: hence the saying photographs never lie. But a visual message is always an interpretation of what the producer has selected. His interpretation can enlarge our understanding of an object or distort how it is seen.

> Whether it is one image, or an entire sequence, it is often assumed that the single message, the reality of the "photographic record," will be communicated. But if the "visual message" is always an interpretation on the part of the producer, constructed by a mechanical device, there is reason to doubt that intended crucial aspects of this "record" and "message" will be communicated, as the viewer may be in conflict with the interpretation or even the conventions and products of the photographic device itself. The projection of verisimilitude does not refer simply to the quality of the representation, but is also expected to provide the necessary base for the establishment of an effective communication. Audio-visual communication, as will be seen, has confronted communicational difficulties in the holding of such a simple view of duplication and representation.

13. Most ETV investigators regard the early phase of development of television for education as not very meritorious. A still significant number have been critical and doubtful of the value of many aspects of more contemporary ETV practice, with some even going so far as to negate any worth to the entire project up until the time of their writing. See for example: George N. Gordon, "Instructional Television: Yesterday's Magic," and David Berkman, "The Medium Whose Future Has Passed," *Instructional Television,* ed. Jerold Ackerman and Lawrence Lipsitz (Englewood Cliffs, N. J.: Educational Technology Publications, 1977), pp. 147–52, and pp. 95–108. See also David Olson, *Introduction to Media and Symbols,* pp. 1–24; Ide, pp. 331–32.

14. Television communication remains an area where on-going research continues to unravel complexity. As there appear to be historical, as well as social and organizational factors involved in viewer-television interaction, any understanding of such must be open to new, previously unrealized conditions. See James Carey, "The Ambiguity of Policy Research," *Journal of Communications,* vol. 28, no. 2 (Spring 1978), pp. 114–19, and *Broadcaster/Researcher Cooperation in Mass-Communications Research,* ed. James D. Halloran and Michael Gurevitch (Leeds: J. A. Kavenaugh & Sons, 1971). Furthermore, as is pointed out in UNESCO documentation on mass communications, knowledge of the effects of television is not very broadly based, both in terms of producers and consumers. There has been a need for on-going media education which would inform viewers on the effects of television communication in a variety of forms. See Minkkinen, *Model for Mass Media Education* and *Media Studies in Education.*

15. Ide, "Potentials and Limitations," p. 356; George N. Gordon, "ITV, Media and Contemporary Education," pp. 138–42.

16. ETV has been the most researched area of educational technological development, and it remains in demand and well financed. This is evidenced by the high degree of investment in software and hardware development by large multinational electronics and information processing corporations, the development of Public Television Stations in the United States, TV Ontario, Access Alberta, and Radio Quebec in Canada. A wide variety of trade, professional, and scholarly journals as *Audio-Visual Instruction, Media and Methods,* and *Audio-Visual Communications Review* frequently feature articles on television applications in schools.

17. Gordon, "ITV: Yesterday's Magic," pp. 147–52; pp. 8–10.

18. For examples see: *Media and Symbols* for a wide variety of psychologically based media methods. See also E. U. Heidt, *Instructional Media and the Individual Learner: A Classification and Systems Appraisal* (N.Y.: Nichols Publishing Co., 1978) for an in-depth, cognitive psychology-based classification of media and media use; and Leslie J. Briggs, Peggy L. Campeau, Rogert M. Gagne, Mark A. May, *Instructional Media: A Procedure for the Design of Multi-Media Instruction, a Critical Review of Research, and Suggestions for Further Research.* Report prepared by the Center for Research and Evaluation in Applications of Technology in Education (CREATE) (Pittsburgh: American Institute for Research, 1967). The latter is a widely used handbook of production methods based on behaviorist-Skinnerian notions concerning learning.

19. The child reacting with boredom to a taped lecture and favoring an adventure or variety show may be arguably reacting to the practice and ideology of a paternalistic pedagogy.

XXI

THE CONSOLIDATION OF THE AMERICAN FILM INDUSTRY 1915–1920

George Mitchell

By 1920 most of the pioneering U.S. film producers, firms like Edison, Kalem, and Biograph had been bankrupted or swallowed up in a wave of consolidation and rationalization that swept over the movie business in the mid-teens. No aspect of commercial film production was left untouched by a series of fundamental changes in the organization of the industry such as the transition from low-capital to high-capital film production, and the integration of production, distribution, and exhibition. After 1918 a few U.S. producers dominated not only the domestic but also the world market for films. This hegemony on leisure was maintained in the U.S. until the early 1950s and the arrival of television as a mass entertainment.

These new directions had a striking effect on film content and cinematic style. It is no exaggeration to say that the advent of monopoly in the film industry had a more profound effect on the content and technique of films than any technical innovation, change in the composition of the audience, or epochal event. The impact of consolidation becomes clear when we compare early production practices (c. 1908–1914) with those generated by the consolidation of the mid-teens.

One

The single most important change in production methods brought on by the economic consolidation was a shift upward in the control of the filmmaking process. The control was removed from the workers directly engaged in the making of films—directors, actors, cameramen and others who assisted in fabricating films—and placed in the hands of managers who reported to corporate heads. In this, the movie business resembled many other American business enterprises which, during the first quarter of the twentieth century, reorganized managerial and shop-floor practices in order to intensify production.

While the pre-nickelodeon era (1895–1906) had sizeable producers (Edison was one) production was also carried out cottage-industry fashion by technician-entrepreneurs directly involved in making and sometimes exhibiting films. As the business grew more complex after 1906, filmmaking became increasingly special-ized, yet control of the production process remained in the studio. The director continued to exert considerable authority over most aspects of film production until his power was undercut by the changes of the mid-teens. In the highly competitive years before consolidation, the main concerns of the heads of film companies were less with the specifics of content and form, and more with co-ordinating finances, securing markets, and maintaining an adequate supply of the product. As Terry Ramsaye said of the period, "the calamitous demand was for film, film, film, regardless of the content."[1]

In the nickelodeon period, a booming market, production by small firms, worker controlled methods of film production, and a pro-working class perspective in films all appear to be related. The casual attitude toward the making of films can be seen by Biograph's test of D. W. Griffith's fitness to occupy the director's seat: namely, to check if a film shot under his supervision (and photographed by Arthur Marvin, a studio cameraman) was in sharp focus or not.[2] And these instructions to the dime novelist William Wallace Cook from the Essanay Film Manufacturing Company in 1910 are typical of the rough guidelines that came to story writers and directors from management: "the stories should be refined but not highbrow," wrote Essanay to Cook. "They should appeal to the middle class people. Your scenes may be laid in either a Fifth Avenue drawing room or Mike O'Toole's shanty. And we want to emphasize this point: there must be plenty of plot and the stories must be funny."[3] This looseness is also clear in what comes down to us about how films were put together during this early period.

In selecting plots for films, directors, producing as many as two to three short films per week, casually mined a variety of sources such as daily newspapers, dime novels, other films, classics, and theatrical pieces, often disregarding copyrights. In actual production, since the films were not rigorously scripted, anyone might suggest an idea. According to Robert Henderson, D. W. Griffith's biographer, "it made little difference to Griffith what the source of his film stories was. He was as willing to accept a story from a member of the acting company as from Dougherty and the Biograph story department."[4] Joseph Henabery, who played the part of Abraham Lincoln in *The Birth of a Nation,* remembered that before shooting started on his scenes he had received "no instructions, no script, no idea of what I was supposed to do. When it came to the Ford's Theater scenes, he'd tell me what he was going to do in the long shots and I'd tell him what I'd read that Lincoln would be doing."[5] In selecting story material and techniques for telling the story, directors were supposed to use their common sense, plus what they knew about audience likes and dislikes. Intelligence about audience preferences was often gathered by attending films and observing the response to the program.

Yet another factor distinguishing earlier production methods from post World War One practices was the relationship between the movie business and major industrial centers: pre-war facilities were usually close to these centers and drew on them extensively in the making of films. Film companies, for example, were located in the midst of, or very close to major cities that held their markets; metropolitan centers like New York, Chicago, and Philadelphia. Extensive cinematic use was made of city streets, the city skyline, and real crowds. In producing *Cry of the Children*, the 1912 anti-child-labor film, the Thanhauser Company shot factory scenes in a real mill located near its New Rochelle, N.Y. studios (which were housed in a converted skating rink). During his Biograph days Griffith and his crew held their planning sessions in a workingman's saloon in New York, not far from their studio, a converted brownstone.[6] This proximity to, and use of real life was in keeping with what the movie business was supposed to be about as a business. While the medium's capacity for illusion and fantasy was exploited early on by Méliès and others, early movies were all prized for their evocation of actual life. In the decade of movie-making preceding the rise of the story film, "actuality" films depicting major cities, famous landscapes, and news events were a mainstay of the trade. In the 1890s some companies even practiced setting up their cameras on busy downtown intersections, photographing pedestrians, and then showing these films at local theaters. People were urged to see themselves, their neighbors, and their city. Interesting examples of these scenes would then be selected for general distribution. Thousands of films were issued offering glimpses of typical metropolitan scenes, films like *Panorama of Flatiron Building* (1903), *Crowds, Ruins, New York* (Edison, 1905), *Seeing Boston* (Biograph, 1906), *Cleveland Fire Department* (Biograph, 1903), *Ambulance at the Accident* (Edison, 1897), and *Lower Broadway* (Biograph, 1903). Story films like *Child of the Ghetto* (1910) were promoted on the basis of their "actuality" footage, in this case real slum scenes. This extensive use of metropolitan life as a backdrop continues on into the teens. "Location" shooting was part of a general policy in the competitive era to keep individual film costs as low as possible. This policy of keeping things cheap and simple is also plainly visible in the inexpensive movie sets of the period. As late as 1911 the Biograph company used the same basic backdrop for three different scenes in the film *Lily of the Tenements:* an office, a slum tenement room and a room in a middle-class dwelling.

The content and point of view of the story film during the competitive era also demonstrates this proximity to ordinary life. Before 1916, films dealing in one way or another with exploitation in the workplace, usually at the hands of the landlords, and the manipulation of trusts, were commonplace.[7] In general, the working class was viewed with a paternalism characteristic of social gospelism and middle-class reformism, two popular movements in pre-World War One U.S. One example of this sympathy and interest in the plight of the poor can be seen at the Biograph studio where, under Griffith, actors and actresses playing lower-class types were told to familiarize themselves with their real-life models. Mae Marsh remembered that "in several of my earlier plays, Mr. Griffith sent me down to the New York slums on an observation tour. We all made such tours. In *Intolerance* I visited sick and stricken mothers in baby hospitals. We spent half a day once in a jail . . ."[8] In his unpublished autobiography, Griffith boasted of his first-hand knowledge of the slums, noting that early in his career when he was down on his luck he lived in a flop house in Manhattan and got to know "practically every foot of the Ghetto,

Mulberry Bend, the Bowery and Chinatown."[9] A paternalistic approach to working class life is also evident in other prominent early directors such as Thanhauser, Ince, and Porter.

One final note on the subject of control: that control was primarily in the hands of the director and his crew is also evident in the freedom to innovate. In the early years there was considerable leeway to experiment with new techniques, especially in camerawork and editing. Though studio heads often balked at stylistic innovations, the small investment in any one film made the risks inconsequential. Moreover, examples of rigid managerial control over the actual process of fabricating a film are rare (such as highly detailed, management-supervised scripts) so that innovations could be slipped by and announced as fait accompli. This latitude contributed to considerable experimentation and creativity in the U.S. film prior to World War One. Afterward the restructuring of the movie business along modern corporate lines led to a strict clampdown on directorial control, on innovation, and, finally, on the open approach to everyday life. As basic narrative techniques were brought to the point where individual films could generate high-level profits, film form was frozen and deviations in content and form were condemned as lunatic. Innovation in the U.S. film henceforward was permitted only where the needs of the business were clearly forwarded.

In the final analysis, the innovations in cinematic technique in the pre-war period and the social and political critique contained in these films cannot be separated. Griffith's social critique, with its emphasis on the human injury brought on by industrialism and ubanization gave impetus to his experimentation with editing. And when, in the twenties, the possiblities of such a critique were severely restricted, his technique became flat and static.

Two

In spite of the ever increasing demand for films by 1920, most of the pioneering U.S. companies had closed their doors or merged with other firms. None of the seven major producers who pooled resources in 1909 to form the Motion Picture Patents Company remained intact. Two of the earliest and largest producers, Edison and Biograph, had shut down. Vitagraph, Lubin, Selig, and Essanay had merged. Those firms that sprang up after the nickelodeon boom, Kalem, IMP, Rex, Nestor, Thanhauser, Bison, Keystone, Powers, Lux, Helen Gardner Picture Corporation, Morosco Pictures, and Palls Pictures, disappeared through bankruptcy, merger, or acquisition. In their place appeared new and much more powerful corporations like United Artists, Fox, Famous Players, Triangle, and Paramount.

The look and content of films also changed drastically during this period. Comparing the typical film made in 1915 with one made in 1910 one notes striking differences: there are improvements in the mechanics of filmmaking (lighting, for example) and a greater mastery of narrative technique: but the most notable difference is the longer length of films. Individual films lasting an hour or more became standard by the middle of the decade. While the typical film program of

1910 might last an hour in total length, most films ran 12–16 minutes. Another trend obvious by the middle of the decade was a much more costly, elaborate film, the expenditures for which were manifest in the sleek, ostentatious "up-front" aspects of film production.

In explaining the disappearance of the old small producers and forces giving impetus to consolidation in the movie business, film historians often point to the feature film and the huge increases in capitalization it required. According to this analysis the upheaval in production, distribution and exhibition going on in the teens was a response to a new, more costly film which, in turn, was a result of an increasingly sophisticated and better heeled audience. The changes, the argument goes, were rooted in the market: as result of a larger and more sophisticated audience and the popularity of feature films, the motion picture improved into something long, glossy, and expensive.[10] Following the lead of the market, new improved film companies came on the scene to make and distribute the better product. Companies that faltered did so because they lacked the vitality, ingenuity, and flexibility to make the films that would keep them in the running.

This analysis is inadequate and misleading, however, for it obscures the main driving force behind all the important developments of the period, namely the movement to concentrate production and profit in the hands of relatively few firms. Among the keys to this concentration was the film itself, its content and form. That the longer film in itself was not responsible for the increased cost of film production can be seen by comparing film expenditures at various intervals. In 1909 major producers such as Biograph spent around $400–500 on a one-reel film; smaller companies perhaps half that amount. Feature films produced after 1914 ran anywhere from 5 to 10 reels. Using 1908 production costs, a 10 reel film running about two hours could be made for around $5000. And indeed, some of the early feature films made around 1912 were shot on budgets under $8000. In 1914, however, the new Paramount Company was contracting with independent producers, paying them $25,000 per film plus a generous cut of rentals. Blockbuster films like Griffith's *Birth of a Nation* and Ince's *Civilization* were running up budgets of $100,000 or more. By the 1920s the average feature cost hovered around $200,000 and blockbusters like *Covered Wagon* cost close to a million. This incredible inflation in the cost of film production was not a matter of longer films but of a much more expensive film, the Hollywood Style. Nor was this Hollywood style the result of the entrance into the market of the middle-class and the rich, for while the middle-class began to consume more films around this time, the numerical significance of the higher income groups in the film audience was never significant when compared to the presence of the working class, the factory, office, and farm worker. The Hollywood Style was not simply a result of demographic shifts in the audience but the introduction of a strategy enabling relatively few firms to dominate the booming world-wide market for cinema entertainment. In short, the inflation in production costs that took place in the decade 1910–1920 was a direct result of the introduction, piece by piece, of a whole new kind of film. The enormous potential for profit from the films could be realized only by well-organized corporations with large-scale all-weather studios, extensive capital resources, and, most important of all, solid control over production, distribution, and exhibition. Those who fashioned such a system would lock up the market and enjoy returns dwarfing the profit of earlier firms. As a leading producer, George Zukor described the scene in 1918, "of 250 producers it is said that only ten are making money; of these ten, four are making millions."[11] A review of the dynamics of this consolidation shows how content and style were key features.

The Hollywood Style (i.e. the star system, lavish production values, plots increasingly divorced from everyday life, etc.) began to emerge in the mid-teens as firms like Paramount, Triangle, and Famous Players entered into production and distribution. These were by no means the first attempts to dominate the market for films. From the earliest days of the movie business such efforts were always underway. Most of the early attempts hinged on patent claims, like those of the Edison Company over projection and camera equipment. The most elaborate and famous early attempt at monopolization was the Motion Picture Patents Company, formed in 1909, which tried to restrict filmmaking to seven domestic and two foreign firms on the basis of camera and projector patents. A year later MPPC bolstered its efforts by establishing an exchange with the General Film Company, which in a matter of months took over dozens of film distributors throughout the U.S. On paper, all films made and shown in the U.S. should have been produced by this cartel. MPPC films went only to exhibitors who ordered MPPC film packages and paid a license fee for the use of projection equipment. The paper arrangements did not succeed, however, and in spite of this elaborate system, MPPC was successful only in the short run (if that) in controlling the market for films. Years before anti-trust action clamped down on its operations, the arrangement faltered everywhere. Rival firms from the start ignored its patent claims, as did exhibitors. Policing these claims through legal and extra-legal means proved futile. Behind the cartel's failure to monopolize production lay this: films were cheap and easy to produce and profits were high. Means other than patents had to be found to lock up the market. By the middle of the decade it was clear that the film medium itself, that is, modes of production, was one key to this domination.

The transformation brought on by consolidation can be expressed qualitatively in the tremendous increases in capital outlays per film; investments in production facilities, exchanges, and theaters; and of course in the profit sheets. At the time when the movie business, new screen magazines, and other media were spreading the word about the spectacular possibilities of success in Hollywood, monopolization was closing off entry to all areas of the business. Up to 1912 movie-making was still a relatively low-capital process, as we noted in our discussion of film budgets. The costs of individual films had been rising steadily for years, but this was primarily a reflection of the gradual lengthening of films, from a minute or less in 1895 to five minutes in 1905 (these are approximate figures) to 12 minutes in 1908, to anywhere from 12 minutes to an hour or longer after 1912. In the earliest days very little capital was needed to enter into production or exhibition. Vitagraph began production in 1896 with $1000; two years later it was showing profits of $4700. In 1907 profits had risen to a quarter-million and in 1912 to $924,000.

Kalem began in 1905 with $600 according to the film historian Lewis Jacobs, and was clearing $5000 a week by 1908, from two pictures costing $200 each to produce.[12] In 1909 the cost to the new Bison Life Motion Pictures to produce a one reel film was $200. Baumen and Kessel of Baumen and Kessel Pictures, like many early producers, kept expenses down by acting in their own films. In 1909 they were able to turn them out at a cost of from $200–$350 each and make a profit of approximately $1500 per film. In 1908 Griffith was turning out some 12–13 pictures per month for Biograph at a cost of $300 per film. Griffith got the budget increased to $500 in 1909.[13]

The character of operations at this time is also reflected in salaries paid to actors, directors, and writers. In the earliest days jobs in the film business were not strictly categorized and apparently there was a good deal of upward mobility. Edwin Porter, for example, went in the 1890s from projectionist to director in the space of a few years. Indeed, it was possible to be cameraman, actor, director and exhibitor all-in-one. Job specialization increased as the industry grew. Working the camera and directing were separated. Acting and writing became discrete tasks as the story films became more complex. As for salaries, we know that actors were paid five dollars a day at Biograph in 1908, and that talent was casually recruited from New York's pool of unemployed stage performers. A synopsis or film treatment could bring a writer about $30, though films were often put together without "treatments." Writing for the films was, at that stage, still open as were many jobs as late as 1912. Anita Loos, a 16-year-old amateur, sent the Biograph Company a film script in that same year which became *The New York Hat,* earning her a $25 fee. The salary paid a director at this time was probably not a great deal more than what was paid an actor (nor did it carry high status) for when Griffith was offered the chance to direct for Biograph in 1908 he did not jump to accept, but began on a tentative basis with the condition he could have his acting job back if he failed.

By 1912 the cost-per-film was significantly higher, reflecting the introduction of the feature, but film capitalization was still at the low point of a geometric upswing. A detailed breakdown of the Famous Players' feature *The Count of Monte Cristo,* made in that year, shows that the major expenditures of film production were still for the basic materials such as raw film stock and film processing. Actors' fees were a mere $1025, hotel and travel expenses, $83, costumes and props, $142.[14] Advertising was of growing importance, running $1674 for this film; royalties were a significant $1397. Yet the physical production costs came to only $13,000; Kenneth MacGowan writes that the film grossed $45,000 for the year 1913.[15] Accordingly, the price of entry into the business was still modest. As late as 1913, C. B. DeMille, Jesse Lasky, and Samuel Goldfish (later Goldwyn) were able to enter production with their Lasky Features Company with $26,500 in captial. They became a major force in the business almost immediately.

Actors' salaries were part of the reason for this upswing in costs. A central problem for the movie business was product identification: how was a producer to influence consumer demand for his studio's product?

The "name" director was one possible solution. Zukor reportedly offered Griffith, the best known director of the pre-war era, $50,000 a year to work for him.

But it was soon clear that the most effective way to create product identification (as well as limiting entry into the market) was extravagant outlays on "production values," actors' salaries, and advertising. Whereas a few years earlier it was common practice to keep actors' names out of advertising, identifying talent only by the house name (the Biograph girl, the Vitagraph girl, etc.), in the mid-teens films were increasingly promoted through the names of star actors. By 1920 a whole pulp magazine industry had been built, with the direct and indirect support of the film industry, on the exploitation of the careers and social lives of the stars.

Mary Pickford and Charles Chaplin were among the earliest of the new movie stars. Pickford began her movie career at Biograph earning the standard $5 a day; in 1911 Majestic pictures paid her $250 a week; and in 1915 her salary was $104,000 a year and rapidly climbing. In 1913 Charles Chaplin started in the films at $150 a week; in 1914 he commanded $1250 a week and from there his "salary" climbed up to $30,000 a week in the twenties. MacGowan (noting the probability of exaggeration) lists the following weekly earnings for major stars in the twenties: Harold Lloyd, $40,000; Douglas Fairbanks, Sr., $30,000; Gloria Swanson, $19,000; Tom Mix, $19,000; and Colleen Moore, $8,000.[16] Rough calculations suggest that overall production costs for one minute of film were one hundred times greater in 1925 than in 1908.

The exhibition end of the business also followed these trends. The cost of setting up a small travelling or stationary theater in the pre-nickelodeon period could run from $200 to $2500 for the basic equipment. At this time films were shown in two basic formats: at peep shows where the audience paid from one to five cents to look at films through closed projection devices, and at vaudeville shows with their longer-screened programs. Viewing films at vaudeville however, was still relatively expensive and it was not until nickelodeons appeared that movie-going was a regular possibility for the many. "The man or woman who would hesitate long or who can not afford to pay fifty or seventy-five or even twenty-five cents for a ticket to an ordinary dramatic or vaudeville performance will gladly patronize the five cent theatre," noted a catalogue promoting movie projection devices.[17] A few years after the arrival of the nickelodeon, however, larger and more elaborate theaters appear in big cities, charging higher admissions, often with a system of class-pricing seats. Around 1914 some lavish metropolitan theaters charged from 25 cents to $1.50 per film. The higher prices were for the new blockbuster films. The elaborate Strand theatre opening in New York in 1914 had a 3,300 seat capacity and had class-pricing which ranged from 10 cents to 50 cents per head.

These transformations reflect the development of the movie business along capitalist lines. Star salaries, for example, were not a measure of intrinsic worth but a product of the artificial scarcity created by mass exposure, a phenomenon exploited by the industry to create product identification. Huge salaries were tolerated and even promoted because, in the end, they served vital corporate needs. Launching a star into the upper-income brackets put her or him in the national limelight and made Hollywood a focal point on the global map. Many of these stars became idols of consumption—trend setters on the frontiers of acquisition—and of great use in promoting habits and tastes vital to the growth of the new consumer goods sector. One learned in the twenties, for example, that Gloria Swanson received $10,000 a month living expenses, had a $100,000 penthouse atop the Park Charles Hotel in New York, a $75,000 country estate and the title, via marriage, Marquise de la Falaise de Coudray, and that Cecil B. DeMille had yachts, rare collections of jewels, and Indian relics, not to mention a gold phone. Of Douglas Fairbanks, Sr., one Hollywood writer noted: "the rotogravure editors can always fill a spare corner with a new picture of Fairbanks putting grand dukes . . . at their ease."[18]

Not only did the star system generate priceless quantities of print-media exposure, but once established as a method of "rating," promoting, and distributing films, it limited entry into the market in various ways since star-making, like oil exploration, was a costly and risky business. The small-time producer who could neither afford to make or purchase a star (or imitate the Hollywood Style in other ways) found that his films were automatically classed as inferior "B" grade or lower productions. Furthermore, without stars, chances of getting financial support, good distribution, and publicity were slender. The odd director who wanted to work with unknown actors was battling a whole system of production and distribution.

Production values and stars were critical links in the system, but concrete measures were needed to insure a tight grip on distribution and exhibition. One way of achieving this goal was for producers to buy controlling interest in film exchanges which acted as middlemen. A few film companies, now earning huge profits on films, were in a position to go ahead with this task after 1916. Block-booking was also tried, a distribution system in which producers forced exhibitors to buy packages containing up to 52 films a year. The uncertain legality of this system plus exhibitor resistance, showed the importance of more direct economic control. Since producers could not buy all the theaters in the country, they concentrated on purchasing or building flagship theaters. These lavish showplaces were mainly built between 1918–1929 and carefully placed in major cities for maximum accessibility and visibility, not only for the convenience of patrons but also to attract metropolitan based media. By 1919 Famous Players Lasky Company dictated what films were shown at about 400 movie houses nationally through outright ownership and controlling interests. The 1926 Seabury study focusing on movie monopolies noted that "the first class theatres were so located throughout the country and were so pretentious in their appointments that the exhibition of pictures in them became a privilege anxiously sought by all producers of pictures, because of the great and far-reaching influence which the exhibition of pictures in these first-class theatres exerted upon the balance of the 1,400 or more theatres throughout the country."[19] In the later twenties, according to Lewis Jacobs, three companies, Paramount, MGM (through Lowes Inc.), and First National, had a tight grip on the nation's theaters: "By 1927, with close to 600 exchanges in 46 key American cities, and 20,000 theatres, exhibition had become almost entirely monopolized by chain theatres, all in the hands of the major producer-distributor-exhibitor combinations."[20]

The economic rationalization of the movie business quickly made itself felt on the studio floor, transforming not only the methods by which films were put together, but their content as well. By the middle of the decade the days were numbered for the kind of loose collaborative filmmaking described above. The Triangle Film Company for example, founded in 1915, was planned from the bottom up with the idea of producing films on a rational, efficient, assembly line basis. In order to give management (many new executives had come to the motion pictures not through filmmaking but from exhibition as well as a variety of other business enterprises) an authoritative voice in the filmmaking process, the new Triangle Company hired three leading masters of the filmmaking craft, Griffith, Ince, and Sennett, whose jobs were not only to direct films but supervise the work of other directors. The leaders of the industry, following the example of other mass producers, introduced "scientific management" into the production process. The basic principle of scientific management was that the worker should be confined to the physical execution of the tasks of production, while management designed and regulated each stage of production. This school of management theory instructed employers on how to re-arrange the work process so as to achieve greater productivity and profit.

Thomas Ince, more than any other individual at this time, exemplifies the efforts to apply modern management theory to the production of movies. Ince was acutely aware that the work of the modern film manager was to reduce the risks inherent in mass entertainment production. As he put it, "the guess work starts with the selection of the script and the first payment made to the author."[21] Ince, who, like DeMille and Griffith, began in legitimate theater, commenced his motion picture career in 1910 at IMP Pictures. Hired by Triangle in 1915, he set to work out a system of greatly increased managerial control over the chaos of production. Kenneth MacGowan described Ince's attack on the director's craft: "He wouldn't let a director shoot off the cuff, which meant developing scenes and sequences from a sketch outline. Ince worked closely with his writers . . . until he could approve a shooting script. He gave his director this complete blueprint of a picture and insisted that he follow it in every detail. Years later, men like Irving Thalberg, Darryl Zanuck, and David O. Selznick adopted the Ince policy when they managed big studios."[22] Ince also devised a system of cost accounting which enabled management to keep detailed tabs on production on a per-foot basis. The new enormously expensive Hollywood Style made this kind of record keeping a necessity. The old, off-the-cuff style disappeared even from the older studios that had ventured into feature production. An actor after visiting Edison Company Studios in 1915 wrote in his diary, "the entire atmosphere breathes organization."[23]

Around this time producers also tried to reduce the risks of production through "scientific" techniques of determining audience responses. Through trial screenings, audience card surveys, and box office returns they sought to isolate those elements in film content which yielded a profit from those which did not. In 1918, writing in *System: The Magazine of Business,* a film executive characterized the pre-war years as the "old days" when "nearly every film was a leap in the dark, for we had no reasonably scientific means of discovering what the public would like."[24]

The application of modern management techniques to film production spelled the demise of the director as an "artist" or mastercraftsman guided by purely creative and artistic impulses. The breakdown of the filmmaking process extended to all aspects of production, including the writing of films. Edmund Wilson captured the industrial nature of the "thinking side" of film production in an essay he wrote in the 1930s: "the writers, shut up by day in small cells in large buildings, which like mills, have armed guards at the doors, compelled to collaborate in two's just as a pair of weavers is given so many looms and reporting like schoolchildren to supervisors who commend or suppress or censor, or display, even outside the studios, a psychology of mill-hands or children."[25] Joseph Mankiewicz, the producer and director, described the matured process as "constructed, distorted, into a system as closely allied to the producing of wash-basins as it could have been."[26]

A more detailed review of this transition period shows how the social portraiture of the motion pictures was also transformed by being integrated into the overall strategy of the movie business.

As late as 1913 no one in the U.S. business could say exactly what a commercial film was, and was not. There was, for example, a lively debate over the question of how long an individual film should play. Many other unknowns bedeviled producers and exhibitors: should the business encourage or discourage the prominence of the movie actor; should large amounts of money be invested in an individual film? Some Italian and U.S. firms were producing lavish epics with huge casts, although the films were expensive and risky and consequently were not in regular production. And then there was the thorniest question of all: what was the relationship between movie social portraiture and existing cultural norms? How much sex and violence should be in the films? What perspective should be taken on the state, on capitalist development, and other features of modern society? How did one deal with minority groups, with social problems and other controversial areas?

On the question of movie values the business had nothing against tradition as long as tradition turned a profit. Certainly most leaders in the business personally prized and supported bourgeois values; yet there were disturbing indications that old values were a drag on profits. Obviously the great mass of people, as well as bourgeois opinion, actively supported these values but advocacy of them in movies did not generate sufficiently rapid movement toward the theaters. The notion of stimulating demand through a more sensational and provocative social portraiture was gaining ground.

The screen's conservative approach to cultural and moral values was rapidly invalidated by the discovery that movie profits were usually not enhanced by support of the status quo but rather by the advocacy of cultural drift. The confusion within the industry on this question is evident in the pre-war correspondence of the prominent producer-distributor George Kleine. In 1915 an associate wrote to Kleine, "recently I have been hearing the criticism from exhibitors who watch the motion picture audience very closely, that most of the pictures that are being offered are too colourless and lack dramatic excitement."[27] Kleine answered, "we are sitting up nights, trying to be up-to-date in analyzing the public preference in the matter of films."[28]

One approach which appeared more and more promising at the box office was to have the plot deal with some form of 'sex' problem. In 1912 Universal released *Traffic in Souls,* promoted as "the sensational motion picture dramatization of the destruction of the Vice Trust by District Attorney Whitman."[29] A spate of similar films followed, all claiming to be based on real-life happenings and dedicated to the cause of sexual purity. Many middle class critics felt that profit was the aim of these films, not enlightenment. A reviewer wrote of one such production, "such a film represents the commercialization of the subject and the exploitation of it for private gain in the worst degree."[30] Unconvinced, the studios pushed forward. In 1915 the lavish *Daughter of the Gods,* with prurient appeal, was a big box office success, and so were the films of Fox's Theda Bara, the sensational sex "vampire."

The industry soon became a leading propagandist for revisions in the moral code. Theda Bara, in a magazine article "How I Became a Film Vampire" revealed that the "good little girl is just as bad as the bad little girl is good."[31] Carl Laemmle, a studio head, wrote that "instead of discovering that 95 percent favoured clean pictures, I discovered that at least half, maybe 60 percent want the pictures to be risqué."[32] In 1917 one of George Kleine's correspondents quoted an article on a Chaplin film in the *Washington Star* which claimed that "an extraordinary development of the motion picture enterprise is the evolution of a capacity on the part of a large proportion of the public to enjoy vulgarity."[33] Kleine's reply stands as an epitaph for the old perspective. "It is seriously to be questioned" he wrote back, "whether any description that indicates clean living or decency is fitting in trade advertisements."[34]

The result was that traditional norms were no longer actively supported in the film perspective as large corporations aiming to refine the profit potential of movies came to dominate the industry. By the mid-teens, more and more films deliberately veered away from a perspective which supported the virtues of family, hard work, saving, piety, and the modest life. This change is apparent in everything connected with the films, but especially in the new perspective on sex, class, and consumption. The new approach offered a highly ambiguous and often positive view toward (among other things) adultery and consumption. These shifts were justified in the name of corporate expediency (in trade journals) and economic and cultural progress (in popular magazines). Movie makers, hooking up with wider trends, became champions of moral relativism. As DeMille put it later, "what's moral in Africa is unmoral in Asia". The movies did not simply reflect the wider changes taking place at the time, they took an active part in transforming attitudes about work, social relations, and patterns of consumption and leisure.

Let us examine some of the ways in which the new social portraiture served corporate needs. As noted, during the mid-teens eroticism was factored out of the overall human condition and made a key element in the new movie formulas. It is true that eroticism had long been part of the appeal of films; nor was there anything new in using eroticism to give depth and vibrancy to a popular art form. But eroticism in the story film prior to World War One was locked into a strong negative perspective, an approach which severely limited the exploitation of sex. Pre-war films like *Traffic in Souls, Civilization, The Cheat* and *Intolerance* have prurient moments (bare breasts, adulterous relations, rape scenes) but these elements were contained by the old traditional perspective; the sex in these films is supposedly there for an object lesson.

While early producers undoubtedly recognized the potential profit of more erotic films, they faced serious risks in exploiting sex. In the era of small firms, the individual producer did not have sufficient political or economic clout to stand up against the well organized partisans of the status quo who were already breathing down his neck for the sex and violence in the films, the cheap five cent theater etc. The new corporations, larger and much more powerful, found they did have the financial, legal and political wherewithal to proceed in this area. Once this was clear, the old traditional moral code was jettisoned, one part after another. Always in pieces, it should be noted, never with a consistency that could clearly be construed as political or social deviance. Just as the rise of mass production and distribution in other areas of the national economy led to manipulation of the yearly model, so now the mass production of movies subjected the view of society to a similar fiddling. The filmmakers learned that it was not only in their interest to exploit social and cultural phenomena in this fashion, but that only by going against the grain of established values, by offering for public consumption what was officially taboo (or on the borderline of taboo) could their movies generate profits at a sufficient rate. Cultural norms became a kind of natural resource to be steadily mined by the industry.

As the movie industry threw itself against established norms with increasing intrepidity it generated a massive amount of resistance that mushroomed into wide support for stringent public controls. The industry in turn found it necessary to pour money into efforts to maintain autonomy. This effort was always couched in the language of artistic and political freedom but in practice the industry had little use for these freedoms. The industry was motivated to protect its control over film content because its leaders knew that profits, monopolization, and the relative freedom to manipulate the social portraiture were all intertwined. To take one example, anyone comparing the early story film with films made in the twenties cannot help noticing how important a role the wealthy play in the later films and how scarce are realistic stories about working-class life. The popular anti-capitalism of the pre-war film (the idea of wealth as an evil force, anti-urbanism, anti-consumption, the attack on monopoly) virtually disappears after the war and does not appear again until the crisis of the '30s. This was largely a result of the economic consolidation of the industry. The rationalization of the movie business, in combination with wider social, economic, and political changes generated by other sector rationalizations, necessitated a new perspective on wealth, poverty, and class relations. A subtle but pervasive ban was laid down against stories that were critical of the existing economic and political structures. Only rarely, in the twenties, does one see films about economic exploitation, degrading working conditions, or the tactics of powerful businessmen. Even in the thirties, a time of considerable political and economic strife, the critical element is tepid and diffuse. This closure was the result of a conscious position the movie business had assumed vis-à-vis economic, political and cultural questions.

That this shift is something more than another reflection of the post World War

One move to the right is evident in the way the movie-makers rushed to cooperate with strong government policy statements against criticism of the social and economic system while at the same time fighting tooth and nail against the much more popular, broad based movements to resist the model of U.S. life propagated by Hollywood. When its real interests, profits, were threatened, the industry waved the banner of free speech, and where freedom of expression was of dubious profit (as in 'political' films) it policed content as effectively as any government censorship body. The state-subsidized films of Germany and Russia in the twenties show the reactionary nature of the Hollywood approach on aesthetic and political levels.

The new view of sex, wealth, and consumption served corporate aims in a number of intersecting ways. What did movie sex have to do with movie consumption, and how did the promotion of both of these further the interests of the movie business? We noted that movie-makers learned that certain forms of abrasive content brought people to the theaters and kept them coming back. But if the movie-makers were going to present a more liberal view of sex, what would be the social context for this liberalization and what would be its nature? Clearly the working class neighborhood would be unsuitable at this moment for sex high-jinks and wild debauched sprees. A more liberal screen attitude about sex among the working class would, from the viewpoint of the late-teens and early twenties, probably seem as risky as promoting worker-radicalism. Indeed, radicalism and free love were continuously linked in the anti-left propaganda of the time. Here is where a more positive view of the upper class was crucial. A positive view of the wealthy neighborhood allowed producers to move ahead faster with profit-making erotic content, because upper-class sex, cleansed by money and opulence, and linked to a viewpoint supportive of the status quo in economic and political matters, was the only kind of sex that would pass.

The revised social portraiture served corporate purposes in a variety of other ways. The wealthy neighborhood glorified on the screen, helped upgrade the status of the film business by association, conferring bourgeois respectability on an industry still plagued by its reputation as a poor people's theater. This upgrading also had important implications for industry autonomy. Hence the industry endlessly advertised that the classy trappings of its films were proof of the superior character of its films. Vice-versa, industry leaders warned that realistic, austere films about working class life and poverty were sordid, low quality entertainment. The capital investment manifest in sets, gowns, hardware, and manpower were promoted as the "high cost of quality films." In actuality, of course, the classy surfaces had little to do with "quality" and much to do with strategies of consolidation. Finally, this mystification of wealth and consumption was right up the alley of the bourgeois media and its backers in the rapidly expanding consumer goods sector. In the movie business, as in other sectors of commodity production, schemes to insure a stable market were of critical importance; more and more attention and investment had to go to insure demand. This was yet another force pressuring filmmakers to adopt a bourgeois perspective.

To stimulate demand, then, movie-makers tied the social perspective of films up with the mainstream of American economic life after World War One, linking with the rapidly expanding consumer goods industries. A symbiotic relationship evolved between journalism and the film, for example. Great amounts of money were poured into newspapers and magazines for the promotion of films; newspapers, especially big metropolitan dailies and important chains, tended as a result to take a favorable attitude toward the film establishment. Another example of cooperation was the publicity tie-in: plot and content of films were manipulated so as to involve retailers of consumer goods and film exhibitors in schemes of mutual promotion. Speaking of a 1918 high-life extravaganza, a trade magazine advised distributors that "the star wears some very attractive gowns in some of the scenes so that the gown shops . . . will be anxious to show her picture in their windows or on their counters inside of the stores."[35] A suggested promotion line for *The Grand Duchess and the Waiter* was to "play up Menjou and Miss Vidor, photos of Miss Vidor used in tie-ups with jewelry stores, beauty parlors, style shops, showing her with brilliant jewels, her new boyish bob and her Parisian gowns."[36] *Fifth Avenue,* a 1926 Paramount release, was described by promotional literature as a picture which "fairly glows with ornate setting and fine backgrounds." The "exploitation angle" recommended playing up the title, stressing "contrast between Society and Bohemian atmosphere" and "boost style show."[37] The exploitation angle suggested by Paramount for *Speeding Three* (1926) ("comedy drama of rivalry between auto manufacturers with the daughter of one defeating the other with the help of a college boy who wins her love") was "many possibilities for a tie-up with automobile manufacturers."[38] This kind of promotion became very common as the movie idea of contemporary life was shaped around consumer goods. Pictures routinely had their quota of gowns, autos, jewels, and lavish interiors. By the mid-twenties Hollywood's role in disciplining consumers was well appreciated in political, industrial, and commercial circles.

This outlook on materialism was in sharp contrast to the earlier screen perspective on wealth which argued that material goods and money counted for little or nothing. As a company ad for Biograph's *Gold Is Not All* (1910) put it: "there was never a truer maxim framed . . . what a moral those four words teach." Beauty was identified with simple tastes, corruption with extravagance. In the postwar period the screen version of the human predicament increasingly depended on commodities for interest and appeal.

These transformations on the social portraiture can be traced in the ongoing internal debates over the content and format of the film. In the earlier, more competitive era, as noted, business wisdom held that production costs in any single film should be kept as low as possible. Longer films, high actor fees, big outlays on sets were resisted by many producers because of the risk involved. After seeing *Birth of a Nation,* in February, 1915, William DeMille wrote to Samuel Goldfish in New York: "remember how sore Biograph was with Griffith when he made *Judith of Bethulia* and how much money that lost though it was only a four reeler. So I suppose you're right when you say that there is no advantage in leading if the cost of leadership makes commercial success impossible."[39] But the stunning financial success of *Birth of a Nation,* evident in the coming months, demonstrated the advantage of high investments in an individual film. In 1915 we find the Kalem Corporation promoting one of its productions on the basis of a hotel set that cost $15,000 to build. And *The Moving Picture World* anticipated the ideological shifts that would be necessitated by the new business wisdom when it announced in 1915 that "half the world is more interested in how the other half dresses than how it lives."[40]

The idea that lavish production values were motivated by a quest for excellence in films was readily swallowed by the media (and by many film historians). A *New York Times* reviewer stated in 1917 that "a motion picture stands or falls by the measure of its interior scenes . . . too often they are palpably things of paint and canvas, tasteless and tawdry, with no illusion of solidity."[41] After 1920 it was endlessly repeated in industry propaganda that outlays on sets and actors' fees was the measure of a picture's worth. The high-cost film, at first resisted by producers, became the iron-law of filmmaking. The script that could not be shaped to these ends was unlikely to be produced. A film which somehow attacked these values (except in comic form, spoofs on Hollywood such as *Ella Cinders* and King Vidor's *Show People*) was considered subversive.

The connection between excess and the profit sheets is clearly outlined in an anecdote related by Lillian Gish. Gish, playing in a film version of *La Boheme* complained to the producers: "These are poor Bohemians . . . they can't live in a big beautiful house." According to Gish, the front office responded: "How are we to get exhibitors to pay big prices for your pictures if they don't see the production values? "The executives finally agreed to let Mimi live in a big attic," Gish wrote. "I couldn't accustom myself to their strange set of values."[42] Neither could D. W. Griffith, who never adjusted to the new screen perspective that his early epics gave rise to. In 1923 he took to the pages of *Arts and Decoration* with a curious attack on the view of wealth in the film, the exaggerations of which he saw as a kind of cheap "Latin" parvenu influence. "Motion pictures have received and merited much criticism about the style of rooms they photograph to represent the homes of the rich," Griffith wrote. "Men and women in evening attire depart to the opera or arrive from it. Persons of wealth, family and education flash their jewels in the atmosphere of a furniture shop, or an auctioneer's showroom. The rooms are crowded with objects that stridently quarrel. I concede the bad taste of such interiors."[43]

The keystone of the new corporate edifice was the flagship theater which, in conjunction with control and exhibition, the star system, lavish production values, and promotional efforts, provided the means for a relatively small number of producers to dominate the global market for films. To cite the twenties Seabury study again, "the effect upon the public was and is that the producer who also controls the theatres upon a substantial scale can exhibit to the public anything he wishes to exhibit. The spur of competition for the business of these theatres is gone. The man who makes the picture owns the theatre and his picture is exhibited not because it is artistic or has other merits, but because he owns or controls the theatre."[44] The importance of these factors for the social portraiture cannot be over-stressed, for it was the metropolitan audience (and in particular the metropolitan press) which was the gateway to national distribution and promotion of films.

At the start the film was a commodity, but it was a commodity that, for better or worse, still absorbed values and ideas rooted in tradition, and in the community. As the movie business learned that the social portraiture was a key element in growth and monopolization, this popular and traditional influence waned. Now popular culture was processed into the social portraiture only to the extent that it was economically sensible to do so. Important aspects of traditional bourgeois and popular culture (anti-capitalism, nativism, the work ethic), were not adequately represented because they were inconsistent with corporate goals. All discussion of social imagery in the post World War One films must bear in mind that the crucial mediating factor was not "public opinion" but the needs of the movie business.

NOTES

1. Terry Ramsaye, *A Million and One Nights* (New York: 1926), p. 467.

2. Robert Henderson, *D. W. Griffith: His Life and Work* (New York: 1972), p. 39.

3. Letter from the Essanay Film Manufacturing Company to William Wallace Cook, November 1, 1910, New York Public Library Manuscript Collection, hereafter NYPLMC.

4. Henderson, pp. 86–87.

5. Quoted in Kevin Brownlow, *The Parade's Gone By* (New York: 1968), pp. 48–49.

6. Henderson, p. 87.

7. Some examples of early story films with a pro-working class perspective are *A Corner in Wheat* (1909), *Child of the Ghetto* (1910), *The Userer* (1910), *Cry of the Children* (1912), *The Italian* (1914), *The Immigrant* (1915), and the modern segment of Griffith's *Intolerance*, called, when it was released as a separate film after the war, *The Mother and the Law*.

8. Mae Marsh, *Screen Acting* (Los Angeles: 1921), p. 108.

9. Henderson, p. 54.

10. The contention that Hollywood was wired into the minds of its audience is another variation on the consumer sovereignty argument (that the productions of American film content emerge out of a freely operating consensual process). This interpretation of film content and shifts in content is advanced in a great number of works on the American film going back to the twenties. See Lewis Jacobs, *The Rise of the American Film* (New York: 1939); Margaret Thorpe, *America at the Movies* (New Haven: 1938); and Iris Barry, *Let's Go to the Movies* (New York: 1926).

11. *System: The Magazine of Business*, March 1918.

12. Jacobs, p. 57. All these figures have been derived from secondary sources and should be taken as approximations.

13. Henderson, p. 49.

14. Kenneth MacGowan, *Behind the Screen* (New York: 1965), p. 160.

15. Ibid., p. 247.

16. Ibid.

17. *Chicago Projecting Company, Special Catalogue No. 15*, published in 1905.

18. Allen Talmey, *Doug, Mary and Others* (New York: 1927), p. 36.

19. William Marston Seabury, *The Public and the Motion Picture Industry* (New York: 1926), p. 34.

20. Jacobs, p. 291.

21. *San Francisco Call Chronicle,* February 1, 1920.

22. MacGowan, p. 173.

23. Diary of Rogers Lytton, Feb. 15, 1915, NYPLMC.

24. *System,* March 1918.

25. Edmund Wilson, *The American Earthquake* (New York: 1958), p. 399.

26. Joseph Mankiewicz, interview, Oral History Papers, *Popular Arts Project,* Series One, vol. 6, Part Two, p. 3, Columbia University Manuscript Collection.

27. Letter of Denis O'Brien to George Kleine, June 21, 1915, George Kleine Papers, Library of Congress (hereafter cited as the Kleine Papers).

28. Letter of George Kleine to Denis O'Brien, August 12, 1915, Kleine Papers.

29. See also Jacobs, p. 148.

30. *Outlook,* February 14, 1914.

31. Ibid.

32. Quoted in Donald Ramsay Young, *Motion Pictures: A Study in Social Legislation* (Philadelphia: 1922), p. 10.

33. Quoted in the letter of L. W. McChesney to George Kleine, July 23, 1917, Kleine Papers.

34. Letter of George Kleine to L. W. McChesney, July 24, 1917, Kleine Papers.

35. *Exhibition Trade Review,* March 16, 1918.

36. *Motion Picture News,* September 11, 1926.

37. Ibid., Feb. 6, 1926.

38. Ibid.

39. Letter of William DeMille to Samuel Goldfish, Feb. 10, 1915, NYPLMC.

40. *The Moving Picture World,* July 3, 1915.

41. *The New York Times,* Feb. 25, 1917.

42. Lillian Gish in Talmey, p. 45.

43. D. W. Griffith, "Are Motion Pictures Destructive of Good Taste?" *Arts and Decoration,* September 1923.

44. Seabury, p. 55.

XXII

SONG OF THE SHIRT

THE FILM AND HISTORY PROJECT
AND THEIR ATTEMPT TO MAKE A RADICAL,
FEMINIST FILM ON THE NEEDLE TRADE
IN BRITAIN IN THE MID-FIFTEEN HUNDREDS

Alison Beale

> Would that its tone could reach the rich
>
> *(The Song of the Shirt)*

The Song of the Shirt was first presented at the *Feminism and Cinema* event at the 1979 Edinburgh Film Festival. It was produced in London by the Film and History Project and co-directed by Sue Clayton and Jonathan Curling. The film is about the history of dressmakers and seamstresses in the England of the 1830s and 1840s, and the reform movements and appeals to bourgeois conscience and philanthropy that addressed the problems of these "Distressed Needlewomen." During this period, which saw the repeal of the Corn Laws and a shift in power from the aristocracy to merchant capitalists, thousands of single women whose labor had been integral to family agricultural and artisanal production moved into the cities to take up industrial and servant work. However, many of them became engaged in the production of clothing, a trade with the uncertain status of mass nontechnical labor. The terms of employment ranged from independent dressmakers who began as apprentices, to "slop-house" workers who did the rougher sewing on a piece work basis as it was distributed to them by middle-men.

The media of the period, serialized novels, magazines, newspapers, cartoons, and even songs, took up the case of these workers. The "slop-house" workers were a favorite of both the bourgeois and radical presses. They were horrified by the picture they saw of the single woman in this casually organized and over-supplied trade. Her independence and misery disturbed the hypocritical convention of the "protection of women" in the family and in the law. Her image, starved and sexually active, disturbed the womanly ideal, the passive domestic consumer, that accompanied the rise of the bourgeoisie. She presented problems for the propaganda of social reformers and conservatives alike.

However, the film is not a piece of historical detective work, awarding the unknown figures their proper (and final) recognition. The presence of the seamstresses was acknowledged in certain ways: the film is concerned with the forms which that recognition took. The motivation for making the film lies partly in the persistence of comparatively bad working conditions for women today in the garment trade. But in addition to its specific historical material, *The Song of the Shirt* also constitutes a confrontation with a problem-area which has arisen within the economic and cultural conditions of independent filmmaking in England, and within feminist film analyses and practices.

On the basis of the concerns which have arisen from these areas, the suggestion is being put forward that filmic representation (paradigmatically of women, or of history) and film production, distribution, and exhibition have a relationship which exists not only in after-the-fact exegesis of a film text. Instead, the relationships importantly referred to by these terms are those (a) between the audience and the film, and (b) between the audience and "history."

A key feature of this argument is the centralized and monopolized international film industry, which means that the viewing of most film is part of "mass entertainment" or its marginal opposite, art cinema. Given this fact, the role of the audience is to consume and to perform a "suspension of disbelief." Disbelief in the illusion, but also cynicism (and in much of the world, cultural estrangement) with respect to the rightful authority of its presentation must, supposedly, be laid aside, and as if they were the same. This temporary, "voluntary" forfeiting of reason for pleasure is frequently joked about in commercial film, and by its apologists, as though in a conspiracy among equals. But it is temporary only in one sense, because it is an attitude that is maintained by the repetition, at nearly every occasion of viewing, of the same exhibition practices. Film practice of this kind is part of the system of the social production of knowledge, which includes, as in the common-sense rationalization of the audience's position, the construction of the relationships between producer and consumer, or exhibitor and audience, within which knowledge is categorized. Thus we have notions of "common-knowledge," and so also "entertainment" and "history," which are apparently arrived at not by struggle but by a consensus whose machinery is invisible. What can be argued though is that a common-sense approach to being a member of the audience, repeated and ritualized, is disguised as choice but rests on a partial knowledge by the audience of its own position. *The Song of the Shirt* treats this partial knowledge as directly analogous to the type of knowledge of the situation of the needlewomen possessed by the bourgeoisie, by the reforming parties, and by the women themselves.

In this film common-sense Victorian attitudes to class, to gender difference and sexuality are taken apart in such a way as to call into question attitudes of the present. In doing this work the filmmakers were faced by two areas of opportunity and constraint—the financial and organizational limitations placed on the production, film technique, research, and so on, but also the availability of some historical sources and at the same time a lack of records left by the women themselves. These were the material and circumstances at hand for treating the subject of how the ideology of "woman's place" in one particular time partnered the largely unequal relationship of women workers to capital.

With regard to *The Song of the Shirt,* it is important to note the problem posed by the film theory concerned with reading films, in terms of structural or intersubjective models developed from linguistic semiotics and psychoanalysis. The interrogation of the film text, its relationships to the constructed/constructing viewing subject, and even the description of the film as at the conjuncture of a number of cultural and historic discourses[1] are formulations limited in a specific way. This is because the political nature of representation is being handled (if not theorized) at the "viewing" end of the production process. Simply to say that meaning is constituted at the point of viewing detaches this point from the points of producing and distributing and can lead to a reformulation of the liberal gesture to audience free will and common sense. Here, production, distribution, and exhibition must be considered together, especially where a critique is based on a dominant pattern in film practice.

The political nature of representation can be emphasized by the reformulation of a classic communications formula to read: "Who is representing what, and for whom?"[2] The priority in the question is not only representation in general (as if this were possible) but also "who represents" the inequality of the audience to the film production, distribution, and exhibition processes. To achieve a different relationship to the audience, the Film and History Workshop, in the process of research and production for *The Song of the Shirt,* has consulted and planned screenings and discussions with specific constituencies, for example feminist historians, educational associations, and labor organizations.

This formulation of the problematic of the audience and the filmmakers response to it must be seen as relating to four areas of recent film theoretical and practical work in England. Firstly, debate at the 1979 *Feminism and Cinema* event at Edinburgh centered on the relationship of theory to practice in representations of and for women (especially with respect to women's sexuality) in the form of strategies for dealing with pleasure and narrative in "women's" films. Filmmakers were also very concerned about appropriate production and distribution methods. Secondly, socialist and feminist historians in England, such as the History Workshop and the Feminist History Group have suggested both in terms of historical material and in the methodology of recovering "minority" history, how it is that political filmmaking can be concerned with the connection between ideology and historical representations. Thirdly, work on the spectator, the viewing subject, is now challenged and expanded by the interface between psychoanalysis and semiotics. Finally, the film has an integral relationship to the political and aesthetic strategies of independent filmmaking in England, in the face of the current state of English media production and consumption.

The Silent Sex

With fingers weary and worn
With eyelids heavy and red,
A woman sat in unwomanly rags

> Plying her needle and thread—
> Stitch—Stitch—Stitch—
> In poverty, hunger and dirt,
> And still with a voice of dolorous pitch
> Would that its tone would reach the rich
> She sang the Song of the Shirt.

The Song of the Shirt, in black and white, runs for 135 minutes and has been constructed in three parts with a postscript so that it can be screened in classrooms and in situations which allow discussions between or after the episodes. All three parts begin at the same point, a shot of one or two women in a London cafe in which there is a television visible to the right of the picture. On the TV screen there appear interviews with contemporary working women, with slop-house workers of the 1830s and 1840s and voiceovers and titles reading from and presenting visually the texts of documents of the period about the working and health conditions of the workers. This device loosely frames the larger part of the period content of the film—its dramatized, reconstructed documentary and montage sections (using film, video, graphics, synchronized speech and voiceovers and music)—within a contemporary setting. But in the end such formal devices do not close off the historical material. While the cafe TV is zoomed in on at the opening of each section to take up the whole of the film-screen space, video screens and segments also appear within what are perceived of as film sections. In effect, there is no fixed correspondence between time period or theme, and any particular medium within the film.

To take the opening of part one for example: we see a woman sitting in the cafe and a video screen to the right. The woman on the video speaks about her work as a waitress and reveals that her husband is too humiliated to face the prospect of Social Security: "No man's going to like being told . . . that he's suddenly got to start supporting a woman and a couple of kids." As she says this the camera zooms in and the video screen, over which the credits and quotations and titles have been rolling right to left, enlarges to fill the film screen. The picture cuts to the woman who was talking on the video screen now walking through the garment district of London, and to reflections of these streets in shop windows. This is followed by a slow sequence beginning with reflections in canal water and a bridge with the sign "Frog Lane Bridge," over which a woman in Victorian dress walks. The original woman's voice continues: ". . . cottage manufacture being ceased, if the girls cannot obtain places as servants, and but a small number can, they must remain at home idle or else leave home to seek other work." The camera moves across period drawings of industrial canals and then cuts to a grainy shot of girls climbing a canal bridge like the first one, but steeper, wearily carrying bundles of clothes. Within this shot the camera moves across to another screen with close-ups of the girls washing clothes and dipping their feet in the water. Further cuts and camera movements establish railway tracks, canal boats, a period cartoon of a lady leaning out of a railway carriage, and drawings of railway carriage interiors and of open railway carriages bearing frenzied looking workers. The camera comes to rest on a gentleman (an actor in period dress) in a train interior reading to us about the division of labor from Adam Smith's *The Wealth of Nations.*

Two sets of images are repeated throughout the film: the women in the cafe and the seamstresses. The latter are mostly to be found seated around a table working together, though they are also seen at a commission of inquiry into their moral and physical health, and carrying work to and from their lodgings. Their customers are represented by a series of scenes in a grand house, tableau-like, in which a girl is measured and fitted for a gown—these scenes also include the dressmaker and servants. The main scenarios are supplemented by political and satirical cartoons, sketches, and drawings and by the sequence of stills which accompany the reading of a reformist novel *A Woman's Wrongs,* and by an occasional foray into the present with the actresses as historians and presenters. Unlike the male figures Jones and Mayhew (reformist writers), Morrison the Co-operative, Harney the Chartist, Ashley the arch conservative, and Cobden the Free-Trader, no historically "real" women are named. The only exceptions are the titled ladies who sanctioned an "association for the relief and protection of young persons employed in the dressmaking and millinery department in London," and they appear in name only.

The contextualization of the narrative and historical film by the video is incomplete and in fact allows complex correspondences to be made between identities and time periods "inside" and "outside" the film. The actresses each play several roles and appear in modern and period dress at different times. This is not only a formal device, or one that refers in some general way to the question of identity—it is a device that points to the correspondence between individual names being unknown to history (as it has been recorded) and to the indistinct identities of individual women in the film. This correspondence is commented on when actresses change from historical subjects to historians from one scene to another, and when the use of video and film within the film questions the "drama" or "documentary" nature of the various sections. When the actress who plays one of the slop-house workers also plays the part of the tragic Anna (in the stills sequence) both the workers' and our identification with the character(s) is comically and dramatically noted. However the effect is not Brechtian—if one accepts the characterization of Brechtian theater as distancing.

Sex and Economy

The reason for this is that the film is concerned with what is present, not with what is absent from an ideology of woman's place. It can come as a shock, to anyone used to sexual oppression in the guise of tolerance, or used to the titillation of TV costume dramas, to see how clearly Victorian documents and pictures link an ideology of sex to production and consumption, and to the fetishism of the female person. Lord Ashley, 1844:

> What is the ground on which the woman says she will no longer pay attention to her domestic duties or give the obedience which is owing to her husband? Because on her devolves the labour which should fall to his share and she throws out the taunt, "If I have the labour, I will also have the amusement." Where, Sir, under these conditions, are the obligations of domestic life. How can its obligations be fulfilled?

This excerpt from a speech in Parliament is just one piece of documentary evidence that illustrates the significance placed on woman's work and sexuality, and the fear of women controlling these aspects of their lives. The control of women's work and sexuality by regulated domestic life, which is supposedly ahistorical and "natural" can appear here as the subject of a film because it has been talked about and written about as a political issue, as much in Victorian England as in the Welfare State. The film uses the words of Conservatives like Ashley (who was concerned about decent living conditions for workers as contributing to a moral basis for class society), and contrasts them with Free-Traders like Cobden, who in his opposition to the Ten Hours Bill (limiting the working hours of women and children) was more concerned with the profit to be had from these workers, and with force as the social regulator.

In the documents and drawings of the period women appear as either innocent or guileful. For example, the seamstresses very often prostituted themselves to make a living, and since they were not allowed their children with them at their work, they left them with wet nurses in whose care they often died. These were personal tragedies. However, their "moral laxity," their living habits and diseases, which were very much determined by their working conditions, were regarded as transmissible in the work which they produced. Several parts of the film illustrate the imagined political economy of disease and sexuality that connected them to wealthy women, to whose seasonal whims they sacrificed their health.

In the film this economy is centered visually around the dressing of a young lady which appears in a sequence of dramatized scenes in which she stands in her drawers, petticoat and mob-cap and is measured, pinned and fitted to the accompaniment, sometimes, of only the sound of silk rustling. No one but the dressmaker moves. These stylized improvisations (no one speaks), the high camera angle and its distance from the scene (greater than in the scenes with the women sewing around a table), and the dim lighting, emphasize the deathly eroticism of the dress-fitting process. It culminates in the dress being carefully folded in tissue paper, which is the last scene of the film.

This sequence stands in contrast to cartoon drawings of a debutante's Season (in which she wears out milliners and seamstresses on her way to a proposal), to a vignette about the origins of the term "pin money," and to lectures about the responsibilities of upper class to working class women. The film demonstrates that this problem of responsibility is transferred from the sphere of class relations to the woman's individual conscience—her guilt about her comparative advantage and her own commodity status. The composition of several shots in the grand house echoes Tenniel's drawings, for example in the use of mirrors. Editing allows the spectator to recognize similarities between the composition of several scenes and one of his drawings in which a girl is admiring herself in a new dress, while the expiring form of the seamstress can be seen in a mirror. In both cases the mirrors reflect more than a reversed image. In another connection of the classes it is the dressmaker who brings to this house a copy of the novel *A Woman's Wrongs,* which is concealed by a maid in the top of a dolls house, where it is found and read by the daughter (she of the dress-fitting) as the maids watch and listen.

The quoted words of the reformers and conservatives alike confirm the sexual hypocrisy which defined the laziness and greed (or gentility) of the decorative, appealing consumer, and the helplessness (or sluttishness) of the producer. The interesting thing about the way these links are made in the film—from cartoons by Cruikshank, Lynch, et al., mainly published in *Punch,* to speeches about the emigration of "surplus" women, and to the weak sympathy for the seamstresses aroused through the publication of novels like *A Woman's Wrongs* (featuring Anna, who, starving and homeless, "falls" in the arms of a student) is that they do not seek to diffuse the reality of the sex-economy connection. In one improvised scene the slop-house women mockingly act out Anna's seduction, which they have been reading, and in another banter Mayhew about the real reason for his wanting them to emigrate. It is important that in this scene, at the same time the women imply that they know full well why they are candidates for the colonies—"Like bleedin' criminals"—that they also ask why it is that others are making the decisions about their lives: "Come to write more articles, have you, on the terrible conditions of the sweated trades?"

Hysteria

The changes which were coming about in the 1830s meant extended leisure for some and extended work for others. Reactions to these conditions—"nervous" diseases, genuine illness due to working and living conditions, as well as political agitation, tended to be labeled hysteria, or irrational frenzy, by the middle-class press. This hysteria was located in their bodies in the forms of unruly undomesticated sexuality and social diseases. It was not their conditions, but women and workers who were irrational. The materials—cartoons, pamphlets, and speeches—which the filmmakers have used make reference to women's hysteria, and also to hysteria in a more general sense, as for example in the reports of revolution in Europe in 1838. Sexual anarchy, mob rule, and disease were connected, as in Lord Ashley's appeals for sanitation measures during the Cholera epidemic, to lessen the risks of revolution. The logic with which equations such as his were made could not conceal the ideological nature of their common sense assumptions.

In its treatment of this subject the film has to deal with the same problem as all "feminist" film—to know how to treat female sexuality without exploiting it. Since its encounter with the representation of women is both in terms of historical examples (and a trade which emphasized the appearance) and its own filmic devices, the material and tactics of *The Song of the Shirt* make an important case.

A major part of the film's effect is the concentrated presentation of selected texts and cartoons, stressing this hysteria as something present in them, not below their surfaces. But in its handling of a sexual and political ideology and its negotiation of the representation of female sexuality, the film owes a great deal to the musical score. Like the visual sequences, it is composed of a few themes or "narratives," using some Victorian lyrics and tunes. It is a complex instrumental and voice composition, self-referential both in terms of repetition (which does not strictly follow the repetition of the various strands of "narrative"), and variation on a few main themes, lyrics, and songs about Chartism, the Cholera epidemic, the Great Exhibition of 1851, and also about the slop-house workers (such as "The Song of the Shirt") all of which have been used in such a way as to connect or counterpoint certain messages in the film. By slightly altering a normal range of tempo and pitch, by using an ensemble of piano, reed instruments, cello, clarinet, guitar, and voice (with additional saxophone, trumpet, and electric bass), the music plays just "off" the sounds of a Victorian musical evening at home.

At several points in the film, but expecially the end of part three, the tempo is faster, the pitch of a strident tenor more extreme, and a soprano voice beyond the usual range. The songs have distinctly pronounced lyrics, and they are songs of political protest. The satire and the sentimentality that can be heard in their words were features of the political campaigns of which they were a part. They are not an imposition or rationalization by the filmmakers. For example, during the dress-making scenes in the dim room, there is a melancholy introduction to an obsessive lyric sung by two soprano voices in close nasal harmony: "Females work too hard I'm told, Stitch goes the needle." It disappears desperately and abruptly off the soprano register—"Stitch goes the needle!" And a camera movement from the head to the respectable hem of a drawing of a lady, with the caption "As I Was," and across and up the picture of her in a shorter skirt "As I Am," is accompanied by the following lyrics:

> The pretty girls that roam about
> Begin to raise their voices
> They say they're going to turn out
> And ask for higher prices
> They say that times are very hard
> And for to work they're willing
> But what they charged you three pence for
> They'll charge you now a shilling.

The displacement of discourse about social oppression from the mechanisms (relations) of that oppression to the bodies of the oppressed is located, and therefore can be revealed by the film, in the displacement of effects in language to the register of music. The analogy is to be found in Victorian representations, that is, in the drawings and music. Nevertheless, if the music and visual elements were to be given a formal documentary status "borrowed" from the category of historical material, their impact could remain closed off. Through the deconstructive, narrative, and episodic elements of the film and the music this hysteria, or protest, is legitimated as it builds emotional and intellectual sympathy with the audience. The point is that if there is ambiguity in representations of women, it is there for a reason. Therefore we are not encouraged to patronize Victorian attitudes, but to engage with them.

History

In contrast to the silent women, the male figures in the film are those who have spoken, written, and formed "history." Especially in parts two and three of the film, we see and hear the reformers, free-traders, unionists, and Chartists in competition with one another. They declare and quote, haranguing audiences in a present-day London street market, addressing blown-up drawings of skeletal tailors, and arguing with each other through the use of video screens set up on an area like a stage which is used elsewhere in the film as well. Even an uninformed viewer is able to get the gist of the debate and the alliances that were formed for mutual interest. It is clear too that the interests of women and men workers were not identical since women's piece work undercut the prices charged by the male tailors. In fact, when it comes to these scenes of the film, which rely more on documentary evidence, women seem to be largely left out because there is little evidence of their participation in the labor movement at this time. What is interesting is the comparative distance from the male historical characters which one experiences. How much is it a question of the film technique taking a cue from the nature of the material, i.e. the fact that men are historically distinct and are understood through their own words rather than representations of their experience by others (though this idea ignores the illiterate working class man), and how much is it the reproduction by the film and by the viewer of the more sympathetic and "general" character of women, which has its filmic conventions?

The film tends to bring this problem to the foreground. As the story of Anna, written by Jones and Mayhew, is reaching its climax, Mayhew interrupts the composition:

> Jones: ". . . And the flame of love this kindled was to bear through the bitter nights to come."
> Mayhew: "Jones, we cannot have them setting up house together. She must commit suicide—there you are—in the canal."
> Jones: "But that's undercutting the very point of my story. I had intended that he give up the benefits of his superior position, and they continue living together untainted by considerations of class and property."
> Harney: "There are said to be 40,000 starving women in the clothes trade, Mr. Jones, most of them no doubt syphilitic old hags and not at all like your gracious heroine. I've yet to see the 40,000 young gentlemen that'll rescue them. Does your magazine offer them any help?"

Mayhew's and Jones's voices had been heard over a sequence of still photographs referring to the story they were telling. As Mayhew interrupts we see the two authors standing in a garden by the canal composing, then debating the story. When Harney (a Chartist) interrupts them he is seen shouting down at them from a balcony over the garden. This short sequence moves from the absurd but sympathetic romance to the authors' opposing but equally idealistic views of how to continue it, which reveal the ways in which they expect to influence their middle-class readership. Harney's interruption points out a few of the realities of the situation, as well as his own disbelief in the usefulness of serials as a political weapon. He goes on to talk about the stamp taxes that restricted the radical presses (which nonetheless had not prevented the wide circulation of the Chartist papers) and the support for the movement to be gained by working class literacy, by the removal of the Stamp Act, and not by the mere sympathy of the middle class to a melodramatic story. So here the film is dealing explicitly with the politics of representation through arguments about it in the period concerned. The presence of this type of discourse within the film is verbal, certainly, but it owes its form of existence, i.e., the possibility of verbal encounters like those between Jones and Mayhew and Harney to the filmic treatment. Even further, the absence of women from the discussion is noted by a shot of women washing clothes on the other side of the canal.

The direction in which to move the argument now is not further into the layers of representation but into the arena where these are produced, the relationship of the audience to history.

The Audience

A major problem which the film has to handle is the notion of ambiguity—visual and historical. That is, representations of women can be read in different ways, and so can events, as for example in present-day judgments of the effectiveness of strategies taken by the reforming groups of the nineteenth century. The two kinds of ambiguity tend to defeat discursive treatments; representation can be less well handled in pure (i.e., linear) discourse, but so also discourse itself. The problem which has been encountered by oral historians and by feminists is that accounts of history, especially sought-out interviews with participants in recent history, provide a version of events which is personal, oppositional, and does not even seek to be synthetic, analytical, authoritative, or "historical." Therefore it is not only a problem of the production of facts but of the production of forms with which historians must deal.

The film handles this problem in two ways, connecting the production of readings of the film to the production of history both within the text, but also in its production, distribution, and exhibition processes. In the treatment of the sexual and political economy of women, within the text, the nondiscursive does not have to mean the politically ambiguous. But the intended engagement of this film is also with a variety of audiences, who depending on their interest will produce correspondingly "interested" readings. Feminists, feminist historians, historians, school children, people interested in labor history, and so on will produce readings affected by their existing knowledge of this period, by whether or not they see the film in episodes with an opportunity for discussion, by whether they see it repeatedly, and so on. (The variables are not purely mechanical, nor are the results predictable.)

Even more importantly, the production and use of this film cannot stand apart from the project of the Independent Filmmakers Association, and from the movement to validate "Popular Memory." In other words, the relationships between the film and the audience and between the film audience and history are not singular. It is not a question of filling in missing historical information. More accurately, one must take the view that any society provides a limited space for communication, limited both physically and through direct political control. The women's movement, the oral historians, and the independent filmmakers (in England) have all been engaged with criticizing the results of this communicative restriction, but also with opening it up.

The independent film movement in England encounters the same problems as elsewhere. Independent film has effectively been marginalized with the label "alternative" in its relationship to commercial cinema, which increasingly since the war is American, and which, partly due to television, has many fewer outlets. Following the initiative of groups like Cinema Action which have worked by consultation with their film subjects and with practices like discussion at screenings, the Independent Filmmakers Association has in recent years been able to advocate by the means of shifting from an alternative to an oppositional stand, and by refusing its own marginalization (as Art Cinema, for example) to refuse also the marginalization of political movements, ideas, and modes of representation. This development is also to a large extent the responsibility of women within the I.F.A., and the issues of representation, especially of women's daily life and history as they have been treated in films such as *Women of the Rhonda* and *The Nightcleaners*. More generally, the women's movement practice of consciousness raising suggested the need to develop screening "spaces" which did not duplicate the sealed cocoon of the film theater. *The Song of the Shirt* shows the influence which the concern for representation of women's experience has had on the treatment of "popular" history, urging it out of sentimental, humanist, or party-labeled margins.

The work which this has included has involved setting up film production co-ops and distribution outlets, with a stress on collective work and a certain degree of regional autonomy. Most recently the I.F.A. has been involved in negotiations over the terms on which its members will contract production grants with the British Film Institute—to include such specifications as a collective (i.e., nonhierarchical and nonauthorial) mode of production, beginning with the proposal of hourly wages for workers in independent film (an enormous departure from their artisanal "alternative" status), and the guarantee from the outset of sufficient funds for publicity and distribution. (The I.F.A. has also acted as a lobby against the domination of Britain's fourth channel by the commercial Independent Television Network.)

This is not to suggest that there exists among English independent filmmakers a consensus about how to approach their political work, but the existence of this strategy represents a carefully worked out position, which is meaningful, regardless of its success in the face of the monoliths of communications. It is the background against which the production of *The Song of the Shirt* has taken place; therefore the relationship of the film to its potential audiences needs to be seen in this light.

The relationship is open-ended, or, to be more precise, it is defined by the character of the audience and the circumstances of each screening, and by the expectations of that audience and those of the filmmakers, as represented in the film. My experience with screenings of the film to date suggests that the filmmakers are right to hope for situations in which the audience is engaged in some way with the historical period represented by the film, and indeed these are being worked toward in association with teachers and others. Nonetheless this ideal situation is not the only one in which the film has impact. At screenings the filmmakers have been caught between emphasizing the historical and polemic (which tends, falsely, to suggest a linear argument in the film) or emphasizing the issues of representation (which tends, equally falsely, to suggest the lack of any argument). Only in the sense of a film as both a text and a text (literally) in circulation can any message the film has about the history and politics of representation make corresponding and legitimate sense. To the occasional surprise of the filmmakers, audiences have been very receptive to this idea as it affects the issues in the film in which they have the most interest.

Conclusion

The Song of the Shirt engages, in addition to its historical subject matter, with the history of filmmaking practices and theories. The point which I have wanted to stress most is the necessary unity of the film's subject with all aspects of the film's practice. Therefore I have not stressed certain other features, in particular labor history, largely because this writing is not conceived of as a catalogue or review. In particular, this film is only part of a project and it is false to take it out of that context.

One important implication for film practice is the problem of the fetishizing of the feminist film heroine. Fetishizing a feminist heroine is not a visual or narrative sleight-of-hand, but a practice which works because among other factors the "feminist" element (not a group but a tendency) in the market can be sold a symbol of itself as a substitute for an experience. But it is insufficient to suggest that all of the practices which have built up around representations of women, and those such as the camera's habitual voyeurism with respect to the female body, can be deconstructed by the removal of filmmaking from this commercial sphere, since cultural practices are not isolated in such a way. Furthermore, avant-garde film, which has dealt with the formalism of images of the female has not usually concerned itself, other than visually, with the conventions of meaning with which it plays. There is some hope in increased opportunities to present women in a greater variety of roles and visual contexts, but sheer pluralism needs to be checked by movements for more democratic control of the media and by making encounters with the visual media rather less passive experiences than they have been to date. In addition, some work, like *The Song of the Shirt* will be able to show the economic and social reasons for phenomena like the fetishism of the female, which are so transparent and so easily ignored. One discovers through this film that such work is possible.

The second implication is similar but more general. The work which has been done on the audience in the last few years largely owes its development to feminist film theory's encounter with psychoanalysis. This work is visible in *The Song of the Shirt* (the flow of identities, the mirrors, etc.) but both within the film and in similar film distribution and exhibition practices, it has also gained a sharper political edge which now connects the politics of representation in the imaginative and social realms. In other words, the connection is active—it has moved from analyzing the position of the viewing subject in relation to film, to altering that relationship through the reconstruction of film practice.

NOTES

1. See for example the analysis of the film *Nightcleaners,* by Claire Johnston and Paul Willemen in "Brecht in Britain: The Independent Political Film," *Screen,* vol. 16, no. 4, 1975.

2. This reformulation was suggested by Sylvia Harvey at an introduction to the film at a screening in London in October of 1979.

CONTRIBUTORS

Jeanne Allen teaches in the Communications Department of Temple University and also lectures at the University of California at Los Angeles.

Alison Beale teaches at Simon Fraser University and was a member of the editorial board of *Ciné-Tracts*. She recently completed a film on Harold Innis.

David Bordwell is Professor of Film at the University of Wisconsin, Madison, and is the author of *Narration in the Fiction Film, Ozu and the Poetics of Cinema,* and co-author of *The Classical Hollywood Cinema.* His new book is entitled *Making Meaning: Inference and Rhetoric in the Interpretation of the Cinema.*

Ben Brewster teaches in the Division of Film Studies at the University of Canterbury. He was the editor of *Screen* for many years and is the author of numerous articles including "From Shklovsky to Brecht: A Reply," in *Screen* and "Notes on the Text 'John Ford's *Young Mr. Lincoln*' by the editors of Cahiers du Cinéma," in *Screen.*

Ron Burnett, Associate Professor of Film and Communications and Director, Graduate Communications Program, McGill University and a Senior Lecturer in the Division of Cinema Studies, LaTrobe University, founded and was the editor of *Ciné-Tracts Magazine.* He has published numerous articles in a variety of journals including *Take One, Cineaste, Framework, Filmnews, Copie Zero, Borderlines, Filmviews, Discourse, Canadian Journal of Film Studies, Continuum,* and *Cinema Papers.* He is the author of the forthcoming *These Images Which Rain Down into the Imaginary.*

Teresa de Lauretis is Professor of History of Consciousness at the University of California, Santa Cruz. She has written extensively on film and feminist theory including *Techniques of Gender, Alice Doesn't, Feminist Studies/Critical Studies* (editor), and she co-edited *The Cinematic Apparatus* with Stephen Heath.

Mary Ann Doane is Associate Professor of Modern Culture and Media at Brown University and is the author of *The Desire to Desire* and co-editor of *Re-Vision: Essays in Feminist Film Criticism* (1984). She is currently working on a project on the relationship between technology, representation, and the body.

Thomas Elsaesser teaches English and Film at the University of East Anglia. Former Editor of *Monogram,* he has contributed to *Screen, Positif, New German Critique, Wide Angle,* and *October.* He is the author of *New German Cinema: A History* (1989).

John Fekete teaches at Trent University, and his books include *The Critical Twilight: Explorations in the Ideology of Anglo-American Literary Theory* (1978) as well as *The Structural Allegory: Reconstructive Encounters with the New French Thought* (1984), which he edited.

Stephen Heath is fellow and lecturer at Jesus College, Cambridge. His books include *The Nouveau Roman: A Study in the Practice of Writing* (1972), *Vertige du deplacement* (1974), *Questions of Cinema* (1981), and *The Sexual Fix* (1982). He is the co-editor with Teresa de Lauretis of *The Cinematic Apparatus*.

Judith Mayne teaches in the Center for Women's Studies and the Department of French and Italian at Ohio State University. She recently published *Private Novel, Public Films* and *Kino and the Woman Question: Feminism and Soviet Silent Film*.

Patricia Mellencamp is Associate Professor of Film in the Art History Department at the University of Wisconsin-Milwaukee. She has two books forthcoming from Indiana University Press, *Indiscretions: Avant-Garde Film, Video, and Feminism* and (as editor) *Logics of Television: Essays in Cultural Criticism*.

George Mitchell teaches in the film program of the Arts and Media Department of Vanier College. He was on the editorial board of *Ciné-Tracts* and has published numerous articles in *Jump-Cut Magazine*.

Margaret Morse is Assistant Professor of Critical Studies in Cinema and Television at the University of Southern California. She is completing a book entitled *Television Reality* and has published widely on television and video theory.

Peter Ohlin is Professor of English and Film at McGill University and the author of *Agee* (1966) as well as a book on the self-reflexive narrative cinema 1960–70 and articles on American and Scandinavian literature and film.

Claire Pajaczkowska is Lecturer in the Art, Film and Design Department of Middlesex Polytechnic, London, England. She recently completed a doctoral dissertation on psychoanalysis and gender, entitled *Before Language*. She is the translator of *Freud or Reich: Psychoanalysis and Illusion,* by Janine Chasseguet-Smirgel and Béla Grunberger (1984).

Kaja Silverman is Professor of English and Film at the University of Rochester. She is the author of *The Subject of Semiotics* and *The Acoustic Mirror: The Female Voice in Cinema* and a forthcoming book on male subjectivity.

Will Straw is Assistant Professor in Film Studies at Carleton University and has published in the areas of film theory, popular music, and cultural studies. He has recently completed his doctoral thesis entitled *Popular Music as Cultural Commodity: The American Recorded Music Industries, 1976–1985*.

Phil Vitone teaches in the film program of the Arts and Media Department of Vanier College. He was on the editorial board of *Ciné-Tracts*. He is presently completing a doctoral thesis entitled *Lay Knowledge and Popular Media*.

Peter Watkins is a well known filmmaker whose most recent work, *The Journey,* examines the impact of the nuclear question on a variety of different cultures. Most recently he has taught at Queen's University, Kingston, and has done extensive research on the effects of the media.

Linda Williams teaches at the University of California, Irvine and is the author of *Figures of Desire: A Theory and Analysis of Surrealist Film* (1981). She is the co-editor, with Stephen Heath, of *Cinema and Language,* and, with Mary Ann Doane and Patricia Mellencamp, of *Re-Vision: Essays in Feminist Film Criticism* (1984).

Raymond Williams was fellow of Jesus College and University Reader in poetry and drama at Cambridge University. He was the author of many books on literature, drama, and the media, including *Culture and Society* (1958), *The Country and the City* (1973), *Television and Cultural Form* (1974), and *Marxism and Literature,* as well as *Keywords* (1976).